The Labour Government's Economic Record:
1964–1970

The Labour Government's Economic Record: 1964–1970

EDITED BY

Wilfred Beckerman

Professor of Political Economy in the University of London, and
Head of the Department of Political Economy at University College London

DUCKWORTH

First published in 1972 by
Gerald Duckworth & Company Limited
3, Henrietta Street, London, W.C.2.

ISBN 0 7156 0608 5

Printed in Great Britain by
The Anchor Press Ltd,
and bound by William Brendon & Son Ltd,
both of Tiptree, Essex

Contents

Notes on Contributors

MICHAEL ARTIS is a Senior Research Officer at the National Institute of Economic and Social Research and Editor of its *Review*. He was previously a Lecturer and Senior Lecturer in Economics at Adelaide and Flinders Universities, South Australia.

WILFRED BECKERMAN is Professor of Political Economy in the University of London and Head of the Department of Political Economy at University College London. He was previously a Fellow and Tutor in Economics at Balliol College, Oxford. He was an Economic Consultant at the Department of Economic Affairs, 1964–5, and Economic Adviser to the Board of Trade, 1967–9. Publications include *The British Economy in 1975* (with Associates) and *An Introduction to National Income Analysis*.

ANDREW GRAHAM is a Fellow of Balliol College, Oxford, and a University Lecturer in Economics. He was previously an Economic Assistant at the Department of Economic Affairs, 1964–6, an Economic Assistant at the Cabinet Office, 1966–7, and an Economic Adviser attached to the Prime Minister's Office, 1968–9.

JEREMY HARDIE is a Fellow of Keble College, Oxford, and of the Oxford Centre for Management Studies.

ROGER OPIE is a Fellow and Lecturer in Economics at New College, Oxford, and a Special Lecturer in Economics in the University. He was Assistant Director of the Planning Division of the Department of Economic Affairs, 1964–6, and has been a member of the Monopolies Commission since 1968.

MICHAEL POSNER is a Fellow and Director of Studies in Economics at Pembroke College, Cambridge. He was Director of Economics at the Ministry of Power, 1966–7; and Economic Adviser to H.M. Treasury, 1967–9, and, on a part-time basis, 1969–71. His publications include *Italian Public Enterprise* (with S. J. Woolf) and *Fuel Policy* (forthcoming).

DEREK ROBINSON is a Senior Research Officer at the Oxford University Institute of Economics and Statistics, and a Fellow of Madgalen College. He was a Senior Economic Adviser at the Department of Employment and Productivity, 1968–70, and had been an Economic Adviser at the National Board for Prices and Incomes, 1965–7. His publications include: *Wage Drift Fringe Benefits and Manpower Distribution* and *Local Labour Markets and Wage Structures* (editor).

DUDLEY SEERS is Director of the Institute of Development Studies at the University of Sussex. He was Director-General, Economic Planning Staff, Ministry of Overseas Development, 1964–7. He has been a consultant to many developing countries and other bodies concerned with economic development. His publications include *Cuba: The Economic and Social Revolution* (editor), and numerous articles on development economics.

MICHAEL STEWART is a Reader in Political Economy at University College London, and a former Senior Economic Adviser at the Cabinet Office. He is the author of *Keynes and After*.

PAUL STREETEN is Warden of Queen Elizabeth House, Director of the Institute of Commonwealth Studies, and a Fellow of Balliol College, Oxford. He was Professor of Economics at the University of Sussex, a Fellow of the Institute of Development Studies and Deputy Director-General of Economic Planning at the Ministry of Overseas Development. His publications include *Economic Integration; Value in Social Theory; Unfashionable Economics; Commonwealth Policy in a Global Context; Diversification and Development: The Case of Coffee; Aid to Africa;* and *The Frontiers of Development Studies.*

Preface

During the twelve months before the Labour Party won the General Election in October 1964, a group of Oxford economists joined forces to write a book, under the editorship of P. D. Henderson, entitled *Economic Growth in Britain*. Several years later, some of the contributors decided to revisit some of the topics covered in the original book in the light of the events of the period 1964–70. The present book is the result, although in this book more topics have been covered, some contributors have not written about the same subjects as before and many new contributors joined the team. Also, because this book is designed to be less a collection of speculative essays and more a critical record of a specific period in the past, an attempt has been made to document the story much more than in the previous volume. Nevertheless, we have also tried to keep the treatment reasonably non-technical and comprehensible to the layman.

Most of the contributors to this book have served, on a temporary basis, in Government departments during the period of the Labour Government. Naturally, those of us in this category have not drawn on any confidential information in writing our chapters, but we have probably emerged from our period of service in Whitehall with more appreciation of the constraints on economic policy and of the fact that the problems are always much more difficult than they appear to be from the outside.

All the chapters have been read by the editor and some chapters have been read by other contributors. Although, in many cases, this process led to amendments, no attempt at all has been made to reach an agreed view on any topic covered and the chapters represent purely the views of the authors concerned.

Wilfred Beckerman
January 1972

Introduction: Economic performance and the foreign balance

Andrew Graham and Wilfred Beckerman

1. THE INTERDEPENDENCE OF POLICIES

In this book an attempt is made to survey the economic record of the Labour Government during its period of office from October 1964 to June 1970. No judgment can be passed on the degree to which this record is a good or a bad one without identifying the objectives to which that Government aspired – or ought to have aspired. The difficulties of identifying these objectives are discussed in Chapter 1, which also includes a survey of the main findings of the subsequent chapters. The latter comprise more detailed analyses of the policies pursued by the Labour Government in various fields, such as overseas aid and development policies, regional policies, industrial relations and income policies, and so on.

In addition, as discussed at greater length in Chapter 1 and in the individual chapters, one of the main obstacles to a fair assessment of the efficacy of some of these special policies is that their effects, if any, could be completely disguised or smothered by failures in a quite different area. In the period in question the main failure of the Labour Government was that they did not take appropriate action to overcome the balance of payments difficulties inherited in 1964. The simplest view of the Labour Government's policy towards the balance of payments is that they failed to devalue early enough. As a result they abandoned their objectives of full employment and growth, and so failure to deal correctly with the balance of payments led to the failure of their other policies. The other chapters of this book show only too well the distorting effect of the balance of payments. Stabilization policy became destabilizing. Industrial policy became an attempt at a series of hidden subsidies to exports or import replacement. Incomes policy was forced into a legally imposed freeze in the second half of 1966 and in 1968 it was used as an instrument of demand management – thereby almost destroying any hope of a *long-run* incomes policy which must be *primarily* voluntary and which must therefore restrain prices at least as much as wages.

However, this is too simple, and leaves aside many interesting questions. For example, why did the Labour Government not devalue earlier? Why did the balance of payments assume such an important role and become an objective instead of just a constraint on the extent to which more basic objectives were pursued? What alternative balance of payments strategy was adopted? An attempt to provide a partial answer to the first of these questions is made in the next chapter, but all three questions – and others – are inseparable, and there is something to be learnt, perhaps, from an attempt to answer them together.

II.   THE CHOICE OF A BALANCE OF PAYMENTS POLICY

The questions just posed are complex. Politics and economics overlap – and rightly so. Here we shall concentrate on the economic choices. If a country faces a balance of payments deficit, then broadly speaking the choices fall into three groups:

1. A deficit can be *financed* from:
   (*a*) reserves
   (*b*) government borrowing by international agreement
   (*c*) private borrowing (e.g. short-term capital inflows encouraged by raising interest rates relative to other countries or long-term capital encouraged by tax inducements).
2. A deficit can be *corrected instantly* by:
   either (*a*) floating. If Government intervention is removed the currency floats to a level at which foreign exchange inflows and outflows (including speculative ones) are equal, i.e. it sinks initially.
   or (*b*) suspending convertibility by introducing exchange controls on all external transactions.
3. A deficit can be *corrected gradually* by:
   (*a*) devaluation
   (*b*) import tariffs and/or export subsidies
   (*c*) physical controls such as import quotas or controls on travel expenditure and overseas investment. (These are like 2(*b*) above but they apply only to particular sorts of expenditure. If extended far enough they become equivalent.)
   (*d*) any policy (such as prices and incomes) which succeeds in gradually lowering home costs relative to foreign costs (i.e. like devaluation but more slowly).
   (*e*) deflation. (However, unlike 3(*a*)–(*d*) above, this necessarily means abandoning the objective of full employment.)
   (*f*) last, but by no means least, action by *other* countries in the opposite direction to 3(*a*)–(*e*), e.g. revaluation, cuts on tariffs, reflation, etc.

However, if there is to be a deficit, it *must* be financed. The basic choice is therefore between *alternatively* (1) on its own if the deficit is self correcting, *or* (2), *or* some combination of (1) and (3). Moreover, if the country has no reserves (or runs out) and cannot borrow further then (2) is the *only* possibility.

This is the framework from which policy has to start. However, these convenient distinctions ignore certain complications.

The choice of policy depends partly on an assessment of:

(*a*) where the economy *is*

(*b*) where it *will* be and what *will* happen to the balance of payments in the absence of policy – is the balance of payments going to correct itself or is policy needed, and would this correction occur at full employment or is the domestic economy off line?

(*c*) what will be the *effect* on subsequent events of the various policies that are available.

Yet the answer to each of these questions is often extremely unclear. Data can be inaccurate or inconsistent. Forecasts can be misleading. Policy effects may be relatively unknown and will often depend on reactions by other countries. Thus conflicting interpretations both of the past and the future are not only possible but likely.

The choice of policy also depends partly on the particular circumstances of the country and on the extent to which different policies may conflict with basic objectives. For example, if the economy is already fully employed, the balance of payments can be corrected only if *domestic* expenditure (or at least its rate of growth) declines – more goods and services have to go to foreigners so less are available at home. Sad to say, many people do not understand that in these circumstances *any* policy has to be accompanied by deflation. Moreover, even when this is understood there is still a resistance to sharp deflation, and policy makers prefer (quite reasonably) to adjust gradually. However, slow adjustment requires large reserves or large borrowing and this creates its own problems, depending on the particular financial circumstances of the country concerned. Large *ad hoc* short-term borrowing is sometimes possible in a crisis situation (e.g. central bank swaps) but longer-term borrowing usually has strings attached – the more one is in debt the more the creditors call the tune. How acceptable are the strings depends, of course, on the objectives of the Government concerned – e.g. how willingly it will accept heavy deflation as the price to be paid for international financial support.

III.   THE SPECIAL POSITION OF THE UK

These complications are particularly important in the UK for three reasons:

1.   *Reserve currency*

In 1964 sterling was still an important reserve currency. This had the consequence first that other countries (particularly the USA) while expecting the UK to correct the balance of payments deficit did not want this to be achieved by devaluation. Central bankers did not want the existing international monetary system disturbed and the USA did not want the dollar to move into the front line. This meant that there was both pressure not to devalue and the means not to devalue – loans were readily forthcoming. Secondly, the then Governor of the Bank of England (as well as much of the City and of the Conservative Party) seemed to think there was a moral obligation to protect the reserves of the bank's overseas customers. Thirdly, quite apart from the moral issue, the devaluation of sterling would have reduced the liquidity of countries holding sterling reserves and some people thought that this could lead to a decline in world trade.

2. *Illiquidity*

It is normal for a reserve currency to be in an illiquid position and this causes no problems provided the standing of the reserve currency is not in doubt or there is no other feasible alternative. Neither of these was the case in 1964. The UK had a large deficit on current account and devaluation was expected – particularly from a left-wing Government apparently committed to full employment. Also the dollar and gold were available as alternatives. Moreover, at the beginning of October 1964 short-term liabilities were more than four times as large as short-term assets. The result was that if even a proportion of those who held sterling thought that a devaluation was likely and decided to switch out of sterling, the only way that the UK could avoid a forced devaluation was by borrowing from central banks and the international monetary institutions, *and/or* by taking sufficient measures to persuade the holders of sterling that devaluation would not occur. Also it appears to have been thought that devaluation itself might increase the expectation of a *further* devaluation.

3. *The diagnosis of the UK*

There was considerable disagreement within the UK about the causes of the recurrent balance of payments deficits that had been incurred since the war. This led also to disagreement about the policies to pursue in future. Four broad schools of thought can be identified:

(a) Treasury
The conventional view held by many within the Treasury was that the balance of payments deficits were the outcome of too high a pressure of demand.[1] The result in the *short run* was that imports rose rapidly (as

[1] See S. Brittan, *The Treasury under the Tories* (Harmondsworth 1964) and *Steering the Economy* (Harmondsworth 1971).

in 1960 and 1964) leading to a deficit, and in the *long run* this deficit tended to increase because the pressure of demand also caused wages and prices to rise rapidly. In this view, devaluation might or might not be needed in the short run, but long-run price stability and hence balance of payments equilibrium could only be achieved if unemployment were kept at about 1·8%.

(b) Demand management
A second school attributed the problem not to the *level* of demand but to its *rate of change*. They argued that reflations had been too rapid so that capacity had not had a chance to respond to the increase in demand. As a result demand had been satisfied by imports and customers tended not to switch back to home suppliers so there was an adverse 'ratchet' effect.

(c) Exchange rate
A third school argued that the £ had been overvalued for some time and was certainly overvalued by 1963 (when there was a small surplus but high unemployment) and even more so by 1964. (The cause of this was thought to be partly internal inflation, and partly the dynamism of the European economies and of Japan.) Moreover this overvaluation was seen as the cause not just of balance of payments deficits but also of the UK's slow growth.

(d) Structuralists
A fourth school argued that:

(*i*) the major problem was the UK's tendency to inflate and that this was a problem in its own right (of which the balance of payments problem was a symptom);

(*ii*) this inflation could *not* be checked by demand management (except on a completely unacceptable scale);

(*iii*) the balance of payments problem was not *just* the outcome of inflation, but also the result of: (1) slow growth in the UK leading to a sluggish supply of exports, and (2) excessive commitments inherited from the past. The UK could no longer play the part of both policeman and banker to the rest of the world. Nor could she afford to go on investing overseas given her existing illiquidity;

(*iv*) devaluation might be avoided *if* and *only if* a workable incomes policy could be evolved with the co-operation of the trades unions. However, if devaluation proved necessary this did *not* remove the need for an incomes policy—it increased it.[1]

These diagnoses overlap but the emphasis for policy is significantly different. The first two attach primary importance to demand manage-

[1] This school is particularly associated with Thomas (now Lord) Balogh. For a fuller statement of his position see *Planning for Progress: A Strategy for Labour*, Fabian Tract 346, 1963.

ment, the third to the exchange rate and the fourth to incomes policy. However, the fourth is also different in character from the others. Demand management and the exchange rate are directly within a Government's control – a voluntary incomes policy is not. Moreover, establishing an incomes policy is heavily dependent on policies in other fields (see Chapter 9) and the complexity of this approach is both its strength and its weakness.

IV. THE STRATEGY AND POLICIES ADOPTED

The actual strategy proposed by Labour in the period preceding the election was obviously most influenced by this last school of thought – though it was hardly fully implemented after the election and this may be partly because of the greater appeal to Ministers and civil servants of the simpler analyses. It is worth noting, however, that if one accepts the last approach the explanation for Labour's apparent failure has shifted, indeed turned on its head. Putting it crudely, this last view would suggest that it was *not* the balance of payments which caused the failure of incomes policy. It was the failure of incomes policy which caused the failure of the balance of payments. But this also is too simple an interpretation and we must look in more detail at the policies pursued and at their inter-relation with each other.

Commercial policy

First, to diverge slightly, it is useful to clarify the relationship between balance of payments policies, in the sense of policies designed to achieve balance of payments equilibrium and commercial policies. The latter are intended to maximize real incomes (subject to the usual constraints) irrespective of whether there is a balance of payments 'problem'. The normal protectionist case is not that in the absence of protection there will be a balance of payments deficit and that with the protection there will be equilibrium or a surplus. It is that in both cases trade can be balanced, but that with protection (and given certain supply and demand conditions), the *terms* of trade will be more favourable. As a result of balancing trade at a lower level of trade, less home goods have to be exported to pay for a given amount of imports, so that on balance the protectionist country gains in terms of real income.

If the supply and demand conditions are such that a protectionist policy can raise real incomes then it should be introduced as long as raising real incomes is the only objective of policy. If the conditions are such that a protectionist policy will fail, and possibly even reduce real incomes, then it is not the existence of a balance of payments deficit that will change these conditions. Moreover, if a certain protectionist policy is likely to reduce real income rather than raise it (e.g. through the attendant resource mis-allocation) then its introduction will only make it more difficult, not less difficult, to reconcile domestic real income targets with external equilibrium. In other words – at least in theory – one should choose the optimum commercial policy to raise real income and use the exchange rate to achieve the balance in trade.

Of course, in the real world life is not so simple. Real income is not the only objective of policy, and even if it were there are widely divergent views on the long-run dynamic effects of 'protection' on the one hand and on the invigorating effects of competition from abroad on the other. Moreover, in a situation where devaluation is ruled out as a matter of policy then import controls and tariffs come back into their own. It becomes justified to evaluate particular projects (such as import saving projects) with the aid of some notion of the 'shadow' exchange rate, i.e. the exchange rate necessary to achieve equilibrium (given actual or desired levels of interest rates, etc.). Indeed, in a situation in which every other alternative except deflation is ruled out as a method of eliminating a deficit, the shadow price of labour in import substitution projects is zero. Thus, for projects that have large labour inputs but short lives, there are good economic reasons for a high rate of protection when unemployment is the only alternative.

As devaluation was rejected for so long it is surprising that protectionist policies were not used more vigorously. There seem to be four main reasons for this:

1. Unless a country is *either* very small (so that it is insignificant for world trade) *or* is in a very strong bargaining position, it cannot easily pursue an independent commercial policy. Other countries will retaliate, or at least threaten to do so, which is enough to frighten many officials and Ministers. This retaliation possibility frequently rates only a footnote in the theoretical literature because it spoils the beauty and sophistication of the theory. If countries retaliate there is no longer anything of a general character that one can say about whether the protection will pay off or not; all the elegant elasticity formulae become quite irrelevant and the fun goes out of the game. Hence, while the retaliation possibility must be recognized, such unsporting behaviour is not to be given much prominence in the theory. But in the real world such behaviour (*or* the fear of it) is *the* major objection to a protectionist policy.

2. Many protectionist measures were contrary to international agreements to which the UK had subscribed, such as the General Agreement on Tariffs and Trade and the European Free Trade Area Convention. The one important measure which the UK did introduce, namely the import surcharge, had to be removed for this reason.

3. Those measures which (under certain conditions) were not contrary to these agreements – the most important of which was import quotas – faced administrative objections. The variety of goods which the UK imports means that a quota system is a much more technically difficult problem than in a relatively underdeveloped economy.

4. Finally, although some Labour leaders probably expected to use controls and tariffs to help overcome a balance of payments constraint, they did not have any specifically 'socialist' commercial policy objectives.

In fact, the combination of these features, plus the influence of some domestic pressure groups (e.g. Lancashire textiles) plus the complexities surrounding the whole issue of agricultural policy, were such that the degree of freedom enjoyed by the Labour Government in the conduct of commercial policy was very limited. Hence, there were few innovations of a major character to report about commercial policy during the period in question.

Of course, there were various minor measures that could be classified as falling under the heading of commercial policy but these were mostly prompted either by balance of payments considerations or by considerations such as the pressure from our exporting interests to help them compete with what they often felt (and often rightly) to be special assistance to overseas competitors from other governments. Given the fact that some policy makers did not understand one or two very basic aspects of commercial policy, it was easy for mercantilism to gain adherents at any time and never more so than when the slogan 'export-or-die' was restored to popularity as a result of the continuing balance of payments deficit. Some policy makers thought that the mere fact that certain measures would be 'good for exports' was enough to justify them. Until devaluation this was often true given the level of protection that was acceptable (at the correct 'shadow' exchange rate). But it was not true for projects which went on after devaluation, nor for those started after it. Policy makers did not always realize that exports are not 'good' in themselves. Economic welfare is greater insofar as one can enjoy the fruits of other countries' labours, and it is less insofar as we have to give up the results of the sweat of our own brows in order to pay for our imports. Unfortunately, in the wicked world that we live in, foreigners expect to receive our goods in exchange for the goods they supply to us: in other words we must export enough to pay for our imports (taking objectives for capital investment and reasonable changes in reserves, etc., into account). But to export more than this is foolish. To achieve this balance – but no more – is the aim of balance of payments policy.

Balance of payments policy

The Labour Government's balance of payments policies were dominated by the initial situation with which they were confronted – both economic and political. Their attempts to transform a large deficit into a surplus fall into the following phases:

1. *October 1964 to March 1966*
During this period virtually all economic policy was subservient to

the need to maintain unity within the Labour Party and to achieve re-election with an increased majority.

2. *April 1966 to July 1966*
On 31 March the Labour Party was re-elected with an overall majority of 97. Thus they were no longer constrained by the political situation.

3. *July 1966 to November 1967*
On 20 July the Labour Government took its major turning point. Until then they had tried both to maintain full employment and to correct the balance of payments. During this third phase they introduced an incomes 'freeze', deflated and increased unemployment – thus they abandoned their strategy of high growth stimulated by a high pressure of demand and seriously damaged the prospects of a voluntary incomes policy.

4. *November 1967 to May 1970*
Devaluation was eventually forced on 18 November 1967. Policy in this last phase was dominated by the desire to make devaluation work.

Phase 1: *October 1964 to March 1966*
On taking office the Labour Government found themselves faced with an economy at full employment, but with a large and rapidly increasing balance of payments deficit. All their previous policy statements had indicated that their aim was to maintain unemployment at a low level. Indeed this was to be the major means by which investment was to be stimulated and growth increased. The crucial issue was therefore how to do this while at the same time correcting the balance of payments. In the *long run* this was to be achieved through establishment of a prices and incomes policy (see Chapter 9, Labour market policies) and by increasing productivity (see Chapter 5, Industrial policy and Chapter 4, Economic planning and growth).

The need therefore was for policies which bought the time needed to allow the longer-term policies to work. Thus the initial policy measures in October 1964 consisted of:

(*i*) direct action to reduce imports through a 15% surcharge on imports of manufactures and semi-manufactures,

(*ii*) a small subsidy (of about $1\frac{1}{2}\%$ to 2%) for exports by rebating indirect taxes on oil, petrol and vehicle licences,

(*iii*) discussions with the IMF about the use of UK drawing rights to finance the deficit.

The Government's reasons for choosing a surcharge on imports rather than a system of import quotas seem to have been fourfold. First, it was administratively easier. With controls there are so many 'special cases' that very low quotas are necessary on other goods to achieve the required overall impact. Secondly, there is also the danger that to make the controls effective they may have to be spread to other goods or include the rationing of certain categories of domestic consumption – and as a party they wished to avoid further identification with controls and rationing. Thirdly, the surcharge was preferred on conventional economic welfare grounds. It allowed the price mechanism to operate still and therefore improve the terms of trade to the extent that suppliers absorbed some of the tariff. Finally, a surcharge has less *net* effect on the pressure of internal demand than import quotas. In both cases domestic demand is transferred from imports to domestic suppliers but in the former case the Government revenue increases and some of this is paid by domestic consumers. As a result the Government thought that large *additional* deflationary measures were unnecessary. This was particularly appealing from a presentational point of view, given the Labour Government's small majority after the October 1964 election and the commitment to end 'stop go'.

However, this desire to keep internal demand high and to be seen to be doing so for internal political reasons contained the seeds of its own destruction. The basic dilemma facing the Labour Government was that international financiers and traders probably *expected* a Left-wing administration to devalue rather than deflate into external balances. The only ways to remove this expectation were either to fulfil it (and they had apparently rejected this option) or to be *more* orthodox than the Conservatives (which again they rejected), or to present a *convincing* alternative strategy. But the surcharge did not provide this. Thus in the next few months there were a series of speculative crises. Moreover, the weak trend in the balance of payments which had emerged early in 1964 was made worse by the movements of sterling area reserves. These had been built up in the first half of the year when the sterling area was in surplus. The effect was to hide the deterioration of the balance of payments which was occurring and to intensify the speculative pressure when the inflows were reversed.

This situation came to a head in the middle of November. Sterling outflows in the week beginning 16 November created the expectation that Bank Rate would be raised on Thursday – the normal day for changes. It was not. The outflows accelerated. On 23 November – the Monday – Bank Rate was raised from 5% to 7%. But this was neither orthodoxy nor an alternative strategy. In the past Bank Rate had always been part of a package deal in which the other part of the package had been measures to decrease internal demand. This time there were none. The increase on a Monday signalled a crisis instead of signalling measures to deal with one! At the same time the US Federal Reserve responded by increasing its discount rate from $3\frac{1}{2}$% to 4% and Canada followed with a move from 4% to $4\frac{1}{2}$% on the Tuesday. The result was a massive outflow of short-term funds. A forced devaluation was only avoided when on the Wednesday 25 November the Bank of England was able to announce credits of $3,000 million from Western European central banks, Canada, the US, Japan and the Bank for International Settlements.

Rather more important for the longer term was that the import surcharge was no more to the liking of the members of EFTA. They complained about the lack of consultation and argued that the surcharge was in contravention of EFTA and of the General Agreement on Tariffs and Trade which allowed the use of import quotas but not of tariffs. When the surcharge was introduced it was called 'temporary' but no date had been given for ending it. However, the pressure from the EFTA Ministerial Council and the GATT Council led to an announcement in February 1965 that the surcharge was to be removed in November 1966 and was to be reduced from 15% to 10% at the end of April 1965 – in fact the more rational thing at this stage would have been to have increased it.

In spite of this no other major measures were taken to correct the balance of payments (although in the 1965 Budget stricter control of foreign investment and exchange was introduced, and it was hoped that the introduction of Corporation Tax would encourage the repatriation of capital). As a result of this and of the fact that the home economy was more buoyant than expected – a failure of stabilization policy (see Chapter 8) – the balance of payments continued in large deficit. The visible trade deficit increased from £14 million in March to £22 million in April and to £37 million in May. Thus in spite of acceptance by the TUC Conference of the Government's prices and incomes policy in April renewed speculation occurred and a further crisis budget had to be introduced in July 1965. This included tighter exchange controls, reduced import finance (administered through the banks), and measures to deflate the home economy. The result was that (according to the figures available at the time, which are those that matter for policy) the deficit on current and long-term capital account for 1965 was £354 million as compared with £769 million in 1964, and the current account was actually in small surplus (£8 million) in the last quarter.

However, this proved to be the first of several false dawns. In the first part of 1966, according to the National Institute of Economic and Social Research (NIESR), domestic demand was again higher than expected. Incomes, consumers' expenditure and imports were all above the levels forecast. So also was the long-term capital outflow of £73 million in the first quarter (probably in fear of further exchange controls in the Budget).

Phase 2: April 1966 to July 1966
Election victory in April with a majority of 97 removed the political constraint, but the basic dilemma between full employment and the balance of payments was now even sharper. In spite of agreement on paper to the prices and incomes policy it was clear that it was having little effect in practice. (Partly of course because domestic expenditure was higher than expected so that there was a high *level* of demand – unemployment was low and still falling.) For the first 4 months of 1966 earnings were 9½% higher than a year earlier. Then in May 1966 the seamen's strike began, so that in June and July the visible trade deficit was at £40

million and £43 million respectively – even worse than the 1965 position.

Although there had been some deflation in the Budget in May with the introduction of Selective Employment Tax (SET) the effects of this were not expected until the second half of the year. The turning point in Labour's economic strategy, therefore, came with the next major exchange crisis in July 1966. The political room for manœuvre had increased but the economic choices were more clear cut. On any medium-term view which took account of the risks involved it was increasingly clear that the *existing* measures to correct the balance of payments (the surcharge was due to be removed at the end of the year) and the *existing* state of incomes policy did not provide a strategy for combining full employment with balance of payments equilibrium. Moreover there was still the pressing short-run problem of financing and correcting the existing deficit (*in*cluding the movement of short-term funds). The only options were either to devalue, or to introduce increased import controls plus cuts in overseas expenditure (private investment and defence) or to abandon full employment. Moreover at this stage the unpopular deflationary measures which would have had to accompany either devaluation or import controls were now politically possible given the Government's majority – and certainly at least as acceptable as the prices and incomes legislation which was forced through against the wishes of a large section of the Parliamentary Labour Party. Given that import controls would only have bought time and given their commitment to full employment and growth the natural – though still unpleasant – policy choice was to devalue. They did not. Why not is one of the major political puzzles of the 1960s.

Phase 3: July 1966 to November 1967

As the result of the combined deflation of May and July and the associated de-stocking there was a large improvement in the balance of payments in the second half of 1966. Moreover at the end of 1966 there was a further temporary run down in stocks as importers delayed goods until after the end of the import surcharge on 30 November 1966. Thus, there was actually a surplus on visible trade of £86 million in the last quarter of 1966.

At the same time the forecast for the future probably looked satisfactory. The Treasury's forecasts for that period are not published but in its February *Review* the NIESR (which uses virtually identical methods) forecast a 'basic' balance surplus of £200 million at an annual rate in the second half of 1967, and £300 million at an annual rate in the first half of 1968! Moreover the Chancellor stated that he expected to be in balance by the end of 1967 so it seems as if the Treasury forecasts were showing a similar picture.

In fact, with a 'no change' budget in April 1967 and with only mild reflation from the relaxation of hire purchase controls at the end of August the eventual 'basic' deficit for 1967 was £480 million. Of course, there are several explanations for this turn round. The forecasts did not foresee the 'Six Day War' in June 1967 which closed the Suez Canal and thus significantly increased the cost of imports, nor did they allow for either the dock strikes or the slow down in world trade at the end of 1967 – and, of course, devaluation itself increased the deficit in November and December.[1] Finally, there was a very large public sector deficit for this year so that the reflation was probably much larger than the 'no change' Budget suggests.

The combination of these features causing lower exports and higher imports (both volume and price) led to a deteriorating balance of visible trade throughout the year. From about mid-summer onwards devaluation must have seemed almost inevitable. But any doubt was removed by the dock strikes of September, October and November, and devaluation was virtually forced on 18 November 1967 – though the formal decision was taken somewhat earlier.

Phase 4: November 1967 to June 1970
In this last phase, with the Government now committed to achieving a balance of payments surplus (even if it achieved nothing else), everything was concentrated on making devaluation work. Devaluation itself was accompanied by some deflation, and this was reinforced first in the public expenditure cuts announced on 18 January 1968 and then in the huge deflation of the 1968 Budget (see Chapter 8). In spite of this the balance of payments deteriorated in 1968. This was to be expected because it takes time for the reduced price of exports (to foreigners in foreign currency) to result in a substantial increase in sales and hence offset the immediate deterioration in the terms of trade. What was not expected was the large increase in the *volume* of imports in the first half of 1968. The explanation appears to have been partly that stocks were abnormally low in 1967 (which is one of the reasons why the picture looked so good only a year previously), partly that the propensity to import was shifting upwards faster than expected, and partly that the *level* of national income at the end of 1967 (and consequently throughout 1968) was higher than suggested by the original estimates of national income.

Given this continuing deficit, the large international debts already accumulated and the uneasy situation in the world international money markets (it was in March 1968 that the gold crisis occurred with a run on the dollar backwashing on to sterling) it is not surprising that policy became so dominated by the need to achieve a surplus. By this stage there was no other option. If the country was not to run out of finance altogether the *trend* in the balance of visible trade had to be got right – and *fast*!

Thus, in November 1968 following speculation against the franc (and

[1] The initial effect of a devaluation is to worsen the trade balance, for there is an immediate deterioration in the terms of trade (rise in import prices relative to export prices) but this is not offset by a cut in imports and an increase in exports until after a considerable time lag.

to some extent the £) and in favour of the mark there was a further deflation (the 10% regulator) and a prior deposit scheme for imports was
introduced. This covered about one-third of imports and required importers to deposit 50% of the value of imported goods with a bank for 6
months before obtaining customs release. It was intended to reduce
imports mainly by squeezing the liquidity position of importers (though
also partly through the implied higher price for imports – about 2% with
an interest rate of 8%). This was reinforced further in 1969 by a monetary
squeeze as a result of pressure from the IMF. The effect of the import
deposit scheme in the circumstances was probably more to cause a large
inflow of funds to the UK for import finance than to reduce imports.

As a result of all these measures – devaluation, deflation (both fiscal
and monetary) – and aided also by a rapid growth in world trade, the
monthly trade figures eventually moved into surplus around the middle
of 1969. Moreover, in May 1969 research by the Board of Trade revealed
that beginning as long ago as 1963 the export figures had been underestimated because exporters were failing to lodge documents with customs.
It was estimated that by 1968 the error was of the order of 2%. In spite
therefore of the fact that as late as August 1969 the balance of visible
trade showed a deficit of over £200 million in the first half of the year, in
August 1970 the deficit for the same period was thought to be only
£150 million and in 1969 as a whole there was a deficit of only
£24 million. This corresponded to a large surplus of £415 million on
the overall current account. Thus it was only in the last nine months of
the Labour Government's administration that the balance of payments
constraint began to be removed. It is only with hindsight that one can
see that the *cumulative* deflation in 1968 and 1969 was too large.

v. APPRAISAL

There is little doubt that the failure to deal with the balance of payments
for so long was the major mistake of the Labour Government. There is no
single simple reason for this. Those who assert that the pound sterling
should have been devalued in 1964 know their economics but not their
politics. A major point about correcting a balance of payments deficit
from a starting position of full employment is that it is a painful adjustment
– however achieved. Real wages have to fall or stop growing. They may
stop growing less with devaluation than deflation but that is not the point.
A prerequisite is still the political will and the political situation to carry
through the unpopular accompanying measures.

But this is not the whole story. By April 1966 the Government had a
clear Parliamentary majority and were guaranteed 5 years in power yet
still devaluation was rejected. The exact positions of the Prime Minister
(Mr Wilson) and the Chancellor of the Exchequer (Mr Callaghan), the
Secretary of State for Economic Affairs, the Treasury and the Bank of

England in this failure to devalue remain unknown. And it is highly likely that opinion inside the Treasury and the Bank of England was not completely unanimous. Yet some, at least, of the responsibility for not devaluing lies also with those who fostered the strange mixture of the historical mystique and symbolism which equated the strength of sterling with the strength of the economy – shades of 1925! What is known is that both the Bank of England and the Treasury were opposed to devaluation at this stage largely because of the special role of sterling. Many people thought that we had a moral obligation to overseas holders of sterling (though we also had an obligation to those who became unemployed by the UK's refusal to devalue). Moreover, particularly in the earlier years of the Government, it seems that the USA was opposed to devaluation by the UK *and* was providing much of the finance to prevent it becoming unavoidable.

However, political failure and economic analysis overlap. There seems little doubt that in the period from October 1964 to July 1966 the Government *thought* that they were deflating the economy slightly – this is certainly the NIESR's interpretation from July 1965 onwards. Yet the pressure of home demand stayed higher than expected so that the balance of payments was worse and incomes policy was trying to fight a demand pull inflation. From July 1966 to November 1967 fiscal policies certainly created the deflation but now the improvement in the balance of payments was less than expected. Indeed if one took the NIESR forecasts for February 1967 (including their longer-term look to 1970) at their face value, the implication was that if one accepted an unemployment level of 2% or a little above, then a modest surplus on the balance of payments was possible *without* devaluation – and as we have seen there are reasons for thinking that the Treasury's views were similar.

Yet even here there are three separate strands. First, the data on which policy was assessed were inadequate (e.g. the revisions to both the national income and the export figures). Secondly, the forecasts assumed that previously existing relationships (e.g. import propensities) would continue unchanged. This proved unjustified. Thirdly, and most important, there was a failure by the Government to appreciate the risks involved in the strategy. An error of just 1% in both exports and imports could throw the balance of payments out by over £100 million – quite apart from errors originating either from an inaccurate forecast of the domestic economy or a misjudgment of the effects of policy.

In fact, the failure throughout was that the Government never achieved any room for manœuvre. Admittedly the political and economic situation with which they started did not contain many options but they did little to increase them. They decided not to devalue and tried to present an alternative strategy but the *execution* of this strategy was never wholly convincing. It is little wonder that they were eventually blown off course.

VI.   EXCHANGE RATE POLICY IN THE FUTURE

Is there a balance of payments 'problem'?
It may seem paradoxical to ask such a question at this stage. However, there is a lot of truth in Samuel Brittan's frequent assertion that the balance of payments 'problem' is a 'non problem' even though it has dominated the British economic scene, as well as the international one, for many years. Those who maintain that the balance of payments does not constitute a real problem do so on the grounds that the real problems are how to increase productivity and output, to avoid heavy unemployment, to move towards a desired distribution of income, to prevent a rate of inflation that is socially undesirable, and to remove glaring disparities in regional living standards, job opportunities, etc. These are difficult tasks and there are no simple instruments or magic wands that will achieve them. But the balance of payments is a quite different proposition. As explained in Chapter 1 below, what matters about the balance of payments is that it constitutes a constraint on the extent to which other, and more basic, policy objectives can be fulfilled.

The events of the last few years in the international monetary scene – particularly in the last year or so – have indicated a much greater acceptance of the need and justification for changing the exchange rate before the balance of payments becomes a false constraint to which other objectives have to be sacrificed. During the international monetary 'crisis' beginning in August 1971 not only have exchange rate pegs been withdrawn they have not even been officially reinserted at different points. The rates have been allowed to 'float' through with considerable control from the central banks. Such a situation would have appeared to be unthinkable only three or four years ago. Hence, provided there is not an outburst of protectionism, it is unlikely that chronic balance of payments difficulties will dominate internal economic policies in the future to the extent that they did in the late 1960s. It is doubtful now whether any of the major countries would accept as many sacrifices of *genuine* economic objectives as did Mr Wilson and Mr Callaghan during the first few years of the Labour Government *just* in order to defend the parity of the £.

Exchange rates can now apparently be changed at the stroke of a pen but this does *not* mean that they should be changed at the drop of a hat. There are three reasons why this is so:

(*i*) As a matter of pure logic as long as other countries are free to vary *their* exchange rates no one country can fully determine its own rate *vis-à-vis* all the others.

(*ii*) More important in practice is that although many countries may want to improve their comparative positions at the same time they cannot all achieve this. However, if they all *try* to do this in an unregulated manner then there could be a series of competitive devaluations or alternatively a growth of competitive protectionist policies. This is why it is still essential that exchange rates – if not irrevocably fixed – should still be determined by some form of international agreement, perhaps of a flexible and informal kind.

(*iii*) Finally, there is the asymmetrical nature of wage movements – they tend to react upwards but not downwards. Thus the danger of fully floating rates, or rates that can be changed too easily, is that depreciation of a currency can exacerbate an already existing inflationary problem. There would therefore be much to be said for balance of payments adjustments being made primarily by *re*valuations rather than *de*valuations. Inflation is now an international problem and one in which the surplus countries must play as big a part in looking for a solution as do the deficit countries.

There is room for much discussion about how exactly greater flexibility of exchange rates should be achieved and about the international context within which greater flexibility by *this* country should be operated, but it is against the above criteria that alternative schemes should be judged.

The unwillingness of the Labour Government to recognize that the exchange rate should be the means to other ends and not an end in itself was Labour's real mistake. The consequences of the exchange rate policy and the resulting weakness of the balance of payments were felt, in fact, in most of the areas covered by the various chapters in this book, and it seemed more appropriate to deal with them in their special contexts rather than to attempt to bring them together in a separate chapter. This procedure provides a fairer and more accurate assessment of the more specialized policies in the field of industrial relations, income distribution, regional development and so on than would otherwise be the case. When allowance is made for the way that policies in many fields were hampered by the balance of payments situation (and for the fact that a longer period free from balance of payments constraints was needed in order for them to bear full fruit), it is clear that these various policies were more successful than might otherwise have appeared to be the case.

1 Objectives and performance: an overall view

Wilfred Beckerman

'Socialism is what the Labour Government does.' HERBERT MORRISON[1]

In this book an attempt has been made to assess the economic performance of the Labour Government from the time it took office in October 1964 to the time it left office in June 1970. There are many difficulties in making an overall assessment. For example, the benefits of some policies may have been obscured or disguised by the failures of others, and some policies may have needed more time to bear fruit. Also, it is impossible to know whether any alternative government would have been more successful in solving the economic problems that have faced the country during the last ten years or so.

But the first difficulty is to identify the objectives with which the performance of the Labour Government is to be compared. Presumably these should reflect the particular objectives of the Labour Party.[2] To an economist, however, these are not adequately described by a shopping list of the usual items such as faster growth, full employment, stable prices and so on. These items are included in the shopping list of both the major parties. Yet different parties may attach very different priorities to the individual objectives.[3] Consequently, if it were found that there was some conflict between some or all of these objectives, as is likely to be the case, the parties might differ considerably in the extent to which they were prepared to sacrifice one or more objectives in favour of others. In the economics jargon a simple list of objectives tells us nothing about the 'trade offs' or the 'preference patterns' relating the objectives to each other.

If two consumers have the same incomes and face the same relative prices and one of them spends more on meat, say, than does the other, one can conclude that the former must like meat more than does the latter. But one cannot perform the same exercise for two political parties. For in the different periods during which they are in office the relevant con-

---

[1] Quoted in Peter Jenkins, *The Battle of Downing Street* (London 1970), page 101.

[2] Of course, anybody is free to decide that he doesn't like those objectives and wants to assess performance in the light of his own objectives, but in that case he is passing judgment on the objectives as much as on performance.

[3] The parties can hardly be expected to indicate their priorities in any precise numerical form. As Michael Lipton points out, 'If party A says "Growth is 1·5 times as important as equality", and party B replies, "No, 1·3 times as important", it is going to be very difficult to have a well-informed election on the issue . . .' (*Assessing Economic Performance* (London 1968), page 36).

straints, corresponding to the incomes and relative prices of the two consumers in the above example, will be different.

The record of a government clearly cannot simultaneously indicate its
objectives and the extent to which it has succeeded or failed in achieving
them. At the same time, one cannot expect that analysis of the policy
statements by the Party or by individual politicians will provide a consistent and independent picture of the objectives of the Labour Party in
terms of the relative priorities attached to specific detailed objectives.
Political pamphlets are designed to serve electoral purposes; and different
Labour politicians will have different views on the relative priorities to be
accorded to various objectives. On the other hand, if one abandons
the attempt to establish independently the objectives of the Labour Party
with what does one compare actual performance and achievements?

In this book we have largely followed the usual way out of this dilemma.
That is to say we have, to some extent, compared actual performance
with certain widely accepted key objectives of policy, such as faster growth
and full employment. But we have not followed this path as closely as
have other commentators on the economic performance of this country,
like Messrs Brittan, Dow, or Shonfield, since we have gone further in
attempting to establish what have been the particular objectives of the
particular Labour Government with which we are concerned here.[1]

Is there a 'Labour' economic policy?

The importance of the 'Left-Right' distinction in British politics

Simply to compare the Labour Government's record with a set of objectives that is assumed to be shared by everybody would, of course, be consistent with the widespread view that party politics is all a great sham and
that there is barely any real difference between the two major parties in
this country even though the parties try to present different packages to
the electorate. This view of British politics was summed up, about twenty

[1] J. C. R. Dow, *The Management of the British Economy 1945–60* (Cambridge and NIESR
1964); Andrew Shonfield, *British Economic Policy since the War* (Harmondsworth 1958);
Samuel Brittan, *The Treasury under the Tories* (Harmondsworth 1964) and *Steering the
Economy* (Harmondsworth 1971). Michael Lipton's book, referred to above, also constitutes, to a large extent, an appraisal of economic performance in this country in the
context of a sophisticated discussion of the whole problem of defining a sensible pattern
of economic objectives in the light of the pure theory of economic policy. Of the other
three commentators referred to here, Dow probably takes slightly more trouble to
establish the objectives and economic philosophies of Labour and Conservative Governments respectively, in Chapters 2 and 3, except that his book concentrates much more
on the demand management objective than the other two books, and also contains far
less questioning of the wisdom of certain other objectives than is contained in, say,
Chapter 5 of the first edition (1964) of Brittan's book or at various points in Shonfield's.

years ago, in the term 'Butskellism', which was intended to indicate the alleged convergence of views between Hugh Gaitskell and R. A. (now Lord) Butler.

Recently, this interpretation of British party politics has been set out more fully in a stimulating book by Samuel Brittan, who has attempted to show that the distinction between the Left and the Right in British politics today 'obscures more than it illuminates'.[1] According to Mr Brittan there is barely any systematic difference between Left and Right on most issues, the main exceptions 'centring around the concept of "equality" '.[2] After arguing that there is no clear difference of view as between Left and Right on matters such as the price mechanism, planning, compulsory incomes policy, or even over attitudes to change, he states that 'the most plausible case that can be made for the continued relevance of Left and Right hangs not on change at all, but on attitudes to social and economic equality' and that 'voters in each camp are unified by views on a very narrow range of class matters. Left-wing voters favour measures which they think will put money into the hands of the lower paid, while Right-wing voters are concerned to gain more for the middle class and are also more hostile to trade unions'.[3] For Mr Brittan all this is really an inadequate basis for political classification; it no longer corresponds to the really important issues; and some alternative grouping or classification should replace the present 'Left–Right' political classification. While Mr Brittan's well-informed analysis of the way that the same views on numerous aspects of economic policy can be found in both of the main political parties provides a salutary check to facile generalization and instant prediction about political attitudes, I believe that he goes too far in denying the importance of the Left–Right distinction in British economic policy. There are four main reasons for this.

First, as explained above, two parties may both list the same aims under the heading of economic policy without necessarily attaching the same relative priorities to them. Economics is about choice, so that in economics everything is relative. (Even with respect to the equality issue there will still only be a difference of degree; the Conservatives might not want the income distribution to become far less equal than it is and the Labour Party might not want complete equality of income distribution.) Both parties may include high employment, fast growth and so on among their objectives, but one cannot conclude from this that there is no difference between them with respect to the relative importance they attach to the various objectives. To maintain that there is no difference between the parties apart from the equality issue requires evidence that their priorities are the same, and no evidence of this has been provided. The sort of consistency tests carried out by Finer or by Blondel, and to which Mr Brittan refers, tell one nothing about the extent to which parties have the same

[1] Samuel Brittan, *Left or Right, The Bogus Dilemma* (London 1968), page 11.
[2] Ibid.
[3] Op. cit., page 67.

relative priorities among competing objectives.[1] Furthermore, concepts such as 'growth' and 'equality' are very vague and agreement as to their desirability might conceal differences in interpretation of what is meant by these terms.

Secondly, insofar as the parties do differ with respect to whether or not they are in favour of greater equality of income distribution, this is surely of major importance in its own right, quite apart from its implications for other objectives. It is true that concern with the issue of equality of incomes fell somewhat into the background during the period when capitalism was working so inefficiently that it was clear that the greatest contribution to the welfare of the majority of people would come through full employment and economic growth, rather than through redistribution of incomes. But now that these two problems seem to be less acute, interest among economists has shifted back to the equality issue.[2] This may not always take the form of a redistribution of income, and is often bound up with policies concerned with the pattern of output in the economy. For if it is thought that there should be greater equality of consumption of some goods or services, such as medical care or education or housing, than would emerge from the desired distribution of income, then policies designed directly to achieve the desired distribution of consumption of these goods or services will be pursued.

Thus the equality issue is so important that if political parties differed over nothing else the distinction between Right and Left in British politics would be important and useful. To complain that the two main parties differ only over the equality issue would be like complaining, at the time of the English civil war, that since men on both sides could be found with identical views on the role of the episcopacy in Scotland, land enclosures, the prerogatives of the monarch in foreign policy and so on, the two sides differed only over the trivial matter of whether the king should have his head cut off for trying to assert his power over Parliament. The equality issue is what divides the 'have-nots' from the 'haves'. It has probably been the most common basis for party politics through the ages. In the absence of violent religious dispute, it is doubtful whether any other basis can ever be found until 'the' economic problem of scarcity has disappeared. As long as scarcity dominates the scene, it is doubtful whether party politics can be explained except in terms of what is in the economic interest of the main groups in the community. Of course, the pure milk of Labour Party doctrine may not be so materialistic as this would suggest. Equality of *income* is only one aspect of equality, and much of Labour Party philosophy

[1] Op. cit., pages 46 and 47, and 52 ff. The Blondel results show a lack of connection between beliefs on policy and party allegiance among individuals interviewed in opinion polls, and so do not relate to official party policies anyway. The Finer results are about the views of MPs but are more concerned with the correlation between views over a very wide field including relatively non-economic issues, and anyway are subject to the point made above concerning relative priorities attached to different objectives.

[2] See James Tobin, 'On limiting the domain of inequality', *Journal of Law and Economics*, October 1970.

is concerned with equality in a wider sense. This does not mean merely extending the concept of equality to embrace equality of consumption or living standards, or to include equality of wealth; it goes beyond economic concepts completely and includes social and political equality defined very broadly.

Thirdly, it is doubtful whether any other basis for distinction between parties would be less prone to fuzziness at the edges than the Left–Right distinction. Alternative criteria, such as 'radicalism', 'authoritarianism', 'elitism' and so on, are just as vague and open to varying interpretations as 'equality'. Furthermore, as soon as one has more than a handful of people and a few economic objectives about which they might differ, it becomes impossible to group the people into two completely distinct and homogeneous parties. Kenneth Arrow showed, years ago, the impossibility of combining the preference patterns of a number of individuals into some clearly defined aggregate preference pattern. How then could one expect to find two clearly defined and distinct aggregate preference patterns, each one representing millions of people? A casual acquaintance with the work of Arrow, Anthony Downs and others should have protected us from any illusions on that score.[1] Hence, no two-party system will exhibit a clear distinction between the parties with respect to any large number of objectives, so that there is little point in complaining about the weakness of the present system in that respect.

The fourth reason for not concluding that the distinction between Left and Right is a sham battle simply because the two main parties differ only with respect to whether they advocate greater equality of income distribution is basically that there is hardly any other *independent* objective of policy about which they could conceivably differ anyway. This is because most of what commonly pass for 'objectives' of economic policy are not really independent objectives desired for their own sake but are desired mainly because they promote one or other of two more basic economic objectives: namely higher standard of living and some desired degree of equality of income (and wealth) distribution. It is true that other subsidiary objectives, such as price stability or full employment, may also be desired partly for their own sakes, but they are chiefly wanted for the contribution they are believed to make to one or other (or both) of the two basic objectives. And many other 'objectives' of policy have even less independent status than price stability or full employment. For example, balance of payments equilibrium should not be desired for its own sake at all, but only because the balance of payments sets a constraint on the extent to which a country can maximize other objectives, such as high consumption or growth.

Of course, this is an over-simplification of the problem since, as indicated

[1] For example, Kenneth Arrow, *Social Choice and Individual Values* (New York 1951); J. M. Buchanan and G. Tullock, 'The Calculus of Consent' (Oxford 1962); Anthony Downs, *An Economic Theory of Democracy* (New York 1957). The Arrow result rests on certain assumptions which might be regarded as unduly restrictive, such as incomparability of different individuals' satisfactions.

above, the concepts of 'standard of living' and 'equality' are open to a wide variety of interpretations which could, in principle, be the subject of party differences. One can imagine, for example, strong party differences over the weight that should be attached to working conditions, or to public rather than private consumption, in any definition of the standard of living. But it is doubtful whether such strong differences would arise if they did not have implications for the other basic objective, namely the equality of income distribution.

The basic objectives of economic policy should reflect the value judgments of the Party about what it is ultimately striving to achieve – i.e. the economic aspects of the sort of society we should live in. They may, and probably usually do, reflect the interests of particular groups, and it is reasonable and natural that such a clash of interest or fundamental value judgment can rouse political passion. If a sharp distinction could be drawn between ultimate, or basic, independent ends and the means of achieving them, the latter would not be matters of value judgment or of special interest, but would reflect merely the technical realities of the world. For example, suppose that price stability were desired solely because it was believed to facilitate faster economic growth. Then two people having the same preference for faster economic growth could only disagree about the desirability of inflation insofar as they disagreed about the purely technical matter of whether or not it was really true that inflation hampered economic growth. And it is difficult to see why this should arouse strong feelings or be a cause of clear party difference.

In the same way, it is difficult to see why parties should be expected to differ strongly over a host of subsidiary objectives except insofar as these have different implications for the basic objectives over which they can differ since these are matters of value judgment, or – to be less charitable – of clear difference in self-interest. And if there are only two important *independent* objectives of policy that make sense, namely higher living standards and greater equality, then, insofar as both parties can hardly differ in a general way about the former, there is only one independent objective that they can disagree about – viz. the equality issue! And this is, apparently, all that they do disagree about; the facts are consistent with more or less theoretical prediction, and there is no call to be surprised if the only fundamental difference between the two main parties is with respect to equality.

Why the parties differ over the instruments of economic policy

To expect parties to differ systematically about technicalities, which is what difference about the *means* of policy would amount to, would be like expecting them to take sides as between the 'big-bang' theory or the continuous creation theory of the nature of the universe. Such issues do not involve value judgments, or impinge on the interests of different groups in society, which is why political parties have not grown up around them.

And since there can be legitimate differences of opinion as to what means will achieve certain ends, the science of economics being in such a rudimentary state, it is also possible for a group of people sharing the same ends to embrace a wide variety of schools of thought as to the means to be used. Anthony Crosland, in *The Future of Socialism*, argues that a confusion between ends and means can lead to the label 'socialist' being applied to political groupings that, in his opinion, differ very widely from the sort of modern democratic socialism that he wishes to expound and advocate.[1] In particular, he thinks that it is for this reason that the Labour Party includes people who advocate some radical Marxist solutions to the problems of contemporary society, which, in his opinion, are no longer relevant.[2]

Conversely, the scope for many different views as to the means required to achieve any given ends not only explains the diversity of opinions about policies within one party dedicated to specific ends; it may also help to explain the similarity of policies between different parties having conflicting ends. For example, some socialists support British entry into the Common Market because they believe that socialism is essentially international in character, whereas some Conservatives support it because they think that freer movement of labour and capital will weaken the power of British trade unions.

But in spite of all this, the degree to which the two main parties do differ about what are basically mere instruments of economic policy is not negligible. There are probably two main reasons for this. First, the distinction between ends and means is not quite as sharp as the preceding discussion might appear to suggest. There are hardly any pure 'instruments' of policy that do not have some end value, particularly because of some impact on income equality. Almost any economic measure one can think of will have some effect on income distribution and so will involve a political or value judgment. For example, one might think that there can be very little scope for value judgments to enter into the parties' preferences as between investment grants and investment allowances looked at purely as means of stimulating overall investment. One might have thought that this is purely a technical matter, open to empirical verification, and that there is no reason why Socialists and Conservatives should differ systematically as to the likely results of such enquiries. But, in fact, if it is believed – rightly or wrongly – that investment grants favour small and new firms then some people may prefer them, not as better instruments for promoting an overall increase in investment but as a means also

[1] C. A. R. Crosland, *The Future of Socialism* (abridged and revised edition, London 1964), pages 64–6.
[2] In an article in the *Sunday Times* (March 1970) entitled 'Where we go wrong'. Mr Crosland went to some trouble, however, to point out the dangers of a Labour Party that tried 'to seek the esteem of the liberal audience of columnists and television commentators, college graduates also, with essentially middle-class values', and he urged a shift back to 'Labourist popularism'.

of leading to a more equal distribution of output as between firms, reducing the power of the large corporations and thereby, perhaps, reducing the degree of monopoly power in the economy.[1]

In the same way, almost any other 'instrument' of policy that one cares to think of can be shown to affect possibly the privileges, or lack of them, of some group in society and hence have some independent end-value for some people. For example, many business men, and possibly some prominent politicians, might oppose 'planning' because they fear that any substitute for the price mechanism and the profit motive must lead to some redistribution of income away from profits.

The second possible reason why the parties may appear to advocate very different economic policies in spite of what has been said above is that it is partly a sort of sham battle, as Mr Brittan has maintained, arising out of the existence of a virtually continuous election campaign.[2] As a result, opposition parties feel obliged continually to attack whatever the government of the day is doing and to argue that they would do it differently or better in some way or other. In the search for ways of differentiating their product from their rival's they have to exaggerate differences in purely technical instruments of policy. Investment grants rather than allowances, Value Added Tax rather than Corporation Tax or Selective Employment Tax, and so on, are the counterpart in the battle for political power of 'controlled biological action' rather than 'extra stain removing power' in the battle for the detergent market. Detergent producers do not need to argue about what detergents are supposed to do; we all want cleanliness. So, according to this view, why should politicians worry the public with debates about what it is all in aid of and what sort of society we should live in? This will only confuse them and they won't understand it anyway. All that is left, in this view, is to reduce political activity to a battle about who will be the most competent at giving the public what it is thought to want. Such a battle can only be about instruments. If we cannot differ about ends, we can fight only about means.

But there is nothing necessarily 'sham' or 'phoney' about such a battle. If the ends are worth pursuing then it is right for the public to be interested in the question of which party will be most competent at pursuing them. And the claim to greater competence was also one of the major planks in the Labour Party's 1964 election campaign, with its attempt to cultivate an image of white-hot technological revolutionaries who worked everything out on computers instead of with matchsticks. In fact, the battle between the parties is very much a battle about which is likely to be the most competent in achieving common objectives. To some extent the party

[1] The idea being that large firms can offset allowance against certain profits on some part of their total operation whereas smaller firms will get the grants whether their investments prove profitable or not but might not get the benefit of the allowance unless the particular investment concerned does prove to be profitable. (See, for example, the speech in the House of Commons by Mr Eric Heffer, 6 May 1971.)

[2] Brittan, op. cit., page 114.

leaders genuinely differ about which means are most likely to be effective.

Nevertheless, it is not true that the parties do not really differ over objectives at all. For the reasons given above, a difference over the equality issue would be an important one, and there may be others; either derived from this one, or differences that take the form of different priorities, or different interpretations of what a high 'standard of living' means. In the rest of this chapter, therefore, we shall consider what the major objectives of the Labour Party appeared to be and how far these objectives, or the instruments selected to pursue them, were specific to the Labour Party. Of course, no clearly defined unique set of Labour Party objectives actually exists, so there is no point in spending too much time searching for it; different members of the Party attached different degrees of importance to individual ingredients of policy. But unless commentary on the effectiveness of a Party in achieving its particular objectives is to cease, some effort must be made to see what their objectives actually were.

THE MAJOR OBJECTIVES OF POLICY

The classification of the policies

The various aspects of economic policy that are the subject of the later chapters of this book can be roughly classified into three main groups. The first group covers two topics that appear to be vitally important to the claim that the Labour Party does really represent a significantly different policy from the Conservatives; these are policies in the field of income distribution and in the field of overseas aid, since this is merely an international – as distinct from national – form of income redistribution. The equality component of Labour's economic policy probably, therefore, calls for prior discussion and, as we shall argue, poses perhaps the most difficult problems for the Labour Party in contemporary conditions of trade union organization and attitudes.

Following this are a group of sub-policies which are all, in a sense, largely different instruments by which a certain common objective, namely faster economic growth and higher standards of living, is to be reached. These areas of policy include planning, industrial policy, the operation of nationalized industries, and regional policy – though the latter could be guided also, to some extent, by a concern with the reduction in regional income differentials for its own sake as well as for the sake of the contribution that regional policy could make to the overall level of output and growth.

Thirdly, there are important ingredients of economic policy which might be regarded as being concerned with the general 'management of the economy'. These are (*i*) stabilization policy, which is concerned largely with maintaining the desired overall level of demand in the economy and preventing excessive fluctuations around this level of demand; (*ii*) incomes policy, which has been regarded as contributing mainly to the prevention of inflation, though, as is discussed below, it has also been seen as a means of contributing to social justice as well as an instrument for improving industrial relations and, hence, perhaps industrial productivity; and (*iii*) balance of payments policy (discussed above).

In the rest of this chapter we shall survey briefly the policies carried out under these various headings, during the period 1964 to 1970, in the light mainly of pronouncements by the Labour Party or by its leaders. Of course, one can always select statements that match the particular gloss that one wishes to put on the argument; one of the duties of politicians is to talk a lot. It is impossible to demonstrate that the following selection is a representative one. Also, one must make allowance for the fact that it is politicians that we are using in evidence, and what they say is usually said with some eye on wider political implications for the Party and for themselves personally. Thus if, for example, one finds that Mr Callaghan hardly ever said anything between 1960 and 1970 about any economic issue without mentioning social justice and equity whereas Mr Douglas Jay hardly ever said anything over the same period without forgetting social justice and equity, this does not necessarily mean that only Mr Callaghan is concerned with social justice, and that Mr Jay is not. It could also mean that Mr Callaghan is more the astute 'politician' and Mr Jay more the Fellow of All Souls.

Similarly, it is possible – indeed highly probable – that some of the themes recurring in Labour Party statements of policy will reflect much more what the Labour politicians think is essential to electoral victory than what they really care about themselves. And this is not necessarily a sign of cynicism at all. Far from it, it is often a sign of a genuine desire actually to get something done about the ills that one sees in the world rather than simply a desire to wallow in the pleasures of moral indignation. If one seriously wants to do something about old-age pensioners, there is little point in taking a high-and-mighty line about the corrupting influence of greater material benefits, since this would ensure that the Party would never be elected for at least fifty years, by which time all the present old-age pensioners and a lot of new ones would long be dead. But we are not concerned here with what Party leaders really want – if that could be said to exist – but with what they set out to provide. That is a difficult enough task anyway, without having to psycho-analyse the motives behind the statements of what the Party promised to provide.

Equality: at home and abroad

There is no doubt that equality has long been the key theme of serious discussions and statements of socialist economic policy. In *The Future of Socialism* Mr Crosland listed five traditional basic socialist aspirations, but of these five he notes that two which were 'censures on the material results of capitalism' are no longer very appropriate, since they concerned mass unemployment and poverty and squalor and these particular 'aspirations relating to the economic consequences of capitalism are fast losing their relevance as capitalism itself becomes transformed'.[1] The remaining three basic objectives which are described as 'stemming either from a concern with the "bottom dog", or from a vision of a just, co-operative and class-less society, have clearly not been fully realized. . . . We have plenty of less fortunate citizens still requiring aid; and we certainly have not got an equal or classless society, nor one characterized by "co-operative" social relations.'[2]

In essence, therefore, according to Mr Crosland, socialism is basically about equality – as other socialist leaders have confirmed, and as is per-fectly clear from the emphasis given to this theme in most, though not all, of the more recent summaries of Labour Party policy. For example, at the beginning of the 1964 General Election Manifesto it is stated that 'until sixty years ago when the Labour Party was founded, the ending of economic privilege, the abolition of poverty in the midst of plenty, and the creation of real equality of opportunity were inspiring but remote ideals. They have now become immediate targets of political action.'[3]

Similarly, although the popular, brief, version of the 1965 National Plan[4] echoes a speech made in the House of Commons by Harold Wilson in 1961 in restricting the list of key objectives to production, exports and prices,[5] numerous other statements emphasize the importance of social considerations, particularly income distribution. In *The Relevance of British Socialism* published in 1964, Harold Wilson argues that 'the economic dynamic will have no sense without social purpose', and many other state-ments[6] refer to the need for economic progress and social redevelopment to go hand in hand or to the fact that industrial expansion must not be accelerated by means which would undermine social priorities, or the im-portance of the 'balance between public and private expenditures', and even of the aim of ensuring that 'the fruits of higher production and technological advance [be] distributed in accordance with Socialist principles' as distinct from what, in 1961, Mr Wilson believed to be a 'manifestly unjust distribution of the national dividend'.[7] There is no sign of the Party having lost sight of its declared concern with equality during its years of office. For example, in the 1969 statement of the Party's

[1] Crosland, op. cit., page 69.
[2] Ibid.
[3] *New Britain*, 1964, page 5.
[4] *Working for Prosperity: the National Plan in Brief*, 1965.
[5] *Hansard*, House of Commons, Vol. 645, Col. 440.
[6] *The Relevance of British Socialism* (London 1964), pages 28 and 99; *Time for Decision*, Labour Party Manifesto for 1966 Election, pages 4 and 7; *Economic Policy*, A Statement by the National Executive Committee to the Annual Conference of the Labour Party, 1966, page 1.
[7] *Hansard*, House of Commons, Vol. 638, Col. 982.

National Executive it is stated that 'economic policy is about the distribution as well as the creation of a higher level of national income'.[1]

References to incomes distributions that are manifestly 'unjust' or to the 'notorious' pay pause of Selwyn Lloyd, which is alleged to have been 'unfairly' directed at lower paid workers, and similar adjectives are characteristic of the flavour of moral righteousness which is invariably found in Labour Party statements about the objective of greater equality of opportunity. Somehow or other most Labour supporters seem to be deeply convinced that their aim of greater equality is morally 'right'.[2] And it is probably true that many Conservative supporters have an uneasy feeling that their own opposition to greater equality is founded not on moral righteousness but on practical policies in a world in which human nature cannot be changed.

But there is no reason why equality, particularly if defined as equality of opportunity, should be readily accepted as being virtuous, if impracticable. If the present distribution of income and wealth, which may largely reflect the accident of birth, is to be replaced by one which results from equality of opportunity, and will therefore largely reflect the accident of ability, what is so virtuous about the change? For the distribution of ability is presumably just as much a matter of the luck of the draw as is the distribution of inherited income or capital. Furthermore, if it were the Conservative Party – i.e. the Party that, by and large, represents the wealthier classes – that advocated greater economic equality one could well applaud its virtuous self-denial. But since the Labour Party – again, by and large – represents the less wealthy section of the community, it is difficult to see what is so virtuous about advocating a more equal share out, since this means that Labour supporters will, on the whole, tend to gain at the expense of the others. In other words, if equality of opportunity or greater equality in the distribution of income or wealth is a virtue then Labour supporters are in the fortunate position of being able to equate virtue with expediency. Conservative supporters cannot oppose equality quite so easily, which is, perhaps, why they try to overcome a sort or moral inferiority complex by presenting the issue of the freedom of the individual as a major difference of moral principle between the parties.

Of course, the Labour Party comprises different groups whose interest in equality varies. It could well be that concern with equality has come

---

[1] Labour Party National Executive statement, *Labour's Economic Strategy*, 1969, page 9.
[2] This contrasts with an old and now defunct classical tradition in economics to the effect that the marginal productivity theory of wages provides a moral basis for inequalities of income on the ground that 'incomes must be earned on the open market. A person who renders services to the community is remunerated by the market mechanism. Should someone end up with a low income, this is due to his small contribution to the national product – pardonable, perhaps, but nevertheless his own fault. It is not the rich who are criticized in this reasoning but the poor; they have been deficient in productive capacity.' (J. Pen, *Harmony and Conflict in Modern Society* (English language edition, New York 1966), ch. 3, page 35. Professor Pen is not subscribing to this view, merely describing it.)

mainly from the more middle-class elements that would lose by it – at least by greater equality of incomes or wealth – and that the trade union elements are concerned mainly with the maintenance of income differentials at the lower end of the income range. It is not surprising that the middle-class element in the Labour Party has tended to be regarded with some suspicion by their working-class colleagues; one can hardly rely on people who, when it comes to the crunch, are quite capable of putting morality before expediency. One of the problems of the Labour Party is that of being a pro-equality party relying heavily on support from an organized pro-differential element.

The prime importance of the equality objective in differentiating the Labour Party from the Conservative Party adds importance to the much neglected fact that, in this sphere, the Labour Government did go quite a long way towards achieving its egalitarian objectives. Failure to appreciate the Labour Government's achievements in this respect may be partly because there are so many aspects of equality that it would be difficult to agree on which of them are most important to measure. But it is also partly because even if one concentrates on changes in the degree of inequality in the distribution of income it is far more difficult to interpret the statistics than to say, for example, whether the balance of payments has become much better or worse, or whether full employment has been maintained.[1] To begin with, allowance must be made for the way benefits of various kinds affect the different groups in the economy, as well as the incidence on different groups of various kinds of taxes, both direct and indirect, and Government expenditure on goods and services, which constitutes income in kind. In addition, there are considerable conceptual and other limitations on the data, which are discussed by Michael Stewart in Chapter 2.

Nevertheless, if all the main elements in the picture are brought together in the way that Stewart has done, it appears that, on the whole, Labour policy measures have improved the income distribution between 1964 and 1969. This did not arise on account of any measurable change in the distribution of original incomes (i.e. pre-tax wages and profits), though the Labour Government did attempt to help low paid workers in that the criteria of the prices and incomes policy specified that low paid workers would be given special consideration in applying the policy. And over the period 1965 to 1969, the earnings of lowest paid workers did rise slightly faster than the average, though this improvement seems to have been lost during the acceleration of the rate of increase in earnings in 1969–70.[2] The main cause of the reduction in inequalities of income under the Labour Government was the rapid increase in cash benefits, including pensions, supplementary benefits and family allowances, and of benefits in kind in the form of health and educational expenditures. As a result,

[1] Not that either of these concepts is by any means straightforward.
[2] See Chapter 2, page 83, and *General Problems of Low Pay*, National Board for Prices and Incomes, Report No. 169, Cmnd. 4648, 1971, page 14, para. 39.

net taxes and benefits have added proportionately more to the incomes of the poorest groups in 1969 than they did in 1964. Most of the people in the lowest 10% or so of the income range are unemployed, in fact, so that their main income is from national insurance benefits, or retirement pensions, or supplementary benefits. And, on the average, those in receipt of state benefits of one kind or another did better in terms of increases in real disposable income between 1964 and 1969 than the average manual worker or salaried employee. Also, the Labour Government succeeded in persuading many people to draw assistance to which they were entitled but which they had not drawn before for one reason or another. Furthermore, the Labour Government raised family allowances significantly.

Thus it is clear from Stewart's tables that cash benefits rose as a percentage of income for everybody between 1964 and 1968 but rose proportionately much more for the poorer than for the richer households. There was also a considerable increase in benefits in kind and, according to Stewart: 'it seems indisputable that the high priority the Labour Government gave to expenditure on education and the health service had a favourable effect on income distribution'.[1] For example, for a family with two children in the income range £676 to £816 p.a. cash benefits rose from 4% of income in 1964 to 22% in 1968; whereas for a similar family in the income range £2,122 to £2,566 the rise was only from 1% of income to 2% over the same period. For benefits in kind the changes over the same period for similar families were from 21% to 29% for the lower income family and from 9% to 10% for the upper income family.

The problem of providing adequate pensions for everybody without the burden of flat rate contributions pressing too heavily on low paid workers during their working lives is another problem that the Labour Government set about tackling in the form of a national superannuation pensions scheme with graduated contributions and pensions. One of the key features of this scheme, which was very much the brainchild of Richard Crossman, was that lower paid workers would receive a higher proportion of their previous earnings than the better paid workers. But these proposals did not reach the statute book by the time of the 1970 General Election.

While the main factor in increasing the equality of incomes (defined very widely) was, as just explained, the increase in benefits and Government expenditures on goods and services, there were some measures on the taxation side that were designed to have a similar effect. For example, the regressive nature of local rates was mitigated to some extent by the measure to provide rate rebates for low income recipients, and the Labour Government also tended to concentrate increases in indirect taxes on items such as motoring, wines, furs, jewellery, cameras and so on, which are least likely to hit the poor. The Labour Government also introduced the Capital Gains Tax. But as regards the distribution of wealth, it appears that although there may have been some shift in the direction of greater equality, this probably owes more to factors such as an increasing propen-

[1] Chapter 2, page 105.

sity to save by the lower income groups and a relative rise in the prices of the sort of assets they hold (such as houses, life insurance, etc.)[1] than to very mild measures designed to effect the distribution of wealth that Labour introduced.

Thus contrary to some impressions (e.g. the article by Professor Peter Townsend in *The Times*, March 10, 1971), the Labour Government did achieve a reduction in the inequality of incomes when all taxes, benefits and Government expenditures on social services are taken into account. This must be reckoned an achievement, especially when contrasted with the very regressive first major budget of the Conservative Government. Anybody who can still maintain that the equality issue is not sufficiently important as a dividing line between Labour and Conservative can have very little contact with the mass of the electorate.[2]

The Labour Government's record on equality of income distribution within the country contrasts, unfortunately, with the same Government's record on international equality – i.e. aid and overseas development.

Insofar as the Labour Party tries to equate greater equality with virtue rather than expediency, the acid test of its sincerity is presumably the extent to which it is prepared to distribute incomes more equally as between countries – i.e. give more aid to poorer countries – since this combines principle with the practice of having less, not more, for oneself. In their chapter below, Dudley Seers and Paul Streeten draw attention to the long standing internationalist element in Socialist policies and to the fact that that Labour Party pioneered international solidarity before even the First World War. The present generation of Labour leaders have been equally committed to the relief of world poverty (e.g. Mr Wilson's 1953 book *The War on World Poverty*). And when Labour finally came back in power in 1964 the Minister put in charge of aid and overseas development was none other than Barbara Castle, famed as the conscience of the Left. Nor were the noble intentions of the Party allowed to be foiled by a 'group of somewhat archaic but intelligent officials in the Foreign Office (and in the Commonwealth Relations Office as it then was)',[3] for a new Ministry was set up, headed by Barbara Castle and staffed with nearly as many economists as the rest of Whitehall put together (not that this was saying much in those days).

Thus, if it were purely a matter of intentions and administrative machinery, aid policy got off to a better start than almost any other area of Labour economic policy. Yet, as Seers and Streeten show, the central theme of their chapter 'is one of political sociology; how with the assumption of power by Labour, "responsibility" made for nationalism'.[4] For in

---

[1] This suggests that the poor are really smarter than the rich, which makes the present inequality of income distribution even more inequitable!

[2] Actually, it appears that Mr Brittan has somewhat changed his mind recently over the importance – or lack of it – of income equality, judging by his article in the *Financial Times* (29 April 1971), 'Incomes, and the argument about equality'.

[3] Chapter 3, page 121.

[4] Chapter 3, page 120.

the end less Government aid to overseas countries was given when Labour left office in 1970 than when they had taken office in 1964. Gross aid rose slightly between 1964 and 1966, but even this was on account of commitments already entered into by the Conservative Government; and after 1966 the figure fell. Since national output was rising slightly and aid repayments also rose, *net* aid as a percentage of national product fell from 0·48 in 1965 to 0·39 in 1969, which was back to the level of the mid-1950s.[1] Of course, it is not difficult to find extenuating circumstances; and the authors point out that the fact that the cuts in aid were not even greater during the years of almost non-stop balance of payments crises, when many sacred Labour principles were being sacrificed – free prescription charges, raising the school leaving age to 16, and so on – is to the credit of those involved. For although overseas aid did have some pressure groups at home, these groups did not represent large numbers of voters.

It will never be possible to say exactly how far the dismal record in the end reflected a failure of political will rather than the exigencies of the overall economic situation. Nevertheless, if one takes account also of other policies affecting the poorer countries, such as certain aspects of trade policy, foreign policy and policies affecting the overseas operations of British companies, the Labour Party's record on aid and development is, as Seers and Streeten say, 'discreditable, especially in contrast to the promises before the election'.

Growth and how to get it

The growth of productive potential clearly can be the main means of achieving a higher 'standard of living' defined more widely, though there have recently been increasing doubts about this[2] in view of the growing public consciousness of certain disamenity effects of growth, such as pollution. But there has been very little discussion of this aspect of growth in the usual Labour pronouncements on this subject. For example, it is usually asserted that 'higher living standards, and a fair chance in life for everyone, can only be achieved with a strong, efficient and expanding economy'[3] or that 'economic growth is the key to Labour's social programme. Economic growth sets the pace at which Labour can build the fair and just society we want to see . . .'.[4]

If one looks hard enough one can even find what appear, superficially,

---

[1] Private investment in less developed countries, in contrast with both public aid and with declared government policy, was much higher in 1969 than in 1964 and much higher than the official flow of aid (Chapter 3, page 132).

[2] See, for example, discussion of some of these doubts in chapter by the present writer in *Conflicts in Policy Objectives* (papers presented to Section F of the 1970 meeting of the British Association for the Advancement of Science) edited by Professor N. Kaldor (Oxford 1971).

[3] *Economic Strategy*, Labour Party, 1969, page 27.

[4] *Economic Measures*, Labour Party Talking Points Nos. 15/16, 1966, page 15.

to be assertions that growth is a prior objective for its sake, such as Douglas Jay's statements in Parliament, in 1962, to the effect that 'We really must decide to take rapid growth as our prime objective . . .'[1] and that 'I believe that [the Government] should adopt the OECD target of 4·2% a year. . . . Having done that the Government should then make the achievement of this target the first priority in economic policy. . . .'.[2] But such statements, in the course of Parliamentary debate, cannot be taken as indicators of any real divergence of view as to the function of economic growth and merely reflect the fact that even members of the Jay family cannot, every time they say anything, say everything.

In fact, since official pronouncements of the Labour Party have tended to ignore any discussion of how far growth is desirable and how much priority should be given to it by comparison with other objectives, most Party pronouncements about growth are only about the means by which it is to be achieved.

More broad-ranging discussions of the pros and cons of economic growth can be found only in unofficial writings, notably those of Mr Crosland, who took up some of the broader aspects of the growth issue in 1956, 1962 and again in a recent Fabian tract.[3] But Mr Crosland's discussion of the wider aspects of the growth problem does not really raise any specific party issues. One might expect that anxiety over, say, the harmful effects of growth on the environment is likely to be greater in those Socialist circles that have a William Morris tradition than in business circles, with their tendency to assume that the market mechanism will automatically look after pollution and the like and that firms should not be burdened with extra costs in order further to reduce pollution.

But this would be a travesty of the situation. For a large proportion of the working population, the conditions in which they work and spend most of their time are so much worse than the pollution that is currently fashionable that they are not really very worried about the rise in the carbon dioxide content of the world atmosphere. And, at the top end of the income or social spectrum, opposition to economic growth finds natural allies among those classes that risk losing established privileges, not to mention the dangers to their conservationist interests. For some people, economic growth and pollution mean simply that the grouse moors will have less grouse, beaters and gillies, and more upstarts who don't really know how to handle a gun.

Consequently, as there is no clear class interest in the relationship between growth and the standard of living there is little specifically Socialist content in such discussion as can be found of the growth issue.[4] In fact,

---

[1] *Hansard*, House of Commons, Vol. 656, Col. 143.

[2] Ibid., Vol. 657, Col. 1353.

[3] *The Future of Socialism*, op. cit.; *The Conservative Enemy*, 1962, Chapter 6 ('Production in the age of affluence'); and *A Social Democratic Britain*, Fabian Tract, 1970.

[4] I have argued elsewhere that, if anything, it is the middle classes who stand to lose most from economic growth. See page 44, footnote 2.

even in Mr Crosland's discussion of the growth issue in 1956, in which he set out to select those aspects of the growth issue that he believed, at that time, to be 'most germane to socialist policy', he finished by discussing mainly the need for a higher rate of investment and the problem of inflation. But there was nothing particularly Socialist about either of these, as he would almost certainly now recognize. The former is an ingredient in any Conservative Party programme, and the passage of time has shown that conservative Governments in other countries, such as Germany and Japan, have not prevented high rates of investment. And his discussion of inflation did not raise any specifically socialist issues either, being mainly about the adverse consequences of excess demand. As has now become increasingly recognized, this is not the same thing at all, and if inflation is largely caused by wage push the real problem for a Socialist party is what to do about it if it means curbing union power.

Of course, there are genuine Socialist aspects of the growth issue, given the Socialist concern with income distribution. First, given that the economic problem of growth is the problem of how much present consumption should be sacrificed in the interests of more consumption in the future, Socialists should be asking *whose* present consumption is to be sacrificed. A Socialist might not attach much importance to a further sacrifice of present consumption by the rich. But he might think that the sacrifice of some present consumption by the millions of people that, according to Michael Stewart's chapter below, are still living on or below the supplementary benefit level might not be thought worthwhile in the interests of yet higher consumption by future generations whose standards of material consumption will be much higher than those of today anyway.

Secondly, insofar as it is accepted that some sacrifice of present consumption must be made, there are difficult decisions to be made about how this is to be obtained without either a less equal distribution of original income (notably by raising the share of profits in national income) or the provision of more public savings corresponding to a greater budget surplus. Thirdly, even if the resources for more investment can be released by means of higher public savings, unless the extra investment is to take place in the public sector there is still the question of how to provide adequate stimulus to extra investment in the private sector. This may well require a higher rate of return on capital so that, given the ratio of capital to labour in the economy, this would require a higher share of net profits in national income.

Unfortunately it is difficult to establish how far this is the case. Figures showing changes over time, or differences between countries, in the shares of profits in national income (allowing for the capital-labour ratio) and the rate of investment tell one little or nothing about the direction of causality. For as long as one assumes that the profit receivers save a higher proportion of their income than wage earners, then a higher investment ratio must be accompanied by a higher share of profits in national income. This is a matter of simple arithmetic given the *ex-post* identity of actual investment and savings, and so cannot tell one whether it is the high share of profits that leads to high investment or the other way round.[1]

If it is assumed that the overall level of investment is influenced by the rate of profit then the long-term decline in the rate of profit in Britain might provide much of the explanation of the relatively slow rate of investment in this country. In an analysis of the historical data, in which full allowance was made for changes in the stock of capital and the size of the labour force, Mr Charles Feinstein has shown that the real rate of return on capital in this country has fallen over the very long run, largely on account of sharp falls in the course of the two world wars, but that 'there is some suggestion that the rate has been slipping downwards since 1950–4'.[2] And a very recent study by Andrew Glyn and Bob Sutcliffe has shown that there has been a sharp fall in the rate of profit, both pre-tax and post-tax, during the last fifteen years or so.[3]

For example, the pre-tax rate of profit fell from an average of 18·8% in the period 1950–9 to an average of 12·3% in 1966–8 and finally to 10·9% in the year 1969 (when the pressure of capacity was particularly low, of course). The post-tax rate of profit fell from 8·3% in 1950–9 to 5·5% for the three-year period 1966–8, and 3·2% in 1969. These declines in the *rate* of profit on capital correspond, after adjustment for estimated changes in the capital stock, to a fall in the *share* of profits in national income. And over the average of the last decade the share of profits in national income in this country has been much lower than in the other major advanced countries, though in order to infer that this is responsible for the relatively low investment rate in Britain it would be necessary to take account of the relative ratios of capital to labour in the various countries, the rates of tax, and so on, as well as the even more intractable problems mentioned above of the direction of causality.

But if there is some causal significance in the apparent relationship between the rate of profit and the investment rate then the trade-off between higher growth and greater economic equality needs to be seriously considered. It may well be that the Labour Government's success in achieving a greater equality in the distribution of consumption (including public consumption) has been partially responsible for the slower rate of growth of investment and hence the slower rate of growth of national product. According to Glyn and Sutcliffe, 'to some extent the really amazing decline in the post tax rate [of profit] over the 1965–9 period is the result of less generous investment incentives'. Presumably, this takes account of various increases in the burden of taxation on profits, including the rise in

[1] The latter possibility is the one postulated in a well-known article by Professor Kaldor, 'Alternative theories of distribution', *Review of Economic Studies*, 1955/6.
[2] C. H. Feinstein, 'Changes in the distribution of the national income in the United Kingdom since 1860', in A. Marchal and B. Ducros (eds.), *The Distribution of National Income* (New York, 1968).
[3] Andrew Glyn and Bob Sutcliffe, 'The collapse of UK Profits', *New Left Review*, No. 66, March/April 1971, Table A, page 5.

Corporation Tax. This demonstrates how difficult it is to increase public expenditures on social services, income support benefits and the like, to avoid major increases in tax rates, and, at the same time, to pursue a strategy of achieving faster growth with the aid, partly, of more generous investment incentives. Something has to give and it appears to have been the investment incentives. It may well be that, faced with a choice, the Labour Party may have preferred the more equal distribution of consumption to a faster rate of growth so that the slow growth rate would not be regarded as a failure.

But the choice has never been put this way for the simple reason that the awkward problems of reconciling more equal income distribution with faster economic growth have barely been raised in Labour Party discussions of economic policy. Faster growth was a clear objective since it was claimed that it would come at no cost; largely by changing institutions and people. And then the higher social expenditures could come out of the faster growth. So everybody would be better off and there were no choices to make. Unfortunately, as pointed out above, economics is about choice and a reluctance to recognize this is all too common a human weakness. The choices to be made in the interests of faster growth hardly rate a mention in any of the available political contributions to the debate on national economic objectives. These, as stated above, are almost exclusively about the mere means by which each Party will be more successful than the other in achieving economic growth. The Conservative Party, so we are told, would achieve faster growth by removing the incubus of Government expenditure and intervention, by a more business-like approach to public affairs and by setting the people free and hence tapping those resources of human ingenuity that respond to incentives to work harder. (Personally, since I work too hard already, I am glad that the Conservative Party has not yet found an incentive that will make me work even harder.) And the Labour Party, we are told, has other means of achieving the same growth objective. A discussion of Labour's record under the growth heading, therefore, must be largely about (*i*) what these other instruments to promote faster growth were and (*ii*) how successful they proved to be. As for the instruments of faster growth these comprised mainly planning, industrial policy and regional policy. They all had their part to play, as well as certain changes in the fiscal system – such as the introduction of SET and Corporation Tax – but there is little doubt that the main hope before 1964, and even into 1965, was 'planning'.

Planning
It is true that, as Mr Brittan points out, '. . . it was the Conservatives who took up "indicative planning" and incomes policy in the early 1960s'.[1] But to conclude from this that the two parties did not really differ about the role of planning in improving economic performance would be wrong. It all depends on what one means by 'planning'. Only in a broad and vague

[1] Brittan, op. cit., page 117.

sense can it be argued that there was no real difference between the parties in their attitudes to planning. As David Henderson put it, 'The notion that Dr Erhard and Mr Harold Wilson are equally committed to economic planning, in the same sense of the term, is an attractive one, since it appeals both to the love of paradox and to the desire to believe that all rational men are in agreement on fundamental issues.'[1] As far back as 1956, Mr Crosland had recognized that, in a loose sense, both parties were in favour of planning of a sort, but he pointed out that 'the issue now is not whether, but how much and for what purpose to plan'.[2] In respect both of the objectives of planning and the lengths to which the Party would go in using planning, it is clear that the Labour Party, at any rate, was under the impression that it meant something very different from the Conservatives.

As regards the objectives of planning, the Labour Party's Manifesto for the 1964 General Election states at the outset that '. . . the ending of economic privilege, the abolition of poverty in the midst of plenty, and the creation of real equality of opportunity . . . have now become immediate targets of political action' that can be achieved 'provided it [Britain] wills three things: the mobilization of its resources within a national plan; the maintenance of a wise balance between community and individual expenditure; and the education of all its citizens . . .'.[3] In fact, most of this document was about the wonderful new planning weapon which the Labour Party intended to use to transform the economy and society and to shake it out of the miserable stop-go and stagnation of the thirteen years of Tory rule. Even allowing for rhetoric, there is little doubt that the objectives and scope of planning as set out in this document (and in speeches of Labour leaders) would hardly find a place in a document presented to the annual Conservative Party Conference or to a standard gathering of conservative business men. The same applies to the extent to which it was thought that planning would be used, as well as to the objectives. As a later Labour Party document put it, in connection with Tory planning, 'very belatedly the Macmillan Government had paid lip-service to the widespread demand for planning – but it was a timid empty gesture. The National Economic Development Council, which was established as the new planning instrument, was right outside the ambit of Government policy making and remained so throughout the Tory years.'[4] There was a strong conviction going back very many years in the Labour Party to the effect that 'at the root of the Tories' failure lies an outdated philosophy – their nostalgic belief that it is possible in the second half of the 20th century to hark back to a 19th century free enterprise economy and a 19th century unplanned economy'.[5]

[1] P. D. Henderson (ed.), *Economic Growth in Britain* (London 1966), Chapter 7, page 199.
[2] *The Conservative Enemy*, op. cit., page 354.
[3] *Let's Go with Labour for the New Britain*, 1964 Election Manifesto, page 5.
[4] *Labour's Economic Strategy*, Labour Party National Executive statement, 1969, page 6.
[5] 1964 Election Manifesto, page 7.

Again, as with overseas aid, the new Labour Government in 1964 did not wish its planning intentions to be frustrated by leaving the elaboration and implementation of the plan to the existing Treasury machine with its suspected propensity to see every economic problem solely in terms of maintaining some 'right' pressure of demand. Roger Opie, in Chapter 4, discusses the machinery set up in the new Department of Economic Affairs under the Deputy Prime Minister, George Brown, who, whatever other weaknesses may have been attributed to him, was not likely to allow planning to go by default on account of any lack of personal dynamism or timidity in putting his own point of view in discussion with colleagues. But perhaps that was the whole trouble, for the essence of 'planning', as the very word suggests, is rational and dispassionate calculation. If a policy is to succeed by sheer weight of enthusiasm, drive, energy, dynamism, bullying, and so on there is not much need for a plan. Planning is essentially a matter of sober assessment of alternative targets, honest identification of the obstacles and difficulties, calculated selection of feasible, consistent and coherent solutions, and resolute sacrifice of secondary objectives that involve overstraining the resources estimated to be at one's command. This is a task for cheese-paring economists, not for swashbuckling men of action, unless the latter are prepared to listen to the former. George Brown should have inscribed on his desk Joseph Schumpeter's dictum 'We always plan too much and always think too little'.[1]

The main reason why the Plan failed in the end is certainly, as Opie described, the failure to ensure a satisfactory development in the balance of payments. But this weakness of the Plan was inherent in its conception from the outset. The unlikelihood of overcoming the foreign balance constraint without a devaluation was apparent at the time the Plan was drawn up. But George Brown stuck to the agreed Government policy at the time of refusing to countenance any change in the exchange rate, a position which, it is believed, happened to conform to his own appraisal of the situation until after the Plan was published. It is true that the Plan did include a long list of actions that would be taken to help increase output and productivity. But, as Opie points out, most of these tems could have figured in any policy statement with or without all the paraphernalia of 'planning'.

As far as the specific targets of the Plan are concerned, not one was achieved; indeed this was hardly possible given that the key target, namely the rate of growth, was missed by such a large margin. Over the period 1964 to 1970 gross domestic product was planned to rise by 25% and, in fact, rose by only 14%. The failure of output to rise, on average, by more than 2·2% per annum over the Plan period instead of the planned 3·8% per annum reflected partly a slower rise in employment (employment in 1970 was actually 2% below the 1964 level instead of the planned rise of 3%). But the main cause of the shortfall was the slow rise in productivity. It appears that this might be partly due to the planners having over-

[1] *Capitalism, Socialism and Democracy*. Preface to the second edition.

estimated what the underlying trend rate of growth of output was to begin with, so that not all the shortfall in productivity could be attributed to the failure of policy measures to engineer an acceleration in what was believed, in 1965, to be the underlying trend rate of growth.[1]

Given the failure to achieve the planned growth rate, there was less point in achieving some of the sub-targets and, indeed, in a climate of slow growth, it would have been inconceivable that targets, such as for investment, could have been reached let alone would have been desirable. Nevertheless, whatever the cause (the slow growth of demand, the slack pressure on capacity, the low rate of profit, etc., etc.), the increase in the share of resources devoted to investment, which was a key element in the growth strategy, failed to materialize. In 1970 gross fixed investment was only 18·4% of national expenditure instead of the planned level of 19·5%.[2] This shortfall in the investment share was slightly more than matched by an excess (over the Plan target) in the combined share of private and public consumption of 1·8%. This pattern was, of course, the reverse of Labour Party strategy, which involved a shift of resources in favour of investment which, in turn, would permit faster growth out of which higher consumption of the lower income groups and higher public consumption in general could be provided. Of course, the fact that the pattern of resources moved in the opposite manner does not demonstrate that this strategy is inherently misguided, for the strategy depends on the assumption that there is no external constraint to prevent the pressure of demand from being maintained. It was the error regarding the foreign balance constraint that wrecked the strategy.

The errors in the foreign balance targets in the Plan cannot be seen by comparing the planned targets for 1970 with the outcome, since there was a little matter of a devaluation in 1967 which had not been allowed for in the Plan and which greatly boosted the exports. The most useful comparison, therefore, is between the planned rates of growth and the rates of growth of imports and exports over the period 1964–7. These comparisons show that the forecast increase in imports was not far off target, imports rose by 3·6% per annum as against a planned rise of 4% per annum. But given that the growth rate of national product was much slower than planned, the rise in imports implies that the ratio of the increase in imports to the increase in national product was actually nearly twice as great as had been planned.[3] On the export side, exports were planned to rise by 5.25% per annum and rose by only 3·4% per annum over the period up to the devaluation.

[1] See M. J. C. Surrey, 'The National Plan in retrospect', forthcoming in the *Bulletin of the Oxford University Institute of Statistics*.
[2] See Surrey, op. cit. See also Chapter 5, page 175.
[3] Ibid. According to Surrey, the planned income elasticity of demand for imports was about 1·05, whereas the actual outcome corresponded to a 'revealed' elasticity of 1·8, but that if allowance is made for stockbuilding in the two terminal years used for the estimates the true error was even greater than this.

Given the resulting failure to eliminate the balance of payments deficit the National Plan stood no chance of achieving its main targets. But, although it is argued below that failure to devalue the pound earlier was the major cause of the economic difficulties throughout the period of the Labour Government and that an earlier devaluation would have had numerous beneficial effects, both directly on the external balance and indirectly on the subsequent management of wages and prices and employment, it must not be thought that an earlier devaluation would necessarily have enabled the main Plan targets to have been achieved. Elimination of the external constraint was only a necessary condition not a sufficient one. It is, of course, impossible to calculate exactly by how much an earlier devaluation would have raised the feasible growth rate of the economy, since we do not know how far absence of an external constraint would have stimulated, in the longer term, a greater rise in investment, faster technological progress, etc.

Without making any allowance for this sort of influence of an earlier devaluation, Mr Surrey has calculated that if the pound had been devalued in 1964 the growth of national product over the period 1964–70 could have been 5% higher than it actually was. In other words, it could have risen by 18% instead of 14%, by comparison with the planned rise of 25%.[1] This suggests that the Plan's targets would still have been missed by a large margin. But if it is assumed that a situation in which a favourable external balance was combined with full employment would have led to more optimistic investment behaviour and a faster rate of technological progress, then it may well be that the actual rate of growth would have been somewhere between the 18% figure and the Plan target of 25% over the whole period, so according to whether one puts the final figure near the bottom or the top of this range the failure to devalue earlier explains between one-third and the whole of the failure to achieve the planned growth rate.

Regional policy

Regional policy was to be a central feature of the National Plan, though attitudes to regional policy illustrate the difficulty of making a sharp distinction between the means of policy and independent objectives. Frequently regional policy is described in terms which suggest that it is seen simply as a means of raising total national output, particularly as set out in 1965 in the National Plan or in the January 1966 White Paper on Investment Incentives.[2] Also the 1967 White Paper on 'The Development Areas (Regional Employment Premium)' is almost exclusively in terms of the 'efficiency' and 'management of the economy' aspects of regional policy.[3]

[1] Surrey, op. cit.
[2] *The National Plan* (Cmnd. 2764, 1965), page 11; and *Investment Incentives* (Cmnd. 2874, 1966), page 3.
[3] Cmnd. 3310, 1967.

But this may simply represent the style of official documents rather than any change of emphasis in the Labour Party. Leading Labour politicians invariably emphasized the social equity aspects of regional planning, as in a speech by Mr Callaghan in 1965 in which he represented regional policy as a remedy for 'economic waste and social hardship'.[1] Mr Peart is even more categorical about the social objectives of regional policy in 1968 in saying that the object of regional policy 'has been to bring about a fairer distribution of economic opportunities and social conditions throughout the country' and he only adds as a secondary consideration that 'we also aim certainly to make use of the unused resources of the less prosperous regions for the benefit of those regions and the whole of the national economy'.[2] In the same way, Labour Election Manifestos tend to present regional policy as being bound up with the relief of unemployment in certain regions as an objective in its own right rather than simply, as in the White Paper mentioned above, as a means to more price stability or greater output for the economy as a whole.[3]

The question of how much contribution regional policy made to the overall targets of the National Plan hardly applies given the other developments that torpedoed the Plan anyway. Nevertheless, the Labour Government's regional policies were pursued with more effect than certain other aspects of overall economic policy. Jeremy Hardie, in Chapter 6, describes first the very heavy increase in expenditures under the heading of regional policy that took place under the Labour Government, and although he shows that simple comparison of the figures with those relating to the preceding Tory administration can be very misleading they do seem to lead to the conclusion that the scale of the regional effort was significantly greater than had hitherto been the case. Of course, in some cases the increased effort might have been misconceived; this might apply, for example, to the large increase in transfer payments made, in effect, to the shareholders of oil and of chemical companies as part of the policy of giving heavy investment grants to firms in Development Areas even if such investment did very little to reduce heavy local unemployment.

Nevertheless, there is no doubt that the scale of regional variations in unemployment levels, which had been widening hitherto, began to narrow somewhat,[4] and this is probably due to regional policy measures including, of course, the Regional Employment Premium. Hardie also argues that the Regional Planning Boards, whatever their limitations, introduced some element of rationality and co-ordination into certain of the regional activities of various Government Departments. Furthermore,

---

[1] *Hansard*, House of Commons, Vol. 710, Col. 283.
[2] *Hansard*, House of Commons, Vol. 772, Col. 820.
[3] See especially the 1964 Election Manifesto, page 11, and the 1966 Manifesto, *Time for Decision*, pages 6 and 14.
[4] Table 6.5 in Chapter 6 shows that the ratio of the unemployment percentage in Development Areas to the national average fell steadily from 2·21 in 1964 to 1·67 in 1970, and there was also an improvement in activity rates in Development Areas.

continuity and predictability of policy are very important in this area of policy since results take a long time to achieve.[1] It is likely that some regional policy measures had some indirect and non-quantifiable effects, for example on the quality and outlook of local management, and in this and other ways it has probably improved the basis on which future developments in many regions can build. It may well be that even the installation of capital intensive factories in areas where they did little to resolve the immediate problems of unemployment will, in the longer run, prove to have helped revitalize some of the development areas. Thus, even if regional policy made no significant contribution to economic growth by 1970, this is no reason for writing it off as far as this objective was concerned, not to mention the clear success it did achieve in reducing regional unemployment differentials.

Industrial policy

Industrial policy consisted of the application to industry of the various measures to raise productivity that were implied by the targets of the National Plan and by the general objective of increasing the rate of growth of the economy. The basic strategy for industry, as summarized by Andrew Graham in Chapter 5, consisted of stimulating investment through high demand combined with more effective investment incentives, to use incomes policy as a means of preventing the high demand from being translated into excessive increases in wage costs, to stimulate faster technological innovation by suitable taxation measures or direct intervention and encouragement, and to obtain the benefits of all this on the prices side by means of better policies in the field of monopolies and mergers. Basic Labour Party philosophy had little faith in the expansionary capacity of a corporate sector controlled by managers who would be more concerned, so it was believed, with safety than with genuine enterprise, and operating in a framework of oligopoly in accordance with a pattern of demand that was artificially stimulated to a large extent by advertising. Such an industrial environment could hardly provide the framework for rapid technological innovation or produce a pattern of output that matched social interests and benefits. The 1964 election theme, which presented the Labour Party as the party of the new technocrats, ushering in the scientific revolution in British industry, was not just for the birds and the electors; some of the Party leaders genuinely believed it.

To remedy the deficiencies of the industrial situation called for a whole range of policy measures, which are surveyed by Andrew Graham in Chapter 5. (*i*) Through the NEDC private industries would be associated with the work on the National Plan, so that, if nothing else, the Plan would provide some sort of co-ordinated and informed market research for the individual producers. (*ii*) By forming their expectations there would be more chance that they would respond appropriately and hence help to

[1] Allowance must also be made for the fact that the full package of regional measures was not in operation until September 1967.

make the optimistic predictions of the Plan become self-fulfilling. (*iii*) Investment was to be stimulated, in addition, by changes in the taxation system that would, in effect, discourage dividend distribution (notably the switch to Corporation Tax, accompanied by income tax on dividends out of post-Corporation tax profits). (*iv*) The switch from investment allowances to investment grants was expected to make a greater impact on investment decisions. (*v*) The Selective Employment Tax was introduced partly, if not largely, on the grounds that by shifting labour out of the service sector into industry the latter would be able to reap greater economies of scale and achieve a faster rate of growth of productivity. (*vi*) A more active monopoly and mergers policy would be operated both to keep a closer check on harmful restraint on competition and to supplement the workings of the market by promoting socially useful mergers that might otherwise not easily take place. This was to be carried out through the activities of the IRC, which was set up under the Industrial Expansion Act, in which the inadequacies of the price mechanism and the need to intervene in cases of divergence between private and social interests were clearly set out. In addition to these overall measures, there were also special instances of Government intervention, such as in connection with the establishment of aluminium smelters, or the special measures taken to help the shipbuilding industry. And the impetus behind the technological revolution was to be the newly created Ministry of Technology.

What was the outcome of all this activity and this wide range of industrial policy measures? Graham's chapter shows that from 1964 to 1968 productivity in the economy as a whole or in manufacturing alone rose faster than during the previous four years (see Chapter 5, Table 5.2), but that it is difficult to say how far this represents a continuous acceleration in the underlying rate of growth of productivity. It is also shown that, given the decline in profits and liquidity during the 1960s, manufacturing investment kept up rather better in 1966/7 than in previous cyclical downswings. For example, the worst year for manufacturing investment was 1966/7, when it fell by 2·8% (in volume), whereas in the 1961/2 downswing it fell by 8% and in 1962/3 by 11·6%. But given the uncertainties about what factors really determine investment, it is impossible to demonstrate that this is the result of Government policies. It may well be that investment grants are more likely to be taken into account than were the old investment allowances so that for a given effect on the balance of the Government's budget over a run of years the investment stimulus from grants is greater than that arising from a corresponding investment allowance.[1] But there is little concrete evidence for this view, whereas there is no doubt that the total tax 'take' from profits has increased over

[1] The concept of an equal effect on the budget is not very clear, in fact, since the change from grants to allowances or vice versa involves a change in the time path of Government receipts and expenditures, so that the degree of equivalence depends partly on the Government's rate of time preference.

the last few years. As for the selective character of the investment grant system, with its preferential treatment of manufacturing (and one or two cherished industries) and the Development Areas, this is something that could have been achieved with an allowance system just as well. Also, as mentioned above in connection with regional policy, it is likely that the high rate of investment grants in the Development Areas went partly to add to profits in chemical and oil refining companies and did little, at least in the short run, to contribute to any national economic objectives, even if they did have a beneficial longer run effect on the general economic climate in some of the regions. As for the special privileges accorded to manufacturing industry by means both of the investment grants system as well as the Selective Employment Tax, the underlying theory of this has never been entirely clear, and the absence of any obvious results suggests that this might reflect more than a lack of expository skill by its main protagonists.[1]

Of course, there may have been many other reasons for the failure of the industrial policies to have produced more convincing results in time. Overseas governments were quick to react to what were believed to be special Government subsidies or assistance to any particular industry – witness the considerable agitation in EFTA over the suspected subsidy on electricity prices to be charged to the new aluminium smelters, as well as over the high rate of investment grants in the Development Areas. Also, civil servants in this country tend to be rather shy of exercising much direct control over the market economy and are well aware of the dangers of trying to do so. Superimposed on all this was a wide divergence of view among Labour Ministers about the extent to which the price mechanism could be allowed to get on with the job aided here and there perhaps by a tax gimmick or two, as distinct from a full-blooded Socialist attempt to plan everything down to the last little detail. But as Graham points out, the various weapons of industrial policy might have been far more effective if they had been operating 'in contexts for which they were intended', namely a context of expansion and full employment.

One final ingredient of industrial policy that might have special interest from the point of view of Labour Party philosophy has been its policy with respect to nationalized industries. However, as Michael Posner's chapter shows, the 'sole Socialist step of importance was the nationalization of steel', and the case for steel nationalization can hardly be said nowadays to be one of controlling the 'commanding heights' of the economy. At the same time various steps were taken under the Labour Government to rationalize and modernize the nationalized industries and to put their operating criteria on a more logical economic basis than had been the case in the past. But this was probably simply the continuation of a process of increasing sophistication in the management of nationalized industries in

[1] Of course, like some of the regional policy measures discussed above, it is likely that policies aimed at achieving longer-run structural changes in the industrial situation need a longer run in order to bear fruit.

Whitehall that owed little to the particular inclinations of any one political party.

The management of the economy

There are three main conventional aspects of the management of the economy that have tended to preoccupy all Governments, Right wing and Left wing, in this country and abroad. These are the maintenance of high levels of employment and freedom from severe fluctuations in the pressure of demand, price stability, and a satisfactory balance of payments. High employment is desired largely as a means to maximize consumption, though unemployment is also an evil in its own right on account of the unpleasant psychological effects on the people concerned irrespective of the extent to which their consumption levels could be maintained by means of income transfers. Short-term fluctuations in the pressure of demand are disliked for a variety of reasons: first, the periods of low pressure of demand are necessarily periods in which total national consumption is lower than it could otherwise be, but, secondly, it is believed that fluctuations in demand and output have an adverse effect on the longer-run growth of capacity, though there is very little evidence for this view. As for price stability, there is no evidence that absence of stable prices has any particular effect on economic growth, but there is some evidence and strong prima facie reason to believe that it does move the income distribution against the weaker sections of the community and this conflicts with generally accepted notions of social justice. Finally, the need to maintain some sort of equilibrium in the balance of payments is recognized to be incumbent on nearly all countries in this harsh world.

Thus the responsibility of the Government of the day for the short-run management of the economy, including the prevention of inflation, has not been a matter of party politics. But it may well be that the Labour Party would define 'full employment' as corresponding to a rather lower level of unemployment than would the Conservative Party. Also, there has been a tendency for Labour politicians to assert – pre-1964 – that the Conservatives gave rather too much priority to short-term considerations and not enough to the longer-term development of productive potential. This was the general spirit behind the pre-1964 attacks on the Tory 'stop-go' policies. How much better did the Labour Government fare?

The level of demand

As Michael Artis points out at the beginning of Chapter 8 on stabilization policies, it is not really possible to judge performance by any one objective such as the level of unemployment or the degree of fluctuations around a steady path of growth. The other short-run objectives just discussed, namely price stability and the external balance, have to be taken into account, not to mention the basic longer-term objectives discussed earlier in this chapter. And rarely, in fact, could good intentions in the field of the short-term pressure of demand have been so completely abandoned on account of exigencies arising out of balance of payments difficulties as was the case with the Labour Government throughout virtually the whole period mid-1966 to the General Election in mid-1970.

Of course, attempts to measure the impact of Government policy on the level of demand and hence on the stability of output raise extremely complex problems of analysis and interpretation. If one tries to say how much Government fiscal and monetary action has determined the course of behaviour of the economy one is, in effect, trying to say what would have happened in the absence of the governmental measures. This requires an accurate 'model' of how the economy would have behaved in the absence of governmental intervention and such a model is not available. Also, virtually nothing is known about the longer run impact on the behaviour of the private sector or the knowledge that, in the short run, no Government is likely to allow unemployment to approach pre-war levels.

Nevertheless, a partial estimate can be made of the short-run effect of changes in taxation, which are necessarily the most important fiscal instruments of stabilization policy. On the basis of such estimates, Artis has shown that

(i) in terms of the degree of fluctuation around the longer-run trend of output the Labour Government did not stabilize output any more than previous Governments, although

(ii) the old 'cycle' disappeared.

But this was because the 'go' phase of what would normally have been a 'stop-go' cycle beginning with the 'stop' of 1966/7 never materialized; the economy stayed in the 'stop' position. By 1970 output was over 2% below the trend level, and the trend rate of growth itself had no doubt been depressed by the sluggish growth of output over the whole period and the gradual slackening of the pressure of demand.[1] And the average unemployment rate over the years 1967 to 1969 inclusive (2·5% for the UK) was higher than any previous consecutive three-year period.

Of course, there are some complicating features in the labour market situation, such as the changed relationship between unemployment and vacancies, indicating that there has probably been some rise in the degree of 'frictional' or structural unemployment. It is highly likely that the redundancy payments and income-related unemployment benefits introduced by the Labour Government have meant that a given pressure of demand is associated with a higher level of unemployment than had hitherto been the case. It is also quite possible that the aftermath of devaluation was a certain amount of extra structural unemployment corresponding to some shift into export or import substituting industries. It is impossible to quantify these factors precisely, but it could well be that a figure of 2·5% unemployment post-1967 corresponds to a pressure of

[1] See also Surrey, op. cit. Surrey's estimates suggest that for the pressure of demand to have been as high in 1970 as in 1964, output would have had to be 3% higher in 1970 than it actually was.

demand that would have been associated with about 2·1% unemployment pre-1967 (this would be consistent with the vacancy figures, for example). In that case, average unemployment for the three years 1967 to 1969 inclusive would be 2·1% in the UK which is about the same as during the three years 1958 to 1960 inclusive or 1962 to 1964 inclusive, which were the worst three years, from the unemployment point of view, of the Conservative Government. And, still adjusting downwards the actual unemployment figures for the post-1967 years as indicated above, the average unemployment for the whole period of the Labour Government, which can be taken as roughly 1965 to 1969 inclusive, would be 1·9%, which is less than the average of 2·1% in the preceding six years of Conservative Government (1958 to 1963 inclusive).[1]

The balance of payments and the pound sterling
The Labour Government took office towards the end of 1964, a year in which, in addition to a long-term capital outflow of £354 million, there was a current deficit of £395 million, the largest peace-time current deficit in this century. It is understandable, therefore, that neither of the two men who later were to occupy the post of Chancellor of the Exchequer were able to live up to their brave declarations of earlier years to the effect that the balance of payments should be sacrificed to other objectives, notably economic growth. For example, Roy Jenkins said in 1961 that 'we should be prepared to go through a period of weak balance of payments . . . a period of losing reserves if necessary, in order to get over the hump of stepping up our rate of growth' or that '. . . there is no possibility of solving the balance of payments problem unless Britain goes for a rapid rate of growth'.[2] Mr Callaghan was taking the same line in 1962 in saying in Parliament, 'Which do the Government want most? Do they want stagnation here and a firm balance of payments, or do they want growth and to handle the difficulties that would arise in the balance of payments as they occur? I would choose the second.'[3] It is a far cry from this to the sort of statements that Mr Callaghan was making in 1966 such as that 'I should therefore emphasize that the over-riding task before us is to achieve

[1] Of course, from the point of view of successful demand management or the welfare of the people affected, the adjustment made and the simple averages obtained can be very misleading. For example, if the average unemployment in two periods is 2%, but in one period this represents a steady 2% and in the other it represents fluctuations from 0·5% in one year to 3·5% in another year, it is reasonable to conclude that demand management has been less successful in the second period and also that the loss of welfare was probably greater on balance (though any such conclusion about the welfare aspects, particularly when there have been changes in unemployment benefits, etc., must be subject to very many strong assumptions).

[2] *Hansard*, House of Commons, Vol. 638, Cols. 1040 and 1038.

[3] Ibid., Vol. 656, Col. 51. Similar sentiments were expressed in a debate in the House in November of the same year (Vol. 666, Col. 619), when he added that protective measures could be adopted to deal with any balance of payments difficulties caused by giving priority to expansion.

a current surplus'[1] or the official Labour Party notes for its speakers in the 1966 General Election to the effect that 'for twenty months now the over-riding aim of Labour's economic policy has been to solve the inherited balance of payments problem'.[2] On the other hand, Mr Callaghan's pre-1964 speeches on this subject are entirely consistent with his post-1970 speeches for, in 1971, he has begun again to advocate a policy of all-out expansion over the next five years irrespective of the foreign balance.[3] It was only when he was in office and able to shape events that he took a different view. Mr Jenkins was of course in a similar position, when he became Chancellor of the Exchequer just after the 1967 devaluation, in having to give priority to the improvement in the balance of payments, but he was much more careful to explain that this was not because the balance of payments was an end in itself[4] and when, in April 1970, he believed this objective had been achieved, he added that the time had come 'when we can adopt a more normal balance of priorities'.[5]

The most important aspect of attitudes to the foreign balance, from the point of view of the subject of this book, is, of course, the attitudes to the means by which the balance of payments constraint on the pursuit of other policies can be met. In the pre-1964 statements Labour politicians frequently argued that expansion must not merely be given priority over the balance of payments but that it was the only means of achieving a satisfactory balance of payments since it would lead to a faster growth of productivity and so on, though Mr Wilson is on record about Labour's determination to defend the value of the pound before taking office in 1964.[6] In the first two years of the Labour Government, however, as we all know, the over-riding importance of maintaining the exchange rate was stressed over and over again.[7] The consequences of this misplaced devotion to one particular price (for sterling) in a political party that was believed to be suspicious of the virtues of the price mechanism were, of course, incalculable. By comparison with the effect on the foreign balance of the devaluation that was eventually forced upon the country in November 1967, the effect of all the other policies mentioned above, and many more besides, were negligible. Corporation Tax, SET, investment grants, IRC,

[1] Ibid., Vol. 725, Col. 1107.
[2] *Economic Measures*, Labour Party Talking Points Nos. 15/16, 1966, page 2. In fact, 1966 was the year of Orwellian 'doublethink'. On the one hand this same document conceded that 'the Government has several times announced measures to reduce pressure in order to free resources for export production and to cut back the demand for imports', and the 1966 Election Manifesto was, on the other hand, proclaiming that 'in the pursuit of solvency and the defence of the pound, which were our over-riding aims, the new Government was determined not to repeat Conservative Stop-Go'. (This was shortly before 're-deployment' was invented as a substitute for unemployment.)
[3] Reported by Peter Jenkins, 'Jim goes for growth', *Guardian*, 5 July 1971.
[4] *Hansard*, House of Commons, Vol. 781, Col. 992.
[5] *Hansard*, House of Commons, Vol. 799, Col. 1213.
[6] *The Relevance of British Socialism*, op. cit., page 56.
[7] For example, see Harold Wilson in *Hansard*, House of Commons, Vol. 720, Col. 32; or Callaghan, ibid., Vol. 745, Col. 206.

National Plan, Regional Plans, Regional Employment Premiums, import substitution, the lot. Most of them had no clearly identifiable impact at all during the period 1964 to 1970, unlike devaluation (if with rather greater delay than had been anticipated by many people, including me).

The true story of why the Labour Government did not devalue earlier will probably never be known to the public, but there seems to be little doubt that the initial decision not to devalue when they took office in October 1964 was almost entirely political and was dictated by the narrowness of the majority.[1] In such conditions the probability of being forced to an early election was considerable and the judgment of the Party leaders was that if the Labour Party were to go to the electorate after having devalued almost immediately it had taken office, and given that the previous devaluation of the pound was also carried out by a Labour Government (in 1949), it would certainly be defeated. Labour could not, so it was believed, survive being so clearly marked as the Party that always devalued the pound. Having made this decision, it was necessary to minimize the threat to the pound by increasingly categorical assertions that the pound would never be devalued, and even on the charitable assumption that these assertions were intended primarily for overseas consumption they had the effect of making the leaders of the Party feel publicly committed never to devalue the pound.

Of course, this political judgment is understandable during the period up to the Spring 1966 General Election. But the real mystery is why the pound was not devalued after Labour had won the Spring 1966 election with an overwhelming majority. To some extent it is likely that the sheer euphoria of a great electoral victory left the Government in no mood to come down to earth and face the most unpleasant problem of going back on a public commitment not to change the exchange rate. Also, it is likely that unwillingness to go back on this commitment once the election had been won led to sheer wishful thinking about the extent to which the balance of payments would solve itself anyway, though by early 1966 there was probably hardly an economist in the country who did not advocate devaluation. After the Labour Government won the election of Spring 1966 with a handsome majority and could look forward to five years of uninterrupted power as long as there was no catastrophe, there was no further excuse for not devaluing the pound.

Samuel Brittan has provided a detailed blow-by-blow account of the relevant events in 1966 and 1967. These included, unfortunately, the false dawn that seemed to follow the deflationary package of mid-1966, and which made it easier for the Government to indulge in wishful thinking to the effect that a devaluation was not necessary so that they would not be

[1] One minor contributing factor in the failure to devalue soon after the 1964 election may have been the very strong US support for the pound, motivated partly by the belief that if the pound were to be devalued the dollar would then be in the front line. And, in fact, the dollar did not survive unscathed in the front line for long.

obliged to go back on a strong personal commitment not to change the exchange rate.[1] It also appears from Mr Brittan's account that Mr Wilson and Mr Callaghan differed fundamentally over the devaluation issue from most of their Cabinet colleagues who might be expected to hold informed views on the subject. This is confirmed by Peter Jenkins, the exceptionally well-informed columnist on the *Guardian*, who writes that Mr Callaghan's 'responsibility for the humiliation of forced devaluation was at worst equal with the Prime Minister's. It had been the Prime Minister who had declared the word unmentionable, had even put to the flame the position papers on the subject by the Government's economic advisors.'[2] Peter Jenkins' suggestion, at a later date, that Mr Callaghan bore more of the responsibility than anybody else for refusing to devalue earlier probably refers to relative responsibilities of Ministers other than the Prime Minister.[3]

It is not known, of course, exactly what advice (if any) the Chancellor received on this subject from senior Treasury officials, particularly as the officials had apparently been given to understand that devaluation was simply inconceivable and so not to be officially discussed and studied. In describing events in the summer of 1967, Mr Brittan writes that 'the Treasury itself now regarded it [i.e. devaluation] as a very real possibility . . .',[4] which suggests that it had not been regarded as a practical possibility before the early summer of 1967, though reference is also made to the Head of the Treasury having introduced the devaluation issue in the context of discussion of the Common Market application at a meeting in April 1967.[5] Obedience to a Ministerial directive to the effect that devaluation was not to be countenanced under any circumstances would have meant that although some Treasury officials may well have become finally convinced of the desirability and, indeed, inevitability of devaluation, there was little they could do about it.

There is little doubt that the decision to give absolute priority to the maintenance of the exchange rate was the one great mistake of economic policy. It meant pushing other sensible objectives into the background and weakening the effect of the many other useful policy measures that the

---

[1] S. Brittan, *Steering the Economy* (revised and enlarged edition, Harmondsworth 1971), Chapter 8.

[2] Peter Jenkins, *The Battle of Downing Street* (London 1970), page 81.

[3] In the article in the *Guardian* referred to above (page 60) on 'Jim goes for growth', Peter Jenkins writes that 'Mr Callaghan dedicated himself during his three years at the Treasury to removing the deficit without changing the parity. He tried to do this by progressively stifling economic expansion. With great determination he pursued exactly the opposite policy to the one he now recommends. He put parity before country and before party. He personally saw to it that the growth ticket on which Labour had been elected in 1964 was torn up before an invited audience of the Governor of the Bank of England, Treasury mandarins, the US Secretary of Treasury, and members of the international banking community. . . . When devaluation came, after three wasted years, Mr Callaghan stood head and shoulders above all others in the last ditch.'

[4] Brittan, op. cit., page 350.

[5] Brittan, op. cit., page 349.

Government introduced during its period of office.[1] There is equally little doubt, therefore, that failure to devalue earlier was a major cause of the defeat of the Labour Party in the 1970 General Election, insofar as it was largely responsible for the deterioration on the home front – notably with respect to rising prices, worse industrial relations and higher unemployment – in the last two years of the Labour Government. It may seem extraordinary that so much weight can be placed on one single mistake of policy, but the case for doing so is a strong one. And the electorate cannot be expected to take account of the fact that the Conservative Party had professed to be against devaluation even more firmly than the Labour Party and had violently attacked the Government for the devaluation that was eventually forced on the country in 1967.

Failure to devalue earlier meant that both the deficit that had to be eliminated and the surplus that had to be aimed at in order to pay off accumulated debt were much greater than would otherwise have been the case. This aggravated both the price effects and the demand management aspects of the required devaluation. The size of the devaluation had to be greater with a greater deterioration in the terms of trade, and this meant both a greater addition to the resources that had to be moved into the foreign balance and a greater rise in import prices. The amount of resources that had to be shifted into the foreign balance – i.e. through extra exports or import substitution – allowing for the initial deficit, the target surplus, and the worsening of the terms of trade, came to roughly £1,250 million, which was equal to about one year's normal growth of output.[2] This necessitated the massive squeeze which began, albeit modestly, with the public expenditure cuts at the beginning of 1968 and was followed by the very deflationary budget of spring 1968. Under such conditions many employees tried to obtain a faster increase in money wage in order to enjoy some of the annual rise in consumption to which they had become accustomed.[3] Insofar as the required rise in money wages was held down temporarily by very stringent prices and incomes controls, it only delayed

[1] Mr Crossman is reported to have told a Fabian Society meeting that 'the fact that we did not devalue for three years and then, having tried for three years not to devalue, that we were forced to, is probably the single most damaging fact about the Government' (*Financial Times*, 29 September 1970).

[2] To avoid argument about the precise size of the 'true' underlying deficit in 1967 and of the size of the surplus at which we should have aimed in order to pay off debts, it can presumably be accepted that these were of the order of magnitude of about £500 million each, to which must be added about £250 million representing the real resource cost of a final deterioration of the terms of trade by about 4%.

[3] Other reasons have been given for the 1969/70 wage explosion, such as those referred to on page 65 below, though it should be noted that while Professor Clegg points out that there is no evidence for the view that the 1969/70 wage explosion was caused by devaluation he also concedes that 'there is more substance in the view that the outbreak of militancy (1968 onwards) was a consequence of the delayed effect of devaluation on the price level', and that 'it makes sense, therefore, to treat the pay explosion, at least in part, as a response to a rapid upsurge in shop-floor militancy' (page 61).

the eventual breakthrough. From then onwards it became much more difficult to decelerate expectations and to bring down again the conventional notions of what is a reasonable rate of increase in money wages.

If devaluation had been carried out a year or two earlier, when the underlying deficit had been, say, only about £250 million and when a target surplus of about the same amount would have sufficed to pay off debts, so that a devaluation of only 10% or so would have been required, with an attendant deterioration in the terms of trade of only 2 to 3% (making the usual allowance for some increase in our export prices in sterling and for some fall in import prices in foreign currency), the rise in the domestic price level would have been limited to only 1% or so on account of the devaluation and the total amount of resources to be switched into the foreign balance would have been only about £600 million. This would have represented a difficult task, of course, but it would have at least left *something* for higher consumption, and the chances of a complete breakdown on the wages front would have been that much less.

Before devaluation other objectives were subordinated to the preservation of the exchange parity. After devaluation they had to be subordinated to the need to make sure that devaluation worked. In this over-riding aim the Government succeeded, of course. In 1969 the external current surplus was £437 million, which was far higher than the previous record surplus of £344 million in 1958, when unemployment was about as high as in 1969 (making allowance for the various factors mentioned on page 58 above). And in the last six months of the Labour Government the current external surplus was running at an annual rate of £718 million (in spite of the heavy imports of Boeing planes that helped produce such bad trade figures just two days before polling day in June 1970). But the price that had been paid both to maintain the parity up to 1967 and then to ensure that the devaluation succeeded had been too great for the British electorate.

Labour market policies

If the responsible Ministers really believed that devaluation was not necessary, before mid-1967, in order to eliminate the chronic balance of payments crises, what did they think would restore British competitiveness in international trade? The answer was twofold. First, the technological revolution, stimulated by the National Plan, the newly created Ministry of Technology and the other industrial policy measures referred to above, would accelerate the growth of productivity. Secondly, an incomes policy would prevent this being offset by faster increases in money incomes.

But incomes policy has never been regarded by the Labour Party purely as a means of achieving greater price stability, and although statements can be found attributing solely this virtue to incomes policy other statements can also be found that emphasize the equity aspects of incomes policies.[1] Nor is there any shift away from the equity aspects to the price stability aspect of incomes policy during the period that the Labour Government held office. For example, Mr Callaghan's emphasis on 'the concept of a fair incomes policy' in 1963[2] or Mr Wilson's stress on the need to avoid a socially unjust incomes policy in 1965[3] are still echoed in an official White Paper in 1967.[4] In short, incomes policy was by no means a new weapon designed solely as a substitute for a devaluation. In fact, all post-war British Governments, as Derek Robinson points out in Chapter 9, have made use of some form of incomes policy, if only for very brief periods, though it remains to be seen whether Mr Heath's Government will attempt anything that would be recognized as an incomes policy without too much stretching of the vocabulary.

But in spite of experimentation with incomes policies in one form or another the magic formula that will enable the trade union movement to accept, and to impose on its members, settlements that appear to them to be less advantageous than those that would emerge from a process of free bargaining has not yet been found. As Robinson points out, attempts to implement wage and earning settlements that are different from those that would otherwise have been reached imposes greater problems and strains on trade unions than on management (which did not do much to help either).

Of course, it is very difficult to say exactly how far certain militant trade union leaders have genuinely tried to obtain the acquiescence of their members in an effective incomes policy and how far they really are the prisoners of a more militant membership or shop steward movement. It is true that some of their members and shop stewards are more militant than they are themselves.[5] But the notion that Hugh Scanlon and Jack Jones are really reasonable men who do fully understand that excessive increases in wages and earnings have only slowed down the rate of growth of the economy and have led to much higher unemployment is often difficult to reconcile with their usual statements and postures. Active and alert trade unions, independent of Government, are an indispensable and healthy element in a democracy. At the same time, it is up to the trade union leaders to provide clear guidance as to what kind of active policy really serves the longer-run interests of their members, and to wield the necessary

[1] See, for example, the White Paper *Prices and Incomes* (Cmnd. 2639, 1965), page 9; *Economic Policy*, Statement by the National Executive Committee to the Annual Conference of the Labour Party, 1966, page 4; the 1966 General Election Manifesto, page 7; or the White Paper *Productivity, Prices and Incomes Policy in 1968 and 1969* (Cmnd. 3590, 1968), page 3.

[2] *Hansard*, House of Commons, Vol. 684, Col. 366.

[3] Ibid., Vol. 720, Col. 35.

[4] *Prices and Incomes after 30th June 1967* (Cmnd. 3235, 1967), page 5.

[5] For example, at the policy-making conference of the AUEW at Eastbourne, on 23rd April 1971, Mr Scanlon was obliged vigorously to defend his role in the settlement of the Ford dispute that had just been reached against attacks by very militant members of the union, including some holding official positions of one kind or another (Mr Sid Harraway and Mr Reg Birch). See also Hugh Clegg, *How to Run an Incomes Policy and Why We Made Such a Mess of the Last One* (London 1971), page. 80.

moral authority and powers of leadership to get this policy accepted. The public must be forgiven if it feels that few trade union leaders have made any effective attempts to do this.

The inflationary effects of the existing machinery for wage determination in Britain combined with the increasing public discontent with what appeared to be chaotic industrial relations, gradually led to a widespread public belief that the present structure and organization of collective bargaining only served to hamper social progress and to further the interests of a few unions in a particularly strong bargaining position. In 1969 the Prime Minister and some other Ministers became increasingly convinced that something had to be done about industrial relations, even though this meant a threat to the traditional relationship between the Party and the trade union movement. 'For it was obvious by now that trade unionism left to its own nineteenth-century devices was in no sense working towards the achievement of a modern Social Democracy. The reverse was the case: the trade unions were one of the elements in the insoluble post-war equation in which full employment and free collective bargaining had somehow to be made to produce a satisfactory rate of economic growth.'[1]

The battle over the reform of industrial relations was a long and bitter one and, in the end, the Labour Government gave way. At the same time, one of the results of the battle, according to Robinson in Chapter 9, was that it became even more difficult to engage in any constructive dialogue with union leaders about incomes policies and the reform of industrial relations. This deterioration of relationships and hardening of union attitudes is a more important, if less tangible, indication of the failure of Labour Government's policies than any precise figure of the rate of increase of incomes or the incidence of strikes.

Robinson also suggests that the particular developments of 1969/70, including the wage explosion, had been partly aggravated by the fact that, in the eyes of many trade unionists, the incomes policy side of industrial relations was identified with the heavy deflationary measures of the immediate post-devaluation years. But even though this is probably true the root causes of the present state of British industrial relations, and of the absence of any machinery that can provide a framework within which wages negotiations can take account of the overall national interest, including the real interests of the working classes, go much deeper than this. They involve the whole organization and functions of the trade union movement in a fully employed economy,[2] the quality of the people who

---

[1] Jenkins, op. cit., page xi.

[2] For example, Hugh Clegg argues (op. cit., ch. 8) that the 1969/70 pay explosion has been largely the culmination of a process of growing workshop power that has been developing for many years. At the same time, whilst these various factors help to explain the British wage explosion, the international phenomenon of acceleration of inflation in 1969/70 suggests that other factors may also be contributing to the rise in wages and prices in Britain.

lead it, and the nature of their relationship with the Government.

In the early years the Labour Government was probably somewhat more successful than previous governments in obtaining the support of the trade union movement in its industrial relations policies and its prices and incomes policies. This support continued even against a background of the deflationary policies pursued since mid-1966. But it proved far too weak to withstand the strains of the 1967 devaluation and the associated measures, though it must be recognized that this was asking a lot of it. It is too easy to write off incomes policy on the ground that over the whole period 1964–70, which included the post devaluation period, earnings seemed to have risen as fast as before, if not faster. It is also too easy to write off such minor improvements in the industrial relations machinery that were introduced (e.g. the 1969 Concordat signed by the unions which reduced inter-union disputes, and the TUC vetting machinery which did at least initiate some central discussion of differentials and other matters) on the grounds that industrial disputes seem to have been more serious and widespread during the last year of the Labour Government than during the previous years. But it is necessary to take account of the great strains imposed by the overdue, and hence very heavy, devaluation discussed above.

Nevertheless, from a political point of view, what mattered may well have been the acceleration in the rate of increase of wages and the deterioration in industrial relations that marked the last year of the Labour Government. One of the hopes of Labour supporters in 1964 had been that a Labour Government would be able to succeed where Conservative Governments had failed, namely in obtaining the effective support of the trade union movement in some radical reform of industrial relations and the wage negotiation machinery. And neither the developments over the period of the Labour Government taken as a whole nor the events of the year leading up to the General Election lived up to these hopes.[1] Given that the labour market difficulties and inflationary pressures of 1968 and 1969 were, as argued above, partly the result of devaluation having been left until too late, it is ironic that Mr Callaghan, who must bear a major share of responsibility for this, emerged as the champion of the workers and defender of the traditional privileges in the face of the industrial relations reforms originally introduced by Mr Wilson and Barbara Castle.

THE OVERALL ASSESSMENT

With the best will in the world, the record as summarized above and as set out in more detail in the following chapters cannot be interpreted as anything but disappointing. As such it is in striking contrast to Labour's outstandingly civilized and enlightened record in many areas of social and

[1] See also Jenkins, op. cit., page xi.

educational policy. It is true that the 1964 Labour Government inherited a substantial deficit on the foreign balance and came to power with a slender majority that may well have excluded any recourse to the one instrument of policy – the exchange rate – that has proved its effectiveness over and over again in eliminating chronic external deficits in various countries. But, at best, that can only explain the events up to Spring 1966 and there is little excuse for the failure to devalue after the 1966 election victory.

We have seen above that some progress was made during the six years of Labour Government to achieve the goal that, more than any other, characterized the Labour Party's economic policy, namely greater equality of incomes. This arose largely through the increase in benefits, in cash and in kind, to the poorer groups in society, though efforts were also made in taxation policy and in prices and incomes policy to improve the relative position of the lower paid. If the heavy strains of the impact of an overdue devaluation had not led to an acceleration of inflation in 1969–70, with an attendant deterioration in the position of lower paid workers, the Labour Government's egalitarian efforts might have had even better results. Little merit can be claimed, however, for the record with respect to overseas aid. The share of national product devoted to official aid was lower at the end of the six years of Labour Government than it had been when Labour took office, and not all of the Government's ancilliary policies affecting the trade of developing countries were helpful. The most that can be said for Labour's aid policy is that, given the absence of strong public interest in overseas aid and development, it is to the credit of some of the Ministers and officials concerned that their policies in this field were not even more unfavourable at times when other unpleasant measures had to be carried out at home.

As regards other longer-term objectives of policy, the bare statistical record is, of course, even worse. The productivity target of the National Plan was nowhere in sight of achievement by 1970. Nor did the Government achieve the shift in the pattern of resources in favour of investment that was one of the key objectives of the Plan. And in the field of short-run demand management, the closing years of the Labour Government saw the economy operating with levels of unemployment that were as high as during the worst years of the Conservative Government. There seems to have been some narrowing of regional unemployment differentials, and possibly some longer-term intangible contribution to the future growth of some of the poorer regions, but it is impossible to verify this sort of claim, let alone weigh such benefits against the heavy expenditures incurred in the interests of regional policy or the possible social cost of these expenditures. As regards the foreign balance, it is true that there was a large surplus on the balance of payments during the last year or so of the Labour Government, in sharp contrast to the situation that the Government inherited. But the success of devaluation in inducing a large favourable swing in the foreign balance only serves to underline how mistaken were those who had earlier refused to believe that devaluation could do the trick. Finally, as regards incomes policies and industrial relations, the minor improvements painfully extracted from an unwilling trade union movement during the early years of the Labour Government were completely overshadowed by the industrial unrest and the collapse of the incomes policy that marked the last months of the Labour Government and which were very much the consequence of having devalued too late.

It is in the field of labour relations and income policy, perhaps, that one can identify the greatest – and also the most excusable – failure of the Labour Government. Although the over-riding 'mistake' was the failure to devalue earlier, and the small and slow acting improvements resulting from many other policy measures were largely swept out of sight by this mistake, devaluation would not have achieved, by itself, all the other major policy objectives. It would probably have led to faster growth and hence would have made it easier also to pursue other objectives, such as full employment and a greater increase in public expenditures. But it would not have solved completely the problems of internal financial stability and improved industrial relations, which are important to the public and which may also be important from the point of view of their contribution to other, and more basic, objectives of economic policy.

If failure to devalue earlier was a great mistake, it is at least one that is not likely to be repeated in the same circumstances, at least not by another Labour Government. The term 'mistake' implies that there was an alternative; i.e. that the correct theoretical solution was not only known but that the means of applying it were available. The same does not apply to the problems of inflation and industrial relations, which are still with us. There is widespread agreement in the Labour Party that something urgently needs to be done about incomes policies and industrial relations but little agreement about what it is that ought to be done. In this field any claim to have found an answer that is both theoretically convincing and workable in practice must be treated with the greatest suspicion, and it is in this field that the greatest efforts still need to be made. (Instead much more energy seems to be expended on relatively unimportant matters, such as the Common Market issue, which, on account of political motives has been blown up to an extent which is out of all proportion to its true significance.)

It is partly for this reason that it is easy to draw the wrong conclusions from the failure to devalue earlier, and to assume that as long as the same mistake is not repeated, all problems of economic management have been solved. But there is a danger that if Governments become too ready to change the exchange rate at the drop of a hat their resolve to deal with the problems of internal price stability is lessened. Hence, provided that price stability is an objective of policy irrespective of its effect on the balance of payments, greater readiness in future to change the exchange rate does not mean that Governments need not worry about the threat of inflation. Peter Jenkins is right when he says: 'It can be argued that had not the exchange rate of the currency for so long been given absolute priority the Government would have turned in a better performance in promoting growth. Even so, at any given rate of exchange, the tendency for wages and costs to be pushed up faster than the increase in national productivity is a problem which no government can ignore.'[1]

Of course, one can cite academic studies showing that inflation does not necessarily lead to a worsening of the income distribution or a collapse of organized society. But it would be a foolish Government that took risks with the stability of the currency in the light of generalizations based on a handful of cases such as the inflationary experience of Chile in the 1950s, Austria in 1921 or post-war Mainland China![2] There simply is not enough experience of prolonged inflation in advanced Western democracies for anybody to make confident predictions of what the consequences would be in this country. There is thus no escape from the need for the Labour Party, if it is to provide a convincing alternative to the Conservative Government instead of riding back to power on the usual swing of the political pendulum, to work out some new policy on industrial relations and the settlement of wages and incomes.

Thus, how the Labour Party is to handle its relations with the trade union movement must be one of the major issues to be sorted out over the next few years.[3] This goes back to the discussion at the beginning of this chapter of what a Labour Party is supposed to represent in contemporary society. According to Peregrine Worsthorne, 'British socialism stands or falls on faith in its moral content, and if this slackens, then those who are operating it, those who have their hands on the levers of power and privilege, have no conceivable justification.'[4] This may exaggerate even the sub-conscious importance of moral issues in politics, but there is little doubt that the British public regards inflation as one of the major sources of inequity and social injustice, and the heavy burden of responsibility that can be legitimately laid at the door of the Labour Government for its failure to devalue earlier must not distract attention from the continuing problem of what to do about incomes policies and industrial relations given our trade union structure, traditions and leadership.

Of course, most trade union leaders are responsible people who realize fully how much harm the trade union movement is doing to its public image; and many of them may even recognize how much damage excessive increases in earnings may do to the longer term interests of the men

[1] Jenkins, op. cit., page 165.
[2] See, for example, H. G. Johnson, *Essays in Monetary Economics* (London 1967), Chapter 3, page 134; P. Cagan, 'The theory of hyperinflation', reprinted in R. J. Ball and P. Doyle (eds.), *Inflation* (Harmondsworth 1969), pages 118–19; and A. G. Hines 'Inflation and economic growth' in Kaldor (ed.), *Conflicts in Policy Objectives* (Oxford 1971).
[3] See also Thomas Balogh, *Labour and Inflation*, Fabian Tract, 1971, page 6.
[4] Peregrine Worsthorne, 'Going nowhere', *Encounter*, March 1971, page 78.

they are supposed to represent. But they seem to lack the determination to push through policies that would achieve any serious reform of industrial relations and the wage bargaining structure. 'They realized the considerable impotence of their position as they conducted, on the one hand, high diplomacy with the Government on behalf of the whole trade union movement while, on the other hand, they struggled with constituents over whom they had little control. They purported to be the authoritative representatives of the unions but they knew that they were seldom in a position to enter into a firm bargain on their behalf.'[1] In fact, the leading trade unionists present to the public the image of always being able to provide plausible reasons why anybody else's reforms are unworkable or unnecessary, but of being quite unable themselves to present any convincing and effective alternatives. Indeed, the public statements of many trade union leaders give the impression that many of them do not see the necessity of any wage restraint to begin with.

The case for a workable incomes policy as a key instrument of economic policy in conditions of full employment is not new. It is not a matter of the balance of payments, for which the exchange rate is the appropriate instrument when there is a clear fundamental disequilibrium. It is true that if Governments attempt to correct a fundamental disequilibrium in the external balance by means of deflation then the faster the rise in wages the more will the Government deflate and the heavier will be the consequent unemployment. But that is largely the fault of the Government's refusal to employ the appropriate instrument of policy when it could perfectly well do so.

It is also true that if a Government believes that inflation can be checked only by massive unemployment, then the faster the rise in wage costs the greater will be the unemployment, and again this is partly the fault of the Government's persistence with a doomed policy. But in this case the trade union movement must share some of the responsibility since, unlike the devaluation instrument for dealing with the external problem, there is no simple instrument for preventing inflation that a Government can turn on or off as it likes. An incomes policy, which is the instrument required for price stability, can only be applied if the trade union movement cooperates. If it fails to do so, it may be true that greater unemployment will only make things worse in that unemployment and inflation are worse than inflation by itself. But if the Government does not create unemployment in the face of the inflation, there will still be the inflation, and that can be bad enough, and that would be very much the responsibility of the trade unions, although the need for the Government *and* employers to play a constructive role should by no means be overlooked.

Even if there is merely a *risk* that inflation could have damaging effects on the economy, risks are to be avoided unless there are clear counterpart gains to be had. In any case, nobody knows enough about the mechanics of inflation under all conceivable conditions to be sure that some extra

[1] Jenkins, op. cit., page 53.

unemployment will not slow down the rise in prices to some extent, if by nothing like as much as to achieve the degree of price stability that the public and the Government would prefer. Thus an incomes policy is required primarily in the interests of internal price stability and, to some extent given the world we live in and the reactions of Governments, it is also required in the interests of continued full employment, faster growth, and improved standards of living for the working classes.

Consequently, even if militant trade unionism as practised in this country has raised the share of wages in the national income by two or three percentage points, this has been much more than offset by the resulting higher unemployment and slower rate of growth. In other words, it has been against the interests of the working classes. Mr Jack Jones and Mr Hugh Scanlon are either incapable of understanding this or are guilty of cynical betrayal of the interests of their members. Their cries of outraged astonishment – in which many of their colleagues join – at the Conservative Government's legislation in the field of industrial relations are hardly likely to meet with much sympathy among those who were telling them throughout most of the period of Labour Government that if they did not co-operate and help the Labour Government improve industrial relations and slow down the pace of wage-push the result would be a Conservative Government that would introduce legislation that would be even 'nastier' as far as they were concerned and probably to even less effect.

Lord Balogh, who was one of those who frequently warned of the eventual consequences of a failure by the trade union movement to help the Labour Government overcome the problem of rising prices and industrial relations, summed up the situation as follows: 'The direct total social gain from "industrial action" was not merely negligible; it might well have been negative. . . . The increase in *money* wages has been frustrated by rising money prices. These robbed the wage earner (or rather his wife) of the expected gain; frustration and anger were the result.'[1] According to Peter Jenkins, Barbara Castle was also one of those who took the view that 'if a Labour Government did not act on the union question the unions might find themselves in the less tender grasp of a Conservative Government with far more extensive powers at its disposal. She was saving the trade unions from themselves, public opinion and the Tories.'[2]

Some sort of deal with the trade unions, in the interests of price stability, is thus politically essential for the Labour Party irrespective of the effects that inflation may be believed to have on the foreign balance, income distribution, resources allocation, hyper inflation, etc. etc. 'Because of its institutional and historical ties with the trade union movement the sins of unofficial strikers were visited upon the Labour Party, even in opposition.

[1] Balogh, op. cit., page 34.
[2] Jenkins, op. cit., page 43.

Bad industrial relations were bad for a Labour Government politically.'[1]

Furthermore, if the Labour Party is to recapture any public faith in the moral virtues of socialism, it must undo the damage done during the last two years of its office when 'fewer and fewer people believed that a steadfast redistribution of income was one of its main policy planks'.[2] As mentioned above, in connection with Michael Stewart's chapter, the gains that the lower-paid workers made during the early years of the Labour Government were lost after 1968 with the 'fatal spiralling of costs and prices that gave small privileged minorities – mostly of the middle class type such as doctors, pilots, petty managers, technicians, but also . . . strong unions – an opportunity to snatch advantages from their less privileged fellow workers'.[3] How then is the Labour Party to do a deal with a trade union movement that, for all its rhetoric, is essentially concerned with the maintenance of the existing machinery even if this means preserving existing differentials between the weak and the strong, and is impervious to the effect of this philosophy on the well-being of weak and strong alike? The basic dilemma of being a pro-equality party that relies heavily on support from a pro-differential pressure group is one from which the Labour Party must, some day, escape. 'For if Labour is one day and soon to form the Government again it will have to restore its credibility as the party of growth and sound economic management. Therefore it will have to persuade the people once more of its will and capacity to govern the trade unions and not be governed by them. . . . Barbara Castle was surely correct in believing that a more constructive relationship between unions and a Labour Government, a changed balance of rights and responsibilities, was necessary for the successful achievement of Social Democracy. The more so if Labour in opposition discovers new radical purposes, for the trade unions are in many of their aspects forces of conservatism, slow-moving and defensive organizations which cannot in their present form and with their present attitudes serve as effective and willing partners for a party of reform.'[4]

How a new relationship with the trade union movement is to be reached is not easy to see. The financial dependence of the Party on the trade union movement precludes any great show-down accompanied by some formal change in existing relationships. At the same time the ordinary British man in the street will not pay for his politics by any other means than through the organized trade union movement. Perhaps there is some hope of gradual informal relaxation of the ties that bind the Party to the trade union movement without any overt or official change in the financial support of the Labour Party through the trade union organization. But whatever the final policy adopted, the elaboration of the policy is clearly the number one problem for socialist strategy in the years to come. In the past,

[1] Jenkins, op. cit., page xii.
[2] Balogh, op. cit., page 45.
[3] Ibid., page 41.
[4] Jenkins, op. cit., pages 169–70.

the basic problem of the socialist movement in Britain has been the relationship between the Labour Party and its trade union allies, on the one hand, and the rest of society and the economy, on the other. The problem now is one of the relationship between the Labour Party, on the one hand, and the trade union movement on the other.

2 The distribution of income

Michael Stewart[1]

1. INTRODUCTION

Equality has always been one of the great watchwords of the Labour movement; to reduce existing inequalities has always been one of the professed objectives of Labour Governments. The citizens of Great Britain have for many years enjoyed equality in the political sense (one man, one vote) and in the legal sense (equal rights before the law). But equality in these two senses may mean little as long as vast social and economic inequalities remain. What a community also requires, to quote Tawney, is

a large measure of economic equality – not necessarily in the sense of an identical level of pecuniary incomes, but of equality of environment, of access to education and the means of civilization, of security and independence, and of the social consideration which equality in these matters usually carries with it.[2]

This definition comprehends aspects of equality which would today be regarded as social rather than economic, and much of the territory surveyed by Tawney must remain outside the purview of a book concerned with the economic performance of the 1964–70 Labour Government. But although this chapter is confined to an examination of changes in the distribution of income and wealth, the quotation serves as a reminder that these are not the only areas in which a Labour Government should be seeking to promote greater equality. This remains true even if one includes within the definition of 'income' the benefits received by different income groups in the form of Government expenditure on the social services. For – to quote Tawney again –

the disparities between classes which cut deepest are a matter, not merely of income, but of life. The contribution to the increase of equality made by developments of the kind summarized above [i.e. social service expenditure] is not, therefore, to be measured merely or mainly in terms of a quantitative alteration in the distribution of wealth. Their most significant aspect consists in the qualitative change in the character of a society which is produced when

[1] The author is indebted to Theodora Cooper, Howard Glennerster and J. L. Nicholson for helpful comments on an earlier draft of this chapter; however, they bear no responsibility for the final version.
[2] R. H. Tawney, *Equality* (4th edition revised, London 1952), page 32.

disabilities afflicting particular classes are diminished or removed, and advantages formerly restricted to a minority are made more nearly a general possession.[1]

One might reasonably infer from this that a greater equality in the distribution of income and wealth, though not a sufficient condition of achieving the kind of society that socialists want, is none the less a necessary condition. For the purposes of this chapter, therefore, the objective of policy is assumed to be an improvement in the distribution of income and wealth, and the question to be answered is whether such an improvement occurred between 1964 and 1970.

Traditionally, the distribution of income which has most interested economic theorists has been the distribution of the national income between wages and profits. By this test, the Labour Government's economic record is easily summarized (Table 2.1). The share of company profits in the national income fell steadily from the year Labour assumed office until the year it left it, and in the latter year was only about three-quarters as big as in the former.[2] But one only needs to glance at these figures to see that they raise more questions than they answer.

The most immediate question raised is how permanent the change might be expected to be. Unemployment was much higher in 1970 than in 1964, and capacity utilization much lower, and such cyclical movements have nearly always been associated with a contraction of profit margins. One might, therefore, expect that when the economy, and capacity utilization, recovers, so will the share of profits. Much the same applies to dividends, though the rather modest decline that occurred here could also have been influenced by the introduction of the Corporation Tax, which had the effect of taxing retained profits less heavily than distributed profits, and may have inhibited dividend payments for this reason.[3]

It has been argued[4] that the fall in the share of profits during the late 1960s was greater than could be accounted for by the cyclical downswing alone, and that other factors, such as an intensification of international competition and the marked acceleration in the pace of wage increases in 1969–70, also played a part. While there may be some truth in this, it is not clear why the effect of such factors should be regarded as permanent rather than temporary: changes in the pattern of world exchange rates, and the

[1] Tawney, op. cit., page 251.

[2] If stock appreciation – which was substantially higher in 1970 than in 1964 – is excluded, the decline in the share of profits was even greater (see Andrew Glyn and Bob Sutcliffe, 'The critical condition of British capital', *New Left Review*, 66, March–April 1971).

[3] In this case shareholders might expect to see lower dividend payments offset in time by higher capital gains, so that the adverse effects on them might have been more apparent than real. This avenue of escape was, however, partially blocked by the introduction of Capital Gains Tax (see page 85).

[4] For example in the more analytical part of Glyn and Sutcliffe, op. cit.

TABLE 2.1. WAGES AND PROFITS

Per cent of total domestic income[a]

	1960	1961	1962	1963	1964	1965	1966	1967	1968	1969	1970
Income from employment	66·3	67·7	68·4	67·4	67·1	67·5	68·8	68·5	68·0	68·7	70·4
Gross trading profits of companies[a]	16·3	15·0	14·2	15·2	15·6	15·1	13·4	13·3	13·5	12·5	11·6

Per cent of total personal income

	1960	1961	1962	1963	1964	1965	1966	1967	1968	1969	1970
Rent, dividends and net interest	11·3	11·5	11·5	11·9	12·1	12·2	11·9	11·9	11·7	11·6	10·8

[a] Before providing for depreciation and stock appreciation.

Source: 1971 *Blue Book*.

lapse of enough time to permit price-setting to respond to the faster growth of wages, might be expected to restore profit margins over a slightly longer period.[1]

But it is not only the possibly temporary nature of much or all of the decline in the share of profits and dividends between 1964 and 1970 that makes it such an unsatisfactory measure of Labour's success in improving the distribution of income. Nor is it even the broader suspicion that a decline in profit margins which makes new investment more difficult to finance and less attractive to undertake, and is itself one aspect of a policy of deliberately restraining the growth of output, cannot augur well for the relative position of the poorer and weaker members of society. It is also the fact that a decline in the share of profits and dividends, though undoubtedly in an overall statistical sense resulting in an improvement in income distribution, not only tells one very little about who gains, and who loses, and by how much, but is in any case only one of many factors that can influence the distribution of income between individuals or households.

The decline in the share of profits in the national income between 1964 and 1970, then, itself less an indication of the Labour Government's success in improving the distribution of income than of its failure to achieve certain other economic objectives such as faster growth and a slower rate of inflation, is silent on the questions which are of the greatest interest.

A much more relevant measure of Labour's success in this field has been suggested by Harold Wilson:

Given a Labour victory, the test is this: will there be, twelve months from now, a narrowing of the gap between rich and poor, quite apart from any general upward movement there may be as the result of increased national production? The answer is, quite simply, that there will.[2]

Unfortunately, although this is all right as far as it goes, the problem is a bit more complicated than that. There are over twenty million income receivers in the UK.[3] Some are undoubtedly rich; some are unquestionably poor. Over a period of six years the incomes of most of these income

[1] There is some evidence that the share of labour in the national income has been creeping upwards in recent decades (see for example references cited in Report No. 169, National Board for Prices and Incomes, *General Problems of Low Pay*, April 1971, Appendix B). But it is too early to be sure that this trend accelerated in the later 1960s.

[2] Harold Wilson in the *New Statesman*, 3 October. But it is perhaps not without significance that the year in which the piece appeared was not 1964 but 1959. The theme of greater equality was rather less in evidence in Labour's 1964 Election Manifesto than in its 1959 one – partly, no doubt, because deficiencies in other aspects of Britain's economic performance, particularly growth and the balance of payments, were more glaring in 1964 than they had been in 1959.

[3] As defined by the Inland Revenue, which meant (until the changes foreshadowed in the 1971 Budget) counting married couples as a single taxable unit.

receivers (whether considered before or after taxes and social service benefits) will change. But how is one going to decide whether the net result of these myriad changes is an improvement or not?

Statisticians have devised various ways of measuring the distribution of income, and thus comparing the distribution of income of different countries, or the same country at different times. (Both the theoretical and the practical difficulties of assessing changes in income distribution are discussed in the Appendix.) But at bottom the problem is not one of devising sufficiently precise techniques of measurement, but of deciding which of two situations is better. If middle income groups gain at the expense of both the rich and the poor, is this an improvement or not? No statistical formula is going to provide an answer.

Another way of looking at the problem is to ask what distribution of income a Labour Government should be seeking to bring about. Is the ideal distribution of income one in which all incomes are equal? If so, does this mean that all families should have the same income, regardless of size? Or if that were thought unreasonable, should per capita income be the same for everybody in the community, regardless of age, number in family, type of work, length of working week or anything else? One cannot altogether evade these questions by answering that one does not need to define an ideal income distribution in order to recognize an improvement. When looking at the 'vertical' distribution of income (i.e. the range of incomes received by families of a particular size and structure) this may be so: a reduction of the dispersion would be regarded by most people as an improvement. But what about changes in the 'horizontal' distribution of income – i.e. changes between households of different sizes and structures? Many people might agree that a redistribution of income from rich bachelors to poor families with six children was a good thing, but what about less glaring cases? Is a family with four children and an income of £1,000 a year better or worse off than a family with three children and £900 a year? What change in their relative incomes would constitute an improvement?

These difficulties have been raised (and are discussed at greater length in the Appendix) in order to emphasize that whether, and how far, a Labour Government has succeeded in improving the distribution of income is likely to be a more controversial question than whether, and how far, it has succeeded in achieving its other economic objectives. Whether a Government has maintained full employment, increased the growth rate, reduced the rate of inflation and secured a healthy balance of payments surplus, is likely to be apparent to the naked eye. Whether it has improved the distribution of income is not.

But one must not be too agnostic. To most people who supported the aims of the Labour Government the most objectionable feature of the distribution of income that existed in 1964 was probably not the relatively large proportion of the national income that accrued to the 1% or 2% at the top of the pyramid – offensive though that was – but the relatively small proportion that accrued to the 10% or 15% at the bottom.[1] There are many aspects of the changes in the distribution of income between 1964 and 1970 that need to be looked at, but this one needs to be looked at most carefully of all.

Broadly speaking, there are three ways in which a Government can improve the distribution of income. First, it can attempt to influence the *original* distribution of income, both earned and accruing from the ownership of property, that emerges from the interplay of market forces. Secondly, it can modify the original distribution of income by means of *taxation*, direct and indirect. Thirdly, it can modify this original distribution of income by means of *benefits*, in cash or in kind. The next three sections discuss the Labour Government's record in each of these three broad areas in turn. A more general evaluation of the effect on the distribution of income of all these measures taken together is attempted in Section V.

II. ORIGINAL INCOME

Earned income

The distribution of earned incomes is notoriously resistant to change. It would seem, for example, that the dispersion of the earnings of adult male manual workers in Britain was much the same in the 1960s as it had been in the 1880s, despite all the institutional changes, and the twentyfold increase in the level of earnings, that had occurred over the period.[2] The fact that the Labour Government approached the possibility of improving the distribution of original earnings with a certain amount of circumspection is therefore hardly to be wondered at. Nevertheless the circumspection was not total. One of the Government's first actions was to reduce by half the increases in the salaries of Government Ministers proposed by an independent committee, and one of its last ones, five and a half years later, was to do exactly the same in the case of senior doctors. However, it would require the assistance of an electron microscope to detect the effect of these decisions on the distribution of income; and it would require a good deal of innocence to fail to detect, in both cases, political considerations of a short-term nature. The examples do perhaps indicate that in the

[1] *Signposts for the Sixties*, an important policy statement published by the Labour Party in 1961, had talked of 7 or 8 million people (i.e. about 15% of the population) living 'close to the poverty line' (page 24). A more recent estimate (A. B. Atkinson, *Poverty in Britain and the Reform of Social Security* (Cambridge 1969), page 42) suggests that between 4% and 9% of the population have incomes *below* the poverty line – i.e. below the Supplementary Benefit scale (see page 81); this may mean that as many as 5 million people are living below the officially defined minimum standard.

[2] A. R. Thatcher, 'The distribution of earnings of employees in Great Britain', *Journal of the Royal Statistical Society*, Series A (General), Vol. 131, Part 2, 1968, page 163; and National Board for Prices and Incomes, op. cit., Appendix B.

case of highly-paid people, for whose salaries it was directly responsible, the Labour Government was sometimes willing to give the distribution of original earnings a nudge in an egalitarian direction; but such action could be regarded as little more than window-dressing unless it were accompanied by equally effective action to reduce the dispersion of earnings at the lower end of the scale. For, after the elderly, low-paid wage-earners and their families constitute the largest group in poverty in contemporary Britain.[1]

The seriousness of the problem of low-paid workers was amply demonstrated by an official survey, published in 1967,[2] which showed that of the 3 million families receiving family allowances in which the father was in full-time work, more than 2% (70,000 families containing more than 250,000 children) had earnings which fell below the National Assistance scales then in force.[3] Since the National Assistance scale – subsequently polished up a bit and re-christened the Supplementary Benefit scale – is in effect the Government's own estimate of the amount of money required to give people a standard of living below which no one in contemporary Britain should fall, it seems clear that anyone whose income is below this is not merely poor, but unacceptably poor by society's own standards. Moreover the problem is accentuated by the fact that it is not only those actually in employment who are hit by low wages: because it is felt undesirable for people to have a higher income when unemployed than when they are working, the 'wage stop' operates in a way that prevents low-paid workers from receiving Supplementary Benefit living standards when unemployed as well.[4] Altogether there were in 1966 160,000 families, with half a million children, living on incomes below the National Assistance level either because the fathers were in full-time work or because they were out of work but 'wage-stopped'.

In Opposition, Labour had talked of the possibility of dealing with this kind of problem by an 'Incomes Guarantee' – a form of negative income tax which would automatically ensure that no one's income fell below a particular (and newly-established) minimum.[5] For reasons connected partly with the well-known difficulties about a negative income tax, and partly with the heavy burden imposed on the Inland Revenue by the introduction of the Corporation and Capital Gains Taxes, this proposal was quietly shelved.[6] As far as low earnings were concerned, an interdepart-

[1] Child Poverty Action Group, *Poverty and the Labour Government*, April 1970, page 6.
[2] Ministry of Social Security, *Circumstances of Families* (HMSO 1967).
[3] Those in full-time employment are not eligible for National Assistance/Supplementary Benefits.
[4] Various steps were taken in 1968 to mitigate the severity with which the wage-stop operates; but the phenomenon still exists.
[5] In the 1964 Election Manifesto, the Incomes Guarantee proposed was to be restricted to those already retired, and to widows.
[6] The change from National Assistance to Supplementary Benefits was regarded as a partial *quid pro quo* for abandoning the idea of the Incomes Guarantee (R. H. S. Crossman, *Paying for the Social Services*, Fabian Tract, page 15).

mental working party of officials was set up in 1967 to consider the feasibility of establishing a national minimum wage. There are many drawbacks of a statutory minimum wage, just as there are many advantages, and the report of the working party, published in 1969,[1] did not fail to point them out. The Government's response to the report was somewhat lethargic: the Secretary of State for Employment and Productivity, in her foreword, contented herself with saying of it: 'It is in my view essential reading for all those with an interest in a subject which touches everyone and provides the basis for a more informed discussion.' It is hardly surprising that no action had followed by the time the Labour Government left office.[2]

Low-paid workers were, however, catered for in the Labour Government's prices and incomes policy, in the sense that they were supposed to receive specially generous treatment. In the original White Paper setting out the criteria which were to guide those concerned with determining prices and incomes, one of the four criteria permitting pay increases in excess of the 'norm' of $3-3\frac{1}{2}\%$ was 'where there is general recognition that existing wage and salary levels are too low to maintain a reasonable standard of living'.[3] Similar sentiments were expressed in subsequent White Papers. How much effect was exerted on the distribution of income by the pronouncement of this principle, and such action as the Government itself took to implement it in cases where it controlled the purse-strings, is difficult to say. No comprehensive data on the distribution of earnings exist for any year between 1960 and 1968,[4] and although summary information on the changes in average earnings in high-paid and low-paid industries between 1964 and 1970 (Table 2.2) constitutes circumstantial evidence of an absence of marked changes in dispersion, it could conceal differential changes within particular industries. A much more detailed examination of what happened to the weekly wage rates of the lowest paid workers in over 100 industries carried out by the Prices and Incomes Board suggests that over the four years April 1965 to April 1969 (broadly speaking the effective period of operation of the Labour Government's incomes policy) those in the lowest-ranking industries did slightly better than the average;

---

[1] Department of Employment and Productivity, *A National Minimum Wage*, 1969.

[2] On equal pay, on the other hand, the Government was more forthcoming: the Equal Pay Act, to ensure that women received the same pay and conditions as men when performing the same work, became law in 1970, just before the dissolution of Parliament. But the full effect of this legislation will not be felt until after the end of 1975. There was no improvement to speak of in the pay of women relative to men under the Labour Government: between October 1964 and October 1970 the weekly earnings of male manual workers in industry rose by 55%, those of females by 56%; and the hourly earnings of males by 62% and females by 63% (*Department of Employment Gazette*, February 1971, page 167).

[3] *Prices and Incomes Policy* (Cmnd. 2639, April 1965), page 8. The successive phases of the Labour Government's prices and incomes policy are discussed in Chapter 9.

[4] The massive *New Earnings Survey* first conducted by the Department of Employment and Productivity in September 1968, and annually since April 1970, will be a mine of information on changes since 1968, but is of little help for present purposes.

TABLE 2.2 CHANGES IN INDUSTRIAL EARNINGS

Average weekly earnings, men 21 and over, in October 1970 (October 1964= 100)

Industry	Ranking		
	1964	1970	
Paper, printing and publishing	First	First	159
Vehicles	Second	Second	154
Metal manufacture	Third	Third	154
Clothing and footwear	Third lowest	Third lowest	153
Certain miscellaneous services	Second lowest	Second lowest	158
Public administration	Lowest	Lowest	155

Source: *Ministry of Labour Gazette*, February 1965, page 50; *Dept. of Employment Gazette*, February 1971, page 166.

TABLE 2.3. INCREASES IN WAGE RATES

Average annual increases in weekly wage rates of lowest paid adult male workers, ranked by industry

Ranking of industry	Average April 1965 to April 1969	Average April 1969 to April 1970
	Per cent	Per cent
Lowest quarter	4·5	5·9
Third quarter	4·0	6·7
Second quarter	4·0	9·5
Highest quarter	4·6	7·4
All industries covered	4·3	7·7

Source: *National Board for Prices and Incomes, Report No. 169*, 'General problems of low pay', April 1971, page 14.

but that this advantage was lost in the following year, when wages in the higher-ranking industries rose much more rapidly (Table 2.3). Much the same impression is conveyed by a similar examination of increases in average weekly earnings.[1] The broad picture would seem to be one of a slight improvement in the relative earnings of low-paid workers during the first four or five years Labour was in office, subsequently lost in the wage explosion of 1969–70. Whether the improvement would have been consolidated had Labour not virtually abandoned its prices and incomes policy in 1969, or whether traditional differentials were bound to re-assert themselves sooner or later, is a matter on which one can only speculate.

Wealth and unearned income

Unearned (or 'investment') income derives from the ownership of capital wealth; the main determinant of the distribution of unearned in-

[1] National Board for Prices and Incomes, op. cit., pages 15–16.

come will therefore be the distribution of wealth. But the distribution of wealth is of interest not only, or even mainly, because of its influence on the pre-tax distribution of income.[1] It is the most fundamental measure of the way that command over resources is distributed between different groups in the community; and it can be a very significant indicator of how egalitarian a society's values really are.

Although some individuals can accumulate or fritter away holdings of wealth at an impressive rate, there are really only two ways in which the distribution of wealth for society as a whole is likely to be significantly changed by deliberate Government action. One is a tax levied on holdings of wealth as such; the other is a tax on the transfer of wealth from one person to another.

As far as the first approach is concerned, the Labour Government's record is easy to summarize: nothing happened at all. There was no wealth tax in Britain when Labour took office; nor was there one when it left it. But this very failure to act is itself of some interest: a case almost of the dog that failed to bark in the night. For there had been a good deal of talk about a wealth tax in Labour circles during the two or three years before the 1964 election, and Mr Callaghan, then Shadow Chancellor, and subsequently Chancellor for Labour's first three years in office, appeared to view it with some sympathy.[2] The rate at which its advocates suggested the tax should be levied rarely exceeded 2% a year on even the largest holdings of wealth, and was often no higher than $\frac{1}{2}$–1% a year. At a time when the gross yield of the very safest investments was likely to be over 6%, these rates could hardly be described as confiscatory: even allowing for relatively high marginal rates of taxation on unearned income, the rates of wealth tax under discussion seemed more likely to moderate the pace at which large holdings of wealth grew than to reduce their size in absolute terms.

Nevertheless, despite the essential modesty of the proposal; despite the respectability of its ancestry (in 'socialist' Sweden, always good for a salute from the Labour Party, there had been a wealth tax for more than half a century); despite what one might have thought its tactical usefulness in securing agreement on an incomes policy; and despite the large egalitarian wedge of which a modest wealth tax might represent the thin edge – despite all this, nothing was done. Indeed there is no evidence that it was ever considered as a serious possibility by most senior members of the Government, and although the heavy burden placed on the Inland

[1] The inegalitarian effects of investment income, though by no means negligible, are not as great as is sometimes supposed. In 1967–8, for example, total (pre-tax) investment income was only 7% as big as total (pre-tax) earned income; it was distributed among more than 5 million families – about a quarter of the number of families who received earned incomes; and half of it accrued to families whose incomes before tax were less than £3,000 a year (*Inland Revenue Statistics 1970*, Tables 52 and 53).

[2] See, for example, *Hansard*, House of Commons, Vol. 671, Col. 1131. Some of the issues, as seen at the time, were discussed in my article 'The proposed tax on wealth', *Bankers' Magazine*, April 1963.

Revenue by other tax reforms may have played a part in this, it can hardly have been the principal reason, for there was no mention of a wealth tax in the 1964, 1966 or 1970 Election Manifestos. Conviction, rather than feasibility, appears to have been the missing ingredient.

But if a tax on existing holdings of wealth was too revolutionary a step to contemplate, what about a tax on transfers of wealth from one person to another? If the Labour Party's predilection for evolution rather than revolution inhibited it from storming the barricades with a wealth tax might it not at least encourage it to infiltrate through them with a reform of inheritance duties? Apparently not. The only significant change was an increase, effected in 1968, from five to seven years in the period that had to elapse between the date a person gave away property and the date of his death if the property was to escape estate duty. But the effect of this change is unlikely to prove very important: it merely requires the wealthy to accept the fact of their own mortality a little earlier in life than before. The truth is that it is very difficult to make death duties an important egalitarian influence unless they operate in harness with a tax on gifts *inter vivos*, and the Labour Government made no attempt to introduce such a measure.

Although there was no direct onslaught on holdings of wealth as such, and little tightening up on the transfer of wealth from one generation to another, the Labour Government did introduce one measure of considerable long-term importance. This was the Capital Gains Tax put into effect in 1965. With certain important egalitarian exceptions (notably wealth in the form of owner-occupied houses), capital gains were now to be taxed at a flat rate of 30% if realized in any period over a year, and at the full marginal income tax and surtax rate if realized in under a year.[1] Provided it is not abandoned or watered down,[2] this measure, although it had probably had little effect on the distribution of wealth or unearned income by 1970, is likely to have a significant effect in the longer run in slowing down the rate at which the wealth of the better-off increases.

In view of the absence of action, and apparently indeed of desire, to improve the distribution of wealth, it is slightly surprising to find that such figures as are available suggest that there was in fact some improvement (Tables 2.4 and 2.5). It is true that these figures are not very reliable, and must be treated with considerable reserve,[3] but they cannot be completely ignored. Moreover the impression they convey is confirmed by figures on the distribution of investment income (Table 2.6), which also

---

[1] The Conservatives had introduced a short-term gains tax in 1962, but this only applied to gains realized in less than six months and the yield, unsurprisingly, was negligible.
[2] The long-term Capital Gains Tax was in fact the only major tax measure introduced by Labour which survived the new Conservative Government's first full Budget in March 1971; the Selective Employment Tax was to be abolished and the structure of the Corporation Tax radically altered.
[3] See Appendix, page 115.

TABLE 2.4.   DISTRIBUTION OF WEALTH

	1964	1968
Per cent of net wealth owned by		
Top 1% of wealth owners	25	24
Top 5% of wealth owners	48	46
Bottom 50% of wealth owners	8	10

Source: *Inland Revenue Statistics 1970*, Tables 122–3.

TABLE 2.5.   DISTRIBUTION OF WEALTH – GINI COEFFICIENTS

1961	1962	1963	1964	1965	1966	1967	1968
72	72	73	72	70	67	67	68

Note: a lower coefficient means a less unequal distribution of wealth.

Source: *Inland Revenue Statistics 1970*, Tables 122–3.

TABLE 2.6.   DISTRIBUTION OF INVESTMENT INCOME

	1963–4	1967–8
Per cent of total investment income accruing to		
Top 10% of income receivers who received investment income	58	53
Bottom 50% of income receivers who received investment income	17	20

Source: *108th Report of Inland Revenue*, Table 62; *Inland Revenue Statistics 1970*, Table 53.

suffer from severe limitations, but are at least derived from a different source.

Just why there should have been this apparent improvement in the distribution of wealth and (pre-tax) investment income is not entirely clear, but it seems possible that one factor may have been a change in the relative prices of different assets. Although no official figures are available which specifically relate the form in which wealth is held to the amount of wealth held, there is little doubt that a much larger proportion of the wealth of 'poor' wealth-holders than of 'rich' wealth-holders is held in the form of houses, insurance policies, and building society shares and deposits, and a much smaller proportion in the form of equity shares and gilt-edged securities.[1] Although the price of equities was for the most part higher in 1968 than in 1964, the price of gilt-edged securities tended to be lower. House prices, on the other hand, rose substantially over the period.

However by no means all of the change in the value of different forms

[1] In 1964 the average wealth of the lowest 50% of wealth-holders was only about £500 (*Inland Revenue Statistics 1970*, Table 122). Since in principle this figure covers not only the value of houses, but also of household goods, cash and bank deposits, the scope for holding such assets as equity shares or gilt-edged securities is obviously not very great.

of wealth-holding over the period (which is illustrated in Table 2.7) can be accounted for by price changes; much of it represents net investment and disinvestment in different types of assets. The above-average increase in the value of life assurance policies, residential buildings, and shares and deposits in building societies seems to have been a reflection in part of an increase in the propensity to save on the part of the less wealthy majority

TABLE 2.7. FORM OF INDIVIDUAL WEALTH-HOLDINGS

	Per cent of total, 1964	Per cent change between 1964 and 1968
Government and municipal securities	4	−17
British quoted ordinary shares	16	+12
Policies of life assurance	14	+30
Shares and deposits in building societies	5	+87
Residential buildings	24	+35
Total net wealth	100	+22

Source: *Inland Revenue Statistics 1970*, Tables 120–1.

of the community. Although the increase in the overall propensity to save does not match up closely on a year-to-year basis with the apparent changes in the distribution of wealth,[1] it could nevertheless have been a major factor behind the substantially bigger flow of funds into private house ownership, building societies and insurance policies, if it were the case that a large part of the extra saving, in absolute terms, was done by people with relatively small holdings of wealth. In so far as this happened, it could provide part of the explanation of the apparent improvement in the distribution of wealth and unearned income between 1964 and 1968.

However, explanations must remain somewhat tentative as long as the phenomenon to be explained is itself somewhat uncertain. All that can really be said is that there are some signs of an improvement in the distribution of wealth and pre-tax investment income between 1964 and 1968, but that it is hard to give the Labour Government much credit for it.

III. TAXATION

In addition to the Capital Gains Tax, already briefly discussed on page 85,

[1] Personal saving, as a proportion of personal disposable income, averaged around 5% in the late 1950s and around 8% in the 1960s (*1971 Blue Book*). The rise reflected, broadly speaking, an increase to a new plateau at the beginning of the 1960s. According to the Inland Revenue figures, all of the improvements in the distribution of wealth took place between 1964 and 1966 (see Table 2.5); but the apparent sharpness of the change may to some extent be an illusion due to quirkiness in the data; and the fact that 1966 was a very bad year for both equity and gilt-edged prices had an important, if transitory, effect on the figures.

the Labour Government introduced two other major new taxes, the Corporation Tax and the Selective Employment Tax. Neither of these taxes was primarily designed to influence the distribution of income, and although they must have influenced it willy-nilly, the effective incidence of both taxes is so controversial that there is little that can usefully be said about them in the present context. Such tax changes as are likely to have affected the distribution of income in a measurable way were changes in taxes that already existed. These can be classified as changes in either *direct* taxation (income tax, surtax and – to be realistic – National Insurance contributions); or in *indirect* taxation (taxes on expenditure, such as purchase tax and excise duties). These are discussed in turn.

Direct taxation

The changes in direct taxation introduced by Labour, though not negligible, were relatively few in number and small in importance. The standard rate of income tax was increased by 6 old pence in the pound (i.e. increased to 41·25% before allowing for earned income relief) in the 1965 Budget; there were various increases in personal allowances, particularly in 1969 and 1970, and the complete elimination of the reduced rate bands (so that people started paying income tax at the effective rate of 32%); there was a temporary 10% surcharge on 1965–6 surtax bills, a temporary special charge on personal investment income in 1967–8, the ending of one minor scandal in 1968 by aggregating the investment income of children with that of their parents, and of another in 1969 by disallowing tax relief on personal interest payments (both of these seem likely to be temporary too – though not intended to be – since in 1971 the Conservatives decided to restore the *status quo*).

In a way, the most significant aspect of the Labour Government's record on direct taxation lies concealed in the account just given. By *not* reducing the standard rate of income tax during the five years after the increase in the 1965 Budget, it permitted the combination of a progressive tax structure and rising money incomes to lead to a substantial increase in the proportion of personal incomes paid in direct taxes, and to a distinct shift from indirect to direct taxation (Table 2.8, see opposite). The overall effect of all this must have been progressive – but how progressive is not easy to say. Table 2.9 shows the proportion of their original income that different kinds of household paid in direct taxes at different income levels in 1964 and 1968.[1] The progressive effect of direct taxes on both the vertical and the horizontal distribution of income comes out clearly: in both years, for every type of household, the proportion of income paid in

[1] This information is also available for 1969, but because of a change in the definition of original income it is not comparable with the information for 1964 (see *Economic Trends*, February 1971, page x). Similarly, it would be more logical to take direct taxes as a proportion of original income plus cash benefits, since the latter are for the most part taxable; but this information is not available for 1964.

TABLE 2.8.   INCOMES AND TAXATION

	1960	1961	1962	1963	1964	1965	1966	1967	1968	1969	1970
Taxes on personal income											
(1) As % of total personal income	9·4	9·8	10·2	9·8	10·1	11·1	11·6	12·2	12·7	13·4	14·0
(2) As % of taxes on income and expenditure combined	41·3	42·5	43·0	42·4	43·0	44·7	44·9	45·9	45·6	46·2	48·0

Source: 1971 *Blue Book*.

TABLE 2.9. INCOME TAX AND SURTAX AS PERCENTAGE OF ORIGINAL INCOME

Range of original income (£ per year)

Type of household		(1) 216–	(2) 260–	(3) 315–	(4) 382–	(5) 460–	(6) 559–	(7) 676–	(8) 816–	(9) 988–	(10) 1,196–	(11) 1,448–	(12) 1,752–	(13) 2,122–	(14) 2,566–	(15) 3,104– and above
1 adult	1964	6	5	9	8	8	8	9	12	15	13	16				
	1968		7	10	10	9	12	11	13	15	18	19	23	20	18	
(a) 1968 (1) minus 1964 (1) etc.			2	1	2	1	4	2	1	0	5	3				
(b) 1968 (2) minus 1964 (1) etc.			1	5	1	1	4	3	4	3	3	6	7			
2 adults	1964	3	2	6	5	4	5	7	7	9	9	10	13	16	16	
	1968		3	3	7	6	8	7	9	10	12	12	13	15	16	24
(a)			1	−3	2	2	3	0	2	1	3	2	0	−1	0	
(b)			0	1	1	1	4	2	2	3	3	3	3	2		
2 adults, 1 child	1964						2	3	5	6	7	10	15			
	1968							3	4	5	8	10	11	14	14	13
(a)								0	−1	−1	1	0	−4	−1		
(b)								1	1	0	2	3	1			
2 adults, 2 children	1964						1	1	1	4	6	7	11	10		
	1968							0	2	3	7	8	10	12	15	19
(a)								−1	1	−1	1	1	−1	2		
(b)								−1	1	2	3	2	3			
2 adults, 3 children	1964								1	2	4	5	9	11		
	1968								3	2	6	6			14	15
(a)									2	0	2	1				
(b)										1	4	2	4	5		

Source: *Economic Trends*, August 1966 and February 1970.

direct taxation rose with income; and for every income group the proportion of income paid in direct taxes fell as family size increased.

What happened between the two years, however, is more difficult to see. In the (*a*) rows in the table, the percentage of income paid in tax in 1964 is simply subtracted from the percentage paid in 1968 for each type of household and each income group. Not surprisingly, in view of the fact that for total personal income the proportion paid in tax rose by 27% over this period, the result of this subtraction is in most cases positive – people were paying more taxes in 1968 than in 1964. But it is hard to see any significant pattern in these results: the increases for the higher incomes, for example, are neither systematically higher nor systematically lower than the increases for the lower incomes.

Inflation, however, can make such comparisons – even over as short a period as four years – very misleading. A one-adult household whose original income was in the range of £260–314 in 1968 would be poorer in absolute terms (and poorer still relative to other people) than a one-adult household with the same income in 1964, and a straight comparison of the percentage of income paid in direct taxes in each case is not very meaningful. There is no fully satisfactory way of avoiding this problem. However the average increase in original money incomes over this period was approximately 25%, which happens to be only a little bigger than the percentage difference between the (log-scale) class-intervals in the table, which is about 20%. The (*b*) rows in the table therefore compare each income group for 1964 with the *next highest* income group for 1968. This is likely to give a generally better indication of what happened to the direct tax burden on particular groups of people, though of course the results of what one might call this 'diagonal' comparison need to be interpreted with considerable caution. In fact, although the figures in the (*b*) rows look rather more sensible than the figures in the (*a*) rows, in that they show some tendency to rise with income, there is too much variation for any very positive conclusions to emerge.

Table 2.10 represents a different way of looking at the problem. It shows the proportion of their income that 18 different households would have paid in income tax and surtax in 1964–5; and the proportion they would have paid in 1970–1 if their income had risen by 50% – i.e. by approximately the national average. This gives one some idea of how households in the same relative position in the income scale in 1970–1 as in 1964–5 fared in terms of the burden of direct taxation. It is clear from the table that every household would have been paying a larger proportion of its income in direct taxes in 1970–1 than in 1964–5, and in some cases a much larger proportion. There is more than one way of assessing the significance of this for different income groups, but the best seems to be to examine the percentage reduction in the proportion of income *retained*. On this basis it would seem that although there were no very marked changes in horizontal distribution, there was a slight improvement in vertical distribution as between low and middle income groups; and a very marked

TABLE 2.10. BURDEN OF DIRECT TAXATION ON EARNED INCOME

Annual income in 1964-5 (£)	Equivalent annual income in 1970-1ᵃ (£)	Per cent of earned income paid in income tax and surtax						Per cent reduction in proportion of original income retained		
		Single		Married		Married with 2 childrenᵇ		Single	Married	Married with 2 children
		1964-5	1970-1	1964-5	1970-1	1964-5	1970-1			
600	900	16	17	5	11	—	2	1	6	2
1,000	1,500	18	23	13	19	5	14	6	7	9
2,000	3,000	24	28	22	26	17	23	5	5	7
4,000	6,000	27	33	26	32	24	29	8	8	7
10,000	15,000	41	55	40	54	38	53	24	23	24
20,000	39,000	61	73	60	72	59	72	31	30	32

ᵃ The figures in this column simply represent the figures in the first column increased by 50%, since this was approximately the average increase in *per capita* earned incomes between 1964-5 and 1970-1 (*Economic Trends*, February 1971, page 29). Thus households in the first column would have to have the income specified in the second column if their *relative* position in the income scale were to be the same in 1970-1 as in 1964-5.
ᵇ Under 11.

Source: *108th Report of Inland Revenue*, Financial Statement and Budget Report 1970-1.

improvement as between low and middle income groups on the one hand, and very high earners on the other. Much the same is true in the case of unearned income (Table 2.11). Whereas the reduction in the proportion

TABLE 2.11. BURDEN OF DIRECT TAXATION ON INVESTMENT INCOME
Married couples

Annual investment income in 1964–5 (£)	Equivalent annual income in 1970–1 (£)[a]	Per cent of investment income paid in income tax and surtax		Per cent reduction in proportion of original income retained
		1964–5	1970–1	
1,000	1,400	22	28	8
2,000	2,800	30	36	9
10,000	14,000	58	68	24
20,000	28,000	72	79	25

[a] The figures in the first column increased by 40%, since this was approximately the increase in investment incomes over the period (*Economic Trends*, January 1971, page xvii).

Source: *108th Report of Inland Revenue*, Financial Statement and Budget Report 1970-71.

of relatively small investment incomes retained was about 10%, for very large ones it was about 25%. In this case as well, therefore, the change in the vertical distribution was favourable. What is, perhaps, disappointing is that the reductions in the case of unearned incomes are little greater than the reductions in the case of earned incomes: those with earned incomes of £1,500–£3,000 in 1970–1 had suffered nearly as much as those with unearned incomes of the same amount.

Although not formally a direct tax, the employee's flat-rate National Insurance contribution is in effect a tax on income, and is appropriately dealt with here. It is notoriously regressive, since it is the same for particular categories of people regardless of their income.[1] Although the rise in the employee's National Insurance contribution while Labour was in office was no faster than the rise in average earnings (both rose by roughly 50%), this of course bore more heavily on those with lower incomes: the rise in the weekly contribution for adult men from 11/8 to 17/8 (58 new pence to 88 new pence) hit those whose weekly earnings rose from £12 to £18 more than those whose earnings rose from £30 to £45.

The regressive effect of the flat-rate National Insurance contributions introduced in 1946 to implement the war-time Beveridge proposals had been appreciated for many years. The Beveridge philosophy had been that everyone, upon retiring (or becoming sick or unemployed, though in terms of cost this was of far less significance), should receive weekly cash benefits sufficient to give them a guaranteed, if minimal, standard of living. These benefits would be largely financed out of weekly flat-rate

[1] A tax is called 'regressive' if it accounts for a smaller proportion of higher than of lower incomes.

contributions by employees and employers. It was recognized that these contributions would represent a bigger proportion of the income of lower-paid workers than of higher-paid ones; but then so would the retirement pension (or sickness or unemployment benefit), which was also flat-rate; so that was fair.

The main snag about this arrangement soon became apparent. If the flat-rate contribution was to be kept low enough not to impose too heavy a burden on lower-paid workers, the level of pension would also remain low, and one of the main objects of the exercise – that people should not suffer a catastrophic fall in living standards when retiring, or becoming sick or unemployed – would be lost. If, on the other hand, the real value of pensions and other benefits was to be kept reasonably in line with the real value of average earnings, the flat-rate contributions needed to finance them would bear very heavily on the lower paid.

One way out of this dilemma would have been to finance an increasing proportion of pensions and other benefits out of direct taxation; but the increase in the standard rate of income tax that this would have required was regarded as politically unacceptable. The alternative was to graduate the employees' and employers' contributions in line with the employee's income. But if this were to be done, and the fiction were to be maintained that by their contributions people were financing their own future pensions, it was difficult to escape the conclusion that benefits should be graduated as well.[1] This in any case made more sense from the point of view of easing people's transition from employment to retirement: to insist that people's pensions should be equal even though their pre-retirement earnings had been distinctly unequal seemed to put the cart before the horse; and earnings-related occupational pension schemes were already enjoyed by many people in the higher income groups.

Considerations of this kind led the Labour Party to propose, in 1957, a National Superannuation Scheme, which would provide half-pay on retirement for the average wage earner, and up to two-thirds for the lower-paid. This proposal, which was repeated in subsequent Election Manifestos, was of great importance. As eventually worked out, the scheme came to grips with the problem of inflation in that it ensured that pension rights were automatically adjusted to changes in average earnings up to the time of retirement, and subsequently adjusted at two-yearly intervals by enough to take account, at the very least, of rises in prices. Unfortunately this scheme, which would gradually (admittedly, very gradually) have eliminated one of the major forms of poverty and insecurity in contemporary Britain, was killed by the result of the 1970 General Election – or perhaps simply by its timing, since at the time of the dissolution of Parliament the Bill was already at the committee stage.

On earnings-related sickness and unemployment benefits, however,

[1] From a national accounting point of view, of course, today's National Insurance contributions finance today's pensions, not the pensions which will be paid in thirty years' time.

Labour had moved more smartly: these came into effect in 1966, and significantly reduced the inequality between a man in work and a man out of work. Whereas in 1964 the net income received by the average wage earner, when on sickness or unemployment benefit, was only 45% of what he received at work, by 1968 the figure had increased to 75%.[1]

Indirect taxation

Whereas direct taxation is distinctly progressive, indirect taxation is inclined to be regressive, and one might therefore have expected to see some shift from indirect to direct taxation under the Labour Government. This did indeed happen: although the yield of indirect taxation[2] rose by 68% between 1964 and 1970, the yield of direct taxation rose by 111% (Table 2.12), and therefore increased as a proportion of the yield of taxes on income and expenditure combined.[3]

TABLE 2.12. CHANGES IN TAXATION YIELDS AND EXPENDITURE

Per cent change between 1964 and 1970

Taxes on income	+111
Taxes on expenditure[a]	+68
Central Government current expenditure[b]	+68
Gross National Product[b]	+46

[a] Excluding Selective Employment Tax.
[b] At current prices.

Source: *1971 Blue Book.*

In addition to this quite marked change of emphasis between direct and indirect taxes, the Labour Government also made a considerable effort, within the field of indirect taxes, to concentrate the biggest percentage increases on those commodities more likely to be bought by the rich than the poor. For excise duties, for example, the rise in the duty on beer and tobacco was modest compared with the rise in the duties on motoring (petrol duty and vehicle licences), and very modest compared with the assault on wine-drinkers (Table 2.13). Within the purchase tax field, the rise in tax on more essential goods such as clothing, furniture and household utensils was much smaller than the rise on less essential

[1] *Social Trends*, No. 1, page 19.
[2] Excluding Selective Employment Tax which, as the name implies, is a tax on employment and not on goods and services. The extent to which SET was passed on in higher prices is controversial, and no allowance is made for it here.
[3] The yield of taxes on income and expenditure combined rose about twice as fast as the Gross National Product. This reflected the fact that Central Government current expenditure also rose significantly faster than the GNP, and that the Central Government's current surplus increased over the period from £500 million to £3,700 million (some of the implications for income distribution of this rapid rise in Government expenditure are discussed in the next section).

TABLE 2.13.　CHANGES IN TAX RATES WHILE LABOUR WAS
IN OFFICE

Per cent change in rates of excise duty

Light wine	+108
Heavy wine	+ 78
Private motor vehicle licences	+ 67
Petrol	+ 64
Spirits	+ 46
Beer	+ 41
Tobacco	+ 30

Per cent change in rates of purchase tax

Furs, jewellery, cameras, records, perfumery and cosmetics	+120
Motor vehicles, radio and TV sets, domestic appliances, gramophones, confectionery, ice cream, soft drinks	+ 47
Clothing, furniture, household utensils	+ 38

Source: *Economic Trends*, January 1971, page xlviii.

goods such as furs, jewellery, cameras and perfumery.[1] The effect of the low increase in the duty on tobacco was particularly noticeable (Table 2.14).[2] For the three types of household shown, the percentage of disposable income spent on tobacco duty declined over the period at many income levels (whether one makes a 'straight' or a 'diagonal' comparison).[3] But there is some tendency for the decline to be greater at the lower end of the income scale, particularly in the case of one-adult households.

One or two other steps were taken by the Labour Government to alleviate the burden of indirect taxes where it was heaviest, the most notable being the introduction of a system of rate rebates for those with low incomes.[4] Over a million households were benefiting from this by 1968–9, and although the sums involved were small (an average of about 40 new

---

[1] It is difficult to make useful comparisons *between* commodities subject to excise duties and commodities subject to purchase tax. This is partly because in the typical case excise duties in 1964 represented a much higher proportion of the selling price than purchase tax did; but chiefly because at a time of generally rising prices excise duties, being 'specific', *have* to be increased if they are not to represent a diminishing proportion of the selling price of the commodity, whereas rates of purchase tax, which is an *ad valorem* tax, do not.

[2] It is also of some intrinsic interest, in view of the heavy pressure for higher duties on tobacco on health grounds. There is no doubt that such a step would be regressive in income distribution terms.

[3] See page 91. But since we are here dealing with the change over the *five*-year period 1964 to 1969, one needs not so much a 'diagonal' as what one might call a 'knight's move' approach, since the increase in disposable money incomes over the period was roughly 35%, and the increase in the class-intervals is only 20%. Clearly any systematic evaluation is impossible.

[4] This followed the publication of the report of the Allen Committee, *The Impact of Rates on Households*, Cmnd. 2582. Rates are not strictly speaking an indirect tax, but they are classified as such by the CSO and it is convenient to include them here.

TABLE 2.14. AVERAGE PAYMENTS OF TOBACCO DUTY AS PER CENT OF INCOME AFTER DIRECT TAXES AND BENEFITS

Range of original income (£ per year)

		216–	260–	315–	382–	460–	559–	676–	816–	988–	1,196–	1,448–	1,752–	2,122–	2,566–	3,104 and above
1 adult	1964	7·7	4·8	6·3	8·7	3·8	5·2	5·8	5·9	4·2	2·8	0·8				
	1969	2·4	2·8	2·7	2·7	3·4	3·7	3·7	3·8	3·7	3·1	3·1	1·6	1·1	2·3	
2 adults, 1 child	1964						5·8	7·5	5·2	5·4	4·7	4·0	4·4			
	1969						6·0	7·9	5·9	5·4	4·7	4·8	3·5	2·7	2·8	2·4
2 adults, 2 children	1964						6·7	6·1	5·2	5·3	3·5	3·3	2·4	2·4		
	1969						5·3	7·4	4·2	4·0	4·0	4·1	3·1	2·8	1·5	1·2

Source: *Economic Trends*, August 1966 and February 1971.

TABLE 2.15. INDIRECT TAXES AS PER CENT OF INCOME AFTER DIRECT TAXES AND BENEFITS

Range of original income (£ per year)

	260–	315–	382–	460–	559–	676–	816–	988–	1,196–	1,448–	1,752–	2,122–	2,566–	3,104–	Average
1964	17	17	20	18	18	18	18	17	18	17	17	17	16	13	17
1969	23	21	22	21	22	23	23	22	22	22	21	21	20	21	21

Source: *Economic Trends*, February 1970 and February 1971.

pence per week), for many of those receiving the rebates this amount was by no means negligible. But the effect on the overall distribution of income was obviously not very great.

Table 2.15 summarizes the impact on income distribution of all the changes in indirect taxes between 1964 and 1969. For all households together, the percentage of disposable income taken by indirect taxes rose from 17% to 21%.[1] To a remarkable extent (whether one's comparison is 'straight' or 'diagonal' or 'knight's move'), this rise of 4 points or so applied throughout the entire income range. Only at the very top and the very bottom, on a 'straight' comparison, is there a markedly bigger rise in the burden and, given the inevitable quirkiness of the figures, it would be fanciful to make very much of it. The tentative conclusion would seem to be that although – as the discussion in the last few pages has suggested – Labour's policy on indirect taxes pointed in the right direction, it does not appear to have been powerful enough to have had much effect on the figures.

IV.   BENEFITS

A Government determined to improve the distribution of income is bound to concentrate a good deal of attention on increasing benefits – more so, probably, than on changing taxation. For it is hard to envisage any really worthwhile improvement in income distribution in contemporary Britain which does not involve significantly increasing the standard of living of the lowest tenth – or even the lowest fifth – of the population in relation to that of the rest. This cannot be done by tax changes: for the most part, the poor do not pay income tax (though it is true that many of them pay National Insurance contributions); and little could be done to relieve them of indirect taxation which did not relieve everyone else as well. Hence any marked success the Labour Government of 1964–70 could have had in increasing economic equality would have rested heavily on what it did about benefits. In this section benefits are discussed under two broad headings: cash benefits, and benefits in kind.

Cash benefits

The great majority of those in the lowest 10 or 20% of the income range are those who are not employed, and therefore not currently earning an income – principally the old, the sick, the unemployed, the widowed; and their dependants.[2] The main source of income of these people is the system

[1] Although this mainly reflected the big increase in the yield of indirect taxes it was also to some small extent the result of the change in definition of original income used in the February 1971 *Economic Trends* analysis (see footnote on page 88). Any differential impact on different income groups is unknown, though obviously small.
[2] The other main category of people likely to be in poverty are those actually or usually employed in the very low-paid jobs, and their dependants (see pages 81–3).

of National Insurance benefits and retirement pensions. To some, of course, state benefits represent only an addition to income derived from other sources such as private pension or insurance schemes, or accumulated or inherited wealth; but these are in a minority. For something of the order of 8 million people – one person in seven of the population as a whole – what happens to their standard of living is wholly or largely determined by what happens to state benefits.

State benefits, however, do not consist solely of National Insurance benefits and retirement pensions. For various reasons, though principally because they have not paid the necessary contributions, a number of people are not entitled to National Insurance benefits, but have no other means of support. Such people are saved from destitution by drawing Supplementary Benefits (essentially the same thing that used to be called National Assistance). Curiously, the level of this assistance, when account is taken of the fact that those receiving it also have all or much of their rent paid for them, has throughout the post-war period been higher than the level of National Insurance benefits. Since Supplementary Benefits are in effect the Government's estimate of the minimum amount of money people need to maintain an acceptable standard of living in contemporary Britain, this has been officially recognized as implying that those receiving National Insurance benefits but little or no other income were entitled to have these benefits topped up by Supplementary Benefits – provided they took the initiative in applying for them.

Because average earnings increase at a fairly steady pace over time, while National Insurance benefits and Supplementary Benefits are increased by discrete amounts at discrete intervals,[1] comparisons need to be drawn with rather a broad brush; much misplaced ingenuity has gone into demonstrating that over particular time-periods benefits have lagged behind earnings, or vice versa. The fairest thing to do seems to be to take the level of National Insurance and Supplementary Benefits immediately after the last time Labour raised them, in relation to what they were immediately after the last time they were raised before Labour took office; and to compare this with the rise in average earnings over the same period. This is done in Table 2.16. It is clear that benefits rose at roughly the same rate as salaries, but not quite as fast as weekly wage earnings. This has been taken by some commentators[2] as an indictment of the Labour Government, since a move towards greater equality obviously calls for bigger percentage increases in the much lower incomes of those in receipt of state benefits. But, in fact, in terms of *disposable* incomes (which is the more relevant concept) this did happen: because of the fairly steep increase in direct taxes and National Insurance contributions over the period, the disposable income of manual workers earning the average

[1] Generally every two years or so, though National Insurance benefits and Supplementary Benefits are often increased at different times.
[2] For example, The Child Poverty Action Group, *Poverty and the Labour Government* (April 1970), pages 6–7.

TABLE 2.16.   INCREASES IN BENEFITS AND EARNINGS

Index numbers, March–June[a] *1963 = 100*

	Oct.–Nov.[b] 1969
National Insurance benefits:	
Unemployment, sickness and retirement benefit (single)[c]; widow's pension	148
Retirement pension (married couple)	149
National Assistance/Supplementary Benefit:	
Husband and wife[d]	150
Weekly earnings of adult male manual workers (all industries)	154
Earnings of male administrative, technical and clerical employees	148[e]

[a] For benefits, date of increase; for earnings, April.
[b] For benefits, date of increase; for earnings, October.
[c] Excludes earnings-related supplements.
[d] Excludes allowance for rent.
[e] Approximately: figures are only available for October.

Source: *Employment and Productivity Gazette, Economic Trends.*

wage rose by only about 40% between the spring of 1963 and the autumn of 1969, while for the average salaried employee the rise was only about 35% (Table 2.17). In terms of *real* disposable income (i.e. after allowing

TABLE 2.17.   INCREASES IN DISPOSABLE INCOMES

Index numbers in Oct.–Nov. 1969, April–May 1963 = 100

	Adult male manual workers	Male administrative technical and clerical employees	Retirement pension, married couple
Gross average weekly earnings/income	154	148	149
Disposable income[a]			149
Single man	141	137	
Married man with two children	139	134	
Real disposable income[b]			115
Single man	111	108	
Married man with two children	109	106	

[a] Gross earnings *plus* family allowances (where applicable) *minus* income tax and flat-rate and graduated National Insurance contributions.
[b] Disposable income deflated by the rise in the appropriate retail price index.

Source: *Employment and Productivity Gazette*, Inland Revenue reports, Dept. of Health and Social Security.

for the 27% increase in the retail price index over the period) the typical employee benefited to the tune of 5–10%. On average, those in receipt of state benefits did considerably better than this, even after allowing for the fact that for many of them prices rose slightly faster.[1] Thus there was in practice some closing of the gap, at any rate in relative terms.

The Labour Government had some success too in persuading people who previously, through ignorance or pride, had failed to draw assistance to which they were entitled, to do so (this was indeed the main reason for the change from National Assistance to Supplementary Benefits and the publicity which attended it). But much of the increase in the numbers drawing assistance seems to have been the result of the increase in the assistance scales;[2] obviously, an increase in Supplementary Benefit scales increases the number of people with incomes below the scales, and therefore entitled to some supplementary allowances.[3] It would seem clear that when Labour left office a large number of people who were entitled to Supplementary Benefits were still not drawing them, and that in this particular sense the problem of poverty had not been much alleviated. Some indicators, moreover, had actually worsened: the number of men who were wage-stopped, for example, had risen from 15,000 in 1966 to 24,000 in 1970. But this does not alter the earlier conclusion, that the disposable incomes of these people – mainly retirement pensioners – increased at a faster rate than that of the average wage earner; in this sense, even after allowing for differential price effects, there was some improvement in the relative position of the poorest members of the community.

National Insurance and Supplementary Benefits are not the only important cash benefits. To a great many families with two or more children what really matters is family allowances; this is particularly true of large, low-income families where the father is in full-time work or wage-stopped. As a method of channelling assistance to where it is most needed the family allowance has many virtues. Because there is no means test – i.e. because everyone is entitled to it, regardless of their income – it has a near-universal take-up. Although it may seem indiscriminate, it is taxable, and its net value therefore bears quite a good relationship to needs: the poor will get the full value of the allowance, the rich only a fraction of it. The total amount received in family allowances automatically increases with the number of children in the family, and at low – and even not-so-low – income levels there tends to be more poverty in large families than in small

---

[1] The retail price index for two-person pensioner households rose by 29% over the period (*Employment and Productivity Gazette*, August 1970, page 684).

[2] This is argued, for example, in Atkinson, op. cit., Chapter 4.

[3] The other side of the coin is that, if the Supplementary Benefit scale is defined as the poverty line, an increase in the scale will automatically, overnight, increase the number of people 'living in poverty' even though no one is in absolute terms any worse off. This is sometimes overlooked. For example, in a much-quoted article entitled 'A million more in poverty since 1966' (*The Times*, 10 March 1971) Professor Peter Townsend said, 'It would be surprising if those with incomes less than the Supplementary Benefit scales numbered fewer than 3,500,000 at the beginning of 1971, or a million more than in 1966.' He failed to point out, however, that at the beginning of 1971 Supplementary Benefits had just been increased (in November 1970) whereas National Insurance and Retirement Benefits had not been increased since November 1969.

ones. Finally, it is payable to the wife and not the husband; this favourably affects the distribution of income within the family, the importance of which is sometimes overlooked.

Unfortunately, family allowances are unpopular in some quarters, partly because they are believed to encourage large families (a belief for which there is no evidence); and partly because they do, in a sense, represent money taken out of a man's pay packet by the state and handed over to his wife. Perhaps these factors account for the derisory level of family allowances when Labour took office in October 1964: at 8/- (40p) a week for the second child and 10/- (50p) a week for subsequent children they were not much higher in money terms, and very much lower in real terms, than when first introduced in 1946.

Labour increased family allowances: when it left office the figure was 90p for the second child and 100p for third and subsequent children, and to people with large families and low incomes this made a lot of difference. For a labourer with four children, earning £15 a week, for example, it meant an increase of £1·50 or nearly 10% in the family's weekly disposable income. The rise in family allowances also had the virtue, by raising the level at which the 'wage-stop' started to operate, of increasing the net amount a low-paid worker would receive in Supplementary Benefits if he became sick or unemployed.

It did, however, take Labour a long time to increase these allowances – nothing happened until 1968 – and when it did, it failed to press the scheme nearly as far as many of those concerned with family poverty in Britain would have wished. The main reason for this reluctance to raise family allowances was simply the enormous cost. In 1964 they cost some £150 million – big money by any standards. Of course the net cost would be significantly smaller than this, because for better-off people, higher receipts of family allowances would mean higher payments of income tax. But while this fact might allay some criticisms, it created others. What was the point of the Government paying out large sums with one hand, it was asked, and taking them back with another?

This latter criticism was misconceived. There is nothing intrinsically wrong with a method of redistributing income which involves giving money with one hand and taking it with another – what matters is the cost-effectiveness of such a method, and its impact on incentives. A more telling criticism of a straight increase in family allowances was that even the wealthiest would benefit from it to some extent, since no one has a marginal tax rate of 100%.

This objection was overcome, in the event, by an ingenious scheme known at the time as the 'give-and-take' scheme, though subsequently, and less elegantly, described as the 'claw-back'. In essence, the benefit that better-off families derived from the increase in family allowances in 1968 was offset by changes in the child allowances income tax payers can set against their tax liability. Broadly speaking, this adjustment was such that standard-rate income tax payers were left in the same position, after the changes in family allowances, as they had been before; those paying sur-tax were worse off; those paying no tax, or tax at less than the standard rate, were left better off. This scheme, despite the controversy it aroused,[1] had one overwhelming virtue: it channelled assistance to one of the places where it was most needed, and it did so without a means test. In fact, it achieved an aim often appropriated to themselves by the Conservatives, by a method traditionally approved by Labour. There is, of course, a limit to how far the technique can be pushed if income tax child allowances are not to become negative; but this point is still some way off. In a rational world, the innovation would have come earlier and been bigger.

An indication of the net effects of Labour's various policies on cash benefits is provided in Table 2.18. It is clear (on the basis of either 'straight' or 'diagonal' comparison) that between 1964 and 1968 cash benefits as a percentage of original income rose for virtually every category of household and income for which satisfactory information is available, and that it rose to a much more significant extent for poorer than for richer households.[2]

Benefits in kind

Although not perhaps always regarded as such, benefits in kind consti-tute a very important form of income. They consist of the goods and ser-vices provided by central or local government, either free or at subsidized prices, out of the revenue they collect in taxes and rates. In contemporary Britain these benefits, in so far as they can be allocated to different families, consist almost entirely of health and educational services, and housing subsidies.[3] Housing subsidies are, in the overall context, so small that for present purposes they can be ignored.[4]

[1] In some quarters it stimulated argument of near-theological intensity. One objection, which would not have shamed a medieval schoolman, was that family allowances were a gift from the state to the individual, whereas income tax child allowances were not the same thing at all, but rather the absence of a gift from the individual to the state; and that it was therefore wrong to consider the two together.

[2] If anything, the figures understate the improvement, because the first instalment of the increase in family allowances did not come until April 1968, and the second one not until October, and thus were not fully reflected in the figures. (No figures are available for 1969 on a comparable basis.)

[3] The benefits derived from health and educational services consist of the value of medical and dental treatment, less prescription charges and other payments made; the value of education received at state schools, and the value of scholarships and education grants (which may be received in the form of cash but represent an income in kind that can – legally – only be spent on education). They also include other miscellaneous goods and services, such as free or subsidized milk, school meals, welfare services, etc.

[4] This is not to say that Labour's housing policies were not egalitarian, for many people in relatively low income groups benefited not only from bigger subsidies to council houses, but also from the offer of 'option' mortgages to those not paying income tax at the standard rate, and the setting-up of machinery under a new Rent Act to establish 'fair rents' for privately owned furnished accommodation. But a detailed scrutiny of the results of the Family Expenditure Surveys fails to reveal any significant impact of all this on the distribution of income.

TABLE 2.18. CASH BENEFITS AS PER CENT OF ORIGINAL INCOME[a]

Range of original income (£ per year)

		216—	260—	315—	382—	460—	559—	676—	816—	988—	1,196—	1,448—	1,752—	2,122—	2,566—	3,104 and above
1 adult	1964	60	38	20	9	8	2	1	1	2	1					
	1968		77	54	43	26	17	10	4	5	2	2	4	0	1	
2 adults	1964	120	102	86	51	27	17	11	5	2	1	1	1	1		
	1968		137	112	91	66	51	27	18	8	5	3	2	1	1	1
2 adults, 1 child	1964						11	4	2	2	1	1	1	1	0	
	1968							20	9	4	3	1	1	1		0
2 adults, 2 children	1964						8	4	4	3	2	2	1	1		
	1968							22	13	7	4	3	3	2	1	1
2 adults, 3 children	1964							9	7	6	6	3				
	1968								12	12	8	5	5	4	3	2

[a] Because of a change in the definition of original income in the C.S.O./D.H.S.S. analysis of the 1969 Family Expenditure Survey, the 1968 figures are probably a better guide to trends under the Labour Government.

Source: *Economic Trends*, August 1966 and February 1970.

Unlike cash benefits, benefits in kind only help those who consume the services provided. Thus there is no simple relationship between benefits received and original income. A bachelor who is poor but enjoys excellent health will receive little direct benefit from free health, education and welfare services,[1] whereas even a wealthy family with a large number of children and a tendency to chronic illness will benefit enormously. Nevertheless, benefits in kind are distinctly progressive both vertically and horizontally: they decline as a proportion of income with increasing income, and they form a higher proportion of the income of large than of small households. One must therefore expect a favourable effect on income distribution during a period when expenditure on health and education rises as a proportion of the Gross National Product; and it is clear (Table 2.19) that under the Labour Government this happened to a very marked extent.[2]

TABLE 2.19.   EXPENDITURE ON HEALTH AND EDUCATION

	Per cent of Gross National Product	
	1964	1970
Health		
Current expenditure	3·6	4·5
Total expenditure	3·9	4·9
Education		
Current expenditure	3·9	5·1
Total expenditure	4·8	6·1

Source: *1971 Blue Book.*

But although in broad terms it seems indisputable that the high priority the Labour Government gave to expenditure on education and the health service had a favourable effect on income distribution, any precise attempt to quantify the size of this effect is fraught with difficulties, the most intractable of which is the problem of satisfactorily allocating the benefits derived from higher education (this problem is discussed in more detail in the Appendix, pages 116–7). But even if it were possible to overcome this difficulty, it seems unlikely that it would make much difference to the broad picture that emerges from Table 2.20. In both 1964 and 1968, benefits in kind were steeply progressive; and over the period those in the lower half of the income scale appear to have benefited more than those in the upper half. The increased provision of benefits in kind by the Labour Government, then, seems to have been an important element making for an improved distribution of income.

[1] He will, of course, benefit *indirectly*, in that he is less likely (than he would be if these services were not provided to anybody) to contract typhoid or cholera, and more likely to find someone who can mend his motorbike.
[2] Far more than can be accounted for by demographic changes.

TABLE 2.20. BENEFITS IN KIND AS PER CENT OF ORIGINAL INCOME[a]

Range of original income (£ per year)

		216—	260—	315—	382—	460—	559—	676—	816—	988—	1,196—	1,448—	1,752—	2,122—	2,566—	3,104 and above
1 adult	1964	11	9	6	4	4	3	2	1	1	1	1				
	1968		14	17	8	6	5	4	3	3	3	2	1	1	1	
2 adults	1964	24	26	16	10	8	6	6	4	3	2	2	2	1		
	1968		32	23	20	20	13	10	8	6	4	4	3	3	2	2
2 adults, 1 child	1964						14	14	12	10	8	7	6			
	1968							20	17	13	11	9	8	7	7	3
2 adults, 2 children	1964						23	21	18	14	12	13	12	9		
	1968							29	22	20	16	14	13	10	11	7
2 adults, 3 children	1964							33	25	24	18	17	19	17	12	9
	1968								35	26	27	21	17			

[a] See footnote to Table 2.18.

Source: *Economic Trends*, August 1966 and February 1970.

V. OVERALL ASSESSMENT

In the last three sections an attempt has been made to summarize the Labour Government's record in the three main areas affecting the final distribution of income – namely the distribution of original income, the impact on this of taxes, and the impact on it of benefits. Broadly speaking, the distribution of original income does not seem to have changed very much, but tax changes probably had some favourable effect, and changes in benefits, particularly cash benefits, a favourable effect on a more substantial scale. Can one therefore conclude that the overall effect on income distribution of all Labour's measures, taken together, was a favourable one?

On the assumption that the distribution of original income did not change very much (and certainly not as a result of Government action), Table 2.21 provides, in the simplest possible form, an answer to this question. It shows, for fourteen different income groups, the percentage by which original income was increased or reduced by all taxes and benefits in 1964 and 1969.[1] It is, in other words, a measure of how far the final distribution of income is different from the original distribution of income as a result of the intervention of the state. It is clear[2] that whereas the effect of all taxes and benefits on those in the top half of the income scale was to reduce their original income in 1969 by as much as, or more than, in 1964, the effect on those in the bottom half of the scale was to increase their original incomes by significantly more – the effect being strongest for the lowest incomes. As far as it goes, this table is powerful evidence of an improvement in income distribution as a result of the Labour Government's policies.

The same data are broken down in more detail in Table 2.22. The full complexity of this table cannot be summarized in a sentence, but it is broadly true that for each type of household the same thing happened: in the lower half of the income scale (particularly towards the lower end) the net effect on final income of state intervention was more favourable in 1968 and 1969 than in 1964; in the upper half it was less favourable, or unchanged.

The significance of the figures in Table 2.22 is brought out more clearly in Table 2.23, which shows a measure of the dispersion of income after all taxes and benefits. The table takes income after all taxes and benefits as a percentage of original income for the two highest comparable income categories, and calculates this as a percentage of the same figure for the two lowest income categories.[3] For each type of household there is a reduc-

---

[1] Because the 1969 figures are not strictly comparable with the 1964 figures, the 1968 figures are given as well. With one or two exceptions, the 1968 and 1969 figures are remarkably close to each other.

[2] On the basis of either 'straight' or 'diagonal' comparison.

[3] No significance can be attached to the very different absolute figures obtained for different types of household, partly because the range of incomes for which satisfactory information is available varies for different types of household.

TABLE 2.21. PER CENT CHANGE IN ORIGINAL INCOME RESULTING FROM ALL TAXES AND BENEFITS

All households

Range of original income (£ per year)

	260–	315–	382–	460–	559–	676–	816–	988–	1,196–	1,448–	1,752–	2,122–	2,566–	3,104 and above	Average
1964	+59	+47	+31	+6	—	−6	−9	−13	−17	−19	−22	−25	−27	−34	−15
1968	+109	+82	+58	+32	+19	+2	−5	−12	−17	−21	−23	−25	−27	−29	−16
1969	+109	+83	+59	+41	+20	+6	−2	−9	−15	−20	−23	−24	−26	−33	−16

Source: *Economic Trends*, August 1966, February 1970 and February 1971.

TABLE 2.22. PER CENT CHANGE IN ORIGINAL INCOME RESULTING FROM ALL TAXES AND BENEFITS

Selected households

Selected households		216–	260–	315–	382–	460–	559–	676–	816–	988–	1,196–	1,448–	1,752–	2,122–	2,566–	3,104 and above
								Range of original income (£ per year)								
1 adult	1964	+30	+13	−9	−24	−17	−31	−31	−36	−30	−31	−34				
	1968		+53	+34	+14	−2	−16	−24	−33	−31	−36	−36	−35	−37	−32	
	1969		+45	+40	+11	+8	−10	−23	−29	−32	−34	−35	−38	−32	−38	
2 adults	1964	+98	+91	+66	+20	−4	−11	−16	−24	−28	−30	−28	−29	−29		
	1968		+112	+84	+64	+44	+19	−5	−14	−26	−31	−32	−33	−33	−35	−35
	1969		+92	+91	+72	+43	+25	+1	−18	−20	−28	−32	−33	−33	−35	−41
2 adults, 1 child	1964						−7	−13	−17	−19	−20	−23	−31			
	1968							−3	−11	−18	−22	−25	−25	−28	−27	−21
	1969						+19	−9	−6	−20	−21	−27	−25	−26	−27	−32
2 adults, 2 children	1964						−2	−5	−7	−12	−13	−14	−17	−18		
	1968							+16	—	−7	−15	−16	−18	−19	−21	−26
	1969						+56	+19	+11	−4	−12	−15	−21	−24	−21	−28
2 adults, 3 children	1964							+13	+6	+2	−2	−4				
	1968								+11	+5	—	−7	−10	−10	−14	−26
	1969							+18	+11	+12	+1	−4	−8	−14	−14	−21

Source: *Economic Trends*, August 1966, February 1970 and February 1971.

TABLE 2.23. CHANGES IN THE DISPERSION OF FINAL INCOME[a]

	1964	1968	1969
1 adult	56	45	45
2 adults	37	33	34
2 adults, 1 child	81	79	80
2 adults, 2 children	86	74	67
2 adults, 3 children	89	85	84

[a] The concept represented by the figures in this table is explained in the text. A *reduction* in the figure constitutes an *improvement* in income distribution.

Source: Table 2.22.

tion in dispersion – i.e. an improvement in the distribution of income – between 1964 and 1968 or 1969; and except for one-child families the change is quite marked.

Tables 2.22 and 2.23 bear on the vertical distribution of income – i.e. the distribution of income for the same type of household at different levels of income. Table 2.24 provides some information on the horizontal distri-

TABLE 2.24. INCOME IN 1969 AS PER CENT OF INCOME IN 1964

	Original income[a]	Income after direct taxes and benefits	Income after all taxes and benefits
1 adult (excl. pensioners)	118	125	124
2 adults (excl. pensioners)	138	137	131
2 adults, 1 child	143	140	134
2 adults, 2 children	146	140	137
2 adults, 3 children	147	142	137
2 adults, 4 children	145	146	141
All households	136	135	130

[a] Old basis (see Appendix).

Source: *Economic Trends*, February 1971.

bution of income – i.e. the distribution of income between households of different types. Over the period 1964 to 1969 the rise in income after all taxes and benefits was greater, the larger the family. Although there are conceptual problems here (discussed in the Appendix) this would probably be widely regarded as an improvement in income distribution.

It would appear, then, that there was an improvement in the distribution of income, both vertical and horizontal, under the Labour Government. The main reason for this seems to have been the increases in cash benefits – National Insurance and Supplementary Benefits, and family allowances. Increases in benefits in kind, taking the form of a rapid rise in the provision of health and educational services, were also an important influence. Less important, though not completely insignificant, was the impact of an increase in the effective rates of direct taxation.

To have promoted a measurable improvement in the distribution of income against the background of the deplorably slow rate of growth of output permitted by its macro-economic policies was one of the Labour Government's main achievements – though, ironically, one that has received very little recognition from many of Labour's own supporters. What might be achieved against the background of a reasonable growth rate? One day, perhaps, we may see.

APPENDIX.   ASSESSING CHANGES IN THE DISTRIBUTION OF INCOME

This note attempts to indicate in broad outline some of the main problems involved in trying to assess how the distribution of income has changed in Britain in recent years. Theoretical difficulties are discussed first; then practical ones.

1. *Theoretical problems*

The 55 million people in Britain are divided among more than 20 million households, or families. In any given week or year, each of these families will have a certain income; in any given week or year some time later, they will (ignoring the problem of new households which are formed and old ones which disappear) also each have an income, which will probably be different from their previous one. The fundamental theoretical problem is to express these 20 million changes in a sufficiently summary way to be intelligible, yet a sufficiently disaggregated way to bring out changes in the relative position of different income groups.

One of the best-known methods of describing the distribution of income is the Lorenz curve (Figure 2.1), which shows the cumulated percentage of total income which is received by a cumulated percentage of income receivers. If all incomes were equal, the Lorenz curve would coincide with the diagonal, since 1% of income receivers would get 1% of total income, 10% would get 10% and so on. The extent to which the Lorenz curve in fact sags below the diagonal is an indication of how unequally income is distributed: evidently, the further the curve from the diagonal, the more unequally is income distributed.

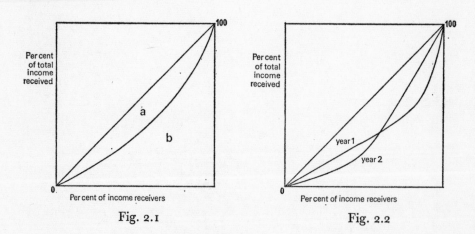

Fig. 2.1   Fig. 2.2

Another way of representing the same information is the *Gini coefficient*, or *Gini concentration ratio*, which is the area between the Lorenz curve and

the diagonal expressed as a percentage of the triangle under the diagonal –
i.e. $\frac{a}{a+b}$ in Figure 2.1. Thus a reduction in the Gini coefficient indicates
a reduction in the degree of inequality, and vice versa.

The basic difficulty about using these two indicators in order to assess what has happened to the distribution of income over a period of time is that they may not tell one very much about what has happened to the particular groups (probably those at the top and the bottom of the income scale) in which one is likely to be most interested. In certain cases, indeed, the answers these indicators provide may be ambiguous, because the Lorenz curves may intersect each other.[1] In Figure 2.2 is the distribution of income more or less equal in Year 2 than in Year 1? Or is it – assuming the Gini coefficient to be the same in the two years – the same? Evidently, there is no single answer to this question. Between Year 1 and Year 2 there has been a shift of income away from those at both the top and the bottom of the scale in favour of those in the middle; in other words, the rich have got relatively poorer, but so have the poor. Whether one regards this as an improvement in the distribution of income or not is really a value judgment or gut reaction: it depends on whether one thinks it is more important to soak the rich or succour the poor.

Because of these ambiguities, any detailed investigation of changes in income distribution is likely to require an examination of what has happened to particular quantiles – e.g. the income of the family which occupies the position 1% or 10% or 20% up the income scale.[2] Quantiles can be expressed as a proportion of the median or of other quantiles in order to give a simple but useful measure of dispersion. However, any such measure inevitably conceals detailed shifts, since it provides no systematic information about what has happened to income between the quantiles used. Alternatively, therefore, one can look at changes in the share of total income accruing to particular quantiles (see Budd, op. cit.). This approach can bring out major changes in the shares of particular groups, but does not avoid the basic dilemma that if looked at in summary form, it can give ambiguous information,[3] and if looked at in detail can become unmanageable. These difficulties are mitigated by the fact that for practical purposes one may be particularly interested in the 1% or 5% at the top, and the 10% or 20% at the bottom; but the experience of even these relatively small groups cannot always be summed up in an easy way.

[1] For evidence of the extent to which this has happened in the United States in recent years, see Edward C. Budd, 'Postwar changes in the size distribution of income in the US', *American Economic Review*, May 1970.

[2] Strictly speaking, the lowest percentile is the income such that 1% of incomes lie below it; the lowest decile the income such that 10% of incomes lie below it, etc. Any convenient quantile can, of course, be examined.

[3] The change in the share of the incomes lying between the 10th and 15th percentiles, for example, can be different from the change in the share of incomes lying between the 9th and 14th or 11th and 16th percentiles. Where this is so, there is no easy way of saying what has happened to the distribution of income.

More generally, quantile comparisons, being based on the incomes of individual units, can be very misleading where the sample is small.

The discussion so far has tacitly assumed that all income-receivers can be indiscriminately ranked along the same scale, regardless of their composition. In practice, of course, the income-receivers ranked along the horizontal axis of the Lorenz curve diagram will include families of many different kinds, ranging from one-person households at one extreme to households containing three or four adults, or two adults and a large number of children at the other. Because of this, any change in the demographic structure of the population will result in a shift in the position of the Lorenz curve even if in some real sense there has been no change in the inequality of the distribution of income. The shift between Year 1 and Year 2 in Figure 2.2, for example, could in principle be the result of a demographic change involving fewer very small and very large families, and more middle-sized ones. In practice, such demographic shifts are, of course, unlikely to be very important over a period of time of only five or six years; but even if there are no demographic changes at all, the problem of evaluating changes in the distribution of income between families of different sizes remains. Whereas a change in the 'vertical' distribution of income – i.e. the distribution of income among families consisting, say, of two adults and three children – is a readily comprehensible concept, a change in the 'horizontal' distribution of income – i.e. the distribution of income among families of different sizes and structures – is much less so. Attempts have been made to get over this problem of measuring the 'horizontal' distribution of income by calculating scales of 'equivalent adults', or, to put it the other way round, by calculating the incomes which families of different sizes would have to have if their incomes were to be regarded as 'equal'. One ingenious method, which used as a criterion of 'equality' the income at which families of different sizes spent the same proportion of their net disposable income on food, suggested that for Britain 'horizontal' equality of income distribution would require that, if the net disposable income of childless married couples were 100, single persons should have an income of 54, married couples with one child 131, married couples with two children 155, and so on.[1] However, such calculations rest in the last resort on arbitrary assumptions, and no very firm conclusions can be drawn from them. For this reason the distribution of income examined in most studies tends to be either the 'vertical' distribution for each of a number of different types of family, or the overall distribution of income on the assumption that any changes in this are the result of changes in the vertical, rather than the horizontal, distribution. Neither procedure is entirely satisfactory; it is a case of *faute de mieux*.[2]

[1] J. L. Nicholson, *Redistribution of Income in the United Kingdom in 1959, 1957 and 1953* (London 1965), page vii.
[2] For a more detailed discussion of some of these theoretical problems, see J. L. Nicholson, 'Redistribution of income—notes on some problems and puzzles', *Review of Income and Wealth*, September 1970.

2. Practical problems

The main practical problems which beset any assessment of recent changes in income distribution in Britain lie in the accuracy, the comprehensiveness and the comparability of the available data.

Broadly speaking, there are three main sources of data:

(*a*) Inland Revenue figures based on tax returns;
(*b*) Department of Employment earnings enquiries;
(*c*) The annual Family Expenditure Surveys.

(*a*) The Inland Revenue figures are comprehensive, but tend to be rather out-of-date (at the time of writing, in April 1971, the most recent year for which a full breakdown of the distribution of personal incomes is available is 1967–8 – i.e. a period which ended more than three years ago, and more than two years before the Labour Government left office). A further difficulty about the Inland Revenue figures is that they tend to be unreliable at the lower end of the scale (where people pay little or no income tax); and perhaps at the upper end of the scale as well, because of avoidance and evasion of tax on incomes not subject to PAYE. Avoidance and evasion also constitute a difficulty in the case of death duties. Inland Revenue figures of payment of estate duty at present constitute the only data on which estimates of the distribution of wealth can be based. Close examination suggests that the margins of error involved in this process are so great that little weight can be placed on the figures of the distribution of wealth published by the Inland Revenue; and certainly any apparent small changes in the distribution of wealth need to be treated with the greatest reserve.[1]

(*b*) A very comprehensive survey of the earnings of employees was carried out by the (then) Department of Employment and Productivity in September 1968, and a great deal of information was obtained about the distribution of these earnings. Unfortunately, although similar surveys are now being conducted annually and one will be able to analyse in great detail changes in the distribution of earnings since 1968, this is not true of the period immediately before 1968 (the nearest year for which there is even remotely comparable data is 1960). For the purpose of analysing changes between 1964 and 1970, then, the data are of no help: one can only look at changes in averages (on the basis of the long-established twice-yearly *average* earnings enquiries) and not at changes in dispersion.

(*c*) A great deal of information is collected by the Family Expenditure Surveys conducted each year by the Department of Employment, and although the published reports concentrate on the expenditure rather than the income pattern of households, the original information obtained

[1] See, for example, the various studies discussed in Richard M. Titmuss, *Income Distribution and Social Change*, London 1962; and Michael Meacher, 'Wealth: Labour's Achilles heel' in Nicholas Bosanquet and Peter Townsend (eds.), *Labour and Inequality: a Study in Social Policy 1964–70*, Fabian Society, 1972.

is analysed in great detail from the point of view of income distribution by the Central Statistical Office and the Department of Health and Social Security. These analyses, which are published annually (generally in the February issue of *Economic Trends*) form the main source of accessible information about the distribution of income in the United Kingdom.

This information, and the analysis based on it, is distinctly sophisticated by comparison with what is available in most other countries. In particular, the analysis takes account not only of the influence on personal incomes of cash benefits (such as old-age pensions and family allowances) and direct taxes (such as income tax and surtax), but also of indirect taxes and of benefits in kind – such as the value of the health and education services provided by the state. It attempts, in short, to show the effect on the distribution of income of all the activities of the state which are relevant to income distribution, excluding only certain types of expenditure (such as expenditure on administration, defence, and general environmental services) and certain types of taxation (principally taxes on undistributed profits and capital gains) which are virtually impossible to allocate.[1]

For present purposes there are three main drawbacks about the detailed information presented in the *Economic Trends* articles. The most important is the relatively small size of the sample that co-operate in the Family Expenditure Survey. Although the sample was increased in 1967 and the number of households co-operating is now about 7000 instead of about 3000, this is still too small a sample on which to base conclusions about many of the sub-groups. Thus for some types of family at some income levels, information is not even published; and for those for which it is published, it is not always very reliable.

The second drawback is that because of changes of definition it is sometimes difficult to make detailed comparisons over time. For example, the data for 1969 are for the most part not strictly comparable with the data for 1964 because of a change in the definition of income.[2] This change is not in fact so great as to vitiate comparisons, but in some cases it makes them more difficult.

The third main drawback arises from the treatment of young people aged sixteen and over, who are treated as adults even if they are still at school, and of university students, who are not treated as part of their parents' household if they are away from home at the time of the survey. As a result, the substantial benefits in kind received by those who continue with full-time education (including university education) after the age of sixteen are very difficult to allocate in a satisfactory way. Families with university students living at home at the time of the survey will be counted as three-adult or four-adult households, and lumped together with other three-adult or four-adult households of entirely different composition;

---

[1] For a full account, see 'The incidence of taxes and social service benefits in 1969', *Economic Trends*, February 1971.
[2] Op. cit., page x.

while the benefits derived by families with university students away from home at the time of the survey will not be included in the statistics at all. This would not necessarily matter, for present purposes, if there were no correlation between income level and higher education, but in fact children from higher-income families are still very disproportionately represented in sixth forms and at universities,[1] and there is thus a danger of exaggerating the extent to which benefits in kind from education have a favourable effect on income distribution.

Although there is no fully satisfactory answer to this problem, it is probably fairly safe to ignore it in the context of the present exercise, on the grounds that (1) although very disproportionately represented, children from professional and managerial families (perhaps accounting for the top 5% of income receivers) only account for about a fifth of the total undergraduate population (itself still a very small proportion of the total of those receiving full-time education); (2) other forms of higher education, including teacher training, also expanded very rapidly under the Labour Government, and children from lower-income families are much more heavily represented in these courses than at universities;[2] (3) it is in any case not clear how far the benefits derived from a university education should be allocated as income in kind accruing to the parents rather than to the actual recipient.

---

[1] For a discussion of the way different social classes have benefited from recent increases in educational expenditure, see Howard Glennerster, 'Education and inequality' in Nicholas Bosanquet and Peter Townsend (eds.), op. cit.
[2] Ibid.

3 Overseas development policies

Dudley Seers and Paul Streeten [1]

In some obvious ways the world seems to be much more 'one family' than it was over thirty years ago. Jet aeroplanes have brought us together and television has destroyed old images. An advertisement for the Concorde airliner said: 'The world is about to be halved in size'; Marshal McLuhan tells us that 'the new electronic interdependence recreates the world in the image of a global village'. The numerous activities of the United Nations, the stupendous growth of the multi-national business corporation, the attempts to weld continents into common markets, the flourishing voluntary organizations have provided us with an institutional framework for international co-operation.

But this framework is unused. In many ways we have turned inwards, with an increasingly short-sighted view of the interests of our own nation and its citizens. The socialist parties of the industrial countries of the West were pioneers of international solidarity before the First World War, but now friendly references to international matters in national plans, publications, manifestos, speeches and other declarations are considerably less common (as well as less convincing) than they were sixty years ago. The phrase 'workers of the world unite' would have no appeal, almost no meaning, to a modern British factory worker and is not likely to be voiced at a Labour Party conference. It would in fact not be easy to say unambiguously whether the Conservative or the Labour Party is more 'international-minded'.

The pre-election policy

International policy is, however, a moral issue. If the Labour Party is to have any capacity to inspire people, especially the young, it has to be rooted in humanism, ultimately in the recognition of the essential brotherhood of man – and thus in a revulsion at the scale and nature of world poverty, a revulsion which does not stale with the familiarity and intractability of the problem.

Labour leaders once saw this. They were, when in opposition, committed to the relief of world poverty and to the creation of an integrated world community. This is especially true of Harold Wilson, who in 1953 wrote *The War on World Poverty*, a book pervaded by a sense of outrage

[1] The authors are indebted to Miss Diane Elson and Mr Ron Brigish for material used in this chapter and for help in writing it, and to a number of friends and colleagues for comments.

at the world's social evils, and urging that aid flows should amount to 3% of national incomes, more from richer countries. Through the whole period from 1945 to 1964 he returned again and again to the need for large capital flows as part of an international plan.

Even as late as 1964, in an article for the *Britannica Book of the Year*, entitled 'The relevance of British social democracy', he proposed a solution to the problem of international liquidity which would harness the industrial capacity of the advanced countries 'to increase aid to the under-developed areas to the utmost'. In the section on trade policy, he stressed the need for world-wide commodity agreements, to be negotiated under the aegis of the UN Conference on Trade and Development (UNCTAD) and said:

Commodity agreements, a world food plan, have always been central to our thinking . . . we must recognise that it is idle to talk of world development or of containing communism in the contested areas of the world, if we are prepared to see the earning power of these countries, through their sales of primary produce, subject to sudden and periodic collapse through price instability.

In particular, he suggested that

in addition to existing UN or national plans, we might provide that the IMF be empowered to assign credit certificates, to the tune of say £200,000,000–£300,000,000 a year, to an international investment fund which might be set up in conjunction with, or in replacement of, the existing International Development Association. These credit certificates would be allocated for spending in fully developed debtor countries which at the same time have unemployed resources – such as Britain and the United States in present circumstances.

What is urgent is that western nations should regard [an international economic summit meeting to discuss this type of plan] as a matter of primary importance.[1]

Similarly, Mrs Castle, in the debate on 3 February 1964 on the International Development Association (IDA) Bill[2] made an impassioned plea for more aid and for a more effective and better co-ordinated aid strategy. She castigated motives for giving aid 'which have nothing to do with the prime purpose of securing the economic development of the recipient countries of the world'. Development aid had miscarried, because those providing it had done so 'for reasons of national prestige, or for political motives to sustain certain regimes as against others, or for reasons of rivalry in the cold war, or for reasons of their own internal economic self-interest'.

The Manifesto on which the Labour Party fought the 1964 election was a good deal more cautious, but it showed awareness of the indivisibility of poverty, wherever it occurred in the world. The Party promised that, if elected, it would

[1] Harold Wilson, 1964. *Britannica Book of the Year*, pages 35–6.
[2] IDA is the 'soft-loan' affiliate of the World Bank, designed for very poor countries.

discuss with other countries proposals for expanding the trade of the developing nations;

increase the share of national income devoted to essential aid programmes, not only by loans and grants but by mobilizing unused industrial capacity to meet overseas needs;

revive the concept of a World Food Board for the disposal of agricultural surpluses.

It will give a dynamic lead in this vital field. Labour will create a Ministry of Overseas Development to be responsible not only for our part in Commonwealth Development but also for our work in and through the specialist agencies of the United Nations. This new Ministry will help and encourage voluntary action through those organisations that have played such an inspired part in the Freedom from Hunger Campaign. We must match their enterprises with Government action to give new hope in the current United Nations Development Decade.

The Manifesto also undertook that a Labour Government would strengthen Commonwealth ties. Migration limits would be 'negotiated', a Commonwealth Consultative Assembly established, joint projects (e.g. satellites) adopted and a career service set up for experts working in the Commonwealth. All this would be in the context of the creation of a 'genuine world community' with (eventually) a world Government.

This chapter will attempt to contrast the hopes with the realizations, the election promises with the performance in office. It would be too easy to blame the Civil Service or the inheritance from the Tories or economic adversity or the limited scope set by outside pressures for the gap between promise and fulfilment. These are all – as we shall see – elements in the picture. But the central theme is one of political sociology; how, with the assumption of power by Labour, 'responsibility' made for nationalism.[1]

It is perhaps worth pausing momentarily to discuss what steps were actually implied by the Labour Party's proclaimed policy. Certainly it would have been unrealistic to rush to carry out the promises in the Manifesto. There was a wide measure of public support for lofty ideals, but this would soon have evaporated if these had been made specific, for example, by handing Aden over to the United Nations for decolonization, or shifting the emphasis from military expenditure to development aid in the Persian Gulf.

Yet public opinion is not inflexible. To do what the Manifesto said clearly provided a perfectly feasible role for Britain, as a middling power with trading and cultural links throughout the world. A great bonus of goodwill still awaits the first industrial nation that shows by its actions genuine sympathy for, or even understanding of, the problems of the world's poor countries. What was necessary was a strong and consistent lead from the centre to help keep this view of our role before not only the public, but also official, opinion. Political leadership meant insisting on this international strategy, whatever temporary retreats and compromises might be necessary.

[1] See Gunnar Myrdal, *An International Economy* (London 1956).

The first steps needed (and possible) were, however, organizational. An enlightened international policy – even an enlightened aid policy – was out of the question so long as a group of somewhat archaic but intelligent officials in the Foreign Office (and in the Commonwealth Relations Office, as it then was) determined strategy in all its essentials. It would have required politicians of much greater capacity and moral conviction than those the Labour Party had at their disposal to induce them to accept a decisive change in approach to foreign affairs.[1] The key move would have been the creation of a political and economic staff inside the Office, brought in from outside, to provide an alternative source of advice for ministers, with access to all the papers of officials and to their meetings. The measure needed to complement this was the appointment of an unofficial committee – perhaps a few months later – to suggest how the diplomatic service should be reorganized (as the Fulton Committee did later for the home civil service).[2]

Still, such moves would not have been enough in themselves. It would take many years to reform the Foreign Office (and the other overseas departments). A separate Ministry was needed, at least in the meantime, to take account of the interests of poorer countries in their dealings with us, over a wide range of policies, including aid.

This Ministry was in fact established, and in a way that showed how the Foreign Office too might have been handled.

The creation of the Ministry of Overseas Development

One of the first acts of the Labour Government was, as promised, to centralize the administration of aid in a single department. The previous position had been vividly described by Mrs Castle:

We have no fewer than seven Departments with a finger in the pie, six of them with other responsibilities – the Treasury, the Board of Trade, the Colonial Office, the Commonwealth Relations Office, the Central Africa Office, the Foreign Office and the Department of Technical Co-operation, to say nothing of those Departments which have also a general oversight over the relationship

[1] A particularly memorable occasion was when a member of the foreign service was explaining to a committee how much better it would be to expand bilateral aid than to join in a move for a big replenishment of the resources of IDA. Sir Andrew Cohen pointed out to him that a rise in our contribution to IDA would be a means of obtaining eight times as much in additional funds from other donors; and that India was the chief beneficiary. He paused to consider this. 'Well,' he said, 'our masters' (the traditional ironic term for Ministers) 'would rather India received £1 from us than £9 from an international agency.' (One wonders whether Labour Ministers had entirely lost influence on some aspects of policy – or had they really been brainwashed?)

[2] The Plowden Report (Cmnd. 2276) had already considered many organizational questions, but had not raised the basic issues of the sort of service Britain would need in the closing decades of this century. The Duncan Report (Cmnd. 4107) was to raise some of these issues subsequently, in 1969, but in a superficial and unenlightened way, especially so far as the Third World was concerned – see below.

with the work of the specialized Agencies, such as the Ministry of Agriculture, which deals with the FAO and the international commodity agreements in food, and the Ministry of Education, which deals with UNESCO – and so we could go on.

Many of those working in the field – William Clark of the Overseas Development Institute for example – had been promoting the idea of a single department for some time. The precise shape of the new Ministry of Overseas Development (ODM for short – to avoid confusion with the Ministry of Defence – MOD) was determined by a working group of Fabians set up early in 1964, with Thomas Balogh as Chairman. The central idea was that poverty should be attacked by a coherent strategy, in which the various forms of aid complement and reinforce one another.[1] Moreover they need co-ordinating with many other types of policy – in trade, migration, international monetary reform. ODM was not seen as just an aid Ministry but (as its name implied) a department concerned with all aspects of policy affecting the Third World.

The fact that it was a Ministry outside the Foreign Office reflected the view that development policies should not be subordinate to our own political interests. Making it a Ministry of Cabinet rank underlined the importance attached to its work, and a belief that development policy was something worthwhile.

The first Minister was Barbara Castle, a Minister of outstanding determination and energy, and a close confidante of the Prime Minister. Her Permanent Secretary was Sir Andrew Cohen, previously Director-General of the Department of Technical Co-operation (DTC), set up in 1960. Andrew Cohen, a man larger than life-size in a number of senses, was an open Labour supporter and keenly sympathetic to the aims of the new Minister. The Ministry soon and inevitably acquired the nickname the Elephant and Castle and the tiny Minister and her huge Permanent Secretary were described as a well-balanced team.

Round the old DTC, which had been formed mainly from superannuated colonial servants, were grouped administrators from the Foreign Office, the Commonwealth Relations Office, the Colonial Office, the Treasury and other departments. But the most radical innovation was the creation by Mrs Castle (on the advice of Dr Balogh) of an economic planning staff of twenty economists and statisticians, under the two of us.

---

[1] Aid may be given in the form of technical assistance, or goods (e.g. food aid) or money to buy goods (capital aid); for specific investments, such as a steel mill or a dam (project aid) or for general purposes in the context of an overall plan (programme aid). It may be transferred directly from donor to recipient (bilateral aid) or through an international agency like the United Nations Development Programme or the World Bank Group (multilateral aid). These forms of aid are not, however, true *alternatives*, although they are often presented as such in controversies: thus only a well-worked-out programme can provide the framework for useful projects; capital aid can be more effectively utilized if it is accompanied by technical assistance; multilateral aid should be a means of avoiding competition between bilateral donors, etc.

This consisted of three divisions. One was statistical (the descendant of the old Colonial Office statistical department), one dealt with general economic policy issues, and the third consisted of a group of economists with considerable overseas experience, each working in a geographical department. Through ourselves, who were given very senior positions (perhaps excessively so), this staff had direct access to the Minister.

The overt purpose of its creation was to introduce professional expertise into an area of policy where it had been conspicuously lacking. (The Commonwealth Relations Office had been lending or granting more than £100 million a year, allegedly for purposes of economic development, without the help of a single economist.) In addition to that, however, one motive was to bring into Whitehall those who were sympathetic to the Government's approach to overseas problems, and who saw Britain's role not just as the dispenser of financial and technical help to former colonies but as a pioneer in creating a more equitable world system.

The digestion of this relatively large group was naturally not achieved without some difficulties, both outside and inside the Ministry. The Treasury took the idea in its stride, but the overseas departments, which were in any case resentful of the arrival of a new sister, found it embarrassing to meet 'outsiders' on interdepartmental committees.

One line of public criticism was that where economic expertise was really needed was not in London but in the field, especially in our Embassies and High Commissions, both to help improve policy and also to assist Governments. There was something to this, though perhaps the first task was to create a nucleus in London big enough to affect policy. Its work was supplemented in the field by a number of missions, drawing on non-official economists, to assess aid needs and to advise on development policy (*inter alia* to Tanzania, Malawi, Southern Africa, the Caribbean). In any case, the attachment of economists to overseas posts was resisted by the overseas departments. (There were two economists in the Middle East Development Division in Beirut, one in the Caribbean and one was later appointed to work in the High Commission in New Delhi.)

Inside the ODM a *modus vivendi* was fairly soon established. This was partly due to the Minister, who went out of her way to ask for the views of the economists. (Indeed, every submission had to show whether they agreed with the advice she was offered.) But it was also due to the determination of the Permanent Secretary to make the arrangement work and to see that these foreign bodies, unaccustomed to the ways of the civil service, were quickly integrated into the regular machinery. The decisive step was a conference in February 1965 (at Buscot Park, the home of Lord Faringdon) where the leading administrators and economists met for a whole weekend going over all aspects of policy, with the Minister herself taking a very active part. Most administrators, especially those with geographical responsibilities, came not only to accept but even to welcome the economists. A very senior official recently went so far as to say 'I cannot imagine how we ever managed to operate without the advice we get from the Economic Planning Staff'.

The 1965 White Paper and the volume of aid

The idealism evident in the Election Manifesto and in the creation of the new Ministry seemed to be confirmed by the Ministry's first White Paper. It was published on 3 August 1965, on the same day as an appalling fall in the gold reserves, a conjunction of events that did not augur well.

The White Paper, more than most such documents, reveals signs of multiple parenthood, reflecting the views of officials of many departments. Whenever an assertion is made which appears to commit the Government to a definite moral position, it is immediately withdrawn, contradicted or softened. 'The basis of the aid programme . . . is a moral one' but: 'the provision of aid is to our own long-term economic advantage'. Or: 'it is in the nature of aid that we should accept an economic sacrifice when giving it' but 'we give aid because in the widest sense we believe it to be in our interest to do so as a member of the world community'. Or: 'aid is not a means of winning the friendship of individual countries', though 'we are glad to offer aid to our friends'. And so on. Political security; altruism; commercial advantage and profit seeking; they are all grist to the mill and everyone can take his pick. The variety reflects the then unresolved political conflicts within Government, and between Ministers and officials.

Yet, despite these equivocations and despite frequent references to constraints set by the balance of payments and the 'strength of the economy', the White Paper was positive and struck a completely new note. Unlike previous White Papers in this field, which were largely descriptive, it provided statistical and economic analysis; whereas former documents had been somewhat apologetic, it sounded optimistic and independent. Development aid was intended to accelerate development. The need for forward planning of aid, to avoid disruptive uncertainties for recipients, was emphasized, as well as support for regional co-operation, so vital for the formation of wider markets, and rational investment policies in areas where the political boundaries bear no relation to the needs of development. Greater efforts would be made to co-ordinate aid with other donors; and top priority was given to technical assistance. Stress was laid on the need for multilateral aid, which has the advantage of less direct political pressures, and, unlike most bilateral aid, is not tied to purchases in a particular country.

An important step forward in the White Paper was the announcement that 'in appropriate cases' (which are explained later) countries would in future receive interest-free loans. The decision had been a difficult one. There had been considerable opposition in Whitehall because of the anticipated objection of European creditors. Yet it was clear from the known liabilities of overseas countries that the burden of debt service which was accumulating would soon prove unmanageable.[1]

It might be argued by a hostile critic that debt service can hardly be regarded as a 'burden'. If the yield of a loan exceeds the interest rate and amortization, there remains a net benefit to the borrower; if not, there is no case for borrowing. However, this ignores certain other factors relevant to aid. For instance, even if the total returns to the recipient exceed the cost of the loan, after making full allowance for tying,[2] the debt servicing payments have to be collected in taxes; the fiscal machinery of many less developed countries is not able to cope with this task. Moreover, in international lending, repayments can be made only by generating a surplus of exports over imports, which depends upon (among other things) the willingness of creditor countries to open their markets to goods and services from their debtors. Furthermore, a relatively long period of net resource inflow is required to permit the structural changes essential if development aid is to be successful and provide the means of servicing itself. The harder the terms (i.e. interest rates, grace periods, maturity dates, etc.), the smaller is the *net* flow of resources, the longer therefore the time necessary to do a given job of development, and the more aid is required to do that job.

A lead in the direction of softer terms seemed necessary. The British initiative in making loans interest-free would have favourable effects on the aid debate in the American Congress and possibly on other donors. In actuality, the hoped-for general decline in interest rates on aid loans did not take place (though the British initiative may have checked a tendency for them to rise), but the decision was clearly justified in itself.[3]

---

[1] The public external debt of all 'developing' countries had risen from $8 billion in 1956 to $33 billion by the end of 1964, an average annual growth of over 15 per cent, while the annual growth of their GNP was on average 4%. (As a percentage of GNP this debt rose from 6% in 1956 to 15% at the end of 1964.) Total debt service in 1965 was $4·2 billion (including private investment and non-DAC aid) and constituted over 11% of export earnings of 'developing' countries and more than half of the gross capital transfers from all sources. The growth of debt service between 1962 and 1966 had been 10% per annum, while exports grew by 7·3% annually. Moreover projections made by the Agency for International Development (AID) of debt service to 1975, on various assumptions about loans and their terms, suggested that debt service might by then be claiming up to 22% of export earnings. See D. Avramovic and associates, *Economic Growth and External Debt* (IBRD 1964) and P. Lieftinck, *External Debt and Debt Bearing Capacity of Developing Countries* (Princeton Essays in International Finance, No. 51, March 1966).

[2] In 1967 for instance only 16% of official aid flows remained untied. This has been estimated to reduce the real value of aid by at least 20%. See *Partners in Development*, (New York 1969) page 77.

[3] For the sake of the record, it should be made clear that position papers favouring interest-free loans were prepared in the Treasury before the 1964 election, although one wonders whether this change would have been implemented without the existence of ODM, and the persuasive powers of Mrs Castle. (The reason for the Treasury position may interest students of administration. They resisted concessionary interest rates on overseas loans because they feared that public authorities in Britain would demand that the same rates be applied to them; the Treasury felt confident that no authority would be bold enough to demand interest-free loans!)

But there was a darker side to the picture. Very little was said in the White Paper about other policies (notably trade) affecting development. Moreover, it was silent about the future volume of aid, in spite of its declaration that, to be effective, aid should be planned ahead. All the Ministry was allowed to say was that 'ultimately the amount of aid we provide will depend on the amount of our total resources which we are willing to sacrifice'.[1]

Anyone looking for an indication of what this really meant had to turn to the National Plan[2] published soon after the White Paper and while the Minister of Overseas Development was still a member of the Cabinet. They would have had a shock: British policy towards the 'developing' countries there appears in a very different light.

The Plan shows what the Government's intentions were *on the assumption that economic developments after 1965 would be favourable.* A total growth of 25% was envisaged between 1964 and 1970, or an annual average of 3·8%; somewhat less in the early years, but accelerating to 4% 'well before 1970'. The Plan provided for a 21% rise in personal consumption over the period 1964 to 1970, and a 27% rise in social and other public services.

After allowing for correcting the balance of payments and increasing investment in private and nationalized industry, the rest of the extra production was to be shared between personal consumption and public services. Out of every extra hundred pounds, 25 would go to improve the balance of payments and raise investment, nearly 20 to housing, defence, health, education, roads, etc., and over 55 to personal consumption – i.e. to cars, television, travel, drink, pet foods, cosmetics, etc., etc. The total addition between 1964 and 1970 was to be £8,000 million (in 1964 prices).

How was aid to fare in this opulent world? The lengthy plan document contains three brief references. While always paying lip-service to the importance of aid, 'the amount we give must be subject to restraint while our balance of payments difficulties persist, and we have to plan our aid so that the foreign exchange cost of the programme is kept to a minimum'.[3]

The second reference has an even leaner look:

The Government have decided to restrain two major items of their overseas expenditure. First, they intend to restrict the Defence Budget . . .

The grants and loans which make up the Government's programme for economic aid also place a burden on the balance of payments. . . . The Government are fully aware of the importance of aid to the developing countries, and are taking steps to increase the effectiveness of what aid is given. It will, however, be necessary to scrutinize the aid programme with particular care so long as the United Kingdom balance of payments is under such great strain and we

[1] HMSO, *Overseas Development: The Work of the New Ministry* (Cmnd. 2736, 1965) para. 61.
[2] *The National Plan* (Cmnd. 2746, 1965).
[3] HMSO, op. cit., para. 25, page 6.

are faced with the need to repay the overseas indebtedness recently incurred.[1]

The third passage says that 'the Plan makes provision for only a small rise over the levels of the current financial year' and that 'the reduction in military expenditure will more than offset the increase in aid'.[2] In fact, although no figure was quoted, a ceiling had been clamped on aid.[3] There was no intention to add many million pounds of the extra £8,000 million of output to the £100 million of grants and £90 million of official loans transferred to the 'developing' countries in 1964.

It was – and is – often argued that to give money away while we are in debt was both wrong and absurd. The Chancellor asked repeatedly 'How can I give away a deficit?'. Such objections to more aid would have sounded more convincing if repayment of debts had been given priority over all other claims on resources, i.e. if personal and public consumption had been similarly restricted. As Professor Thomas Wilson put it:

We are in the position of a man who has got into debt by overspending. He is still living comfortably, is exerting himself no more than he did, and expects his income and consumption to continue to rise. But the fact is he is in debt. What a fortunate opportunity for reducing his modest annual subscription to Oxfam![4]

The record

The August White Paper and the September National Plan express the two souls of Labour:[5] one generous and far-sighted, conscious of international responsibilities and opportunities – the other narrow, nationalistic, materialistic; one looking outward – the other inward; the long-hairs against the skinheads.

The levelling off of British aid was more conspicuous because it followed a rapid rise over the previous decade – despite periodic foreign exchange crises. Gross aid which had been running at about £50 to £55 million in the early 1950s climbed to £150 to £160 million, or three times that level, in the early 1960s, much more rapidly than the national product, and reached £207 million in 1966. There it stuck for the next three years. Meanwhile, amortization was rising, and so were prices. So the real value of net aid declined for the first time since the war.

Aid was subjected to a number of assaults. A ceiling of £205 million was imposed, without adjustment for a fall in the value of money, which other

---

[1] HMSO, op. cit., para. 16, page 71.
[2] HMSO, op. cit., para. 3, chapter 7, page 75.
[3] ODM was also singled out as the *only* department for which expenditure targets had to be set in current prices, without automatic adjustment for inflation.
[4] The *Statist*, 4 February 1966, page 282.
[5] There was in fact a political deadlock over the publication of the ODM White Paper, which was put on ice for some weeks. It was only brought out of cold storage (rather hurriedly) to offset the very bad impression that was expected to be created abroad by a policy statement on immigration.

spending departments enjoyed. Then a cut of £20 million (10%) was made in 1966, when other public expenditure was planned to rise by 5%. A loss of about 10% in the real value was suffered due to the rise in export prices after devaluation in 1967. These are indications of the priority the Government gave to aid compared with its other concerns.

Parallel with these slashes at the aid programme were a number of political changes in the Ministry's standing. Barbara Castle was succeeded by Tony Greenwood and Arthur Bottomley. In January 1967 the Minister was removed from the Cabinet – an act of both symbolic and genuine significance.

It is true that gross aid disbursements continued to rise until 1966 (see Table 3.1). But the Government cannot claim much credit for these figures. They were largely determined by commitments entered into under the Conservatives. The point is that a tight rein was kept on *current* commitments. New commitments in 1965 were the second lowest since the late 1950s. The aid levels of 1967, 1968 and 1969 are better evidence for the intentions of 1965 and 1966 than the then current disbursements. Table 3.1 summarizes the figures of disbursements during the period of the Labour Government.

TABLE 3.1.   TOTAL GROSS AND NET DISBURSEMENTS OF
AID TO DEVELOPING COUNTRIES

(£ million)

	1964	1965	1966	1967	1968	1969	1970
Aid Programme							
Gross	191	195	207	201	203	211	214
Amortization	18	26	34	28	30	31	28
Net of Amortization	173	169	174	173	173	180	186
Interest	22	24	26	27	27	24	24
Net of Amortization and Interest	151	145	148	146	146	156	162

Source: Ministry of Overseas Development, *British Aid Statistics 1964 to 1968*, page 8 (London, 1969), *1965 to 1969*, page 15 (London, 1970), and *1966 to 1970*, page 12 (London, 1971).

The increase in gross aid between 1964 and 1969 by 10%, small though this figure is, can be misleading. We must allow for the mounting repayments of old loans and interest payments (shown in the table) and for the rise in prices. If we set it against the growth of Gross National Product, the proportion of net official flows fell from 0·53% in 1964 to 0·39% in 1969 (0·37% in 1970) back to the level of the 1950s. Public expenditure over the same period grew by over 50%. Aid showed the smallest increase of expenditure by any Government department, except defence.

Balance of payments: reasons or excuse?

Balance of payments difficulties, and in particular the much publicized

£800 million deficit inherited from the Tories, figured prominently amongst the explanations for the restraint of aid. This represented a return to an earlier Whitehall view on the treatment of the balance of payments costs of aid. The White Paper issued in 1963 had said that Government overseas expenditure 'is a massive charge on our balance of payments, and aid to developing countries is one of the biggest items in the account'.[1] Yet subsequent calculations showed that in 1963 the burden on the balance of payments amounted to approximately £50 million, less than one third of total gross aid.[2] Even this figure exaggerates the burden. It was obtained by looking at British aid in isolation; if effects on the aid programmes of other donors are taken into account, the British balance of payments, far from being burdened, may well benefit from aid. Britain provided about $7\frac{1}{2}\%$ of the total flow of aid, but received nearly 12% of the orders for the goods imported by the 'developing' countries from the industrial ones. (See the Appendix on the 'true' cost of aid.)

It may therefore be asked whether balance of payments difficulties were the *reason* for the severe constraint imposed on the aid programme during the years of the Labour Government, or whether they served as an *excuse* for the lack of political will of some Labour politicians.

We have already quoted the National Plan and the 1965 White Paper, both of which emphasized the constraint of the balance of payments. In his speech to the meetings of the World Bank and Fund in October 1965, the Chancellor, Mr Callaghan, said:

We naturally regret that in the immediate future we shall not be able to increase our aid as much as we should like to, although we shall continue to improve its quality and effectiveness. Putting it bluntly, we feel that countries with strong balances of payments could and should do more to raise the volume of aid; and we intend to do so as soon as our position permits it.

In view of Britain's large accumulated debt obligations, this position lay safely in the future.

Aid in perspective

In spite of repeated incantations of the balance of payments, the reason for the retreat from idealism – or perhaps from a more realistic view of the post-war world – lies deeper. The test can be found in the Government's attitude to policies which would have been beneficial for the bal-

[1] *Aid to Developing Countries*, Cmnd. 2147, para. 24.
[2] A. Krassowski, 'British aid and the British balance of payments', *Moorgate and Wall-street: A Review*, Spring 1965. The order of magnitude was confirmed by more detailed studies by the Ministry's Planning Staff, initiated by Robin Marris. There was a good deal of resistance to the publication of these estimates, which are inconvenient for those speaking from Treasury briefs. Eventually a revised and more thorough set of estimates was printed under the title 'Aid and the balance of payments' by Bryan Hopkin and associates in the *Economic Journal*, March 1970, Vol. LXXX, No. 317.

ance of payments (or, at worst, neutral), though they would have imposed a sacrifice in real resources. Studies by ODM economists showed that international agreements to support prices of certain commodities, such as cocoa, would probably on balance earn Britain foreign exchange.[1] The same is true of the 'link' between Special Drawing Rights (SDRs) and development aid. It seems clear that the Government's lack of enthusiasm for these measures was due to its unwillingness to give up the engineering goods or tractors or railway wagons provided under the aid programme and that the balance of payments was, to a large extent, a pretext. Whenever a policy with a beneficial impact on development could be shown to be also beneficial for the British balance of payments, objections were raised by the Treasury and the Department of Economic Affairs that it cost real resources or that it was inflationary.

This came out explicitly before the Estimates Committee, when a representative of the Treasury said: 'It really is not true that it is simply because of the balance of payments impact that a ceiling has been placed on aid. This is misconceived. The Government has to decide what resources it is going to devote to aid, and all the other things within its care.'[2]

Further evidence, if this were needed, that aid is available when political pressures are mobilized (for ends other than development) are the items in the so-called 'additional aid programme', over and above the ceiling. This includes the increased contribution to IDA under the second replenishment (it was finally accepted in Whitehall that the British interest in foreign exchange and in development obviously coincide in IDA replenishment), special aid for Malaysia and Singapore (to induce them to acquiesce in reductions in military expenditure), food aid under the International Grains Agreement (which had to be swallowed as part of the Kennedy Round 'package') and contingency aid to Zambia (to offset the damage done by Rhodesian independence).

There is a reply to those who criticize Labour's aid policy along these lines. In the crisis atmosphere of the Government's first two years, when planned public expenditure was cut and taxation raised, a slightly growing aid programme, though it may look feeble compared with its past growth, was not really so immoral. In 1966 both gross and net aid were at record levels; even expressed as a proportion of GNP, the official net flow did not fall in that year. To cut aid drastically would certainly not have been

---

[1] The calculation on cocoa was made by Miss Peter Ady. In brief, the reason for the beneficial effect is that Britain's share in world purchases of cocoa is smaller than her share in additional imports of cocoa-exporting countries, generated by their higher earnings. When cocoa-producers get higher prices, what in effect happens is that other consuming countries contribute to larger purchases from Britain. Similarly, Britain's contribution to IDA is smaller than her share in the orders generated by total IDA disbursements. It is because Britain plays such an important part in world trade that she stands to gain in higher export earnings from most policies that increase the total contributions of industrial countries, whether directly or through commodity agreements.
[2] *Seventh Report from the Estimates Committee*, Session 1967–8, *Overseas Aid*, House of Commons Paper No. 442 (London 1968) para. 1410.

politically difficult. There were few votes in aid, no powerful lobbies for development. It is the considerable achievement of Mrs Castle (the case for the defence goes) to have defended the programme against such attacks. The cuts in US aid are an example of what can happen when anti-aid forces predominate.

But a plateau of disbursements may conceal the forces making for future decline, when new commitments are severely controlled (see Table 3.2).

TABLE 3.2. COMMITMENTS OF BILATERAL FINANCIAL AID

(£ millions)

	1964	1965	1966	1967	1968	1969	1970
Total bilateral financial aid	236·3	114·9	129·6	149·9	175·0	130·4	143·9

Note: The surprisingly large figure for 1964 is explained partly because it was the last year before a ceiling was imposed and partly by a few large long-term commitments, such as that to Malta.

Source: Ministry of Overseas Development, *British Aid Statistics 1964 to 1968*, page 16 (London, 1969), *1965 to 1969*, page 19 (London, 1970), and *1966 to 1970*, page 19 (London, 1971).

After commitments were cut by £20 million in the deflationary measures of July 1966, the alliance between the Department of Economic Affairs, concerned with British economic growth and firmly anti-aid, the Treasury, resisting all forms of public expenditure and overseas expenditure in particular, and the Board of Trade, became almost invincible in suffocating the goodwill, idealism and talent assembled in the ODM, which only got half-hearted support from the (unreformed) overseas departments.

In addition, there are of course powerful voices on the Right against aid. Two voices supporting Labour policy may serve as an epitaph of this period. The Governor of the Bank of England in a speech (in May 1969) attacking aid as a major factor contributing to our deteriorating balance of payments, said: 'This has been extremely worrying and I am glad that at last the increase has been checked and is beginning to give place to a modest fall.'[1] If the first voice comes from the core of the Establishment, the second is that of a Conservative backbencher, Mr Cranley Onslow. At the Select Committee on Overseas Aid he said to the Treasury witnesses:

Since our Chairman said in her introductory remarks how much she agreed with the cut in defence expenditure, perhaps I could say that I find the standstill in aid since 1966 one of the few sensible things the Government has done.[2]

In 1969, the last full year of the Labour Government, Britain's net *official*

[1] Bank of England, *Quarterly Bulletin*, Vol. 9, No. 2, June 1969, page 170.
[2] Select Committee on Overseas Aid, *Minutes of Evidence*, Sessions 1968–9, 1969–70, Monday, 10 November 1969, 348.

transfer to less developed countries was somewhat smaller (at £150 million) in money terms (and considerably less as a proportion of national income or in real terms) than the amount which the Labour Government had inherited from the Conservative Government in 1964 (£153 million). Ironically, the net *private* flow in 1969 at £299 million was substantially larger than the £152 million inherited in 1964 and larger than the official flow. These results, especially the figure for official assistance, but also the figure for private investment, far from being declared Labour policy, ran counter to all declarations and intentions. It is a reflection on the gap not only between words and deeds, but also between intention and result. And it might well be argued that the second gap, the one between intent and outcome, mitigates any charge of insincerity or hypocrisy levelled on grounds of the first gap, the one between words and deeds. The complexities of implementing economic policies, particularly in the private sector, are such that inability rather than unwillingness may account for the discrepancy between Labour promise and fulfilment.

There was, moreover, a marked change of attitude in 1969. A White Paper on public expenditure published in early 1969 gave a target figure of £227 million for overseas aid in 1969–70 and of £235 million in 1970–1. Excluding Britain's special aid to Singapore and Malaysia, because of the defence element, economic aid was planned at some £219 million in 1969–70 and some £227 million in 1970–1.[1]

Judith Hart, the new Minister, revealed further advances in November. From 1971–2 all economic aid was to be consolidated into one official aid programme (comprising both the basic aid programme and the special items). The gross aid ceiling was to be raised from £227 million in 1970–1 to £245 million in 1971–2, £265 million in 1972–3 and £300 million in 1973–4, the last year of the Public Expenditure Survey. Including the defence element in special aid the figure for 1972–3 is £270 million; £305 million for 1973–4.[2]

Taking what was called a 'high estimate for private flows', the Minister hoped that Britain would reach the UNCTAD 1% target not much after 1975 but added 'we recognize the element of uncertainty which is bound to attach to estimates of private flows six years hence. So we shall keep the progress of both official and private flows under review.[3] In any case, the Government intends, unless our balance of payments position should pre-

[1] *Overseas Development*, No. 20, January 1970.
[2] Statement in Parliament by the Minister of Overseas Development on 27 November, 1969, cited in *Overseas Development*, No. 20, January 1970.
[3] Private overseas investment, however useful to development, should, for semantic as well as for political reasons, not be counted as aid. Like trade, it is a transaction into which both parties enter in the expectation of gain, whereas aid, properly defined, involves an economic sacrifice. The UNCTAD 'one per cent' target, which includes net private flows, has therefore, on these grounds alone, little meaning. It is curious that the actual turnout of 1969 was almost on the target which Mrs Hart promised for 1975, or at the latest 1980: total net financial flows were 0·97% of GNP.

clude it, to reach the target of 1% total flow not a moment later than the end of the Second Development Decade [i.e. by 1980].'

This response to the Pearson Report, to pressures of aid supporters inside and outside the Government and to the improvement in the economic situation, somewhat made up for the bleak years that had gone before. But, judged against the magnitude of the problem, against the Pearson target of 0·7% of GNP for *official* aid, against Britain's wealth and allegedly strong balance of payments, and against past declarations, the response was disappointing, especially if one allows for the accelerating price inflation. Moreover, after the experience of 1965–9, one must wonder what pledges are worth. At the first sight of another economic crisis, would not another George Brown have convinced the Cabinet that a ceiling should be set to such electorally unprofitable expenditures?

The effectiveness of British aid

A stereotyped formula, repeated whenever restraint of the volume was mentioned, was the need and the intention to increase the effectiveness of British aid, or to improve its quality.

The meaning of 'effectiveness' is elusive in the absence of a clearly stated set of objectives. But even on the assumption that we know what is meant, it is plain that effectiveness can hardly be improved without increasing staff overseas, and ensuring that they are capable of judging how British resources can most effectively be mobilized to help a country's development – which means that the aid administrator overseas must understand the country's problems and the general lines of their solution (not necessarily the lines that suit British interests). With that understanding, and sufficient staff, he can guide London on the way to respond to requests – what sort of aid 'package' would be most helpful, what types of people are needed for technical assistance, etc. In some cases he could usefully ask questions about projects, since usually it is too late to alter a project by the time it comes to London. A man in an overseas post also can often help steer students to the right courses at home.

The number of people engaged full-time on aid administration in all our Embassies and High Commissions overseas amounted to twenty-three at the start of 1965. This number excludes the Middle East Development Division, a regional pool of advisers who include among their duties assisting governments with project preparation and administering aid policy for the area, and also those British officials in the colonies (that still existed) who were in effect working on aid administration. Still it is a very small figure in relation to aid of more than £100 million to independent countries. And it says, by implication, a good deal about the motives for British aid. A programme consisting of rewards for political and commercial favours needs very little administration compared to one designed to help a country's development. One result of understaffing, in fact, is that the same person is often responsible both for promoting British exports and for aid – making it extremely difficult to separate the two functions (especially in the eyes of recipients).[1]

By February 1968, the number of full-time staff had risen to fifty-five, and another regional Development Division had been created (in the Caribbean). But this number was still very small in relation to their task, especially if one allows for the fact that a number of colonies had become independent in the meantime. To take a rather extreme example, one man in Zambia in 1967 placed over 700 technical assistance personnel, and helped 100 Zambian students and trainees to visit Britain – such a man can be little more than a postbox. The Duncan Report estimated that in 1968 there were altogether 120 officials (in full-time equivalent) of executive officer rank and above administering British aid in the field.[2]

The situation does not seem to have changed dramatically in the meantime. The British Council has taken over much of the administration of the training programme, but the advice of the Duncan Committee has been followed – it 'could not accept that there is an urgent need for an increase in the Diplomatic Service resources devoted to aid administration'. Apart from being based on a very cursory examination of aid administration,[3] this position faithfully reflected the Government's attitude by this time, not merely its views on the amount it was prepared to spend but also on the weight it was prepared to give to the problems of world poverty. In the absence of a genuine overseas development policy, with political and financial resources behind it, the scope for improving effectiveness is narrow, and the declarations of the intention to do so ring rather hollow.

The pattern of aid

The other way of making aid more effective would be to improve its pattern, steering it deliberately towards governments with the intention and capacity to achieve development. This too would not have been easy to achieve in a static programme.

Official declarations by the Ministry of Overseas Development had a tendency to endow with a post hoc rationality a programme that had grown out of history, pressures and short-term responses. We yield here, we give in there and, lo and behold, the result is a grand design! Inability to cast off the millstone is displayed as pride in the adornment by a pearl necklace; inability to cast off the past, as 'the importance of continuity'.

The pattern is difficult to discern anyway, because of the multiplicity of forces at work. British business interests are in various ways pressing for aid to back up their export drive and their investment overseas, and this is

---

[1] In Nairobi, where there are enough officials for a separate aid section, trade and aid administration have for many years been run by a combined group.

[2] *Report of the Review Committee on Overseas Representation, 1968–9.* Cmnd. 4107.

[3] This is shown in a special number of the *Bulletin of the Institute of Development Studies* (Vol. 2, No. 1) devoted to the Duncan Report and the questions of the adequacy and balance of aid administration.

reflected in the positions taken by officials of the Board of Trade and other departments.[1] The military, with the backing of the Ministry of Defence, are concerned with such matters as alliances, bases and over-flying rights. The diplomatic service makes its own amalgam of these into the 'national interest' in some higher sense. There is a welfare lobby, centred on the voluntary agencies, heavily concerned with relieving poverty, and this may converge with commercial and strategic interests in urging the support of colonies (or former colonies) that have limited development prospects. The somewhat lonely voice of the economists in ODM draws attention (*inter alia*) to the development potential of various countries. Lastly there are the influences outside Britain – the big say of the United States, the pressures exerted by potential recipients and the way they play their own hand (an influence which is by no means to be underestimated),[2] and the forces in the General Assembly and other international fora. The pattern of aid is the resultant of hundreds of individual decisions within and between departments – to treat this country well, another badly. Still, we should at least look at it for clues on Government motivation.

Table 3.3 shows the general geographical pattern for 1965, which reflects the outcome of the decisions of several Conservative administrations – who, as we have seen, increased the aid programme and were thus able to shape it as it grew. One striking feature of this pattern is the high share of bilateral aid in 1965. This itself suggests that political and/or commercial bias was considerable. When we ask what countries were being aided under the bilateral programme the impression is strengthened; a large share was going to a group of half a dozen countries which were on the edge of the Communist sphere of influence, mostly in or near the Middle East, and were thus considered by the British Government (and usually by the United States Government as well) to be highly aid-worthy. One can surmise that aid to these countries would have been drastically reduced, possibly eliminated altogether, if there had been a complete detente between East and West; it was essentially Cold War aid.

The rest of the bilateral programme shows a heavy concentration on the Commonwealth, i.e. colonies and ex-colonies. But this is hardly an explanation in itself – we have to recognize the fact that sentimental ties, trading links and British investments were accumulated during the colonial era.

Within the Commonwealth, there is one group where the balance of motives has been somewhat different. This consists of countries which

---

[1] There is no suggestion here that officials consciously favour interests of particular firms – after all, increasing exports is a national requirement. (But it would be interesting to investigate how many senior civil servants in recent years have moved into business after their retirement.)

[2] We have seen delegations depart from ODM with far less generous arrangements than the Ministry had decided to concede to them – simply because they had not done their diplomatic homework.

have been receiving financial assistance not only with capital spending but also with their current expenditure. Britain had in fact not built up their economies to the point where they could, unaided, maintain even a bare minimum of services – a task which geography had in some cases made difficult. If Colonial Office policies of the 1950s had been maintained, these would in fact never have been considered 'ready' for independence,

TABLE 3.3.　GROSS DISBURSEMENTS UNDER AID PROGRAMME, BY TYPE OF AID, 1965 AND 1969[a]

(£ millions)

	1965	1969	1970
Total	*195*	*211*	*214*
Multilateral	*19*	*32*	*20*
IDA	12	20	6[e]
UNDP[b]	5	6	6
other	3	6	8
Bilateral	*176*	*179*	*154*
of which　*primarily strategic motivation*	*29*	*20*	*21*
Turkey	7	3	5
Jordan	3	2	1
Non-Commonwealth Asia[c]	3	6	6
Aden and South Arabia	9	—	—
Cyprus	2	—	—
Malta	6	4	1
Singapore	—	4	8
primarily welfare motivation	*25*	*30*	*30*
Malawi	10	7	8
Former High Commission Territories[d]	9	12	7
Caribbean Associated States	2	3	7
Oceania	3	8	8
other bilateral	*123*	*130*	*143*
India	28	34	45
Pakistan	10	11	11
Indus Basin	4	2	—
Malaysia	4	3	11
Kenya	17	8	11
Tanzania	5	2	2
Uganda	4	4	4
East Africa (regional)	3	2	1
Ghana	1	6	6
Nigeria	10	6	11
Remainder	37	52	41

[a] Includes advances to CDC
[b] Includes UNICEF
[c] Indonesia, Laos, Thailand, South Vietnam, etc.
[d] Botswana, Lesotho, Swaziland
[e] See footnote 1 to next page

Source: Ministry of Overseas Development, *British Aid Statistics 1965 to 1969*, pages 26 ff. (London 1970), and *1966 to 1970*, pages 26ff. (London 1971)

but the political pressures of the 1960s compelled the viability criterion to be set on one side. Of course trade and strategic interests (and the wish to avoid the world's opprobrium) exert their influence here too. Mere destitution, without British colonial links (and all that goes with them) does not play a big part, otherwise our aid would have been flowing to countries like (say) Honduras and Upper Volta – more especially to North Vietnam. But still, we would be justified in saying that the motive for this category of aid was primarily 'welfare'.

A comparison between the patterns of aid in 1965 and 1969/70 might throw some light on the changes in motivation, though we must remember that the official ceiling on aid meant that there was not much room to manœuvre.[1] (This suggests an interesting speculation: was the ceiling imposed partly because of a subconscious desire not to have to face the choices that would otherwise have emerged?)

When one makes a summary comparison of the 1965 and 1969/70 programmes one notices some improvements. Above all, in accordance with declared policy, there was a shift towards multilateral aid. Within the bilateral programme, which fell in real terms, the fall was concentrated on the countries where the motivation appears primarily military.

However, on this point interpretation is not simple. In part it is due to withdrawal from military commitments (Aden), yet this is balanced by increases to offset withdrawal (Singapore), and the rise in aid to South Vietnam and its neighbours might be regarded as a sort of substitute for the regiment to support the US operation there, for which Lyndon Johnson and Dean Rusk pressed so hard. The decline in the case of Turkey (a weak link in the NATO chain) could be attributed to an economic boom rather than to any reduction in the Foreign Office's desire to use aid for strategic purposes.

On the other hand, aid primarily for welfare was increased, despite a reduction of aid to Malawi – where internal revenues rose sharply.

There was only one major new recipient – and this itself throws some light on motives, because the country was Ghana. The resumption of aid to Ghana (this also happened to Indonesia and Ceylon) represented a gesture of support to a regime considered more helpful to British interests, in various senses, than its predecessor. (In these cases, it could also be argued that the new governments could make better use of aid, but this hardly can be a very weighty argument if one considers how much aid certain administrations receive.)

The story behind the sharp decline in aid to Tanzania is even more revealing.[2] Tanzania broke off diplomatic relations in December 1965, in response to the failure of the British Government to stop the Smith regime

[1] It should be noted that the 1970 IDA figure of £6 million is misleadingly small because it represents exceptionally low drawings from the IDA and for this item the 1969 figure would be more representative.

[2] The other big decline, to Kenya, is due to the fact that in 1965 substantial sums were paid under settlement schemes (in effect to buy out British farmers).

in Rhodesia declaring independence. The British reaction reflected – as so often – a departmental compromise. No new aid agreement would be negotiated (and a loan agreement already drawn up remained 'frozen'), but drawings on existing loans continued and so did technical assistance. By comparison with US reaction in similar circumstances (e.g. to Arab countries when the 'June war' broke out) this was civilized, but nevertheless it revealed an element of spite (the Commonwealth Office still tended to expect grateful compliance from the former colonies). After all, there was no real break;[1] in fact many RAF personnel and other British experts began arriving at this time to help maintain supplies to Zambia.

This rather anomalous aid relationship with Tanzania survived the nationalization of British businesses early in 1967, but not the announcement in July 1968 that Tanzania would cease paying pensions to British administrators who had served there before independence – even though diplomatic relations had now been restored. It is odd that any British Government should have expected this burden to be carried by newly independent countries – and in fact much aid was in effect a way of financing it. It is even odder that the Labour Government waited so long to take over these pensions, which were a perpetual source of petty friction with all ex-colonies (aggrieved pensioners were continually mobilizing their MPs to ask questions in Parliament) especially since President Nyerere had given twelve months' notice of his action. Britain's immediate and petulant response to the blow when it fell was to end aid to Tanzania, though those in technical assistance posts were allowed to serve out their contracts. In March 1970, ODM at last took over responsibility for *all* colonial pensions, a move for which Nyerere must be given the chief credit; by implication not only was Tanzania's lost virtue restored but the general principle underlying his action was conceded.[2]

There is another plane on which the composition of aid can be judged – the proportion spent on technical as opposed to financial assistance. Table 3.4 shows that technical aid has certainly grown in accordance

---

[1] The traditional significance of breaking off diplomatic relations is a prelude to war, but Tanzania had no such intention. The origin of the Tanzanian gesture was a meeting of the Organisation of African Unity which voted to break off relations with Britain if action were not taken to crush the Rhodesian rebellion. Nyerere's action seemed at least partly designed to stop the OAU voting for resolutions which its members had no intention of implementing.

[2] It was done very grudgingly. On 11 March, Mrs Hart said in Parliament that 'the Government had decided that as part of its policy of aid to development it is willing at the request of any government concerned to *consider* assuming responsibility for the cost of pensions to expatriate officers in respect of pre-Independence government service. The assumption of such a responsibility would be *taken into account in determining the total amount of aid* such a country might receive . . .' (our italics). Aid to Tanzania was not actually resumed, however, until the Conservatives took office. An ODM official visited Dar-es-Salaam at the end of June 1970 (though this visit had been planned before the election), and put forward a proposal, accepted in principle, to resume technical assistance immediately and to make a loan on which drawings could begin in April 1971 (the month when Britain would be starting to pay other colonial pensions).

with policy priorities; the 1965 White Paper stressed the importance of skills. But this rise is to some extent illusory. The increase in expenditure on supplying experts, which is responsible for about half of technical assistance outlays, is in large part due to general salary increases (and perhaps

TABLE 3·4 BRITISH TECHNICAL ASSISTANCE DISBURSEMENTS, 1965 AND 1969

(£ millions)

	1965	1969	1970
Bilateral			
Education and training programmes in Britain	3·5	7·8	8·3
Education and training in country of origin	0·9	0·3	0·4
Total education	4·4	8·1	8·7
Experts on technical assistance[a]	14·1	20·4	21·9
Compensation to expatriate officers	7·2	3·0	0·7
Research	2·3	3·1	3·7
Other[b]	3·7	9·0	10·6
	31·7	43·6	45·6
Multilateral	4·6	6·5	6·8
Total	36·3	50·1	52·3

[a] Includes those receiving supplements under OSAS, etc., as well as wholly financed experts.
[b] Consultancies, surveys, equipment, grants for volunteers (and to IUC and TETOC) and (for 1969) expenditure within the British Council's own budget.

Source: Ministry of Overseas Development, *British Aid Statistics 1965 to 1969*, from Table 9, page 23 (London 1970).

to the use of more highly paid types of expertise); the number of experts overseas has not greatly changed, nearly 3,000 a year being recruited in Britain each year (financed from public funds).[1]

There has also been a big increase in the provision for students and trainees. In this case the rise is in some degree a real one, though it is partly due to increases in fees, such as that made in 1967 for university students from overseas.[2] In any case, a serious question is raised by the combination of the increased expenditure on students to come to this country (largely recurrent expenditure) with the reduction in provision for training them in their own countries (largely capital expenditure).[3] Although the two

[1] One campaign promise has been kept, the creation of a 'career' for experts, by giving them long-term contracts – though not many contracts have in fact been issued.
[2] This, however, mainly affected overseas students financed from other sources; these outnumber those assisted out of British public funds.
[3] The rise in disbursements for overseas education levelled off (at about £5 million) in 1967. This implies a downward trend in real terms since then, which will continue, to judge from a fall in commitments. A very dubious policy is the running down of

sets of figures are not strictly comparable, the comparison indicates a shift in the wrong direction. It may be explicable in balance of payments terms but undoubtedly the most helpful type of education in many cases is education in one's own country; much of what is taught in Britain and against a British background is of limited relevance to local problems.

The increased reliance by Britain on imported skills must in any case be considered to have offset any rise in the exports of skills under technical aid. Attention is usually focused on the racialist implications of British immigration policy, especially of the Commonwealth Immigration Act of 1968, which in effect discriminated in favour of white holders of British passports who reside in East Africa and want to migrate to Britain. But there is a development aspect too. The effect of successive changes in the past five years has been to make it easy for doctors and others with professional qualifications to migrate to Britain, very hard indeed for anyone else (except relatives of those already here). Now we have an immigration policy designed primarily to meet the needs of the *British* economy.

Terms of aid

On terms of aid, the record is more encouraging, especially the decision, mentioned earlier, to make most loans interest-free. This did not apply to all loans. In the 1965 White Paper the Government stated:

In offering these concessions we shall have regard to the economic position of the country concerned. We believe that this, rather than the nature of the project or other purpose of the loan, should be the decisive economic criterion for the terms of aid.[1]

In practice, the 'economic position' has been interpreted as poverty (with the IDA limit of $250 a year per capita income as obviously a big influence).[2] Since 1965, rather over 80% of the money loaned has been interest free.

The weighted average rate of interest on British loans had already fallen from 5·8% in 1962 to 4·1% in 1964, largely as a result of the introduction in 1963 of (temporary) waivers of interest on certain loans. The provision of interest-free loans resulted in a further steep fall in the average level of interest rates to 1% (see Table 3·5). The effect was, however, partially

support for research by overseas institutions, and offering instead the services of British consultancy teams, which is presumably believed to create more goodwill. (A conspicuous case here is the fast reduction in British support to the regional research programme of the Department of Agriculture of the University of the West Indies, a sad contrast with all the effort that earlier went into building it up, as the Imperial College of Tropical Agriculture; it also seems inconsistent with declared priorities, both for agricultural development and for regional schemes.)

[1] HMSO *Overseas Development*, op. cit.

[2] But subject to the additional test, for countries below that level, of whether (e.g. because of oil reserves) the balance of payments outlook was such that debt servicing would be easy.

offset by a sharp decline in grants (from £46 million in 1965 to £24 million in 1969), due partly to a big decline in budgetary assistance.[1]

TABLE 3.5 AVERAGE TERMS OF OFFICIAL ASSISTANCE

	Weighted average maturity periods (years)					Weighted average interest rates (percentages)				
	1964	1965	1966	1967	1968	1964	1965	1966	1967	1968
UK	24·0	22·2	23·9	24·1	24·0	4·1	3·3	1·0	1·1	1·0
All DAC countries[a]	28·6	22·6	25·1	24·0	26·0	3·1	3·6	3·1	3·8	3·6

[a] Countries which are members of the Development Assistance Committee of the OECD.

Source: OECD, *Resources for the Developing World* (Paris 1970) page 283.

British financial terms started therefore to comply with one of the OECD Development Assistance Committee's recommendations in the 1965 resolution on the terms of aid.[2] However, there has not been any significant lengthening of either maturities or grace periods (before repayment starts). Indeed because of our rather short average grace period (see Table 3.6), Britain continued to be technically a defaulter on this resolution. Still, as can be seen from Tables 3.5 and 3.6, the best that can be said about the general performance of donors (in which the United States has of course a heavy weight) is that it has not actually worsened since this resolution was passed – the practice of voting for resolutions and then ignoring them is not confined to the OAU.[3]

'Developing' countries, with reason, object to the 'tying' of aid so that it can be spent only in the donor country. This means it buys less. It also cannot be used for local expenses, with the result that highly mechanized projects, requiring expensive imported equipment, are easier to finance than those giving a lot of local employment.[4] British performance has been

[1] The *total* aid going to countries in receipt of budgetary assistance has, however, risen – see above.

[2] The DAC resolution of 1965, which Mrs Castle supported effectively, required either that 70% of aid should be in the form of grants, or that *all three* provisions relating to loans and grants are fulfilled. The provisions are: (*i*) 81% of total commitments as grants and loans at 3% interest or less; (*ii*) 82% of total commitments as grants and loans with maturity of 25 years or more; (*iii*) a weighted average grace period of at least 7 years. A subsequent resolution put forward alternative targets to 70% in grants – either *each* transaction in at least 85% of all official commitments should have a 'grant element' of at least 81%, or 85% of commitments should have an *average* grant element of at least 85%. (The 'grant element' is a statistical device to bring out the concessional element in commitments: in a loan, the 'grant element' is the amount of the loan less the discounted payments of interest and principal.) Britain satisfies both of these alternatives.

[3] The same has happened to many rich-country votes on UNCTAD resolutions.

[4] It is odd that to our knowledge no recipient of aid loans has proposed that repayments should be tied to purchases from *its* country (though repayment in local currencies has been specified in some US food aid agreements under Public Law 480, and Soviet aid agreements in effect provide for this).

TABLE 3.6 PROGRESS OF DAC COUNTRIES ON TERMS OF AID

	Grants as percentage of total commitments					Grants and loans at interest rates of 3% or less as percentage of total commitments					Grants and loans with maturity of 25 years or more as percentage of total commitments					Weighted average grace period of loan commitments (years)				
	1964	1965	1966	1967	1968	1964	1965	1966	1967	1968	1964	1965	1966	1967	1968	1964	1965	1966	1967	1968
UK	54	55	50	57	46	61	70	93	90	91	92	84	95	96	96	5·1	4·8	6·0	5·5	5·6
DAC countries[a]	60	61	62	56	51	84	78	85	78	81	85	76	81	77	78	6·5	4·6	5·8	5·5	6·0

[a] Countries which are members of the Development Assistance Committee of the OECD.

Source: OECD *Resources for the Developing World* (Paris 1970), page 282.

relatively liberal. About two-thirds of the total of British grants and loans are tied in whole or in part to the supply of British goods and services (capital assistance to Asia, Latin America and Turkey being generally wholly tied to procurement in Britain). But budgetary support and investments by the Commonwealth Development Corporation (CDC) are not formally tied, and capital assistance to certain countries (mainly in Africa) can be applied in part to finance 'local costs' of projects – 33% to 40% in East Africa, and there is 'no fixed limit' for Malawi, Botswana or Lesotho. Rather under a half of British aid is tied to particular projects (which normally implies tying to the source of procurement as well). But there was no trend in this ratio while the Labour Government was in office.[1]

The Confederation of British Industries (CBI) in evidence before the Estimates Committee on overseas aid criticized the Ministry of Overseas Development for inadequate 'commercial orientation' of the aid programme. (This phrase means, of course, more than just 'tying'.)[2] Government departments – the ODM, the Treasury and the Board of Trade – did not regard this criticism as valid. In fact the Committee felt that there had recently been some increase in commercial orientation. It could 'find no evidence to support the criticisms made by the CBI. These may have been valid two or three years ago, but they do not appear valid now. Those responsible for the aid programme are aware of the needs of British industry, and they must continue to be so.'[3]

'The Permanent Secretary of the Ministry of Overseas Development admitted that in the early days of the Ministry there might have been a tendency to pay insufficient attention to British commercial and trading interests, but claimed that this was no longer the case.'[4]

Other development policies

The Ministry of Overseas Development has in reality been largely an aid Ministry. This itself says something about the Government's approach to the problems of overseas development. After all, aid is only one of the policies affecting overseas development; as we have already seen, immigration policy also has its effect, though ODM has had very little, if any, influence here. The truth is that many, especially in parts of ODM itself, look on British policy for development overseas as a sort of rearguard action in the recall of the legions of the Colonial Service. There is still a strong ex-colonial flavour about ODM, and many of its officials naturally see it not so much as a Ministry concerned to make British policy in many fields helpful to development but rather as a sort of jumbo version of the old Colonial Development and Welfare operation. At its worst this means

[1] There was a temporary jump in the proportion of commitments tied in 1968, but this was then reversed.
[2] *Seventh Report from the Estimates Committee*, op. cit. page xxvi.
[3] Ibid., page xxvii, para. 78.
[4] Ibid., page xxvii, para. 77.

shoring up the positions of commercial advantage in the former colonies: at its best it represents an attempt to provide financial compensation for our failure to develop them in the past, or even to create the infrastructure that would have enabled them to develop themselves once they had become independent. One must add that neither the Cabinet nor individual ODM Ministers (at least since the departure of Barbara Castle) did much to discourage either of these attitudes, each in their different ways misleading as a guide to policy.

Even if we parochially confine our attention to the former colonies, the most important British policies are not usually in the aid field. The British bungling of the Rhodesian rebellion (remember how the Smith regime was going to fall in a matter of weeks?) had far more effect on the development of neighbouring African countries, especially Zambia, than the aid that was provided subsequently.[1] Indeed some of the work of ODM has turned out to be sweeping up after parties in other departments.

Another area where British policy seriously (and adversely) affected development prospects was in South-East Asia, by supporting American military operations in Vietnam – and indeed in a fairly large area around it. If one is to credit the previous Government with schools and houses it helped to construct in Africa, one must enter on the debit side those which were destroyed, with its diplomatic support, in South-East Asia.

Indeed, if we mean by 'development' more than just 'economic growth', if we allow for the social dimensions which are far more important (and in the long run, we would argue, necessary for growth), then the whole question of the stance of Britain *vis-à-vis* different types of government is relevant. There is always a danger that the Government of a rich industrial country will (as the United States did in Cuba) base its relations on the treatment of 'its own' companies, or upon whether the other Government is friendly with those who happen to be its own enemies. We have already seen that this influences the pattern of aid, but it also affects development less directly through, for example, treaties, sales of arms and support in international disputes. The Labour Government inherited an odd collection of allies from the past. Portugal was one; there were also the various treaty organizations such as CENTO and SEATO. It was the natural practice, especially during the worst blizzards of the Cold War, for Britain (like the United States) to attempt to prop up, by other measures besides aid, Governments which were anti-Communist, often precisely those resisting, or merely paying lip-service to, tax reform, land reform, educational reform and other essential ingredients of development in a wider sense. One cannot in honesty say that Labour had abandoned this practice before it lost office, or that it changed our role in the United Nations as a defender of Portugal and even South Africa.

[1] Perhaps the most revealing of all the Cabinet's decisions on Africa was to entrust the *economic* campaign against the Smith regime to the *administrative* side of the Department of Economic Affairs, which was singularly lacking not merely in economic expertise but even in experience of Southern Africa.

Private British investment overseas also has an impact on development – what sort of impact depends (*inter alia*) on the sector concerned, the extent to which foreign Governments or individuals share in the profits and control, the amount of income and employment generated locally by purchases of materials. A Government of a rich country that says it wants to co-operate in ending world poverty has therefore to draw certain conclusions for its policy on overseas investment (or stand exposed as hypocritical).

This potential inconsistency appears most clearly in its attitude towards the taxation of its own companies by the Governments of poor countries. It looks somewhat odd if Britain is handing out aid to a Government at the same time as it is backing the particular and narrow interests of British companies, especially those threatened by nationalization. The practice of hinting that aid will be easier to come by if British companies are well treated links the two together[1] and one can see the combined implications. What this amounts to is offering money which gains goodwill, which has to be spent in Britain and which has to be repaid, in place of a foreign exchange flow which the recipient Government could spend freely and as of right.

The question is really one of the nature of the support. One hopes we will never again see a Labour Government (or indeed any British Government) behaving as the previous one, the Attlee administration, did in backing a petroleum company's fight against higher taxes (and later nationalization) in Iran – to the point of organizing an international boycott. Indeed diplomatic pressure in support of the interests of British companies is hardly compatible with development objectives or with the political philosophy of the Labour Party, tempting though it may be in terms of short-run politics.

Any company has of course the right to the advice of 'its own' Embassy on legal questions. In practice, however, the big petroleum and mining companies and the large multinational corporations are usually well able to look after themselves, and indeed are already at a decided advantage in dealing with foreign Governments. An industrial country that was really sincere about development policy would in fact be offering objective technical help to Governments in their negotiations with foreign companies, including companies based in Britain.[2]

There was one measure of the last Government that did have a big effect on private investment in the Third World, the introduction of the Corporation Tax. This change removed what had previously been favoured treatment of overseas investment. From a *national* point of view, returns from overseas investment *after* foreign tax should be equated, at the margin, to returns from domestic investment *before* tax; in the case of overseas invest-

[1] Governments which are sympathetic to foreign investors appear in any case as more 'aid-worthy'.
[2] The Commonwealth Secretariat has made a small but imaginative start in rendering this type of technical assistance.

ment, only the returns net of foreign tax accrue to Britain, whereas in the case of domestic investment, the whole return accrues to Britain, either as tax to the Exchequer or as profit to the investor. The old provisions, however, before the introduction of the Corporation Tax, enabled British companies to offset foreign taxes fully against British income tax and profits tax liabilities. This led to a situation in which, from a national point of view (quite apart from considerations of the balance of payments), too much private capital was invested abroad. At the same time, there was some evidence that, in spite of wide dispersions, the rate of return on foreign investments in underdeveloped countries was higher than that in overseas industrial countries.[1]

The Corporation Tax removed this favoured treatment of foreign investment by permitting the company to offset overseas tax against British tax liability only up to the limit of British Corporation Tax liability. Those hit by it looked on the change as a form of unfair discrimination against overseas investment. Transitional arrangements were made to ease its impact, but the new arrangements were designed precisely to deter the outflow of capital. The opposition to the tax demanded general and permanent relief from personal income tax for the British dividend receiver to the extent to which the foreign company tax exceeded the UK Corporation Tax.

The developmental implications of the Corporation Tax are complex. In so far as overseas investment is regarded as beneficial to development, a deterrent to such investment is unhelpful and should be opposed. Probably on balance the effect of continuing what amounts to a subsidy to foreign investment in 'developing' countries is positive, since it means that lower operating profits are needed to justify any act of investment. But private overseas investment in 'developing' countries is only a small proportion of total private overseas investment and only a fraction, though a sizable one, of the total flow of resources to 'developing' countries. The United Kingdom's large capital outflow in 1963–4, mainly to other rich countries, was a principal cause of its economic crisis and necessitated restrictive short-term measures. To the extent to which a measure strengthens the British balance of payments and the British economy, that measure must be supported by those wishing to promote development, for it makes possible more aid and more liberal trade policies.

There are reflex actions in Whitehall. The ODM, almost automatically, was tempted to align itself with the other overseas departments and with the Ministry of Fuel and Power, in opposing the tax. But it was clear to many, including some of the economists in the ODM, that the Corporation Tax made good economic sense, taking all its repercussions into account.[2]

[1] See John H. Dunning, *Studies in International Investment* (London 1970), Table 4, page 57 and W. B. Reddaway, *The Effects of U.K. Direct Investment Overseas* (Cambridge 1967 and 1968).
[2] On a different plane, it could be argued that the irrational system of decision-making in Whitehall justified a retention of the old tax system, amounting to a general subsidy on company profits. Tax alleviation does not count as 'aid', and therefore does not have to

In any case, the Ministry could and did argue that, whatever the general merits, special provisions should be made for private investment in 'developing' countries, especially those with high nominal tax rates (although even there actual taxes paid are reduced by numerous exemptions and special allowances). It would, for instance, not have been difficult to extend the investment grants to certain types of investment in the 'developing' countries.[1] Alternatively, a Labour Government might have increased the flow of official aid to compensate for the deterrent effect on private investment. Or an investment guarantee scheme could have been introduced such as almost all other industrial countries have now adopted. The National Plan had said that it recognized 'the part which private investment can play in overseas development' and the Chancellor of the Exchequer had promised in his budget statement 'to keep the impact on developing countries of all these various measures under review' – this seems, however, in retrospect to have been merely a sop to quieten the opposition.

In addition to changes in taxation, the Government introduced more severe exchange controls on private foreign investment, though so far as poor countries were concerned this affected mainly those outside the Sterling Area. (The 1966 scheme for voluntary restraint on investment *inside* the Sterling Area specifically excluded 'developing' countries.)

Partly as a result of all these measures, private foreign investment (net of disinvestment) in 'developing' countries declined from £157 million in 1965 to £70 million in 1968, with a recovery to £188 million in 1969 and £136 million in 1970. The recovery, however, appears to be the result of a number of financial transactions of oil companies which led to an upward revision of the published figures for 1969 of over two-thirds.[2] The revisions resulted from the failure of anticipated disinvestments or sales of assets to take place. A better picture of the trend is therefore provided if oil investment is excluded; then overseas investment (net of disinvestment) in 'developing' countries moved from £40 million in 1964 to £46 million in 1968. In real terms, whether oil is included or excluded, the figure for the last available year is lower, though not substantially lower, than for 1964.

compete with other forms of assistance where there is a ceiling on 'aid'. But we are raising questions about the way in which policy issues are posed and would not accept the treatment of aid in isolation, still less the imposition of an aid 'ceiling', as necessary constraints on rationality.

[1] In the event, the change from investment allowances to investment grants penalized overseas investment. Investment allowances had applied to British equipment installed at home or abroad, whereas investment grants applied only to equipment used in Britain. Thus a British company whose direct overseas investment consisted largely of the direct supply of British machinery lost a tax concession. This loss was only partially offset by the fact that assets obtained in Britain for use overseas were still eligible for initial allowances, which were raised from 10% to 30%. As a result of these changes, far from applying grants to investment in 'developing' countries, the new investment incentives reduced the inducement to invest in these countries.

[2] Cf. Judith Hart, 'Public aid or private investment?', *Venture*, November 1970, pages 8–11.

More deplorable than the tax changes has been the unconstructive attitude of British delegations in international discussions on trade expansion. Britain declared her willingness to participate in suitable commodity agreements, such as cocoa and tea, but when these were negotiated, the delegation included British trade interests, and often excluded the ODM.

Our own national economic policies showed similar lack of concern with the problems of the Third World. The surcharge on imports hurt some poor countries disproportionately; exemptions or earlier reductions *in favour* of them were *refused*. On cotton textiles, discrimination *against* trade with 'developing' countries was introduced through formal quotas in 1966, due to be replaced by a tariff from 1 January 1972. Beet sugar protection continued and attempts were made from time to time to dismantle the Commonwealth Sugar Agreement, which provides long-term guarantees of purchases at agreed prices. These attempts have failed but, in the renegotiations of the CSA, its term was shortened so as to provide room for manœuvre in negotiations with the EEC.

British attempts to enter the European Common Market have posed a clear danger that the trade of many 'developing' countries would be threatened. Lip-service has been paid in British documents and speeches to the protection of Commonwealth interests, but there is little evidence that the needs of 'developing' Commonwealth countries have been thoroughly considered. Labour's White Paper on the Common Market contained no analysis of this consequence of Britain's joining.

This failure of the Labour Government to advance on the trade front is more difficult to explain, except simply as yielding to vested interests.[1] The strictly national advantages of increased aid are at least arguable, but an enlightened trade policy would beyond doubt be economically beneficial to Britain. A restructuring of British industry so as to draw men and capital from out-of-date, semi-stagnant sectors and move them into those which are expanding was one of the great domestic aims: it is part of modernization, technology, growth, redeployment. Reduced protection of beet sugar and of cotton and jute textiles would have contributed to growth in Britain, as well as in the Third World. It would have created a supply of recruits for engineering and electronic industries, which is (as European experience shows) a condition of economic dynamism – apart from providing employment for the rapidly increasing masses of unemployed in the 'developing' countries. Increased imports of cheap cotton textiles are, from the point of view of the British consumer, equivalent to technical progress in synthetic fibres, but with beneficial instead of detrimental effects on poor countries. Even from the most selfish British point of view, the continued protection of the cotton textile industry is unwise. If the same resources, instead of defending and re-equipping an uncompetitive industry, had gone into the more dynamic sectors, clamouring for skills and capital, levels of living and growth would have risen faster, to the

[1] Though in fairness one must point out that our record is not worse than that of other industrial countries (especially the United States).

benefit of all, except a small, well-organized pressure group (including, of course, trade unions).

On international monetary reform, Britain supported – after some equivocation – the right of the 'developing' countries to participate in the negotiations leading up to the creation of SDRs, against those European countries that wished to confine the discussion to the inner circle known as the 'Group of Ten'. But since there was a clear harmony of interests among all chronic-deficit countries, including Britain, this concern for the interests of others was interpreted, perhaps over-cynically, less as a regard for the needs of the poor than as an attempt to get support for expansionist or – as the opponents would say – inflationary, policies. Britain did not, in any case, back 'the link' between SDRs and aid very strongly, and in fact only gave lukewarm support to the idea, even after the activation of the SDRs. Until this has been done, 'don't rock the boat' was given as the reason for this reluctance, afterwards fear of 'killing a tender plant'.

The conception of the Ministry as a *development* Ministry rather than an *aid* Ministry, with a voice and representation in all issues affecting development, never really took hold in Whitehall. The Board of Trade in particular considered the charge levelled against the Ministry of being a lobby for the 'developing' countries as sufficient condemnation, certainly not as a justification for fuller representation on the key inter-departmental committees. Treasury officials, in particular, rejected the Government's expressed philosophy (which had, in any event, very little conviction behind it). A Treasury witness before the Estimates Committee, asked about the relations between British trade interests and aid, criticized the Government's conception of ODM in the following terms:

If I can say so frankly, there has been a little bit of a tendency in an aid Ministry to say our prime responsibility is towards the recipient country.[1]

As a result, when there were negotiations on immigration, the Kennedy Round, the scheme for generalized preferences for manufactures, agreements for commodities such as cocoa, cotton textiles, entry into the Common Market, or international monetary reform, ODM was either not represented at all, or only very meagrely. Often it was not even consulted. The Economic Planning Staff, which was created to keep an eye on these wider issues, was kept too busy on aid problems and in any case had not the armoury to keep up the unequal battle against the powerful combination of the rest of Whitehall.

Key representational posts, in the field of development, were kept out of ODM's reach. A notable example is the British Executive Directorship in the International Bank, a post in which there is in practice much discretion for policy-making. One of the few battles Barbara Castle lost in the early weeks of the Ministry was the retention of this post by the Treasury. This has ensured that the British voice has been conservative

[1] Ibid. 1377.

(with a small 'c') on the major policies, and that the substantial British vote has been used to help allies and friends, rather than to hasten the gradual conversion of the Bank to a more development-orientated role. The same could be said of British briefs for meetings of the Directors of the Fund, which showed such enthusiasm for monetary orthodoxy as a cure for the problems of 'developing' countries that it became embarrassing as our own foreign exchange problems grew more acute – apart from casting a Labour Government in the role of an opponent of development.

The other key international post, that of leading the delegation to UNCTAD (and providing representation on its Board), remained with the Board of Trade. UNCTAD would have provided the forum for constructive initiatives towards a more integrated world economy, but was treated by Whitehall with considerable suspicion. Ministerial pressure was strong enough to get a bid made for London as the site of the UNCTAD secretariat, against heavy pressure from the diplomatic service ('The Americans would boycott UNCTAD if it were not in New York; besides, it would mean another couple of hundred wogs in London with duty-free privileges' – to run together two separate quotations). But the bid was put forward very feebly – the British delegation hardly bothered to hide their disagreement with their brief.

In the 1968 UNCTAD at New Delhi, British policy was in fact much less sympathetic than it had been in 1964 in Geneva, when the delegation was led by Edward Heath (and produced the proposals for 'supplementary financial measures' to enable development plans to proceed despite unexpected shortfalls in export earnings). The New Delhi Conference took place soon after the 1967 devaluation and there were no signs of improvement in the British balance of payments. Some people argued that since the British crisis was as acute as ever, if not worse, Britain was not in a position to give a lead. But seen in conjunction with all that went before, it is impossible to argue that the British feebleness in New Delhi can be explained wholly by economic difficulties.

Conclusions

On the whole, Labour's record was discreditable, especially in contrast to the promises before the election (which some of us were naive enough to believe). Particularly damaging was the rejection of any attempt to lead public opinion to accept a more international, development-oriented strategy.

This is not to say that all British international policy (including aid) is always just an imperialist plot, necessarily damaging to the Third World. Some types of aid involve a genuine sacrifice, and much of it is on balance constructive in its effects; many countries, notably India, would face a challenge that could well prove catastrophic if aid were withdrawn.

Nor is it to say that the Conservatives would have produced a more defensible set of policies if they had won the 1964 election. Judging from their own record (and allowing for known shifts in attitudes), the history of the past five years would probably have been only marginally different.

It may be that they would also have cut the aid programme after 1964 as they entered a period of inevitable economic difficulties. Our belief, however, is that they would have continued to expand it, because, as we have shown, the cuts were due more to Labour political priorities than to economic difficulties, real though these were. A Conservative administration would have felt less constrained to demonstrate their 'respectability'. On the contrary, Conservatives like to show how enlightened they are – within, of course, the natural limits of their policies. We must not forget that if they had won the 1964 election (the hypothesis), the Labour Party would have still been in opposition and therefore still at least vocally internationalist.

Tories are, in any case, less easily taken in (because less willing to be) by 'balance of payments' arguments and might well have had fewer inhibitions about devaluing sterling, the main requirement for easing the payments problem. It is difficult to believe, once the argument was posed squarely in terms of real resources, that they would have given such an over-riding priority to the increase in personal consumption, already so high by international standards. On immigration, on the basis of post-electoral developments, one is tempted to say that their policy would have been just as destructive, but we must not forget that the present (1971) Government is really following a path pioneered by the Labour Party – if Labour had not made the decisive moves towards an immigration policy with racial and anti-developmental overtones, would the Conservatives have done so themselves? We doubt it.

On the other hand, many of the improvements which Labour did make would have presented, in fact, little difficulty for the Conservatives – the shifts towards multilateral aid and technical assistance, even interest-free loans; one can reasonably conclude that for these it probably did not matter very much which Government was in power.

It is true that 'untying' of aid would have created obvious problems with the backers of the Conservatives. But (as can be inferred from Mr Heath's own strong support of legislation to control Resale Price Maintenance) doctrinal belief in the merits of competition might have opened their eyes to what could be gained from a determined British initiative to achieve an international agreement to untie.

The great question is whether a Conservative Government would not have made aid policy even more political and commercial than it was, especially if we assume that they would have expanded the programme and thus gained increased room for manœuvre. It is reasonable to assume that the pattern of aid would have reflected even more strongly British political and trade interests, rather than those of recipients.

Patience with Tanzania would have been even shorter, one guesses, and it is quite possible that help to the United States in Vietnam would have been less indirect. However, one cannot fairly deduce what the Conservative policy on such matters would have been from their statements in opposition. *In office* they might well have grasped more quickly than Labour did the impracticability of maintaining large military bases East of Suez. One even wonders whether Smith would have tried his breakaway – or have succeeded so completely – if the Conservatives had been in power (though ancestral memories of Carson and Ulster make one hesitate to give them the benefit of the doubt).

Trade policy, however, would hardly have been much better from a 'development' point of view, under Conservative management. Indeed, the post-election withdrawal of the Government grant to the Consumer Council suggests that any alignments of interest between British consumers and exporters of low-cost products from 'developing' countries would have been sacrificed in favour of vocal and well-organized British producer interests clamouring for protection.

These are not purely historical speculations. They are a way of asking about policy in the 1970s. And we shall soon see the shape of the answer.

One thing is certain – the Conservatives would not have made an attempt to take the interests of the poorer countries of the world *institutionally* into account. In other words, they would not have created an independent Ministry with a planning staff with political and economic functions. They would no doubt have created, as they did later, a semi-autonomous unit for co-ordinating aid – probably within what was then the Commonwealth Relations Office.

It has been argued, e.g. when this unit was in fact formed in 1970, that aid policies are weakened, not strengthened, by being handled by a separate Ministry, especially a new one. This vulnerable area of policy needs a powerful sponsor – even if the sponsor does not really approve of, or even understand, the rationale of what he is sponsoring. The same argument has often been used against the creation of a separate Department for overall economic development policy.

It is really not very convincing, given the political views (and the power) of the civil servants in the Foreign Office and the Treasury. Yet the rather spectacular divergence between Labour promise and fulfilment, in the field of overseas development as in growth, has made this institutional issue seem rather less important than it looked in 1964.

Everything seemed to be set up for a new international policy then – a new Ministry, a tough Minister, professional expertise, the right support from some of the most powerful people. How, in spite of these good omens, could things go so wrong? It is now clear that setting up an independent Ministry is merely an empty gesture unless there is real support within the Government for its policies – support strong enough to withstand, and in time change, a public opinion that expects immediate, tangible, national advantages from the proceeds of taxation. When it comes to the pinch, Labour is really *very* parochial.

APPENDIX. THE TRUE COST OF AID

In order to grasp the full implications of the discussion of how much aid we can afford, let us look at the 'true' cost of aid. The simplest reply to the question: 'what is the true cost of aid?' is: its nominal cost. It is simple, but not very enlightening. Any attempt, however, to introduce corrections involves making hypothetical assumptions which are bound at best to be largely unverifiable guesses – or an opportunity to introduce hidden prejudices, at worst.

If our balance of payments were in equilibrium and we had adequate foreign exchange reserves, if we suffered from neither inflation nor deflation and neither bottlenecks nor surplus capacity, if costs indicated forgone alternatives, and if we gave away the aid as grants, the nominal cost of the aid programme would be a rough guide to its true cost to the British economy. Divergencies between the two arise because:

1. £1 worth of foreign exchange is worth more than £1 if there is disequilibrium in the balance of payments and if we are very short of foreign exchange;

2. £1 worth of aid is worth more than £1 if the item is 'rationed' (e.g. reflected in lengthening domestic order books) and less than £1 if we have surplus capacity in the industry producing it or surplus stocks;

3. £1 worth of aid is worth more than £1 if the domestic benefits exceed the nominal costs and less if they fall short of them;

4. £1 worth lent (instead of given away), will yield a return in the future and this has to be appropriately deducted.

1. The main point to note on the divergence between the cost to the balance of payments and the nominal cost is this. If we are short of foreign exchange reserves, the official exchange rate does not reflect the real value of a loss of foreign exchange. While a good deal of aid is spent on British goods and services, some – it has been estimated about a third – constitutes a claim on foreign exchange reserves.[1] A foreign exchange cost occurs if either goods could have been exported for cash (or short-term export debits), had they not been delivered to aid recipients or if, although the aid is tied, recipients buy with tied aid goods they would otherwise have bought with untied foreign exchange and use the money thereby set free to buy from other countries. The latter reason for a foreign exchange cost is known as *switching*; the former might be called *diverting*.

It is sometimes argued that the import content of aid is also a charge on the balance of payments. But to the extent that either 'switching' or 'diverting' occurs, no *additonal* output is necessary over and above what would have been produced otherwise. Therefore, no extra imports are required. Only if *neither* switching *nor* diverting occurs, so that the aid exports necessitate *additional* output, will there be *extra* imports. But these

[1] The references are given above, page 129, footnote 2.

import requirements arise from *all* increases in British production and are not a valid reason for cutting aid rather than, say, industrial investment, in order to save foreign exchange. Suppose, on the other hand, the increase in aid-financed exports is *at the expense of* some other *domestic* activity, then no additional imports are required. (This argument assumes that the import content of aid is no higher than that of the displaced activity.)

Aid can also be beneficial to the balance of payments. Thus aid to transport systems in countries with British-owned mines and plantations can generate a much greater increase in profit remittances to this country. Since countries of this type receive an abnormally high share of British aid (in relation to their population), and since British embassies and high commissions favour precisely the types of project that have this effect, the point is of more than academic significance. In addition, the supply of British equipment in aid programmes makes purchasing departments overseas familiar with their characteristics and thus inclined to place orders outside the aid programme – so the goods financed by aid can have the same commercial significance as 'samples'. A further significant help to exports is that the supply of equipment leads to orders for spare parts – which are rarely financed by aid.[1]

In any case, to say that one third of the aid is a cost to the balance of payments comes nowhere near to answering the important question, what the cost actually is. For, in so far as the loss takes the form of a reduction of foreign exchange reserves, there is no immediate real burden. (The real burden falls on those countries that make this possible by accumulating reserves or extending credits to us.) Only when corrective policies are applied in Britain and the exchange loss is thus halted is a real burden imposed. These corrective policies may take the form of a worsening of the terms of trade, or of domestic deflation with unemployment and loss of production, or of import restrictions with a resulting loss in the form of a less desirable composition of imports – and perhaps of retaliation by foreigners in the form of controls on our exports. The size of this secondary burden may be larger than that of the primary sacrifice although it could, in exceptional circumstances, be negative (e.g. a surcharge on imports that improves our terms of trade).

In order to calculate the 'real' cost, one needs a 'shadow' exchange rate. Since this rate, however, depends on the hypothetical policies that would or will be pursued to put the balance of payments in order, there cannot be a single correct answer. If we have to deflate in order to correct a chronic deficit, the cost is different from what it is if we devalue and again different from what it is with an import surcharge or import restrictions.

Estimates of this shadow rate ran as high as five times the official rate. The argument goes like this: if the propensity to import is one fifth of in-

---

[1] There are even further complications, though perhaps of theoretical rather than practical significance. Thus if other industrial countries increase *their* exports at our expense, for any of the reasons given, they will buy more from us with part of their extra earnings.

come, we have to deflate national income by £5 in order to reduce imports by £1, so £1 loss of foreign exchange imposes a loss of £5 on the economy. Actually, the 'equilibrium' exchange rate before the most recent devaluation was hardly more than 14% above the current official rate (i.e. hardly more than the devaluation that did occur), and the difference between 1·14 and 5 can be ascribed to the stubborn refusal to devalue rather than to the aid programme.

2. Divergencies between nominal and true costs also arise because of bottlenecks and surplus capacity. If an item is in scarce supply but the scarcity is fully reflected in the price, the nominal cost is raised to the true cost. But in manufacturing industry this is not customary. Order books lengthen, i.e. supply is rationed. The true cost exceeds the nominal cost, since some buyers would be prepared to pay more for speedier delivery.

Against this, aid goods from surplus capacity cost less than the nominal cost, for the productive factors would not otherwise have been employed. This has been important for the USA, which supplies surplus food as aid, but is probably not very significant in our aid programme (though more use of second-hand machinery could be important). Even if aid could be supplied from surpluses in, say, railway waggons or ships, it could be argued that this only prolongs the life of an industry that should contract and release labour, skills and capital to industries that are expanding. Therefore only *temporary* surplus capacity, such as occurs from time to time in the steel plant manufacturing industry, can be regarded as a legitimate reason for marking down the cost.

Special problems arise in respect of the services of certain types of scarce skilled manpower (e.g. economists and statisticians) supplied under technical assistance. The salaries of these men often fall short of their true scarcity value (firms say they just cannot recruit certain people) and therefore the apparently low cost of certain forms of technical assistance understates the true cost of the aid programme. (This is, of course, not the same as their value to the recipient country.) Against this, experience overseas may be regarded as a form of human investment which stands the British economy in good stead when the man returns to base. Moreover, even if he is completely unbiassed in his advice, his recommendations are likely to lead to orders for equipment from Britain rather than from other industrial countries, simply because he knows British equipment best and the techniques he recommends may require that any capital goods needed be bought here.

So far we have talked about *specific* shortages and surpluses in *particular* industries. Some might argue that adjustments should be made if *general* inflationary conditions prevail or if *general* underemployment exists. True costs exceed nominal costs in inflation and fall short of them in deflation. But the excess of true over nominal costs exists for *all* forms of expenditure in inflationary conditions and there is no reason to single out the aid programme. Nor is it right to mark down the costs in conditions of general underemployment, for this will normally be the deliberate result of Government policy.

3. There may be other reasons why true costs exceed nominal costs. If a very high priority domestic objective, whose true value exceeds its nominal costs, has to be curtailed or abandoned solely because of the claims of aid, it would be fair to attribute the excess cost to the aid.

4. Finally, much aid is not given away but must be repaid, sometimes with interest. There is a simple method of reducing to a common factor the rag-bag of soft loans and hard loans, short-term and long-term loans, at commercial and subsidized rates of interest, together with free gifts and private investment, which appears now in aid statistics, sometimes gross and sometimes net of repayments. We calculate the nominal value of all forms of financial flows disbursed (or committed) in a year and deduct from this sum the discounted present value of interest payments and loan repayments, discounted at a rate of interest that reflects the alternative employment of long-term public capital. In this way all forms of financial flow are reduced to their equivalent value as a grant (or gift or subsidy). The longer the term of the loan, the lower the interest rate and the later payments start, the greater will be the aid component thus calculated. There is, of course, some doubt as to what is the appropriate discount rate to use – this could vary between periods.[1]

---

[1] The appropriate rate may in any case not be the same for borrowers (and may differ between different borrowers).

4 Economic planning and growth

Roger Opie

The publication by the Government of a plan covering all aspects of the country's economic development for the next five years is a major advance in economic policy-making in the United Kingdom. Prepared in the fullest consultation with industry, the plan for the first time represents a statement of Government policy and a commitment to action by the Government. . . . The plan is a guide to action.

GEORGE BROWN, *The National Plan* (September 1965, Cmnd. 2764)

Since about the mid-1950s it was clear that the growth rate of the British economy was slower than that of most industrialized countries. To many people, it seemed equally clear that Britain's growth rate could be faster. By the early 1960s it also seemed clear, to what is now a surprisingly large number of people, that the problem of achieving a faster growth rate would be partly or even wholly solved by economic planning.

This might well suggest to the cynic that if politics is the art of the possible, economics is the science of the fashionable. For as late as the early 1950s economic planning was not held in high esteem, at least in this country, and at least in peace time. The replacement of Mr Attlee's by Mr Churchill's Government coincided with and partly reflected a growing disenchantment with the practice, if not the philosophy, of detailed, physical micro-economic controls. The irksome restraints of rationing on consumption and of licences on production were regarded as one of the intolerable and inevitable costs of Socialist muddle and meddle, rather than the counterpart of a massive and essential shift of resources from armaments to exports and to capital formation, at a time of overall excess demand and great inflationary pressures. In the 1950s, no one in Britain was a 'planner' in the sense of the word in use in the forties, or again in the sixties.

But experience teaches, even if the lessons are sometimes ambiguous. By the start of the sixties, still with a Conservative Government in power, the wheel had turned full circle. Planning was no longer a dirty word, or even a music-hall joke on a par with groundnuts or white fish. It was about to become a panacea. This remarkable conversion arose from many sources.

The conversion to planning

The first and most potent was no doubt a widespread disenchantment with the performance of the UK economy in the fifties. It was true, in that memorable phrase, that we 'had never had it so good', but that has always been true in each and every year since 1952. It was equally true that in other countries, both in Western and Eastern Europe, to say nothing of Japan, economic growth was not simply faster than here but often at double or treble our rate. In addition, our *actual* growth of output was very unstable. For short periods the economy was fully employed, but for much of the time there were varying degrees of unemployment and excess capacity.

This instability, vilified by critics as 'stop-go', was seen not as a natural phenomenon (which in a decentralized economy it partly was) but as the intended response to a 'stop-go policy'. That policy in turn was intended mainly to halt sudden sharp deteriorations in the balance of payments and partly to restrain domestic price and wage increases which would worsen the long-term trend in the balance of payments.

Poor performance was blamed by many on poor policy. Some laid most of the blame for both the short-term deterioration and the longer-term weakness of the external balance on the 'go' phases of policy. Some, even more cynically, noted the coincidence, to put it no more strongly, between the 'go' phases and the timing of election campaigns, and naturally saw the 'stop' phases as nature's economic retribution for such electoral extravagance.

The critics of official policy divided into two schools. Each wanted to eliminate or at least reduce the degree of instability in economic activity, and each claimed that this would accelerate economic growth. One group was the so-called 'Paish-School'[1] which aimed to stabilize the level of total demand at such a level as would leave a margin of spare physical capacity and unemployed labour. This would eliminate excess demand and hence any inflationary pressures, prevent any weakening of the trade balance, and enable the economy to grow at its *trend* rate of growth.

The other school was much more heterogeneous. It contained, first, those who doubted the *practicality* of the Paish policy. Could the economy be stabilized at *any* level, let alone at the Paish level? But it also contained what might be called the 'expansionists', who questioned the wisdom and the morality of that policy, and who wanted to push up the level of demand, and hence the pressure on capacity, to such a point as would leave registered unemployment not much above one per cent. They rejected the view that 'the Government's object should be to manage aggregate demand so as to *match* the economy's productive capacity, not "stretch" it'.[2] They argued that, on the contrary, pressure on capacity was the surest way to stimulate new investment to add to capacity, to raise productivity per man and thus the rate of growth. They contrasted this possibility with the actual experience of 'a continuing discouragement

[1] See e.g. F. W. Paish, *Studies in an Inflationary Economy* (London 1962), esp. Chapters 7 and 17.
[2] P. Oppenheimer in V. Bogdanor and R. Skidelsky (eds), *The Age of Affluence, 1951–1964* (London 1970), page 150.

to investment, artificially restricted in the period of crisis and crowded out during the consumer boom'.[1]

At the start of the sixties, a number of factors combined to drive opinion away from the orthodox stop-go policies of the fifties and towards planning, or at least to the idea of planning, or at least to a flirtation with the idea of planning. The first was a popular interpretation of the French so-called 'economic miracle'. An increasing number of foreign observers came to see this as 'proof' of the success of French *indicative* planning. For a number of years the Socialist countries of Eastern Europe had also enjoyed high rates of economic growth, but the political costs of their brand of directive planning were unacceptably high. The French experience, however, seemed to show that indicative planning offered all the fruits without the thorns.[2]

The second major factor in the new-found respectability of 'planning' was a remarkable conversion among the managerial establishment. An epoch-making conference was held by the (then) Federation of British Industry at Brighton in 1960 to investigate 'The Next Five Years'. A report published under that title urged the Government, and more particularly the Treasury, to consult more closely with the CBI and the TUC, and to set up machinery for that purpose, in order to pursue policies which would stabilize and accelerate growth and stabilize prices.[3]

Just as important and certainly more remarkable was the conversion of a number of the leaders of both the main political parties to some form of economic planning. Of course, it all depends on what one means by 'planning'. But actions by the Government in setting up some planning machinery, and words by the Opposition, were evidence of an extraordinary shift of established opinion. The then Shadow Chancellor of the Exchequer was Harold Wilson. His words at the time were clear enough:

Trouble lies ahead . . . *laisser-faire* economics provide no answer for the problem and . . . steady industrial expansion and a strong currency in world markets can be achieved only by the introduction of purposive economic planning . . . A comprehensive plan of national development can recreate a dynamic sense of national purpose and restore our place in the world . . . What is needed is a comprehensive plan covering the whole of our industry.[4]

The last factor was the balance of payments crisis of the summer of 1961. The boom which had been deliberately generated by policy in 1958 reached a peak in the spring of 1961, with a characteristic external

[1] Harold Wilson, *New Statesman*, 24 March 1961, page 462.
[2] This interpretation of the French miracle was always questionable, and was increasingly questioned later in the sixties. Cf. *Economic Planning in France* (PEP Broadsheet No. 454); *French Planning; Some Lessons for Britain* (PEP Broadsheet No. 475).
[3] The machinery that was set up in 1962 was the National Economic Development Council, with its supporting Office (both popularly known as 'Neddy') and the ill-fated National Income Commission (known as 'Nicky').
[4] Wilson, op. cit., pages 462–3.

deficit followed by a formidable external crisis. In August 1961 the brakes were slammed on, with a credit squeeze, a 7% Bank rate, public expenditure cuts – all the familiar paraphernalia of yet another British crisis. It seemed obvious that there must be better ways of managing the economy than this. One such way, it seemed to many, was to plan the growth of the UK economy. The first step was to draw up a plan.

The nature of planning

An authoritative survey of contemporary economics, published in 1952, contained a chapter on national economic planning. Its author asserted[1] that 'in the advanced capitalist West, doctrines of economic planning have largely displaced earlier concepts of economic liberalism and exercise a powerful influence upon economic policies and economic thought'. This would strike most observers as a rather extreme judgment, until it becomes clear that national economic planning in the advanced capitalist countries is defined merely as a policy of full employment. Such a definition is clearly too narrow. There is an equal danger of too wide a definition. If a plan is defined as 'a set of policies which together make up a credible strategy for achieving a stated objective',[2] then an economic plan is simply 'a set of *economic* policies . . . for a stated *economic* objective'. In that case, the decisive break is the break with total laissez-faire, which took place a very long time ago.

I would prefer to distinguish between a plan (or planning), and policies. Just as French without tears is not French, planning without policies is not planning. But a plan and a set of policies are not the same thing. A plan is rather 'a consistent, plausible, integrated, comprehensive framework for policy'. It must be consistent (or rational) in the sense that both the ends chosen and the means to those ends are compatible with each other. It must be plausible in the sense that the quantities and the relationships involved bear some resemblance to the real world. It must be integrated in the sense that the parts fit together without loose ends. And a national plan should be comprehensive in the sense of covering the relevant areas of the economy without gaps. Which areas are relevant can only be determined once one knows what the object of the policies is.

If the Baran definition of national economic planning in 'advanced capitalist countries' as confined to full employment is too narrow, French and British planning have been closer in their objectives to Baran's view of planning in the *backward* capitalist world, aimed at accelerating economic growth while pursuing a number of other goals which include full employment. In each case, the original purpose was to influence, if not determine, the whole future shape of the economy. That means in turn influencing the size, the path and the content of total output.

[1] Paul A. Baran in B. F. Haley (ed.), *A Survey of Contemporary Economics, Vol. II* (New York 1952), page 355.
[2] S. Brittan, *Inquest on Planning in Britain* (PEP, Vol. XXXIII, January 1967).

The planning takes the form of setting a target (or projected) rate of growth for the gross domestic product[1] up to a date some years ahead (in the UK that date was on both occasions five years ahead) and hence taking a definite view of the absolute level which that aggregate should reach in the terminal years (1966 in the NEDC plan and 1970 in the DEA Plan).

Note that the rate of growth is not a *forecast* rate, a rate which would happen anyway, but a 'projected' rate which would happen 'only if . . .'. The next stage is then to attempt to discover the obstacles in the way of achieving that growth, i.e. to analyse what are the 'only ifs'. The obstacles, or at least the economic ones, are bottlenecks – shortages of labour, either in total or of certain types; shortages of physical capacity, again either in total or of certain types; or shortages of imports that can be paid for out of export receipts or from a credible volume of loans or aid, i.e. a shortage of 'affordable' imports. To know how tight these bottlenecks will be, we need to know the alternative uses to which resources can and would be put, i.e. we need to know the pattern of the use of resources, as well as their total supply. From that we can calculate how much additional output must be devoted now and over the plan period to capital-formation and the balance of trade (i.e. to exports or to import-replacement).

That is then the framework for policies which will permit or induce or compel the necessary allocation of resources. The best analogy is perhaps that of a combined 'town-plan and route-map' – a picture of how to get there, and one of what it will look like when (and if) you get there. *How* the allocation of resources is achieved provides a boundary between the two main types of planning – imperative or directive planning, as in war-time when resource shifts can be compelled; or indicative planning, as in France (actually) and in the UK (potentially). The Plan itself would indicate where resources should go, and at least in part by that very indication produce the shift.

Much of the 'indication' will inevitably be to the various departments of Government, and if the Plan is to be operational must result in policies and policy changes. There are thus three necessary stages in the planning process – sums, tests of feasibility, and policy.

---

[1] Since the aim of faster growth is a higher standard of living, which means higher consumption per head, it might seem more sensible to set the targets in terms of GDP *per head*, and of productivity *per man*. This would mean in turn (see next para.) that a labour shortage in total would not be an obstacle in itself to a faster growth rate.

In fact both UK plans (of the NEDC and the DEA) were expressed in global terms, a growth of so much in total GDP. This had the political advantage of simplicity, of dramatizing one figure. It had the economic advantage of making it easier for industries and firms to translate the implications of that global target into demands for their own particular product.

On the other hand, it lost nothing in its implications for the supply side of output, since the target overall growth rate can be translated into a target growth rate of productivity as soon as one has forecast the growth of the work force.

The purpose of economic planning

The main purpose of economic planning in the UK was doubtless to achieve faster growth. In a basically laissez-faire economy, this was a new purpose derived partly from new theories of economic growth:

It is unlikely that even twenty-five years ago anyone writing about factors that determine growth would have regarded government policy as an important feature of his analysis. It is a measure of the great change that has come over the economy and our way of viewing it that this consideration should now occupy a central position.[1]

If and insofar as this is true, it justifies a Government in implementing a growth policy, just as the growth of oligopolistic industry and mono-polistic trade unions has so changed the nature of price determination that a Government is justified in having a prices and incomes policy.

But even if Governments would like faster economic growth, and have policies to achieve it, what extra contribution can a Plan make? One answer was given by the Minister responsible for the 1965 National Plan:

The whole point of the National Plan was to identify the areas where there were weaknesses in the existing situation and where we should concentrate our resources. In that way individual industries and sectors could see clearly what they had to do to enable this overall national result to be achieved.[2]

This lays all the stress on industrial action. The earlier NEDC 'Plan' of 1963 attributed three objectives to the NEDC: examining the future potential performance of the British economy; pointing out the obstacles to more rapid economic growth; and seeking agreement on ways to remove these obstacles.[3] There was no suggestion that the NEDC had powers other than the power of persuasion. Indeed, although some saw this as its final condemnation,[4] others saw its purpose as essentially psychological and its effectiveness as a function of its impotence:

The NEDC has at last given body to the idea of expansion: it has been able to demonstrate the immense gains both in income and social benefits of an acceleration of the growth of the national income. There is an immense psycho-logical gain in the present eagerness of all concerned to participate in the work of the NEDC – however futile it looks to the outside observer . . . It is not impossible that the collaboration of industry is secured *because* the NEDC as it is

[1] Sir Eric Roll, *The World after Keynes* (London 1968), page 32.
[2] George Brown, *Sunday Times*, 18 October 1970.
[3] Growth o˙ the United Kingdom Economy to 1966, page viii.
For a short discussion of the NEDC and its 'Plan' see below, pages 18–19.
[4] 'It was a foretaste of its ineffectiveness that it was at once christened "Neddy". It was to be a lovable lion, without claws.' D. Horne, *God is an Englishman* (Harmondsworth 1970), page 229.

organised has *no* power to give effect to its plans, and the Government has no intention to do it either.[1]

So far then, the value of a plan lies in seeking joint solutions, and creating a climate of opinion in favour of growth. The Brookings' view of the National Plan was a little more explicit – 'to develop a co-ordinated internally consistent set of projections of how the economy might develop to 1970 and *thereby create expectations* that would induce private economic decisions to conform to the projections'.[2] This view is an almost explicit assertion of the 'expectations' hypothesis. This can too easily be caricatured as the virtuous circle theory of growth, a virtuous confidence trick, or faith-healing. Put less pejoratively, it is a mixture of a tautology – that faster growth depends on higher investment and faster technical progress: and an analysis of the behaviour of management and labour – that investment and technical progress themselves depend on the expected future growth rate.[3]

On this view of economic performance, a Plan can help to accelerate growth if the indications that it gives of future events and of future policies are sufficiently encouraging.[4] Harrod points to a paradox here:

It may be objected that the 'indications' will not be much heeded, unless accompanied by some guarantee by the authorities that they will use normal policies to ensure that overall the economy achieves its growth potential. And so one might reach this dilemma. If the authorities can give this guarantee, they must have means of their own – apart from indicative planning – of ensuring growth in accordance with potential: then what is the need of such planning? But if they lack such means how can they give the all-important guarantee?[5]

Harrod resolves this dilemma, as do we, by laying stress on the inhibiting effect of uncertainty on entrepreneurs when planning investment, and on the utility of a plan in revealing the sort and size of the problems that faster growth would cause, and hence of reducing at least *one* set of uncertainties. Meade draws[6] the distinction between 'market uncertainties' and 'environmental uncertainties'. Examples of the former are the size of the market for a given product or industry, and of the latter the level of total economic activity, the state of technology, the future rate of exchange. Market uncertainty, he argues, 'is the sort of uncertainty

[1] T. Balogh, *Planning for Progress: A Strategy for Labour* (Fabian Tract No. 346), pages 22 and 35.
[2] R. Caves, loc. cit. My italics.
[3] Cf. e.g. Brittan, op. cit., pages 17–21, and W. Beckerman in P. D. Henderson (ed.) *Economic Growth in Britain* (London 1966), page 65.
[4] It is not necessary to resolve here the dispute as to whether higher investment *causes* faster growth. It is sufficient if it simply permits it.
[5] Sir Roy Harrod, 'Are monetary and fiscal policies enough?', *Economic Journal*, December 1964, page 907.
[6] Cf. e.g. J. E. Meade, *The Theory of Indicative Planning* (Manchester 1970).

which can be removed by a system of forward markets or of indicative planning'.[1]

We can thus list a number of purposes of or benefits from a national plan – the creation of optimistic expectations about future levels of activity; the discovery of the nature, the place, and the size of obstacles to a given faster rate of overall economic growth; the elimination of inconsistencies in the micro-plans of the various but inevitably interlocking sectors of a modern economy – a mixture of brighter expectations, different Government policies and different industrial behaviour.

The NEDC Plan

As we have seen, the NEDC was a milestone along the road from total disillusionment with the whole theory and practice of planning in the UK towards a new willingness to experiment with some form of indicative planning. The NEDC Plan was no more than 'an assessment of possibilities'. It involved no formal commitment, by Government or industry or the unions. It coincided with a shift of policy within the Treasury away from the mainly financial and towards a greater concern with real resources. This surfaced in a more sophisticated control of public expenditure and of the nationalized industries. From 'outside' the Whitehall machine, but from within the forum of tripartite discussions of Government, industry and unions, came the choice of a rate of growth of the UK economy of 4% p.a. from 1961 to 1966 as the basis of such discussion. It was soon elevated into a target rate, partly as a result of the NEDC investigations which showed, so it was argued, the feasibility of the target.

It is ironic that one of the purposes of such medium-term planning is to smooth, as well as accelerate, the rate of growth. But one can only too plausibly argue that the Neddy Plan helped to *destabilize* the UK economy. The main work was done on it in the 1962–3 trough of a stop-go cycle, and the so-called 'Maudling experiment' was at least in part supported by the Neddy calculations as an attempt to drive the UK economy on to a growth path which would achieve 4% p.a. over a five-year period. The Maudling boom and the parallel deterioration of the external balance, which were at least an indirect result of the Neddy Plan, dominated the first three years of the Labour Government, and its own Plan.[2]

---

[1] Op. cit., page 3.
[2] For more details of the NEDC 'Plan', the reader should refer to NEDC, *Growth of the U.K. Economy to 1966*, (HMSO 1963), *Conditions Favourable to Economic Growth* (HMSO 1963) and *Export Trends* (HMSO 1963); C. Sandford and M. S. Bradbury, *Case Studies in Economics: Economic Policy* (London 1970), Chapter 14; A. Shonfield, *Modern Capitalism* (Oxford 1965), Chapter 8; Denton, Forsyth and MacLennan, *Economic Planning and Policies in Britain, France and Germany* (London 1968); P. S. Graves, in Birmingham & Ford (eds), *Planning and Growth in Rich and Poor Countries* (London 1966).

Planning and the Department of Economic Affairs

The election of Mr Wilson's Government in 1964 had a profound effect on the whole planning experiment. The planning machinery was brought inside Whitehall and set up within the newly-formed Department of Economic Affairs. This department, whose Minister was First Secretary of State for Economic Affairs, was intended to be at the centre of economic policy. But although it was a co-ordinating Ministry within Whitehall, and led on many aspects of both macro- and micro-economic policy, it did not have authority over short-term demand management.

In the first twelve months of its life, most of the energy of the DEA and its Secretary of State was devoted to three tasks – to acting as a counterweight to the Treasury and all the other Ministries that, in the committee jungle of Whitehall, exert an influence on economic policy;[1] to producing a Declaration of Intent which was to lay the basis of the voluntary prices and incomes policy in force until July 1966; and to drawing up the National Plan.

The publication of the Plan in September 1965 marked the high water-mark of the planning movement in the 1960s. It stated rather grandly:

The Plan is designed to achieve a 25% increase in national output between 1964 and 1970. This objective has been chosen in the light of past trends in national output and output per head and a realistic view of the scope for improving upon these trends. It involves achieving a 4% annual growth rate of output well before 1970 and an annual average of 3·8% between 1964 and 1970.[2]

This short statement contains many of the targets of later attacks – the choice of a single target rate; the choice of that particular rate; and the unwillingness to map out the year-by-year path to the promised land. It is true that one factor in the choice of the rate was the view that it was a practical one. Perhaps more important, however, was the overriding political need for a Government publicly dedicated to more rapid economic growth to choose a rate not visibly lower than the Selwyn Lloyd/ NEDC rate. The suspicion that this was or might be so was a continual source of public doubt from the very start of the exercise.

Many critics also attacked the choice of only one target rate. What would, or could, happen if, as was to be expected, the actual path were to diverge from the very foggily defined one implicit in the 25% target? This could be made to sound a very damaging attack, but in fact it need not be. The divergence in any given year was not likely to be large, and it ought to be possible to re-work the sums on the basis of the new events and as a result to adapt the policies, as each year went by – indeed, not only possible but necessary. The really damaging point was the evident speed, not to say haste, with which the Plan was produced. This seemed to the

[1] For a view of how it seemed at the time to one participant, see my chapter 'The making of economic policy' in H. Thomas (ed), *Crisis in the Civil Service*, (London 1968).
[2] *The National Plan* (Cmnd. 2764) September 1965, para. 6.

demoniacally energetic Minister of the day a positive merit, or in any case a psychological and political necessity. It meant, however, among other things, that there was certainly no chance, within the eleven months from the election to publication, of exploring in any detail alternative growth paths.

The role of the Plan

The Wilson Government saw its major economic task as a two-fold one. The short-term urgent priority was to eliminate the huge external deficit. The medium-term one was the mixed one of converting that deficit into an adequate surplus to repay the debts incurred, and to speed up the rate of economic growth. This mixture can be seen on the opening page of the National Plan. The very first sentence reads: 'This is a plan to provide the basis for greater economic growth.'[1] The 'central challenge' however is to combine faster growth with an external surplus. 'We must succeed if we are to achieve all our objectives of social justice and welfare, of rising standards of living, of better social capital, and of a full life for all in a pleasant environment.'[2] From the very outset, then, a mixture of a goal and a constraint. 'An essential part of the Plan is a solution to Britain's balance of payments problem: for growth cannot be maintained unless we pay our way in the world.'[3] No one can argue, therefore, that the planners or the Government were hell-bent on faster growth to the exclusion of all else. It might have been better if they were.

But the Plan was not presented as a carefully calculated balance of alternative objectives. If 'heaven rejects the lore of nicely calculated less or more', so too apparently did the Government. Nowhere is there an explicit statement of how much an extra x% in the growth of GDP would be worth, in terms of higher overseas borrowing, or a longer working week, or of higher investment now and hence lower consumption now in order to have still higher consumption later.

Instead the single growth target alone was supreme. From that absolute followed all the other 'requirements' – of extra investment, of higher productivity, of higher exports – and (if the absolute were achieved) the other possibilities, in particular of higher personal and public consumption. But the Plan was not part of some optimizing exercise aimed at balancing a number of goals at the margin.

The making of the Plan[4]

The plan-making procedure is a dual one. Parallel with the econo-

---

[1] Cmnd. 2764, 1965, page 1, para. 1.

[2] Ibid., para. 5.

[3] Ibid., page 1, para. 1, sentence 2.

[4] The most authoritative description available is the Memorandum submitted by the DEA to the Sub-Committee on Economic Affairs of the Estimates Committee of the House of Commons. Cf. *Fourth Report on Government Statistical Services*, Session 1966–7 (HMSO December 1966), pages 290–316, and evidence, pages 317–22 and pages 431–8).

mic model-building of the central staff of the planning body (NEDC or DEA) went an Industrial Inquiry. One can thus distinguish an industrial and an economic or technical section. The first embraced as well the so-called 'Little Neddies', or Economic Development Committees (each one covering an industry or activity and set up under the NEDC), individual firms, research organizations, trade associations, and production ministries (such as the Ministries of Power, Technology and Transport). Their task was to conduct and assemble the Industrial Inquiry covering both the private and nationalized industries sectors of the economy. Their purpose was to provide the check on 'plausibility' in the planning process.

The economic or technical section had the task of providing the 'consistency' of the process: by covering the general relationships of the economic system, e.g. models of consumer behaviour, balance of payments projections, forecasts of money wages, and Government expenditure, and by calculating and applying the technical co-efficients, i.e. the functional ties or the structural relations which can translate the projected final demands into separate gross industrial outputs.

To be *both* plausible *and* consistent required a prolonged dialogue or confrontation between the two 'sides', as it were, of demands and supplies, to provide a test of the feasibility of the overall target, *given* the resources available *and* the policy measures possible.

The Industrial Inquiry started with the basic assumption of a 25% increase in GDP. Firms or trade associations or Little Neddies (as representatives of a particular industry) were asked to answer, to the best of their ability, the following wide range of questions. Year by year, how much output will be generated? How much for the home market and how much for exports? How much will total demand (home and foreign) be, and hence how much will imports be? Output for the home market was broken down by end-use, e.g. consumption, or capital formation, or defence or further processing. This then confronts the 'resources' necessary for this pattern of output – the major materials, fuels and purchased services: labour and capital. These last two were broken down into finer categories. For labour, what extra labour would be necessary (allowing for productivity growth) at national and regional level? What changes of occupation? What occupational and geographical shortages would arise? What training and redundancy problems would arise from the changing occupational and regional trends? And for capital, what extra capital would be required in the form of new buildings and works, and plant and machinery and vehicles? And what regional pattern of investment was necessary? Firms were also asked to calculate their actual investment expenditures in 1963 and 1964, their estimated definite commitments in each year from 1965 to 1967, and their present plans and expectations for those three years. They were also asked what increase in output could they produce with their existing capital stock and labour force (but with no increase in overtime working) and how large was the minimum labour force with which they could produce their current level of output with their existing capital stock.

A number of econometric cross-checks are possible to test the plausibility of the totals and sub-totals thrown up by these micro-economic answers. To test final consumer demand projections, past income elasticities can be used; for investment demand, incremental capital-output ratios can be used; and for intermediate demands, input/output coefficients can be established and used.

Thus the process of drawing up the National Plan consisted essentially of making an initial assumption about the rate of growth of total demand. From this follows the required *pattern* of the growth of demand. How much investment is needed to create the necessary growth of capacity? How much output must be exported or used to save imports in order to pay for the necessary growth in imports? As a residual, therefore, what growth of private and public consumption expenditure will be possible? But even within that residual total some items, e.g. much of the public expenditure programmes, are fixed for many years ahead, even though such expenditure is not 'necessary' to generate the target growth in total output. Thus the flexible elements of public expenditure (which are few in the short term) and personal consumption become the genuine residual. Will the pattern of growth in these items be acceptable? And will the growth be compatible with the savings propensities projected from past behaviour without any increase in tax rates to damp down the growth of consumer demand?

In principle, the next stage should then be to reconsider the initially assumed growth rate in the light of the implied demands for goods and hence resources, and to amend the assumptions, or to foreshadow the necessary policy changes. Somewhere, sometime, somehow a reasonably self-consistent picture should emerge from this iterative process, or process of successive approximations (or as it is sometimes more scathingly described, of going around in ever-decreasing circles).

All this is in order to produce *consistency* at a desired projected rate of overall growth. Is it all necessary? Market forces alone will, after all, produce consistency. Savings plans are made consistent with investment plans by fluctuations in real or money income. Demand intentions and supply intentions are made consistent by changes in prices or order-books or output. Exports and imports are made consistent by changes in incomes or in prices or in exchange rates.

But consistency is achieved without specifying *at what level*. Thus consistency may be achieved (as though there were some merit in that!) at unacceptably low levels of output, income and employment, or at an intolerable level of excess demand, and external deficit or inflation. Economic planning in the UK tried to achieve a superior consistency to that which would have come about naturally. First, it hoped to avoid the 'convoy problem' – that each sector of the economy would be limited to a growth rate determined by the growth rate of the slowest-growing sector. Secondly, it tried to achieve consistency *ex ante* rather than *ex post*:

Instead of the allocation pattern of investment being a product in the first instance of the guesses and expectations of a large number of independent entrepreneurs, in the long run 'revised' by *ex post* movements of market prices, economic planning essentially consists of an attempt to secure a co-ordinated set of investment decisions *ex ante* – in advance of any commitment of resources to particular constructional projects or installations.[1]

The Plan itself put the position in very similar terms:

The projections in the Plan are essentially attempts by Government and industry working in co-operation to break down the global objectives of a 25 per cent growth rate into its implications for particular industries. These projections should help firms and industries to make more informed decisions than if they were left in the dark about other people's intentions and beliefs.[2]

Some would argue that all this arithmetic was the least important part of the whole exercise. The Secretary of State, in his introduction to the Plan, put his emphasis thus:

The Plan is a guide to action. It must show who is responsible for what. The main things that have to be done, and by whom, have therefore been summarized in the check-list.[3]

The check-list contained no less than thirty-nine actions required, a mixture of permissive and causal acts. Among the former were cuts in overseas defence expenditure, limitations on private overseas investment and a ceiling on overseas aid, intended to improve our invisible current and the capital accounts of the balance of payments. On the trade balance, export actions included moves to develop fourteen ports, and to speed up the movement of exports; and an industry-by-industry search for ways to expand exports; plus some moves to improve Government assistance to exports. These were to parallel moves to save imports by a programme of the selective expansion of domestic agricultural output and an industry-by-industry search for ways to save imports.

At home, the permissive steps included a ceiling on the growth of public expenditure (it was to grow at $4\frac{1}{4}$% p.a.) and a rearrangement of the pattern (with a cut in defence spending and a rise in technical training).

The more causal steps included efforts to accelerate the standardization of output (through the Little Neddies) and the rationalization of industries (through the IRC); and to speed up management education and training. Much emphasis was put on stimulating investment – by encouraging the nationalized industries to plan on the basis of the Plan rate of growth; by

[1] M. Dobb, *Economic Planning and Growth* (London 1970), page 5.
[2] Cmnd. 2764, 1965, para. 14.
[3] Ibid., page 1.

switching Government assistance from investment allowances to investment grants; by encouraging new foreign investment in the UK, and longer-term planning of investment among UK firms (and as a by-product of a switch to Corporation Tax). A heavy emphasis was also put upon manpower policy – with schemes for lump-sum payments to redundant workers, earnings-related unemployment benefits and transferable pension rights – and in the related area of regional policy, in an effort to iron out the differences in the unemployment rates in different parts of the country.[1]

But when all is said and done, the critical conditions were three – the rate of growth of productivity and related to it, that of investment, and the state of the balance of payments. The first of these is not a factor on which the Government can act directly but the other two are at least under governmental influence if not governmental control. But in both cases, the cynic could well argue that the only influence actually brought to bear on each was wishful thinking. The 'virtuous circle' theory of growth would itself stimulate the necessary investment, once it was shown arithmetically to be necessary, while the external balance required an increase in our international competiveness which relied essentially on the hope of a supremely successful but voluntary prices and incomes policy.

The actual outcome

The DEA was set up in October 1964, and the National Plan was laid before the House of Commons in September 1965. For many people it was a great moment.[2] But it was to be only a moment.[3] Indeed one could date the life-cycle of the Plan as: 'conceived October 1964, born September 1965, died (possibly murdered) July 1966'. Nor is this unusual in the history of planning in many countries.[4]

The reason in this case was simple. 'Planning cannot . . . be divorced from politics. The ultimate choice among options is a political choice, not to be avoided by greater use of research and statistics.'[5] When it came to the ultimate choice, the Government preferred to sacrifice faster

---

[1] See Chapter 6 below.

[2] 'It is difficult to recall how significant a national event it seemed at the time: an improvement and logical culmination of the Tories' conversion to planning under Macmillan, Selwyn Lloyd and Maudling and their setting up of the NEDC.' Brian Lapping, *The Labour Government, 1964–70* (Harmondsworth, Penguin Special, 1970), pages 41–2.

[3] 'In September 1965, the DEA published the National Plan, 474 pages of it, and on 3 November 1965 the House of Commons resolved without a division "That this House welcomes the National Plan". Then the Government forgot all about it and got back to the sterling crisis.' D. Horne, *God is an Englishman* (Harmondsworth 1970), page 229.

[4] 'There is no doubt about the failure of these Plans. Most Development Plans are put aside soon after they are made: they rest on the shelf, not consulted even by the officials who have made them.' W. A. Lewis, *Development Planning* (London 1966), page 37.

[5] R. G. S. Brown, *The Administrative Process in Britain* (London 1970), page 254.

growth and full employment to the existing exchange rate, and not the other way round. In July 1966 fierce deflationary measures were imposed, together with a statutory wage and price freeze, in a frantic effort to close the external deficit and hopefully to reverse what many held to be a worsening *trend* in our external position.

This meant that growth was abandoned. That was a temporary price that the Government, the press, and presumably the country, were prepared to pay. But a policy for growth and planning had come to be identified with each other. The July 1966 measures destroyed not only growth, but also the Plan for growth and the very *idea* of planning for growth. This suggests that there are three separable views one could hold about the Plan: first, that it was an excellent, valuable, significant contribution to a growth policy which was swept away by outside events; or secondly, that the Plan was deficient in that it did not forecast the external deficit or, if it did, contain measures to deal with it; or thirdly, that the Plan was impotent anyway and was shot down as an innocent harmless bystander.

My view is largely the third, but with elements of the other two. The responsible Minister has argued that 'I still believe there was not all that much wrong with the Plan – it was our failure to adhere to it . . . So orthodox financial control won, and our basic social reformation failed.'[1]

It was, in other words, a political rather than a technical failure:

One of the assumptions we made was that the Plan would take priority and other policies pursued by the Government would be made to fit its provisions. In the event this was not done . . . and as a result the four per cent growth rate was made impossible of achievement.[2]

The blame or responsibility for this can be allocated widely. First is an institutional fact: the Plan was the product of a new Ministry, a new Minister and a new band of (relative) outsiders. If the Treasury had been given the task of producing the Plan, it is possible that it could have *imposed* the Plan at least on Whitehall. Tradition would not have been outraged: *amour propre* would not have become the vital factor in policy proposals and decisions that it undoubtedly was. We would also have been spared the spectacle of the irresistible force meeting the immovable object, head-on, until the former (the Secretary of State) was worn down and out. But politically and psychologically, it was impossible to allow or invite the Treasury to produce a Plan for more rapid growth.

The second factor in the destruction of the Plan was, of course, the continuing external crisis. This was yet another example of the triumph of the urgent over the important. 'Everyone no doubt agrees that faster growth is important', the financially orthodox argued, 'but the first priority must be to get the balance of payments right.' If this means

[1] Lord George-Brown, *Memoirs* (extracted in *Sunday Times*, 18 October 1970).
[2] Ibid.

'getting right' at the then ruling (and sacrosanct) exchange rate, and without any so-called 'artificial' restrictions of trade or payments overseas, the only methods left are a prices/incomes policy, or deflation. Since the former can make a big difference only over a long period, the only way left to deal with an enormous deficit is to abandon not merely more rapid growth, but perhaps any growth at all.

Thirdly, one could argue that the Plan itself was impotent. Far from being directive, or even indicative, it was simply subjunctive. *If* prices and incomes policy (which soon came to seem, with regional policy, the main activity of the DEA and of its Minister) succeeded, and *if* productivity, investment and capacity all accelerated, then . . . But each of these depended on the plausibility of the whole exercise, as well as being necessary conditions of its plausibility. The Plan had no teeth.

But this was not a weakness of planning as such. It was a lack of political will. A social democratic government trying to manage a mixed economy faces a continuing dilemma. Eager to produce results from an economic machine which it distrusts and which distrusts it, it is only too likely to swing between too much intervention and too little. In some areas, the Labour Government intervened swiftly, e.g. with the temporary import charge, but this was a typical 'market' device – indeed, quantitative restrictions on imports were explicitly rejected.

Within the Plan itself there were few weapons designed to *make* the Plan work. The prices and incomes policy was voluntary. The investment incentives were wholly non-selective, except as between construction on the one hand and plant and machinery on the other (where substitutability is nil) and as between the development areas and the rest of the country.[1] But there was no question of e.g. cheap finance for investment necessary for the Plan (by contrast with finance for shipbuilding, essential to match similar subsidies offered in other countries) or the denial of finance to certain industries or firms in order to concentrate resources in the 'worthy' industries or firms.[2]

In other words, the political will to pursue growth failed at two levels. When it came to the point, the maintenance of the exchange rate was preferred to faster growth (or even to any growth at all) and to the maintenance of full employment. But that moment of truth did not arrive until July 1966. Much earlier, indeed throughout the first two years of office, neither the objectives of the Plan nor the necessary conditions of its fulfilment were given top priority. Both macro- and microeconomic policies were tied only loosely if at all to the Plan.

One could also argue that the Plan was *technically* deficient. The data

[1] These operated as part of a distinctive regional policy, and were in fact supplemented by direct controls, in the form of IDCs and a ban on commercial building in London. Later (after the collapse of the Plan) came the regional twist in the SET and the REP. See Chapter 6.

[2] The IRC was invented later to encourage appropriate mergers and rationalizations, with the weapon of ready finance. See Chapter 5.

on which it was based were necessarily out of date and too crude, e.g. the co-efficients used in the input/output matrix were based on a Census of Production taken in 1954: with only rough estimates for 1960 and heroic guesses about trends over the Plan period. And this was the best that could be done as late as 1964! In certain critical areas, e.g. manpower, the data were even more deficient. In the middle of preparing the Plan, the Ministry of Labour 'lost' some 125,000 from the labour force, since they were missing from the mid-year count of National Insurance cards. This played havoc with two crucial steps in the analysis – the implicit past growth of productivity (which now seemed higher) and the size of the future work force. Frantic re-workings of numbers and equations, only for the lost thousands to be rediscovered some weeks later!

Any economist might argue that another glaring deficiency was the absence of any mention of prices, relative or absolute, in the Plan. If relative prices have a crucial allocative role in a market economy, how can this be justified? The answer is a complex one. In a world of administered prices, their allocative role is muted. Secondly, resources are assumed to be so mobile at the margin (or can be made so by policies on the regions, redundancy payments, elastic finance, and so on) that the mere existence of pockets of excess demand or supply will *per se* attract or repel resources.

The absence of any calculations of absolute prices is due to the traditional Treasury terror of giving a self-validating forecast of the rate of inflation. Hence all the calculations are at constant prices, except the rather tricky allowance in the balance of payments projections for an improvement in the terms of trade. Since this is not broken down into changes in export prices and import prices respectively, and since in any case the connection between changes in export and domestic prices for the same product is not stable, no deduction about the forecast rate of inflation can safely be made from this figure.

None the less the analysis of future consumption depends on knowing *absolute* price movements, since consumption is at least partly dependent on *disposable* income, which in turn depends on tax rates and (with a progressive tax structure) on the level and distribution of *money* incomes. But the committee working on prices, savings and taxes was the only Plan Committee whose papers were classified as 'secret' rather than merely confidential.

There is one technical sense whereby the mere existence of the Plan and its projections may be held to have made its own prospects worse. This is in the derivation of a 'norm' for the annual rate of increase of money incomes consistent with the growth of productivity. Those who believe that any norm always becomes a minimum will see the erection of a faster underlying growth rate to a projection of policy as a 'welcome sign' to higher wage demands.[1] Others will argue that, on the contrary, the enormous energy invested in laying the foundations of the prices and

[1] Cf. e.g. R. Caves (ed.), *Britain's Economic Prospects* (London 1968), page 118.

incomes policy over this period must have restrained both demands and settlements somewhat. In so far as such a policy was an essential part of the Plan for faster growth, one must hope so.

1970 – Projected and actual

Although the Plan was abandoned, it is interesting to compare its projections for 1970 with the actual results. Some of the main aggregates can be seen in Table 4.1. Actual growth fell well short of the Plan. But

TABLE 4.1   THE UK ECONOMY IN 1970

	National Plan Projections (1964 = 100)	Actual
Gross Domestic Product	125	114
Personal Consumption	121	113
Public Authorities Current Expenditure	119	112
Gross Fixed Capital Formation	138	120
Exports	136	142
Imports	126	132
Employment		
(i) Total Civil Employment	103	98
(ii) Industrial Production	102	95
(iii) Manufacturing	103	97
Output per man in		
(i) GDP	121	116
(ii) Industrial Production	128	120
(iii) Manufacturing	124	119

Source: *The National Plan* (Cmnd. 2764, 1965) and *National Institute Economic Review*, No. 55.

the productive potential of the UK economy grew faster than the 14% achieved. In 1964 the economy was fully employed (with registered unemployed at 1·6% of the work force), whereas by 1970 unemployment had risen to 2·5%, and was climbing slowly but steadily into 1971. It is hard if not impossible to know exactly how much surplus capacity existed in the economy, but it seems certain that the GDP could easily have been 3–4% higher in 1970.[1] Even allowing for this, economic growth fell short of the Plan's projections (although it reached just about the figure forecast by many of the DEA's more pessimistic critics).

As a consequence, personal consumption also grew by much less (13%) than the lavish projection (21%) of the Plan, and so too did the current expenditure of the public authorities (11 compared with 27%. This latter shortfall is something of a paradox; it partly reflects the policy foreshadowed in the Plan of cutting back severely the defence budget (which by 1970 was 12% below the 1964 budget in real terms). But the

[1] See *National Institute Economic Review*, February 1971, page 32.

civilian items of public expenditure were also trimmed back (in both 1966 and 1968) and that was definitely *not* part of the Plan.

The remaining source of domestic demand (and a vital factor in the growth of productive potential), viz. gross investment, also grew much more slowly (by 20%) than projected in the Plan (38%). The shortfall was very different in the three main sectors (see Table 4.2). 'Productive'

TABLE 4.2   INVESTMENT

	National Plan Projections (percentage increase 1964–70)	Actual Increase (1964–70)
Manufacturing and Construction	55	27
Public Corporations	30	5
Housing	32	−6

Source: ibid.

investment in the private sector grew at only half the projected rate, while in the public corporations it was little higher in 1970 than in 1964. But there was a peak in the middle of the Plan period – investment by these corporations in 1967 was no less than 23% greater in real terms than in 1970, partly in response to the very projections embodied in the Plan. When the economy failed in the event to grow at the projected rate, these corporations faced the imminent danger of surplus capacity, and cut back their investment severely. Part of the purpose of planning, it will be recalled, had been to keep investment on a steadily rising trend. Abandoning the Plan helped to perpetuate the instability of real investment.

Parallel with the shortfall in GDP – as both a consequence and a part-cause – was a shortfall in the growth in output per man. If one looks simply at the statistics, the only success seems to lie with the volume of exports. This outstripped the Plan projections by some $4\frac{1}{2}$%, projections which were dismissed at the time they were published as hopelessly optimistic. No doubt they were at the Plan's exchange rate of \$2.80. Equally extraordinary was the gigantic swing of over £1300m. from deficit to surplus in the overall balance of payments – but this too owes little to

TABLE 4.3   BALANCE OF PAYMENTS

(£m at 1964 prices)

	1964 Actual	1970 Plan	1970 Actual
Balance of Visible Trade	−534	−45	+2
Government Expenditure (Current and Capital net)	−555	−510	−550
Other Invisibles (net)	+561	+680	+1100
Private Long-term Capital (net)	−228	+75	−55
Balancing Item	+35	+50	+125
Overall	−721	+250	+622

anything in the Plan as such. Controls on private overseas investment played some part – but the main sources of the swing were the two factors which had no part, and indeed could have no part, in the Plan – devaluation and deflation. The former was ruled out by decision at the start of the Government's life, before the Plan was even started: and the latter was ruled out by implication as the very negation of planned full capacity growth which was the whole purpose of the Plan exercise.

What difference did it make?

Its essence lies not in the targets which you adopt for each industry but in the measures which are taken to promote private activity . . . The emphasis is therefore on economic policy rather than on figures.[1]

It is now the conventional wisdom that indicative planning, and the UK. National Plan in particular, are not only useless, but are a positive waste of time, a diversion of scarce resources from the real issues. Michael Kennedy writes,[2] for example, that 'the object of planning is not to tell the world what a lovely place it would be if there were no problems, but to look for the problems and solve them. In this respect the National Plan of 1965 must be judged a notable flop'.

This seems a somewhat perverse judgment. The alluring vision of 1970 was certainly presented on the assumption that the problems along the way had been solved – but the planning analysis had itself both identified and quantified those problems. Everyone knew that faster growth would require higher investment and higher foreign exchange earnings, and hence a double restraint on the amount of resources remaining to satisfy the projected demands of public and private consumption. But economic policy is about amounts. The policy-makers need to know, and to know well in advance, just *how big* a shift of resources and hence just how large a restraint on other uses, is necessary.

The most important 'internal' discovery of the National Plan was the dimensions of the crunch-year 1967. By working back from the target level of GDP in the target year, 1970, the level of investment needed no later than 1967 could be calculated, since by then the effective capacity available for the last Plan years would already be in existence. But forecasting from the winter of 1964/5 showed that investment would fall far short of this level.

Just as important were the consequences for the maximum possible growth of real personal and public consumption. Could the two be contained by a sufficient rise in the private savings ratio? And, if not, would the public 'stand for' the necessary rise in tax rates? How do you explain that in order to enjoy faster growth in living standards you may first have to suffer a slower growth?

[1] Sir W. Arthur Lewis, *Some Aspects of Economic Development* (London 1969), page 41.
[2] In A. R. Prest (ed.), *The U.K. Economy* (London, 2nd edition, 1968), page 40.

None of these questions is pointless. Nor are the answers trivial. And those answers are one justification of the planning exercise. But all this *is* a waste of time, energy, talent, morale, if none of it issues in policy. All the so-called 'Actions' in the Action List make sense, and would have made sense without any Plan. What was lacking was an overall strategy, and a subordination of economic policy, at both the macro- and micro-levels, to the Plan objectives. Those sectors of the economy which *were* adjusted to the Plan were the investment plans of the nationalized electricity industry, and the public expenditure totals. But this falls far short of a coherent and convincing overall strategy.

A more substantial criticism is the failure of the Plan and the planners, in conjunction with the short-term forecasters, to foresee the foreign exchange crisis of mid-1966. The Official Secrets Act forbids us to allocate responsibility between these two groups. Let us say simply that the real tragedy lay in the methods chosen to deal with the crisis. Direct action on the external balance would at least have maintained economic growth and full employment, and could have accelerated the shift of resources into the external balance which would have to occur at some date anyway. The actual chosen policy of a freeze and a squeeze destroyed growth and full employment, and did *not* of themselves shift resources. They (temporarily and misleadingly) closed the deficit simply by lowering the pressure of domestic demand – which is *not* a very clever trick.

The result

The deflationary measures adopted in July 1966 to deal with the foreign exchange crisis destroyed not only economic growth and full employment, but the National Plan as well, and the concept of planning, and the DEA as a planning Ministry, and the claim of the Labour Government to be able to manage the economy better than had their predecessors. The passage from panacea through bitter experience to music-hall joke which had been planning's fate in the first decade after the Second World War was repeated fifteen years later.

A wholly demoralized DEA produced another document – 'An Economic Assessment to 1972' – which it was careful to emphasize was *not* a plan but a planning document. It met one criticism of the National Plan by taking not simply one growth target, but a trio of possible paths of high, medium and low growth, which on a graph produced a 'wedge' over the years. This so-called wedge approach could cruelly be taken to mean that almost anything could happen, and its value in *indicative* planning must be (and was) virtually nil. Planning was many months dead already, or murdered.

5 Industrial policy

Andrew Graham

WHAT IS INDUSTRIAL POLICY?

The disagreements in economics are not just about the means used to pursue certain ends but also about whether the policies used can be regarded as ends in themselves – to advocate a policy of increased competition is to advocate a way of life and one in which the weak may suffer. If we are trying to be rational we should only begin to decide on the extent to which government intervention is desirable *after* an assessment of its possible effects. But the effects which can be achieved will depend on the kinds of intervention which are thought acceptable, which brings us back close to where we started.

Moreover, these problems can occur at different levels. An increase in leisure can be the aim and more productivity the means; or higher productivity the aim and more investment the means; or more investment the aim and a tax on distributed profits the means. We must, therefore, make clear our terms of reference. But this is not always possible because we have multiple objectives which interact. It may be that we also want this increase in productivity in order to help reduce costs and thus improve the balance of payments, or the tax on distributed profits to achieve greater equality of incomes – and equality may either be an end in itself and/or a means of achieving an incomes policy.

Nowhere are these difficulties greater than in industrial policy. Here many of the policies are designed to have long-term effects – which is when our imprecision is greatest. At the same time this tends to increase their dependence on related policies in other fields; indeed most other economic policies impinge on industrial performance in one way or another – commercial policy, labour market policy, and policies towards income distribution will all have their impacts on both business confidence and the attitudes of employees. Thus the boundaries of industrial policy are unclear. They are *not* wholly arbitrary, but they *will* shift with the party in power, the policy under discussion, *and* the viewpoint of the writer. The only way to begin, therefore, is to get inside and look sympathetically at the web of ends, means, and constraints that was the strategy of the Labour Party.

The aims

In their presentation to the electorate the aims were stated clearly enough in the 1964 Manifesto:

We want full employment; a faster rate of industrial expansion; a sensible distribution of industry throughout the country; an end to the present chaos in traffic and transport; a brake on rising prices and a solution to our balance of payments problems.[1]

There was also a statement of the means to be used:

None of these aims will be achieved by leaving the economy to look after itself. They will only be achieved by a deliberate and massive effort to modernize the economy; to change its structure and to develop with all possible speed the advanced technology and the new science based industries with which our future lies. In short, they will only be achieved by Socialist planning.[2]

Industrial policy in this period must therefore at very least include planning, and also such policies as were to be used to modernize the economy and change its structure. In addition it must be seen as aiming both at increasing productivity and improving the balance of payments.

The diagnosis

The reason why industrial policy was to take such an active role becomes clear when one looks at the Labour Party view of the efficacy of the usual fiscal and monetary controls.[3] According to the diagnosis of the Party strategists[4] there were four reasons for thinking such policies were likely to be insufficient for reconciling the multiple aims of the Party:

(*i*) The problems were long term in nature.[5] The low rate of growth, the adverse trend in the balance of payments and the regional disparities had all existed at least since the First World War. This did not prove that traditional policies were incapable of correcting them but it did suggest that a basic change was needed.

(*ii*) The problems were interdependent. We grew slowly because of the balance of payments, yet the balance of payments was weak partly because we grew slowly.[6] Moreover, the conventional policies did not

[1] Labour Party General Election Manifesto 1964, page 8.
[2] Ibid.
[3] 'Monetary planning is not enough. What is needed is structural changes in British industry.' Rt. Hon. H. Wilson, Speech to the Annual Conference of the Labour Party, Scarborough 1963.
[4] It is crucial to remember that there is never just one diagnosis nor just one view of what policy should be. The interpretation given here is based mainly on Wilson's speeches preceding the election and on the views of his closest adviser—Thomas (now Lord) Balogh. See in particular *Planning for Progress: A Strategy for Labour* (Fabian Tract 346, July 1963).
[5] See Mr Wilson's speech at Brangwyn Hall, Swansea, 25 January 1964, where he distinguished the short-run balance of payments deficit from the long-run problems.
[6] The first argument is well known. The second assumes that one's rate of inflation relative to other countries is less, the faster the growth in one's productivity, and/or

break into this circle. Deflation to correct the balance of payments not only caused unemployment but also tended to slow down growth, while devaluation was seen at best as buying time and at worst as just increasing inflation.[1]

(*iii*) The price mechanism was increasingly ineffective. First, market valuations were inadequate reflections of true costs or true demands because of (*a*) oligopolies (*b*) trade unions (*c*) advertising (*d*) costs and benefits external to the firm[2] and (*e*) managers who were not necessarily profit maximizers. Secondly, inflation was possible below full employment[3] because of (*a*) and (*b*). And thirdly, policies which assumed profit maximizing responses to price signals were made less effective by (*e*).

(*iv*) Power was increasingly concentrated and promotion to the positions of power remained hierarchical. The result was thought to be the in-efficiency of those already there, combined with an inability to infiltrate new approaches and new techniques into management, the universities, and the Civil Service.[4,5] However, there was also recognition that in industry this power was often associated with large-scale operations and that these could be more efficient – the problem was to control their behaviour.[6]

The means: the strategy in outline

Industrial policy was therefore a reaction to the apparent failure of previous policies and it was in its details that a new approach was to be adopted. The means which were to be used were first spelt out in the 1964 Manifesto and were further developed in the following two years – in particular in the National Plan published in September 1965 and in the Manifesto for the March 1966 election. If one puts the pieces together the strategy ran roughly as follows:

that the faster the rate of innovation the faster the growth in exports. See T. Balogh *Productivity and Inflation* (Oxford Economic Papers, 1958) and M. V. Posner, *International Trade and Technical Change* (Oxford Economic Papers, October 1961).

[1] 'Unless the policies which lead to devaluation – liberalisation, reliance on "free" market mechanism – are reversed and supplanted by a coherent plan for economic development including a balanced social incomes policy, devaluation will be forced upon us but will not solve our problem, but will lead to renewed unbalance due to the same causes.' T. Balogh, *Planning for Progress*, page 25.

[2] For a fuller discussion of (*c*) and (*d*) and the role of income distribution see M. Lipton, *Assessing Economic Performance* (London 1968), pages 67–85.

[3] Assuming that one does not define full employment to be that level consistent with price stability!

[4] '[A] symptom of Britain's declining vigour is the growth of new forms of privilege and the rapid concentration of economic power which has taken place since 1951.' *Signposts for the Sixties*, page 9.

[5] For a discussion of the Civil Service see H. Thomas (ed.), *Crisis in the Civil Service* (London 1968).

[6] 'In terms of efficiency these vast centralised concerns are often, but by no means always, justified. . . . The greatest single problem of modern democracy is how to ensure that the handful of men who control these great concentrations of power can be responsive and responsible to the nation.' *Signposts for the Sixties*, page 10.

(*i*) Productivity was to be increased. At the macro level this was to be achieved by an increase in investment through a combination of a high and steadily expanding level of demand, and by selective investment incentives in the form of cash grants and a change in the corporate tax structure. This was to be further reinforced at the level of the individual industry and firm by policies aimed at structural change, modernization of techniques, and economies of scale. These were to be brought about by financial incentives, by the use of the Industrial Reorganization Corporation to promote mergers in selected industries, by an increase in Government-sponsored research (and by a change in its *direction* from pure to applied and from military to civil), and by Government purchasing policy to encourage standardization.

(*ii*) This increase in productivity was to be accompanied by an incomes policy so that wage costs per unit of output would be decreased by the joint effect of lower money wages and higher real output per man employed.

(*iii*) These reductions in costs were to be accompanied by pressure on prices so as to ensure that the benefits of reduced costs were realized, and so as to stimulate further cost reduction. In industries with large numbers of firms this pressure was to come through increased competition achieved by the continued abolition of Resale Price Maintenance in the retail trade, by the extension of legislation on restrictive practices,[1] by legislation for the provision of greater information in company accounts, and from increased protection for the consumer (via bodies such as the Consumer Council and by legal protection against misleading sales techniques). Alternatively, where competition did not exist, the pressure on prices was to come from Government supervision – 'Labour will give teeth to the Monopolies Commission . . . and take powers to review unjustified price increases.'[2]

(*iv*) In addition, the creation of new monopolies and sources of industrial power was to be supervised (again through a strengthened Monopolies Commission, which was to be given powers to control takeover bids and mergers).

(*v*) Last, but by no means least, this increased intervention in industry was to be achieved without undermining social priorities. 'Technical change tempered with humanity' as Harold Wilson called it at the TUC Conference in September 1964. This meant fiscal policies, such as the introduction of a Capital Gains Tax and equity in the operation of incomes policy. But it also meant greater planning of industrial policy, and this was certainly taken to mean greater consultation with trade unionists on what industrial policies and plans should be – 'high level democracy' as Anthony Crosland called it.[3] Indeed, planning permeated

---

[1] 'Labour is going . . . to close the loopholes in the legislation on restrictive practices in industry.' *The Fight against High Prices* (Labour Party Pamphlet, January 1965).
[2] Labour Party General Election Manifesto 1964, page 12.
[3] C. A. R. Crosland. *The Future of Socialism* (revised edition, London 1964), page 263.

all the other policies. There were to be planned growth of incomes, plans to modernize the economy, and plans for each industry, which were intended to be the guides to action, the background against which decisions on particular policies could be taken.

This then was the strategy. The parts which concern us in this chapter are the measures to increase productivity and investment, the policies for structural change, the supervision of economic behaviour, the control of economic power, and the role which planning played in these. We look first at the ways in which the policies were expected to work, secondly at the results which they seem to have had, thirdly at the doubts there could be about the causal mechanisms involved and the appropriateness of policy, and last, but not least, at the consistency of policy and how it changed during the period.

There are, in fact, three quite distinct phases. The first runs from October 1964 to July 1966[1] during which expansion was maintained. The second is from July 1966 to November 1967 when the Government was trying to avoid devaluation by deflation, and the third from the end of 1967 onwards when the main concern was to make devaluation work, and in which any major initiative of policy was constrained by the approaching election. As we shall see these time periods had a strong influence on the type of industrial policy, in terms of the objectives that were considered important, the speed with which policy was intended to work and the kinds of policy considered acceptable.

THE POLICIES USED

Planning

It was during the first period that the role of planning was at its height. The Department of Economic Affairs (the DEA) was established in October 1964; the Economic Development Committees (the EDCs) were rapidly expanded, and the National Plan was published by September 1965.[2] Planning was intended to help in four interrelated ways:

(*i*) It was a form of large-scale market research in which it was hoped that industry and Government would swap information, become better informed, and as a result take better decisions. More particularly it was hoped that bottlenecks to growth would be identified which could be

---

[1] This is certainly the turning point in economic terms, although one could well argue that politically the dividing line should be the General Election of March 1966. Until then there was a Parliamentary majority of only four so that it would probably have been impossible to have carried through any major change in the direction of policy.

[2] *The National Plan* (Cmnd. 2764, 1965).

removed either by consultation with industry, or by specific policies on the part of Government.

(*ii*) As a result of (*i*), plus a commitment by the Government to aim at a higher rate of growth (and thus by implication to expand demand) it was hoped to shift demand expectations and to encourage firms to plan for long-term expansion. If an important determinant of investment is expected demand, and if increased investment can cause increased growth, then belief in a higher rate of growth may be self-fulfilling – particularly if investments by individual industries and firms are complementary to each other.

(*iii*) Planning was a way of extending consultation and increasing participation in the decision-making process. Through the use of the planning machinery (the EDCs, the Regional Planning Boards, etc.) it was hoped that decisions would be less imposed from the centre and there would be a greater willingness to carry them out.

(*iv*) Finally, it was seen as the framework within which the divergencies between social and private costs could be identified. It was hoped that the plan would indicate the areas in which the market mechanism was failing most significantly which could then be corrected by appropriate policy.

Planning was therefore intended both as an end itself – an extension of democracy – and as a means of changing attitudes, of improving decisions, and of encouraging business men to look further ahead. By these means it was hoped to increase the stability and amount of investment and to improve its allocation.

Fiscal incentives to investment

(a) Investment grants
In January 1966 both the form and the direction of the fiscal incentives to investment were changed.[1] Investment allowances were discontinued and replaced by cash grants.[2] These were obtainable by applying to the

---

[1] Department of Economic Affairs, *Investment Incentives* (Cmnd. 2874, 1966).

[2] Before 1966 all purchases of capital goods had benefited from three main types of allowance which reduced the amount of profits liable to tax. An *annual* allowance – this usually consisted of setting off against tax a fixed proportion of the written down value of the asset at the end of the preceding year; the idea being that the use of the asset should not be taxed with the sum of the annual allowances equalling the cost of the asset. (In effect this still left a small net tax since the present value of future tax reductions is less than the present value of the investment.) An *initial* allowance – this permitted a firm to depreciate an asset in the first year of its life by more than the usual annual allowance in that year. This was equivalent to an interest-free loan since the firms simply benefited from the annual allowances earlier – the total remained unchanged. An *investment* allowance – this allowed an amount *in excess* of the total cost of the asset to be offset against tax. The third of these was the important subsidy to investment and this was the only allowance that was completely removed.

Board of Trade and were concentrated on the manufacturing and extractive industries. In addition the regional variation was increased and assets such as computers and ships received special assistance – Table 5.1 shows the details.

TABLE 5.1   MAIN CHANGES IN INVESTMENT INCENTIVES

Percentages

| | Before January 1966 | | | After January 1966 | | |
| | Grants[a] | Taxation Allowances | | Grants | Taxation Allowances | |
		Investment	Initial		Investment	Initial
Industrial Buildings and Structures	25[a]	15	5	25 or 35[a]	—	15
Plant and Machinery						
(a) Manufacturing and Extractive Industries	—	30	10	20[b]	—	—
(b) Other Industries	—	30	10	—	—	30
Vehicles (other than private cars)						
(a) Special types of mobile equipment (e.g. fork lift trucks)	—	30	10	20	—	—
(b) Other	—	30	10	—	—	30
Computers	—	30	10	20	—	—
Ships	—	40	free depreciation[c]	20	—	free depreciation[c]
Scientific Research						
1. Plant and Machinery						
(a) Qualifying process	—	30	100% write off	20[b]	—	100% write off
(b) Other	—	30	100% write off	—	—	100% write off
2. New Buildings	25[a]	30	100% write off	25 or 35[a]	—	100% write off

[a] These grants were given under the Local Employment Act and were conditional on adequate provision of employment.
[b] 40% in the new category of development areas.
[c] Free depreciation means that tax allowances can be claimed at the time best suited to the recipient.

Source: Cmnd. 2889

The *aims* of the change were (*i*) to help the balance of payments by giving 'priority to those sectors which can make the greatest contribution to the balance of payments',[1] (*ii*) to attract investment in the less prosperous regions, and (*iii*) to encourage investment by firms where current

[1] *Investment Incentives*, page 6.

investment was greater than their current profits and who were therefore unable to take full advantage of the investment allowances. Such firms could be the young and rapidly growing ones so that the cash grant would have helped both growth and competition by encouraging new entrants.[1]

The grants were also thought to be more effective as a *means* of encouraging investment. Inquiries had shown that many firms used very crude methods of investment appraisal – some even assessed projects on a pretax basis.[2] It was hoped therefore that as cash grants were more obvious, paid quicker, and more certain than tax allowances (which depended upon both tax rates and profits in the future) firms would take more notice of them.

(b) Corporation Tax

The intention to introduce Corporation Tax was announced in 1964 and further details were given in the Budget of 1965, but it only came fully into operation in April 1966 when the rate was fixed at 40%. It was intended to contribute to three objectives – equity, investment, and the balance of payments. In terms of equity all incomes to persons were to be treated alike as far as possible irrespective of whether that income accrued from earnings, salaries, dividends or capital gains. To achieve this it was thought necessary to separate personal from corporate taxation.[3]

This was attempted by changing from a system in which all profits were taxed at some 56% (profits tax 15%, plus the standard rate of income tax at whatever rate applied) and then dividends distributed with no further tax liability unless the recipient paid surtax, to one in which total profits were taxed at 40% and then dividends taxed again at the marginal rate for the individual.

The consequences expected from this were threefold. First, to encourage the retention of profits rather than their distribution, secondly to cause a switch from ordinary share issues to fixed interest borrowing (where the interest is deductible), and thirdly to discourage company investment overseas (as the tax exemption of profits earned abroad by overseas trading corporations was lost).

From the point of view of investment it was hoped that the probable higher level of retentions (and the associated lower tax position of those companies who did retain) would lead either to more investment (because

[1] Investment allowances were able to be offset against *later* profits so the major impact of the change to investment grants was on a firm's overall liquidity rather than on the rate of return of individual projects.

[2] See R. R. Neild, 'Replacement policy' (*National Institute Economic Review*, November 1964). D. C. Corner and Alan Williams, 'The sensitivity of business to initial and investment allowances', *Economica*, Vol. 32, February 1965, and *Report of the Committee on Turnover Taxation* (the 'Richardson Committee') (Cmnd. 2300, 1964), page 77.

[3] See the detailed arguments in *Royal Commission on the Taxation of Profits and Incomes, Final Report: Memorandum of Dissent* by G. Woodcock, H. L. Bullock and N. Kaldor (Cmd. 9474, 1955).

of increased liquidity and/or because of reduced costs of finance) or at least to more savings since some of the distributed profits would previously have been consumed. More tortuously, it might also have been argued that if the balance of payments was improved in the short term by lower capital outflows then a higher level of home demand would have been possible which could, in its turn, have increased domestic investment.[1,2]

In addition one must look at Corporation Tax and investment grants together since the introduction of investment grants was an essential accompaniment to Corporation Tax. First, Corporation Tax on its own would have reduced the value of the investment allowances.[3] Secondly, in certain cases, its objective of lowering taxation on companies who retained profits would have been frustrated. The old investment allowances reduced a company's liability to Corporation Tax but did not reduce the income tax payable on the dividends. Thus where a company paid low dividends relative to gross profits but high dividends relative to taxable profits (i.e. after the allowances) it would still have been possible for them to pay more tax under the Corporation Tax even though they were doing the 'right' thing. By shifting to cash grants, which were neither liable to Corporation Tax nor reduced tax liability, the effect was to tax firms as if they were not doing any investment so that Corporation Tax was left free to have the intended result.[4] The firms did of course still get the cash grant and benefit from that.

Harcourt[5] has shown that for those assets which were eligible for a 30% investment allowances before 1966 and a 20% cash grant after that date the change to Corporation Tax reduced the value of incentives, but that investment grants largely restored it.[6] However the net effect depends very much on the length of life of the project, its pre-tax profitability, and on the pay out ratio[7] of the firm. In general the net effect

[1] This argument presupposes first that other methods of improving the balance of payments were impossible or inadequate, and secondly that the effect on the capital account would have been large enough to lead to different policies towards aggregate demand.

[2] It is also worth noting that Trade Unionists on NEDC had urged restraint of overseas investment. They believed that this overseas investment was at the expense of home investment and regarded restrictions on it as part of a *quid pro quo* for an incomes policy. Moreover whether their beliefs are right or wrong it is still rational to take them into account.

[3] Ignoring discounted cash flow then a 30% investment allowance under the old system was worth 30×0.5625 (profits tax and income tax), but under the Corporation Tax only 30×0.40 (Corporation Tax).

[4] See *Investment Incentives,* page 6.

[5] G. C. Harcourt, 'Cash Investment Grants, Corporation Tax and Pay Out Ratios' (*Bulletin of the Oxford University Institute of Statistics,* August 1966) and the correction in *Bulletin,* February 1967.

[6] A similar conclusion is reached by Richard A. and Peggy B. Musgrave in Richard E. Caves (ed.) *Britain's Economic Prospects* (London 1968), page 60.

[7] Distributed profits as a percentage of total profits after taxation and allowances and less depreciation.

will have been more beneficial (or less adverse) the longer the length of life of the project and the lower the pay-out ratio.[1]

The main ways in which Corporation Tax and investment grants later changed were:

(*i*) In December 1966 the rates of investment grants were increased by 5% (from 20% to 25%, and from 40% to 45% in the development areas). This higher level was applicable only during 1967 and 1968 and was intended as a counter cyclical measure.

(*ii*) Hotel building and equipment were made eligible for a 20% grant in March 1968 and extra grants were given in the development areas. This was aimed partly at regional policy and partly at increasing foreign exchange earnings from tourism.

(*iii*) Corporation Tax was increased twice from 40% to 42·5% in November 1967 (at the time of devaluation) and to 45% in the Budget of 1969. The first of these was intended partially to offset the switch in favour of profits expected to follow from devaluation.

One serious anomaly which arose was in the case of investment grants paid for ships. These grants were paid on assets irrespective of whether they were manufactured in the UK. Although this was partially to help the shipping industry by allowing it to purchase wherever it wished, it was much more because to do otherwise would have been to discriminate in favour of home suppliers which would have contravened our obligations under GATT and EFTA. However, this produced the strange situation that foreign companies could set up a subsidiary in the UK, order their ships from abroad, and then operate them between foreign countries with the UK paying 20%.[2] As a result between January 1966 and September 1969 the total of investment grants paid or due to be paid for ships on order amounted to no less than £285 million of which £91 million was for ships ordered by UK companies owned by non-residents.[3] These anomalies were eventually realized and two years after the investment grants scheme began, the arrangements were modified to include a special balance of payments test on orders placed by foreign-owned companies registered in the UK after 1963. But this was still unsatisfactory and in 1969 an Industrial Development (Ships) Bill was introduced so as to apply a similar test to all grants on ships – except that is on ships built in the UK *and* those built in EFTA and the Irish Republic – in other words at least half of the original problem was still allowed to go on!

[1] This ignores, of course, any effects on investment via liquidity or via business men taking more notice of grants than allowances.
[2] This is equivalent to Chrysler buying its equipment in Germany via its UK subsidiary and then installing it in Detroit, in a situation where the Government was trying to improve the balance of payments, restrict overseas investment, and cut public expenditure!
[3] *Committee of Inquiry into Shipping* ('The Rochdale Committee') (Cmnd. 4337, 1970), page 366.

Fiscal incentives for structural change (Selective Employment Tax)

The major fiscal measure aimed at a structural change in the economy was Selective Employment Tax (SET). This was announced in May 1966 and came into effect on 5th September of the same year.[1] In its initial form this was a tax of £1·25 for men, 62·5p for women and boys, and 40p a week for girls. All industries paid it but manufacturing industries received a refund of some 130%, and the public sector plus transport a refund of 100%. It was therefore a small subsidy to manufacturing and a significant tax on construction, distribution, and services. At the time of its introduction its particular attraction was as a new large source of revenue. Moreover it was able to be introduced quickly and it was administratively cheap to operate as it was collected through the existing National Insurance stamp scheme. However, it is in its long-term objectives that it sits most easily with other policies. It was able to have Regional Employment Premium (REP) grafted on to it;[2] it broadened the tax base; and to the extent that services are purchased relatively more by higher-income groups it marginally increased equity.[3]

In terms of industrial policy its major and most contentious claim was that it would increase productivity. At the simplest level this was supposed to occur in the services sector. Here SET was a tax of about 7% on labour cost and a substitution of capital for labour was expected as a result. In practice this might occur less from a change in technique in the individual unit than by a switch within the service sector from one unit to another, e.g. from the labour-intensive shop to Marks & Spencers – at least producing some increase in output per person employed.[4]

A more subtle and influential possibility originates from Professor Kaldor.[5] He argues:[6]

---

[1] *Selective Employment Tax* (Cmnd. 2986, 1966).

[2] This had the attraction of being one of the few large export subsidies consistent with GATT and, in fact, it seems likely that the scheme was conceived as a whole from the start. It was probably not implemented at the same time either because the administrative arrangements were not ready or because the usual budget secrecy had made sufficient discussion by the Cabinet impossible before the budget announcement.

[3] See E. B. Butler and R. Gidlow, 'The Selective Employment Tax', *Moorgate and Wall Street: A Review*, Autumn 1966, pages 81–2. They also discuss the constraints surrounding the introduction of SET.

[4] This may not mean a rise in productivity since capital inputs or other labour inputs (e.g. housewives waiting in queues) may increase.

[5] Kaldor was special adviser on taxation to the Chancellor of the Exchequer at the time when SET was introduced.

[6] N. Kaldor, *Causes of the Slow Rate of Economic Growth of the United Kingdom*, Inaugural lecture at Cambridge (Cambridge 1966). See also J. N. Wolfe, 'Productivity and growth in manufacturing industry: some reflections on Professor Kaldor's Inaugural Lecture', *Economica*, May 1968; N. Kaldor, 'Productivity and growth in manufacturing industry: a Reply', *Economica*, November 1968; and N. Kaldor, *Strategic Factors in Economic Development* (Ithaca, N.Y., 1967).

(*i*) that productivity growth in manufacturing is faster, the more rapid the growth in manufacturing output. This is because, in this sector, there is increasing specialization and learning causing dynamic economies of scale – some of which are external to the firm but internal to the sector.[1]

(*ii*) that labour released by manufacturing in recession tends to be absorbed in other sectors and that, conversely, productivity in these sectors would be *in*creased if they lost labour – and to the extent that economies of scale do exist in services these can be taken advantage of by amalgamating the existing units which tend to be small.

(*iii*) that the transfer of labour to manufacturing does not occur in an economy such as the UK because earnings in the different sectors are at roughly comparable levels. Thus a constraint on the supply of labour to manufacturing would, according to Kaldor, show up in a general rise in wages rather than in a widening differential.

Of course, even if this distinction between manufacturing and services is valid, there is probably no very exact line between them and anomalies are likely to occur. Although, therefore, SET was increased twice (by 50% in the 1968 Budget, and by 28% in the 1969 Budget), a significant number of alterations were made to it – though some of the changes reflect other pressures on the Government. The most important of these were the concessions to quarrying and fishing industries (in May 1966), the exemption of many part-time workers and those over 65 and the refunds to hotels in the rural parts of development areas (Budget 1968), and the small additions made to those industries classified as 'manufacturing' (Budget 1969).

Institutional intervention

(a) The Industrial Reorganization Corporation
The Industrial Reorganization Corporation (the IRC) was set up in January 1966. This was a completely new agency, reporting to the DEA,[2] but financially and executively independent of it, charged with 'promoting industrial efficiency and profitability and assisting the economy of the UK', and with the power to '(*i*) promote or assist the reorganization of development of any industry; or (*ii*) if requested so to do by the Secretary of State, establish or develop, or promote or assist the establishment or development of, any industrial enterprise.'[3]

In order to carry out these functions the IRC was given power to draw

---

[1] '[This] does not require that manufacturers' cost curves be downward sloping, but only that they fall relatively fast through time.' P. N. Oppenheimer, 'Economic theory and the Selective Employment Tax', *Westminster Bank Review*, November 1966, page 23.
[2] Cross links were also established with the Ministry of Technology, the Board of Trade, and other bodies whose work impinged on the IRC to try to avoid duplication of effort or 'getting at cross purposes'. See *IRC Report and Accounts 1967/68*.
[3] Industrial Reorganization Corporation Act (1966).

on financial resources of up to £150 million, which could be used to acquire, and dispose of securities; to form new corporate bodies; to make loans; to give guarantees of loans given by others; and to acquire and place at the disposal of others, premises, plant, machinery and other equipment.

The IRC operated by an initial emphasis on discussions with top management to establish whether apparently desirable mergers, or rationalization, or modernization were occurring. There was a 'two way traffic of ideas, inquiries and proposals',[1] as a result of which useful changes might occur without further help from the IRC. However, if they did not, the IRC was then able to back up its ideas by giving quick and flexible financial support.

Attention was focused first on the electrical and electronics industry. The IRC encouraged the takeover of AEI by GEC,[2] and the merger between English Electric and Elliott Automation,[3] and approved of the subsequent merger between GEC and English Electric.[4] Secondly, it looked at the more fragmented mechanical engineering industry, where as the IRC claimed there was 'an almost unanimous view that structural change is needed'.[5] At the request of the Government it also took a 15% share-holding in Rootes Motors and appointed a director to the Board when voting control was allowed to pass to Chrysler in January 1967,[6] and in 1968 it made a £25 million loan to encourage the merger between British Motor Holdings and Leyland Motors.[7,8]

Its most controversial activities were interventions which it made in the ball-bearing industry and in the scientific instrument industry, in both of which the IRC gave the support of its funds in takeover battles. In the ball-bearing industry there was initially the possibility of a merger between Ransome and Marles, and Skefko (the largest producer with about 27% of the domestic market, and a subsidiary of SKF of Sweden), but this would probably have meant control passing outside the UK. The IRC preferred a merger between the UK-owned companies – Ransome and Marles, Hoffman, and Pollard – who together shared about 35% of the market. As a result in the autumn of 1968 the IRC with the Government's support, asked SKF not to pursue their merger. They were told of the IRC's plans and invited to become associated, but

---

[1] *IRC Report and Accounts 1967/68.*

[2] AEI resisted this. As a result Sir Charles Wheeler (of AEI) resigned from the IRC Board.

[3] The IRC made a loan to English Electric of £15 million interest free until 31 August 1969, and thereafter 8% payable half yearly. *IRC Report and Accounts 1967/68.*

[4] See the detailed statement in *IRC Report and Accounts 1968/69,* Appendix 3.

[5] *IRC Report and Accounts 1967/68.*

[6] *IRC Report and Accounts 1967/68,* Appendix 2.

[7] Donald Stokes was a member of the IRC board. Such interlinks are perhaps inevitable, but they make it more difficult to believe in the impartiality of such bodies.

[8] A subsequent loan of £10 million was made in May 1970 to British Leyland for purchases of machine tools designed to stimulate orders for that industry.

negotiations rapidly broke down over the question of control. Faced either with no merger at all or control outside the UK, the IRC made a cash offer for -- and acquired – Brown Bailey Ltd (who had a controlling interest in Hoffman). As a result the IRC was able to invite Pollard to join the new company. However, Pollard had started negotiations with Skefko and on 8 April 1969 announced agreement on terms with them. But the IRC, using its base in Hoffman had been able to merge this with Ransome and Marles, and after consultation with the latter decided to support Ransome's in a bid for Pollard's which was successful on 21 May. Thus at the end of a long struggle the desired three-way grouping was achieved.

It became clear from these cases and from the IRC statements[1] that the Board of IRC saw its aims as threefold. First, they aimed to increase productivity by improving the logical structure of industry. This was to be achieved by reducing product differentiation and also by reducing the duplication of production where this would lead to economies of scale. Moreover, they primarily did this where they hoped this would help the balance of payments. Secondly, they aimed to promote (or at least not harm) regional development. Thirdly, they aimed at retaining company control in the UK. This last may have been regarded as an end in itself, but more sensibly it should be seen as a means of achieving the first two objectives. The other means used was persuasion which was backed up if need be by loans, and in certain cases by direct intervention in mergers and bids – exactly as had been promised in the manifestos.

(b) The Monopolies Commission

Closely related to the IRC were the changes made in the powers of the Government to inquire into monopolies and proposed mergers. The Monopolies and Mergers Act (1965) carried out the commitment given in the 1964 Manifesto to 'control takeover bids and mergers'. In addition to enlarging the membership of the Monopolies Commission the most important changes were:

(*i*) Power to enquire into the supply of services on reference by the Board of Trade. (Clause 2.)

(*ii*) Additional powers for the Board of Trade to act on the reports of the Monopolies Commission. They were able to 'require the publication of price lists, to regulate prices, to prohibit acquisitions or to impose conditions on acquisitions . . . [and] . . . to provide for the dissolution of monopolies and mergers'. (Clause 3.)

(*iii*) Powers for the Board of Trade to refer mergers, to delay them while a report was being prepared, and to dissolve them if the Monopolies Commission reported that they were against the public interest. (Clause 6).

(*iv*) Special provision to deal with newspaper mergers. (Clause 8.)

[1] See particularly *IRC Report and Accounts 1969/70*.

Essentially therefore the Act greatly increased the discretionary power of the Board of Trade. The Monopolies Commission itself had no executive authority, and there was no *automatic* requirement that a monopoly or merger, however large, be referred to it. The result was that the Act itself was only one small part of the policy. The rest consisted of the machinery for choosing references, the number and type of references which the Government made, and the action which the Government took on any subsequent recommendations by the Monopolies Commission.[1]

In the case of mergers, the first only became clear in 1969 when, in response to criticisms of inconsistencies between the use of the IRC and the Monopolies Commission, the Government gave details of the way in which mergers were given preliminary scrutiny. This publication[2] revealed the existence of an inter-departmental Mergers Panel under Board of Trade chairmanship, and including representatives from other Government departments directly concerned. The mechanism appears to have been that once a merger became known to the Board of Trade (usually through the financial press), they then had to decide whether it came within the scope of the Act. If so, information was collected by the Board of Trade from all available sources (usually including the companies concerned, and, in some cases, their suppliers and customers) and this material was presented to the Panel. On the basis of this a recommendation would be made to the Board of Trade as to whether or not there was a prima facie case for a reference to the Monopolies Commission. Before making their final decision, in a number of cases the Board had further consultations with the companies concerned and this sometimes led to assurances about the companies' future policy. These assurances have been influential and have included such diverse topics as consultation with the unions, the form of company accounts after the merger, future policy on investment and exports where the takeover was by a foreign firm, and due regard for regional policy. Indeed, the Board adds that these assurances[3] were important in their decisions not to refer (1) Chrysler/Rootes; (2) GEC/AEI; (3) International Computers Ltd; (4) EMI/ABPC; (5) GEC/English Electric; (6) General Foods/Rowntree; (7) Ross/Associated Fisheries (trawling interests)[4] and (8) Distillers/United Glass.

Two other features emerge. First, this whole process was conducted extremely rapidly. In 90% of cases a decision was reached within three weeks, and in 75% of cases within two weeks. Secondly, a very small proportion of mergers were examined by the Monopolies Commission. Of some 350 mergers which came with the scope of the Act during the

---

[1] The recommendations are outside the control of the Government except, of course, that they choose the members of the Monopolies Commission in the first place.

[2] *Mergers: A Guide to Board of Trade Practice* (HMSO, 1969).

[3] Though the full details of the assurances were not made public.

[4] It was this case in particular which led to criticisms of inconsistency between the IRC and the Monopolies Commission. Before this the Monopolies Commission had found a very similar proposal to be against the public interest.

period July 1965 to April 1969, only 10 were referred to the Commission (excluding two newspaper mergers). Yet four of these were found to be against the public interest. These were Ross/Associated Fisheries, United Drapery Stores/Montague Burton, Rank/De La Rue, and Barclays/Lloyds and Martins. In the last case of the banks the majority on the Commission (6–4) was not sufficient to constitute a formal recommendation to the Board of Trade, but the Government accepted the conclusion and in this case, as in all others, the parties voluntarily dropped their merger plans without any further action by the Board of Trade.

A similar approach was adopted to monopolies. In the period 1965 to 1969 only fourteen specific and three general references were made, of which nine were found to contain elements which operated against the public interest. Moreover, it was rare for the recommendations of the Monopolies Commission to be carried out by the Government in anything like their original form. For example, in its report on the supply of detergents the Monopolies Commission recommended that Unilever and Proctor & Gamble should reduce their expenditure on advertising and sales promotions by 40% and that there should be some automatic tax sanction on any excess. Instead the Board of Trade negotiated for some six months with the firms before an agreement was reached to keep their prices steady for two years and to introduce a new range of products with little advertising and at some 20% below the price of the existing range. Not surprisingly, as the firms were left free to spend as much as they liked on promoting the other brands, these were a market failure.[1] Even in the case of cinema film where all the recommendations were enacted this was again achieved by consultations with the companies.

Four conclusions can be drawn about the philosophy underlying the operation of the IRC and the Monopolies Commission:

(*i*) Market behaviour was *not* thought to be determined *just* by market structure.

(*ii*) Improving productive efficiency (e.g. by economies of scale) was seen as more important than improving market efficiency (e.g. by increasing competition).

(*iii*) As a consequence of (*i*) and (*ii*) the desirability of a merger was judged on its individual circumstances – some were actively encouraged – and monopolies were judged on their behaviour.

(*iv*) Persuasion was the primary means used, either to encourage a merger, or to control a monopoly. Direct intervention by the IRC in a takeover bid on the one hand, or a reference to the Monopolies Commis-

---

[1] Some people have still managed to conclude that this experiment shows that people preferred more expensive brands! See Frank Broadway, *State Intervention in British Industry 1964–68* (London 1969), page 66.

T.L.G.—G

sion on the other, was only used in the last resort – and even then the implementation of references from the Monopolies Commission did not at any stage result in legislation.

This pragmatic, discretionary policy seems therefore to have been the outcome on the one hand of a desire to pursue multiple objectives (e.g. some mergers desirable in terms of increased economies of scale would be ruled out automatically by rigid criteria on market structure), and on the other hand of the means considered acceptable. For example, there could have been criteria for automatic *reference* to the Monopolies Commission without this necessarily ruling out beneficial mergers. However, this seems to have been regarded as an inefficient method of scrutiny partly because in the eyes of the Government the vast majority of mergers could be seen to be beneficial (or at least neutral) on a quick analysis by the Board of Trade, and partly because much of the work of the IRC would then have been made more difficult – a role as marriage broker is not easy when compulsory divorce may be just round the corner.

Interlinked with this may have been the judgment by the Government about the impact of this detailed supervision of private industry on other policies. In the UK governments depend almost entirely for their statistical information on voluntary co-operation between industry and government departments (particularly the Ministry of Technology and the Board of Trade). In addition, during this period the co-operation of industry was required in planning, in prices and incomes policy and in the programme of voluntary exchange control. Close scrutiny may have been thought counter-productive, politically, if not economically—though whether this view was correct is another matter.

(c) The National Board for Prices and Incomes: price control

The Government also made less use of the Monopolies Commission than they might have done because of the extensive inquiries of the NBPI into price increases. Although the NBPI was primarily concerned with incomes policy (see Chapter 9) its detailed analyses were very much part of direct government intervention in industry and aimed both at increasing market efficiency (by reducing the possibility of monopoly profits) and at instigating increases in productivity and reductions in unit costs. Price increases were allowed if unit costs had risen,[1] provided that cost reductions elsewhere, or a reduction in a return on capital, were not possible. Alternatively, they were allowed if this was the only available way to finance further expansion. Price reductions were urged if productiv-

---

[1] The wage costs allowable were usually those consistent with the criteria for incomes in operation at the time. The ability only to enquire into price *increases* was little restraint in a period when the aggregate price level was rising. The power to delay a price increase was equivalent to a cut in the relative price.

ity growth was above average or profits were the result of excessive market power.

There was therefore considerable overlap and common interest between the Monopolies Commission and the NBPI – they were both trying to control monopoly profits.[1] As a result in 1968 it was announced that the NBPI would bring the Monopolies Commission into cases where prices, and the growth of company profits, were prima facie based on excessive market power; and in 1969 proposals were put forward to combine the NBPI and the Monopolies Commission to form a Commission on Industry and Manpower.[2]

Government intervention

The Government used its own powers to influence research expenditure. For example, in 1965 plans were announced to encourage the use of computers,[3] and under the Science and Technology Act (1965) government grants were given to sponsor new equipment and pre-production models in the machine tool industry. The National Research and Development Corporation (NRDC) was expanded, and attempts were made to shift the emphasis away from research expenditure on defence towards civil expenditure – the cancellation of TSR2 was partly for this reason. Plans were also made to increase the supply of engineers and to encourage them away from pure research into more applied fields.[4]

In 1968 the ability of the Government to support investment schemes was extended by the Industrial Expansion Act. This gave powers to use 'loans, grants, guarantees, the underwriting of losses of the subscription of share capital'[5] where a scheme would:

(*i*) 'improve the efficiency or profitability of an industry'
(*ii*) 'create, expand, or sustain productive capacity'
(*iii*) 'promote or support technological improvements'.[6]

The first use of this Act was in March 1968 when a Government-initiated merger was arranged between the computer businesses of ICT, English Electric and Plessey. A new holding company, IC (Holdings) Ltd was

---

[1] They were, of course, each doing other things as well and the approaches used were very different. The reports of the NBPI show a much greater willingness to question the *status quo* and to examine the overall structure of an industry.

[2] *Productivity, Prices and Incomes Policy after 1969* (Cmnd. 4237, 1969).

[3] See for example *Computers for Research*, Report of Joint Working Group under chairmanship of B. H. Flowers (Cmnd. 2883, 1966).

[4] See *Enquiry into the Flow of Candidates in Science and Technology into Higher Education* (Cmnd. 2893, 1965) and also *Enquiry into Longer-term Post-graduate Courses for Engineers and Technologists* (HMSO 1965).

[5] *Industrial Expansion* (Cmnd. 3509, 1968).

[6] Industrial Expansion Act (1968).

formed with the Government having a 10% shareholding (£3·5 million), and being prepared to put up grants to a limit of £13·5 million for support of research and development.[1]

Aid was also given under this Act to a scheme to build aluminium smelters in the UK which it was hoped would reduce the need to import raw materials and save about £40 million on the balance of payments. After nearly two years of long negotiations it was announced in July 1968 that three smelters would be built in the development areas.[2] First, Alcan Aluminium (UK) Ltd was to build a smelter in Northumberland and was to run it on electricity from its own power station using coal supplied by the NCB under a long-term contract from the nearby Lynemouth Colliery. Secondly, the British Aluminium Co. and a consortium consisting of Rio Tinto Zinc and BICC were each to build smelters with the electricity being supplied on special terms. (The normal price for electricity is related to the average cost of power stations of varying ages and efficiencies, whereas the aluminium companies were effectively sold electricity at the average costs of the most recent nuclear plants.[3]) In addition loans of up to £30 million and £33 million at an interest rate of 7% were given to British Aluminium and the RTZ/BICC Consortium. Finally, all three projects became eligible for investment and building grants.

The case for this project therefore rested in part on pricing electricity at its long-run marginal cost. However the willingness to do this and to make the necessary loans was probably coloured by the regional location of the smelters[4] and, because the projects had originally been conceived before devaluation when the shadow price of foreign exchange was above the market rate.[5]

Significant Government aid was also given to the shipbuilding industry. High levels of orders in the industry during the 1950s had been accompanied by heavy investment – at least by shipbuilding standards – in schemes of modernization. But by 1960 the British industry's order-book was beginning to shrink. Moreover, the combination of high capital costs and lower than expected output meant that there was little correlation

[1] *Industrial Investment: The Computers Mergers Project* (Cmnd. 3660, 1968).
[2] *The Aluminium Industry (Invergordon Project) Scheme 1968, and the Aluminium Industry (Anglesey Project) Scheme 1968.* See Cmnd. 3819, 1969.
[3] They made capital contributions to the Generating Boards equivalent to the cost of the generating capacity they would use, and were then charged the operating costs of this capacity.
[4] Certainly the *ability* to support it was a function of its location. In April 1968 Norway had made a formal objection claiming that the Government had breached the EFTA rules on competition by subsidizing the project via regional policy and the Industrial Expansion Act. The Government did not accept this view but nevertheless the size of the smelters was reduced and an assurance was given that the UK would continue to purchase 100,000 tons of aluminium from Norway.
[5] Whether there is an economic case for subsidizing such projects *after* devaluation depends on whether one thinks the UK has a propensity to inflate faster than other countries.

between the most modern yards and those able to tender the most competitive contracts. This intensified the decline. During 1960 to 1964 the industry attempted to meet this by studying the methods used in yards abroad, and in 1963 the Conservative Government had introduced the Shipbuilding Credit Scheme under which mortgages of up to 80% of the cost were made available to British shipowners ordering in British yards.

The fall in orders was not confined to the UK but our relative performance was poor, so in February 1965 the Labour Government set up a Committee of Inquiry (the Geddes Committee). At the same time the Government driven by George Brown's enthusiasm had become involved in a scheme to achieve large productivity improvements, and new methods of work at the Fairfields Shipyard. When the Geddes Committee reported in 1966[1] it recommended the establishment of a Shipbuilding Industry Board (the SIB) to initiate the necessary reorganization within the industry and to administer Government financial assistance. These recommendations were enacted in the Shipbuilding Industry Act (1967). As a result of this there was:

(*i*) The formation of a new group, the Upper Clyde Shipbuilders (UCS), from a merger of four previous yards, one of which was Fairfields.

(*ii*) £400 million of bank loans[2] (the initial limit of £200 million established in 1967 had to be doubled in 1968) at preferable rates of interest to ship owners to encourage them to place orders with British yards.

In addition, there were successive grants to UCS in June and September 1969, firstly to finance modernization and latterly to stave off bankruptcy. Also Government aid had subsequently to be given both to Cammell Laird and to Vickers. It seems therefore that although the initial aid to shipbuilding was intended to be a short-term measure to ease the process of change, it has ended up being a series of subsidies.[3]

Two conclusions may be drawn. First, the Government gave the impression that modernization could be achieved quite quickly, whereas a long and difficult process of changes in management methods, techniques of work, and attitudes, was needed. Instead, the short period injections of aid probably increased uncertainty in the industry. Secondly, as a result of this, it is likely that a clear decision was never made about the rough level of subsidy that was acceptable.

---

[1] *Shipbuilding Inquiry Committee 1965–66* (Cmnd. 2937, 1966).
[2] Geddes had recommended ceilings of £30 million of credits, £32·5 million of loans and £5 million 'disturbance allowance' (ibid. page 165).
[3] In addition this industry ought to have benefited from devaluation and from the Regional Employment Premium. See J. R. Parkinson, 'The financial prospects of shipbuilding after Geddes', *Journal of Industrial Economics*, November 1968, who suggests that these two facts should have reduced the cost of a ship by some 15%.

The legal framework

(a) The Companies Act (1967)

The Government also attempted to control firms and encourage competition by changes in the legal framework. A Companies Bill was published in 1966 which aimed to increase the amount of information available to the public. First the status of the 'exempt private company' was to be abolished, i.e. all companies including those family-owned, had to file accounts, auditor's reports, and directors' reports with the Registrar of Companies. Secondly, the amount of information required in these reports was expanded to include amongst other things the details of annual turnover, the profitability in 'substantially different' lines of business, the remuneration of directors, details of political and charitable contributions, and the country of incorporation of a company's ultimate holding company. Also companies were required to maintain a register of share ownerships of 10% or more, available for public inspection.

However, the Bill lapsed before it became law. In the period before the next parliamentary session there were warnings of failures by insurance companies,[1] so that when the Bill reappeared in November 1966 an extra section had been added dealing specifically with insurance companies. Liquidity requirements were specified and the Board of Trade was given greater powers of inspection, as well as the ability to stop companies entering into further contracts of insurance.

This legislation was thought necessary because on their own companies will publish less than is desirable collectively. The extra flow of information was intended to increase competition[2] and to improve the allocation of funds within the capital market.[3] There could also be grounds of equity for thinking that shareholders ought to be at least as well informed as managers, and that this should include the shareholders of other companies since they may be affected by takeover bids or mergers.[4] Finally, in political terms concentration of power may be thought less dangerous if the power is open rather than concealed.

Closely connected with the Companies Act was the emergence in 1967 of the City Panel on Takeovers and Mergers. The Companies Act did not deal with accounting practices, nor with companies' responsibility to shareholders of other companies. In particular, there was nothing at all along the lines of the American Securities & Exchange Commission to provide legal protection for shareholders against either fraudulent or

---

[1] London and Midland Insurance Company and Irish American Insurance Company announced their insolvency in January and February 1967, respectively.

[2] Though whether this is always desirable depends on adequate mergers legislation to protect the small, rapidly growing company from its larger and not necessarily more efficient competitors.

[3] That is if one supposes that the past is some guide to the future and if the information is in a useful and comprehensible form.

[4] Similar arguments would apply to the interests of employees but no such radical thoughts emerged in the 1967 Act.

unintentional deception during takeover battles. There was, however, always the threat that this would be introduced and as a result the City Panel drew up a code of conduct, relying on voluntary co-operation from firms. This was not noticeably successful and there were continued suggestions that a further Companies Act would be required, but nothing had appeared by 1970.

(b) The Restrictive Trade Practices Act (1968)

The Restrictive Trade Practices Act (1968) was an amendment to the 1956 Act of the same name. The earlier act was generally agreed to have been largely effective, particularly in the number of restrictive agreements which were abandoned before they came to court, but anomalies and gaps had arisen. Some of the EDCs had come into conflict with the 1956 Act when trying to make recommendations, via trade associations, aimed at improving efficiency or lowering prices. As a result, a number of special arrangements were made for trade associations to pass on the recommendations of the NBPI. There had also been a growth in information agreements.[1] These escaped the 1956 Act although the effects were very similar to the more obvious restrictive practices.

The 1968 Act gave the Board of Trade power to exempt from registration any agreement which was thought to be of importance to the national economy; information agreements were made registrable (and the penalties for non-registration increased); and finally, one other gateway was added to allow through restrictions which did not materially restrict or discourage competition. It is too soon to say how this Act will be used, particularly in relation to the provisions for exemption – though the scheme proposed by the Chemical Industries Association to exchange information about imports of chemicals looks like a form of market sharing which is being allowed an exemption because of the possible benefits to the balance of payments.

(c) The Trades Descriptions Act (1968)

Also to be noted is the Trades Descriptions Act (1968) which made it an offence (with a maximum penalty of £400) to supply a false trades description to goods or services if this was done 'in the course of trade or business'. This Act may have a noticeable influence since in the fifteen months after it came into force there were 1,095 cases notified for court proceedings and of these 958 resulted in convictions. Moreover, one would think that measures like this, which make sure that consumers' choice is correctly informed, would become increasingly worthwhile as economies become more affluent and the techniques of advertising more insidious.

---

[1] These were agreements whereby parties regularly informed each other of the prices, etc., which they are charging.

THE RECORD

The effect of policy

What effects did these policies have? How far did they achieve their objectives? If there had been only a single change in policy in an otherwise regular sequence of events and if this policy had but one objective then to answer these questions would be a sensible and manageable task. However, this is certainly not the picture here. Policies were intentionally chosen because they fitted well with a number of objectives and each objective was influenced by a number of policies. Furthermore, policies can have different effects in different circumstances. There are therefore many interpretations of the same set of facts but we must begin by establishing what happened.

(a) What happened to productivity?

Productivity failed to grow at the rate hoped for in the National Plan. From 1964 to 1968 output per head grew by only 2·7% per annum compared with the objective of 3·2% per annum.[1] Yet in relation to the past the record is quite good. Table 5.2 shows that judged either by output per head in the economy as a whole, or in manufacturing only,

TABLE 5.2   PRODUCTIVITY

		Average Annual Percentage Increase	
	Total Economy Output per head	Manufacturing Output per head	Output per man hour
1960–4	2·3	3·1	3·5
1964–8	2·7	3·4	4·2

Source: *Economic Trends* and *National Institute Economic Review*.

or in terms of manufacturing output per man hour, the performance from 1964 to 1968 was better than from 1960 to 1964. These are naive comparisons between years that have some cyclical similarity, but Reddaway's analysis of the Distributive Trades also found that output per head in 1968 was 5% above what would have been expected if the relationships observed prior to 1965 had continued to operate,[2] and the National

[1] *The National Plan*, op. cit., page 24.
[2] *Effects of the Selective Employment Tax 1st Report. The Distributive Trades* (HMSO 1970), page 93. They also refer to an apparent acceleration in productivity growth in manufacturing, see page 99, footnote 1.

N.B. Since this chapter was first written two articles have appeared which try to analyse this increase in productivity in manufacturing more carefully. See J. D. Whitley and G. D. N. Worswick, 'The productivity effects of the Selective Employment Tax' *National Institute Economic Review*, May 1971, and W. B. Reddaway 'A Reply' *National Institute Economic Review*, August 1971. These agree in finding an increase in manufacturing productivity in 1967 and 1968 in relation to its past trend, but they disagree about the size of the increase (anything from 2·8% to 5·5% depending on the figures

Institute estimated for the whole economy that 'employment in the first half of 1969 seems to be about 300,000 below the figure which would be derived by applying the pre-1967 relationships to the output figures'[1] – which again tends to indicate that productivity increased more than in the past.

But how similar is 1968 to 1964? Cycles can be examined in terms of (*i*) the pattern of demand, (*ii*) the behaviour of aggregate output, (*iii*) capacity utilization, (i.e. output in relation to its past trend), (*iv*) capital utilization and (*v*) labour utilization.[2] However, after 1964 none of the indicators give a clear picture, and any interpretation must take account of the following difficulties:

(*i*) *The pattern of demand* The sources of demand were different. Manufacturing investment was much less cyclical,[3] and such expansion as occurred in 1968 came from exports rather than from public or private consumption.

TABLE 5.3 COMPARISON OF CYCLICAL BEHAVIOUR

1. Gross Domestic Product

	Percentage change on previous year		
1959/60	+5·6	+5·8	1963/64
1960/61	+2·6	+2·6	1964/65
1961/62	+1·3	+1·7	1965/66
1962/63	+3·3	+1·5	1966/67
1963/64	+5·8	+3·9	1967/68
1964/65	+2·6	+2·3	1968/69

2. Manufacturing Output

	Percentage change on previous year		
1959/60	+8·1	+8·7	1963/64
1960/61	+0·2	+3·4	1964/65
1961/62	+0·4	+1·6	1965/66
1962/63	+4·1	+0·0	1966/67
1963/64	+8·7	+6·3	1967/68
1964/65	+3·4	+3·5	1968/69

Source: *Economic Trends.*

used) and also about the interpretation to be placed on these results. This debate is a classic example of the limited ability of purely statistical tests to resolve arguments. An *economic judgment* has to be made and my own is that productivity *did* increase, though *why* is a very different matter (see below, pages 204–6).

[1] *National Institute Economic Review*, February 1970, page 35.
[2] For a discussion of previous cycles in the UK see R. C. O. Matthews, 'Post-war business cycles in the United Kingdom' in M. Bronfenbrenner (ed.), *Is the Business Cycle Obsolete?* (Chichester 1969); and for recent measurement see K. Hilton (assisted by Helen Dolphin), 'Capital and capacity utilisation in the U.K.: their measurement and reconciliation', *Bulletin*, August 1970.
[3] 'The formerly reinforcing movement in private investment disappeared.' (*National Institute Economic Review*, February 1970), page 34.

(*ii*) *The growth in output*   Table 5.3 shows that 1968 was the most nearly comparable year to 1964 but the upswing was weaker and sustained for a shorter period. However, other indicators of manufacturing output derived from inquiries by the CBI suggest a larger expansion in 1968 which continued for longer into 1969.[1]

(*iii*) *Unemployment in relation to output*   From mid 1967 unemployment was *higher* relative to output than was expected.[2]

(*iv*) *Unemployment in relation to employment*   Unemployment was *lower* than expected given what happened to employment. Table 5.4 shows that from June 1966 to June 1969 civil employment fell by 606,000 while unemployment rose by only 230,000. Moreover this was in a period when the labour force was expected to grow by 72,000 so that only about one in every three people who went out of employment became registered as unemployed, which is below the range of 0·4–0·7 found for the period 1958–66.[3]

(*v*) *Unemployment in relation to unfilled vacancies*   Unemployment became higher in relation to unfilled vacancies after 1967 (see Fig. 5.1). More-

TABLE 5.4   EMPLOYMENT, LABOUR FORCE AND UNEMPLOYMENT
(GREAT BRITAIN)

	1966 June	1969 June	Change
			Thousands
Employment[a]	25,330	24,724	− 606
Labour Force[b] (estimated)	26,145	26,217	+ 72
Unemployment[c]	253	483	+230

[a] Civil employment plus HM forces
[b] Official estimates of the labour force prepared on the assumption of a constant (high) pressure of demand, and allowing for changes in the population of working age, changes in activity rates, etc.
[c] wholly unemployed.

Source: *Department of Employment Gazette*, February 1971 and *Ministry of Labour Gazette*, November 1966.

[1] See Mrs Gregory, 'The C.B.I. Industrial Trends Survey as a measure of current manufacturing output' (*National Institute Economic Review*, May 1970). 'For 1969 . . . the official index [was] showing a sharp downswing followed by a recovery, the Survey showing continued expansion and then a marked down turn.'
[2] 'Over the whole period 1958–67 an average output rise of 3·2% a year was accompanied by a mild rise of 13,000 a year in unemployment: this contrasts with the 61,000 increase in the period 1967 III – 1968 III when output growth was again at the 3·2% level,' *National Institute Economic Review*, February 1970, page 34.
[3] See J. R. Shepherd, 'Productive potential and the demand for labour', *Economic Trends*, August 1968.

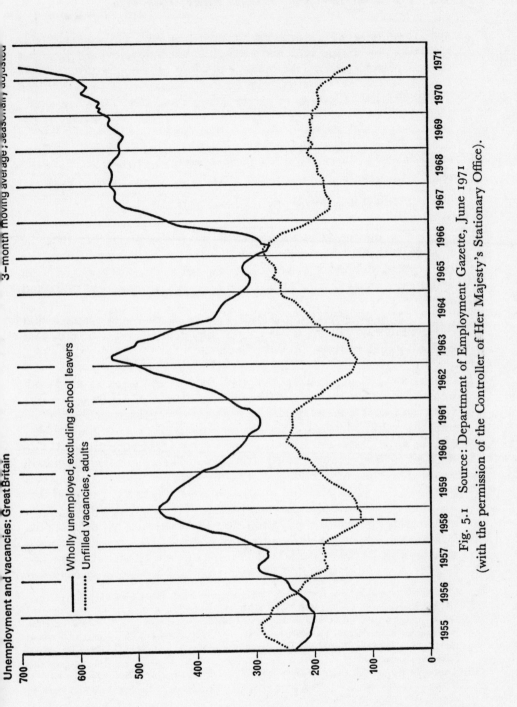

Fig. 5.1   Source: Department of Employment Gazette, June 1971 (with the permission of the Controller of Her Majesty's Stationary Office).

over, there were widely differing situations for men and women. Table 5.5 shows that during 1968 and 1969 male unemployment *and* vacancies for men both increased – the opposite of what one would expect.

TABLE 5.5   CHANGES IN UNEMPLOYMENT AND UNFILLED VACANCIES 1967–9 (GREAT BRITAIN)

	Males	Females
Change in wholly unemployed (excluding school leavers)	+41,100	−17,900
Change in vacancies notified and remaining unfilled	+10,800	+14,600

Source: *Department of Employment Gazette*, February 1971

(*vi*) *The duration of unemployment*   There is slight evidence that the average duration of unemployment increased. On average, of those on the register, only 17·4% were there for less than two weeks in 1968 and 1969 compared with an average of 18·8% in 1962 and 1963 and 20·3% in 1958 and 1959.[1]

(*vii*) *Statistics of the self-employed*   Finally, there is the problem that the last full count of the self-employed was in 1966 and it may be that SET caused an increase in self-employment.[2]

The extent to which the period from 1966 onwards has changed both in terms of the usual relationships and in terms of the policies used[3] – the two are of course interdependent – makes any conclusive interpretation impossible. Indeed, many of the results of the policies are still being felt – and in some cases policies were reversed by the Conservatives before their full effects could have occurred. On the one hand the increase in productivity may have been unreal, either because it did not represent a genuine increase in potential output (because it was the marginal, less productive, workers who became unemployed or left the labour force altogether),[4] or because many people were still working but did not hold insurance cards and were therefore not counted. On the other hand it may be that the fall in the labour force was in age groups who typically do not register – the young tend not to bother to register or may stay on at

[1] See also *National Institute Economic Review*, February 1970, page 36, Chart I.
[2] The self-employed do not pay SET. Whether they are included in the employment figures or not depends on whether they hold National Insurance cards but even here the information is unreliable. The last bench mark was the Census of Population 1966, since then the self-employed have been estimated from a sample of Class II National Insurance cards. See *Department of Employment Gazette*, February 1971, page 158. Self-employment is thought to have increased particularly in construction. See *Report of the Committee of Inquiry under Professor E. H. Phelps Brown into Certain Matters Concerning Labour in Building and Civil Engineering*. (Cmnd. 3714, 1968.)
[3] In addition to SET, the labour market is likely to have been affected by redundancy payments and the introduction of earnings-related unemployment benefits.
[4] Raising the average by putting those with below average productivity out of work is no help to any one!

school because of lack of job opportunities.[1] In which case there was far more slack in the labour market during 1968 and 1969 than the unemployment figures suggest.

The latter view gains some support from an analysis by Sleeper[2] of manpower flows between industries. This found that they were significant in relation to the net change in employment, and that prior to 1966 manufacturing typically released labour to distribution in recessions and re-employed it in expansionary phases.[3] However, Sleeper argues that since 1966 it is likely that SET has reduced vacancies in the services sector. Redundant manufacturing employees therefore had to find jobs in some other sector (which is rather unlikely), become self-employed, unemployed, or leave the labour force altogether. It is therefore very possible that SET is part of the explanation of the large fall in employment and the lesser rise in unemployment. If so, then if manufacturing output were to be re-expanded these people could well re-enter employment. Moreover, *if* the previous cyclical pattern whereby above average increases in output were associated with above average rises in productivity was still to hold[4] then the acceleration in the underlying rate of increase in productivity was *greater* than the naive comparisons in Table 5.2.

Another explanation[5] is that productivity growth was increased as a result of a shift in the pattern of demand which caused a change in industrial structure (either as a result of devaluation and its accompanying measures, or because of SET, etc.). The National Institute found that in a statistical sense the change in the structure of output was just significant after 1967.[6] Productivity could therefore have been increased simply because output was being shifted to the industries with high productivity *levels*.[7] Such a view would also be consistent with the apparent mismatch between job opportunities and people available which is suggested by the

[1] See *Department of Employment and Productivity Gazette*, May 1969, page 416.
[2] See 'Approximate estimates of the flow of employees between industries', *Department of Employment and Productivity Gazette*, April 1970, and the analysis by R. D. Sleeper, 'Manpower redeployment and the Selective Employment Tax', *Bulletin*, November 1970.
[3] See also K. D. George, 'Productivity in the distributive trades', *Bulletin*, May 1969.
[4] An increase in employment of 1% has tended to be associated with an increase in output of about 2%. See W. A. H. Godley and J. R. Shepherd, 'Long-term growth and short-term policy', *National Institute Economic Review*, August 1964, and J. R. Shepherd, 'Productive potential and the demand for labour', *Economic Trends*, August 1968. For an analysis of the cyclical behaviour in manufacturing see F. P. R. Brechling, 'The relationship between output and employment in British manufacturing industries', *Review of Economic Studies*, July 1965.
[5] J. K. Bowers, P. C. Cheshire and A. E. Webb, 'The change in the relationship between unemployment and earnings increases; a review of some possible explanations', *National Institute Economic Review*, November 1970.
[6] See *National Institute Economic Review*, February 1970, page 37. They found the difference in the rank correlation coefficients was significant at the 10% level but not at the 5% level.
[7] These industries may also have had high output growth, and rank correlation tests for the period 1965 to 1969 are consistent with Verdoorn's Law that such industries tended to be those which also have high productivity *growth*.

labour market statistics and by the National Institute findings that the divergence between unemployment and vacancies differed both between regions and between industries.[1] One final twist to these complexities is the possibility that the change in demand was not only between one industry and another but also as a result of devaluation, between one firm and another – a large proportion of exports comes from a relatively small number of large firms.

(b) What happened to investment?

Private investment is also difficult to interpret, because again we do not know how similar this cycle is to previous ones and investment is part cause, part effect. Of course given that output grew much less than in the Plan (2·3% p.a. as compared with 3·8% p.a.) the actual rate of investment was also much lower than intended (manufacturing investment grew by only 3·6% p.a. whereas the Plan target was 7% p.a.). Yet in 1966 and 1967 it fell noticeably less than in previous cycles. Measured from peak to trough (annual figures) manufacturing investment had fallen by increasing amounts in previous cycles (1951–3 minus 7·5%, 1957–8 minus 10%, 1961–3 minus 18%),[2] but in spite of very pessimistic forecasts in 1966 it fell by only 3% from 1966 to 1967.[3] There is also some suggestion that manufacturing investment increased relative to investment in distribution in 1966 and 1967 (see Table 5.6). However, this could be just the different timing of investment in the two sectors.

TABLE 5.6 GROSS DOMESTIC FIXED CAPITAL FORMATION IN MANUFACTURING AND THE DISTRIBUTIVE TRADES

	Manufacturing	Distributive Trades
	% change on previous year, constant (1963) prices	
1959/60	+ 16·8	+ 7·1
1960/61	+ 17·6	+ 9·6
1961/62	− 8·0	− 3·0
1962/63	− 11·6	+ 9·1
1963/64	+ 13·3	+ 14·1
1964/65	+ 9·5	− 4·5
1965/66	+ 2·9	− 9·7
1966/67	− 2·8	+ 3·2
1967/68	+ 4·7	+ 11·9
1968/69	+ 4·1	+ 3·9
% Change 1961–3	− 18·5	+ 5·7
% Change 1965–7	0·0	− 6·8

Source: *National Income and Expenditure*

[1] See *National Institute Economic Review*, February 1969.
[2] Matthews op. cit. page 110.
[3] The CBI Industrial Trends Survey published in October 1966 showed a negative balance of − 39 for expected authorization of capital expenditure on plant and machinery. This was the largest negative since the series began in 1958.

Much more problematic is why this improvement should have occurred, as both company profitability and liquidity were adversely affected. Glyn and Sutcliffe[1] have shown that the *share* of company profits in company value added fell sharply after 1965 and that both pre and post tax *rates* of profit also fell more rapidly than in the past (see Table 5.7).

TABLE 5.7 SHARE[a] OF PROFITS AND RATE OF PROFIT[bc] 1950–69

Percentage

	1950–4	1955–9	1960–4	1964	1965	1966	1967	1968	1969
Share of profits	25·2	22·8	21·0	21·2	20·2	17·6	18·1	16·8	14·2
Pre tax rate of profit	20·2	17·3	14·7	14·9	14·3	11·9	12·3	12·6	10·9
Post tax rate of profit	8·1	8·4	7·3	7·1	7·9	5·8	6·0	4·8	3·2

[a] The measure of the share is the proportion of company profits in value added by the company sector, *after* deducting capital consumption (depreciation) and stock appreciation (that part of profits attributable solely to the increased valuation of stocks as a result of rising prices).

[b] The rate of profit is taken as the return on the book value of ordinary shareholders' assets for quoted companies in UK manufacturing industry. It is therefore on an historical cost rather than a replacement cost basis. In periods of inflation and with substantial net investment so that the average age of assets is declining this could give a downward bias to the trend of the return on capital employed.

[c] All the figures given here should be taken only as indicative of trends. Company profits are Grade B in reliability (±3% to 10%) and both stock appreciation and depreciation are Grade C (±more than 10%) see *National Accounts Statistics: Sources and Methods* (HMSO, 1968).

Source: Glyn and Sutcliffe, op. cit., page 5.

If this was more than the usual cyclical decline[2] – Glyn and Sutcliffe certainly think it was – then one would expect investment to be lower rather than higher. However the squeeze on profits was intensifying throughout the period[3] and it may be that the impact on investment is still to come – there could be a lag before a decline in present profits feeds through on to expected profits and before that is reflected in current investment. Also Glyn and Sutcliffe look at profits *after* deducting stock appreciation. This is correct when measuring the real return to capital but managers may not take it fully into account – or at least not immediately in a situation where inflation is accelerating.[4]

[1] Andrew Glyn and Bob Sutcliffe, 'The collapse of U.K. profits', *New Left Review*, March/April 1971.
[2] For an analysis of the behaviour of profits in earlier cycles see R. R. Neild, *Pricing and Employment in the Trade Cycle* (Cambridge 1963).
[3] There is little doubt that by 1969 the decline in profits share was considerably greater than the normal cyclical behaviour. 'The fall in share over 1969 and 1970 has been ... perhaps three times as much as would "normally" be expected.' *National Institute Economic Review*, February 1971, page 49.
[4] Stock appreciation became particularly large after devaluation. It amounted to £531 million in 1968 and £704 million in 1969. See *National Income and Expenditure 1970*, Table 67.

Company liquidity was also decreased. The ratio of the identified liquid assets of industrial and commercial companies to bank borrowing was 1·16 at the end of 1964. This fell to 0·95 at the end of 1966, and after a small recovery in 1967, fell again to stand at 0·86 at the end of 1969.[1,2] Liquidity is the result of three features – post tax profits, the proportion of profits retained, and the level of investment to be financed. Corporation Tax should have led to an increase in retentions yet companies appear to have continued to regard dividend stability as the main objective and so retentions have been the residual.[3] Despite Corporation Tax, dividends on ordinary shares grew by about the same amount between 1964 and 1969 as did undistributed income (before depreciation and stock appreciation).

Prima facie this decline in profitability and the associated decline in liquidity suggests that investment was maintained *despite* Government policies rather than because of them. However a more detailed analysis would be necessary to establish this. Aggregate figures on profits and liquidity may hide significant differences at the level of the individual firm. These may have been important during 1967 and 1968 when the increase in both investment grants and Corporation Tax would have intensified the redistribution of company income towards those firms that *were* investing. Also, even though retentions did not increase in aggregate, Corporation Tax itself would have redistributed post tax incomes towards firms with a low pay-out ratio and it may be that they had a low pay-out ratio *because* they were growing rapidly and needed high retention.[4] Moreover, the major reason for investment grants was not that they would increase profitability but that they would have more effect than other incentives because business men would take them more into account – and this may have been just what happened.

Finally, it is of course crucial to know whether or not the decline in profits was itself the result of Government policy. Clearly the cyclical part of it reflects the Government's general policy of demand management. In addition, there was downward pressure on retail prices as a result of the gradual disappearance of Resale Price Maintenance,[5] as well as on prices in general through the activities of the NBPI. However, the major

---

[1] *Financial Statistics*, Table 78.

[2] Glyn and Sutcliffe estimate that in the manufacturing sector in 1969 after allowing for stock appreciation 'there were no *real* retained profits at all' and that 'net fixed investment, acquisition of subsidiaries and increase in stocks . . . could only be financed internally by reducing liquid assets'. Glyn and Sutcliffe, op. cit., page 15.

[3] The impact of Corporation Tax is confused by the forestalling provisions of the Finance Act 1965 which sought to limit the payment of dividends out of taxed reserves, and also by voluntary, and then enforced, dividend restraint. However an analysis of 873 industrial companies found that, in the year following the introduction of Corporation Tax, the majority of companies still followed a policy of dividend stability. See R. J. Briston and C. R. Tomkins, 'The impact of the introduction of Corporation Tax upon the dividend policies of UK companies', *Economic Journal*, September 1970.

[4] This possibility is suggested in G. Whittington, 'A note on corporate taxation and dividend behaviour', *Review of Economic Studies*, January 1971.

[5] As a result of the Resale Prices Act 1964, passed by the Conservatives.

impact of the former was probably during 1965 and 1966 and the NBPI usually allowed a rise in price to recoup increased costs, so neither of these offer much explanation for a *continuing* fall in profits. Moreover, the profit share fell further in 1969 and early 1970 despite the relaxation of incomes policy at that time.

An alternative explanation – to which Glyn and Sutcliffe subscribe – is that the squeeze is the result of increased international competition.[1] However, this does not let the Government off the hook either. International competition can be influenced by the commercial policy of governments – and tariffs were, in fact, being cut under the Kennedy Round agreement.[2]

(c) What happened to industrial structure?

Government policy in the form of devaluation and SET caused a change in demand and thus in the structure of output (see page 205 above). The manufacturing sector was the main source of growth over the period, while the relative contribution of mining and quarrying, and of services declined. Within manufacturing, chemicals and engineering increased their share while the consumer goods industries decreased. However, much more dramatic than the overall industrial picture, was the increase in take-overs and the number and value of mergers – particularly in 1967 and

TABLE 5.8   NUMBER OF MERGERS 1958–68

	Total mergers per annum			Average value of net assets transferred All Industry	
	Manufacturing Industry	Distribution and Services	All Industry	Actual values £m.	Constant values £m.
1958–60	55	13	68	2·9	2·9
1961–3	51	18	69	3·6	2·8
1964–5	47	12	59	3·8	2·5
1966	48	18	66	6·4	3·7
1967	61	14	75	9·5	5·1
1968	79	21	100	12·1	6·0

Source: *Survey of Mergers* (HMSO, 1970).

1968 (see Table 5.8). The main increase in these two years was however the result of four very large mergers each involving a transfer of net assets of more than £100 million. When these are left out the apparent acceleration disappears and the constant value figures would then show little change until 1965 followed by a marked rise in 1966 which was roughly maintained

[1] Some evidence for this is that 'the price rise, in response to devaluation, was relatively much less than had initially been anticipated'. *National Institute Economic Review*, February 1969, page 11.
[2] *The Kennedy Round of Trade Negotiations 1964–67*. (Cmnd. 3347, 1967).

in 1967 and 1968.[1] Once again however, we do not know whether these mergers were the result of direct Government encouragement and the climate of opinion at the time, or of the large increase in share prices in 1967 and 1968 which made it easy to raise outside finance,[2] or of an aggressive reaction to the fall in profitability,[3] or some amalgam of these.[4]

The appropriateness of policy

The Labour Government's policies have frequently been criticized[5] for being too discriminatory and for drawing unrealistic boundaries – in particular between manufacturing and services.[6] Paradoxically, however, *not* to discriminate can also be costly. The fiscal measures used to stimulate productivity and investment did not discriminate in enough detail to stop the intra marginal projects receiving as much aid as those on the margin. The difficulty of a more detailed approach was the shortage of the necessary information (and the hostility of firms to providing more information), combined with a shortage of people with the necessary skills to do the detailed appraisals required.

This problem was at its worst in the approach to planning, since planning depends critically on the detail in which it is done. Either people believe in the plan and thus conform to it of their own free will; or they have to be persuaded by a variety of policy instruments ranging from mere Government approval to direct financial incentives or legislation. In fact, the Plan fell between these two stools. On the one hand it lacked conviction during 1965 and 1966 because of the balance of payments situation, on the other hand the Government lacked the detailed policy instruments (and until March 1966 the political situation in which to

[1] See the analysis by the staff of the Monopolies Commission *Survey of Mergers* (HMSO, 1970).
[2] The value of ordinary shares issued in 1968 was more than four times the average for the period 1960 to 1964.
[3] The warlike nature of business actions under conditions of oligopoly is stressed in the classic article by K. W. Rothschild, 'Price theory and oligopoly', *Economic Journal*, September 1947.
[4] See Gerald D. Newbould, *Management and Merger Activity* (Section 3) (Guthstead 1970) – in which he argues that mergers in this period were a reaction to uncertainty.
[5] There have of course been a multitude of criticisms many starting from diagnoses so different from those of the Labour Party and with such different value judgments implied in them that comment here is impossible. However, one that is simply incorrect is the assertion that Corporation Tax must damage the capital market. If a company retains its profits and does not invest them, then presumably this must be because the rate of return on financial assets is higher than that on physical assets (at least as far as that company is concerned). If so, funds would still go back to the capital market and savings would be at a higher level than if the funds were distributed. Moreover, companies are likely to be at least as well informed and rational about their financial investment as are individuals.
[6] Lady Margaret Hall, 'Are goods and services different?' *Westminster Bank Review*, August 1968.

operate them) necessary to reinforce the Plan. Also, if the planning machinery is to have any effect it must be able to impinge on the decision-making level, in this case the firm, which in general the EDCs did not.

One of the roles of the IRC was to help resolve some of these difficulties by establishing direct contact with large firms. It was therefore essential that its strategic approach to 'industrial logic' was linked to the other parts of Government policy. However, by the time the IRC came into operation in 1966 the National Plan was on the brink of collapse and there was then no framework within which the IRC could establish priorities.

In addition, there are contradictions in the approach of the IRC. It was expected to 'earn a commercial return *overall* on its operations'.[1] Yet at the same time the IRC board stated that in its view 'Parliament would not have established the Corporation and authorized the provision of public funds unless it felt that financial support should be made available *on terms which differed from those acceptable to existing institutions*'.[2] It is difficult to reconcile these two views (except by the highly improbable supposition that the IRC charged high interest rates in some areas in order to charge lower ones elsewhere). The IRC's vague terms of reference meant that the personnel who operated it were crucial in determining its shape. In practice, its approach seemed to consist largely of finding good management and then backing it, either in a merger or takeover. But management is not everlasting, nor is the size of the operation that any one man can effectively control unlimited, and it is not necessarily true that good plus bad equals good, in terms of management, nor that large firms are always more efficient than small ones.

There were also attempts to bring the 'public interest' into the decisions of the private firm by means of appointing a director to the board (e.g. the Chrysler/Rootes case). But there must be doubts about the efficacy of this. There may be gains from better information on the part of the firm of what the Government thinks important, and, on the part of the Government of the kind of information that is only obtainable by having someone working for the firm – which may lead to a 'bending' of policy. However, in any real conflict the Government would have to support their director by withdrawing such financial support as it had given – and presumably it could have done this anyway.

The tendency to rely on assurances from firms raises rather similar problems in the case of the monopolies and mergers legislation. There is a spectrum of possibilities for dealing with monopolies. At one extreme the aim is to prevent monopolies occurring at all, at the other, firms are allowed to merge and grow as they like, but are subject to constant supervision of their behaviour. Both approaches have their difficulties. The first means foregoing any benefits that may arise from economies of

[1] *IRC Report and Accounts 1967/68,* page 8. My italics.
[2] Ibid. My italics.

scale and/or from high profits and rapid innovation, the second assumes that adequate supervision is both possible and acceptable. However, monopoly pricing is difficult to identify and skilled manpower may be used by the public sector just checking on the activities of the private sector.

The 1965 legislation and the way it was operated was an unsatisfactory attempt to steer between these two extremes. All references to the Monopolies Commission had to come from the Government which meant that the Monopolies Commission was largely impotent if the Government wished it to be so. It also put great emphasis on a very superficial mechanism for analysing mergers. The Board of Trade was required by the legislation to decide whether or not to make a reference within six months of knowledge of a proposed merger, but in fact an answer was usually given within two or three weeks.[1] Yet even the most perfunctory glance at the questions they supposedly considered[2] suggests that they cannot possibly have given adequate answers in such a short time – particularly as approaches to firms, consultations, a report and a decision, all had to take place within this period. This situation is even more nonsensical in the light of the essential nature of oligopoly which is that action by one firm is likely to cause reactions by others. It is therefore useless to judge a merger between A and B without at the same time asking 'are E and F likely to merge as a result?'

Such rapid analyses could only have been justified if the vast majority of mergers were beneficial or at least neutral to the 'public interest'. However, they can only be beneficial if economies of scale (in the widest sense) are present in some form, but if these exist there will also be a strong tendency for natural monopolies to develop and supervision becomes essential. Equally, there seems no reason why so-called 'neutral' mergers should go unchecked since they will usually result in increased concentration – and to no purpose.[3] Conglomerate mergers which break into new markets can increase competition but it is at least as likely that in many cases their aim is just to reduce risks,[4] so that again scrutiny seems called for.[5]

A more realistic way for the Government to have handled this situation would have been:

[1] There seems to have been no need for this great haste, except for a desire not to hold up bids, which is an odd reason for hurrying.

[2] *Mergers*, op. cit., pages 8–19.

[3] The apparent attitude of the Government to this was strangely at odds with their views on the efficacy of the market system in other spheres.

[4] *Average* profitability seems to be little different for large and small firms but the *variation* of profits is significantly less for large firms. See A. Singh and G. Whittington, 'Growth, profitability and valuation', *Department of Applied Economics, Occasional Papers No. 7* (Cambridge 1968).

[5] For an analysis of a conglomerate which separates financial and real advantages to the firm from real advantages to the economy see C. F. Pratten, 'A case study of a conglomerate merger', *Moorgate and Wall Street: A Review*, Spring 1970.

(*i*) to make more references of mergers to the Monopolies Commission, as well as requiring that large mergers must be *positively* beneficial[1] – not just unharmful (which has been taken to mean anything which did not significantly reduce competition).[2]

(*ii*) to give the Monopolies Commission powers to make ongoing inquiries so that they could look at the *direction of change* of an industry as a whole, rather than just at the snapshot of a firm at only one point in time – in a growing economy the former is far more important.

(*iii*) to conduct its own examinations of industrial structure in conjunction with the EDCs and the IRC as a backcloth against which to judge particular cases.

The aim *should* have been to have used the IRC as a catalyst and the Monopolies Commission as a watchdog – each within a roughly similar overall framework.

The consistency of policy

It has been suggested that it was inconsistent of the Government to be controlling mergers through the Monopolies Commission at the same time as encouraging them through the IRC, and/or to be squeezing profits when trying to increase investment.

However, this is too simple a view.[3] The action which a government takes is the outcome of:

(*i*) how it sees the problem and the importance which it attaches to it (i.e. both the facts and the valuations which interact on one another),

(*ii*) the action it considers possible, and

(*iii*) the success it is having with other objectives and other policies.

These factors are not the same but they do overlap. For example one could decide to use industrial policy more forcibly (e.g. by trying to keep down prices through a reference to the Monopolies Commission) for one or all of the following reasons. New research might indicate that the *extent* of monopoly pricing was more than one had previously thought; it might become more *important* to control prices because of the balance of payments position; or, it might become more *acceptable* to control prices, either because of the new research or because of the changed balance of payments position, or because *other* policies to keep down prices had failed.

---

[1] The Board of Trade had the power to give published directives to the Monopolies Commission but did not use it. See *Mergers,* op. cit., page 5.

[2] This suggestion is argued in slightly more detail by Alister Sutherland, 'The management of mergers policy', in Cairncross (ed.), *The Managed Economy* (Oxford 1970).

[3] In fact, as we saw in the case of the IRC, it would have been *more* inconsistent for the Government *not* to have tried to control mergers!

All these points are well illustrated by the way in which industrial policy changed in its emphasis. During the initial period from October 1964 until July 1966 its role was primarily as an accompaniment to other policies and its major impact was aimed at the longer term. Moreover, until March 1966, policy was critically constrained by the political situation. With a majority of only four, consensus politics was unavoidable. There was a limit to the number of new policies which could be introduced and the only really radical policy at this stage was the creation of the IRC – an *essential* part of the longer-term strategy (even if unpopular). Other industrial policy was confined to setting up the planning machinery and the fiscal[1] and legal framework. Any intervention was entirely of the persuasive sort – a 'dialogue' was being established with industry.

There was however the commitment in the Manifesto to reform the Monopolies Commission. But the Labour Ministers concerned were occupied elsewhere – The Secretary of State for Economic Affairs (George Brown) was heavily involved with prices and incomes policy and the preparation of the Plan, and the President of the Board of Trade (Douglas Jay) was in the middle of the row with EFTA over the import surcharge. Perhaps as a result, the Act which emerged was very similar to the proposals in the Conservative White Paper of a year earlier.[2,3] Moreover, the relatively little use which the Government made of this legislation is understandable in view of their relations with industry at the time – and would have been in line with the traditionally passive attitude of the Board of Trade.

In the second phase, from the deflation of July 1966 until the devaluation of November 1967, the context of industrial policy shifted radically. There was growing agreement that the exchange rate was overvalued and that deflation was not an adequate cure for the balance of payments. Other policies (such as exchange controls and incomes policy) did not seem to be working quickly enough, and open conflict with international obligations (such as GATT and EFTA) appeared to have been largely ruled out – but devaluation was still rejected. Finally, the pressure of demand could no longer be expected to stimulate investment. As a result industrial policy needed:

(*i*) to be effective in the short term,
(*ii*) to ease the balance of payments constraint (preferably by methods subtle enough to avoid too much protest from our trading partners),
(*iii*) to avoid a fall in investment.

It was natural therefore that an attempt was made to change the

[1] Another constraint was the high level of aggregate demand in early 1966 which limited the level of investment grants it was thought possible to give at that stage.
[2] *Monopolies, Mergers and Restrictive Practices* (Cmnd. 2299, 1964).
[3] Indeed the speed with which it was introduced – only five months after coming into office – suggests that the Board of Trade already had a bill in draft form.

style of industrial policy. However, neither the Monopolies Commission nor the IRC had been created with this in mind – 'long term commercial viability' was the latter's criteria, not hidden subsidies to the balance of payments. Moreover, institutions are made up of the people in them, so that it is not easy to graft new functions on to existing organizations.

It was probably partly in reaction to the changed requirements of industrial policy and to the conflicts on the role of the IRC that the powers of the Ministry of Technology were considerably expanded under the Industrial Expansion Act (1968). This Act can be looked at in two very different ways. It widened the powers available to the Ministry of Technology and tidied up Parliamentary procedure. This enabled the Government to respond more quickly to new situations, and avoided the need for separate bits of legislation. Looked at in this way it was just a better means of achieving well-established ends.

However, this Act was also virtually the only time during the whole period of the Government when it was *explicitly* stated in relation to the private sector that the justification for the intervention was 'because of a divergence between national and private costs and benefits'.[1] This compares with the IRC which was *not* allowed to 'support ventures which have no prospect of achieving eventual viability',[2] and the view expressed by the Public Accounts Committee 'that bodies such as the SIB . . . should be guided by strictly commercial principles',[3] – a view with which the Ministry of Technology agreed. Looked at in this second way the Industrial Expansion Act was very much about objectives, not just about means.

Moreover, the Act was *conceived* during Phase 2, that is when other policies to deal with the balance of payments had gone most awry and when there was therefore most agreement on further intervention. Yet it *came into effect* in Phase 3 (after devaluation) when the disagreements were therefore re-appearing. As a result the White Paper announcing its introduction is more interesting in the care which it takes to say what the Act will *not* do, rather than what it will. It points out that the Government would take great care to review projects to see whether devaluation would now make them viable (the Aluminium Smelters?), that the Act was *not* to be used to acquire shares compulsorily and that it was *not* to be used to duplicate work within the province of the IRC.

The other pieces of legislation also tend to confirm this view. The Companies Bill in its initial form was largely restricted to carrying out the recommendations of the Jenkins Committee[4] (i.e. those areas on which there was a consensus). However, before it became law the provisions relating to insurance companies had been added – the intervening failures had made supervision more acceptable. Similarly the Restrictive

[1] *Industrial Expansion,* (Cmnd. 3509, 1968), page 2.
[2] *Industrial Reorganization Corporation* (Cmnd. 2889, 1966), page 3.
[3] *Public Accounts Committee Report,* 1968/69.
[4] *Report of the Company Law Committee* (Cmnd. 1749, 1962).

Practices legislation just filled an agreed gap – apart, that is, from the new exemption for schemes beneficial to the national economy. Was this yet another example of an attempt to find subtle ways of subsidizing industry without openly contravening international obligations?

CONCLUSIONS

In relation to the high hopes with which industrial policy began there is little doubt that it failed. However, industrial policy was only one part of a delicate and interrelated strategy, and it must be judged within this whole. Many policies were forced to work in contexts for which they were not originally intended – SET might have had very different effects if manufacturing output had been expanding rapidly, and investment grants could not be expected to fully offset the effect on investment of depressed output and declining profits. In fact, given this, the record on productivity and investment seems surprisingly good – though we do not know whether this is because of, or despite, the Government's policies!

Indeed, the great majority of industrial policies which look rather tortured in their application are much more understandable viewed against the constraints of a tiny majority in the House of Commons until March 1966, a weak balance of payments, a primarily free trade approach to commercial policy, and a belief on the part of the great majority of civil servants and of industry that the market mechanism was the best guide to the allocation of resources.

It is certainly difficult to find satisfactory alternatives to the last of these, but the market is not always right and intervention – in some cases down to the level of the firm – *is* justified. Coexistence amongst large firms – whether peaceful or warlike – does *not* necessarily guarantee the most logical industrial structure. Also, even within a well-functioning market system, public aid to research is needed. Without this encouragement there will be a tendency to under-invest in research (when there are no patents), or to under-disseminate it (when there are patents) – bygones are bygones and the results of research should be a free good.

Similarly, in shipbuilding there is nothing wrong with a subsidy as such – the more affluent a society is, the less tolerable should *in*voluntary unemployment become. The mistake here was a confusion of ends and means. In evidence to the Public Accounts Committee, the SIB stated that 'it was not their function to take social considerations into account'. But in practice this is what happened and as a result a clear decision was never taken about the rough level of subsidy considered acceptable (there was certainly never any public discussion), and at the time of writing the same seems to be happening with the Rolls Royce RB 211 engine and with Concorde.

Moreover there is an essential similarity in many of these cases between the control and supervision of the large private firm operating under conditions of oligopoly, and the control of the nationalized industries. Both should have special rights *and* special obligations.

However, there was a failure under the Labour Government to appreciate the complexities of this sort of intervention and to be overoptimistic about the size and speed of its effects. Moreover, once one intervenes within the market system all those conflicts which are hidden by the invisible hand become more obvious and the Government becomes the clear object for blame whenever expectations are not fulfilled. Nothing succeeds like success but the reverse is also true. The result was that once the business community became disillusioned all the difficulties – the delicacy, the differing views of what policy should be, the hostility to intervention, the role of the Civil Service, and the constant interaction between these – became worse.

Yet the apparent failure and the apparent inconsistencies which emerged are much more a function of the constraints within which policies were expected to work than an indication of a failure of the policies themselves.

6 Regional policy

Jeremy Hardie

Regional policy and the National Plan

History and ideology make unemployment and poverty crucial political issues for any prospective Labour Government, and it is therefore to be expected that the regional problem – which presents itself most obviously as a problem of disparities in employment and prosperity – should have been an important feature of Labour politicians' plans at the end of 1964. This presumption is not, however, confirmed by the election campaign speeches of the new Ministers. Of course, the issue received attention – particularly from those speaking in or standing for constituencies in the affected areas. But in general regional policy was given little attention in public, except of the most general and casual kind.

There seem to be two reasons for this. The first is that the scale of assistance to the depressed areas had been substantially increased by the Conservatives in the Local Employment Acts of 1960 and 1963. It could well be argued that even with these changes more needed to be done. Nevertheless, as compared with the 1950s, when Conservative policy had been very half-hearted, the situation was much improved, and no longer presented an obvious target for criticism, except on the lines of too little, too late.

The second and more important reason for the neglect of regional policy is that the major innovation which the Labour Party proposed – that regional economies should in some sense be planned – became lost in the wider issue of the management of the British economy, and subsequently of the viability of the National Plan. Economic issues dominated the election (and as it turned out the Government's term of office): and the crucial economic issue, apart from the immediate balance of payments situation, was the contrast between the short-term, stop–go attitudes of the Conservatives, and the long-term, more dirigiste policies to be pursued by Labour. These policies were derived from a commitment to faster growth – of an order comparable with the rates achieved by continental countries in the 1950s and 1960s. For this two instruments were to be particularly important – first, a National Economic Plan: and second the creation of a new Economics Ministry, explicitly designed to administer the Plan and to champion growth against the allegedly short-term preoccupations of the Treasury. If there was to be a National Plan, it seemed to make sense to have regional plans as well: and one of the earliest policy announcements of the new Government was to set up the machinery designed to achieve this.

What regional planning meant in practice, and hence how much of a break with the past the new policy in fact amounted to, is discussed below. Before this, however, there is the wider question of the relationship between regional policy aims and more general national economic goals – in particular, faster growth. The National Plan was designed 'to provide the basis for greater economic growth'.[1] An important obstacle to the achievement of this aim was the slow prospective rate of increase of the labour force. The target rate of growth of 3·8% to 1970 was incompatible with the labour supply which, according to the forecasts, would be available on existing policies. Regional policy – which would contribute to the labour force by drawing on the pool of unemployed in the depressed areas – was crucial in relaxing this constraint, and making available the necessary extra labour. Of the 400,000 manpower gap envisaged, the Plan aimed to meet half by successful regional policies.[2]

The role given by the National Plan to regional policy therefore laid emphasis on the fuller use of national resources – in particular, of unused labour in the depressed areas. In the past demand (and hence growth) had been kept low because expansion might create bottlenecks and other symptoms of excess demand in the prosperous areas. If regional policy were more efficient, and activity were spread more evenly over the country, it would be possible to expand aggregate demand without creating excess demand in some areas before complete utilization of resources had been reached elsewhere. Between 1939 and 1945, when the achievement of war aims required that no potential inputs of labour or capital be wasted, wide-ranging physical and administrative controls had been used to see that, as far as possible, additions to demand fell in those areas which had excess supply potential, and to prevent any excess demand which did develop from having any substantial undesired effects. Full employment throughout the economy was thereby achieved, with unemployment at very low levels even in the areas which had suffered most in the 1930s. A similar uniformity was needed in peacetime if the full potential for growth were to be achieved.

This perspective required that the unemployed be treated as a bundle of unused factors, the location and deployment of which is to be determined in the light of their contribution to the growth objective. Regional policy was to be judged by the success it achieved in making such a contribution to this objective. Plainly, however, governments may have objectives other than growth which regional policy should be used to promote. In particular, a major alternative aim for regional policy is the maintenance of roughly the existing geographical scatter of economic activity, to preserve local communities, cultures and traditions: and to reduce congestion (which is not taken account of in GNP as conventionally calculated) in the prosperous areas. This means, for example, that unemployed Highlanders must be given employment in the Highlands: and

[1] *The National Plan* (Cmnd. 2764, 1965), page 1.
[2] Ibid. page 4.

hence that the criterion of success for regional policy is whether the Highlands are re-established as a viable economic community. But the best deployment of labour on this criterion may conflict with what is best on the growth criterion. Growth may require relocation of labour in the more prosperous areas of the South, where it can readily and cheaply be used by the industries which need it. If minimum cost production for most industries requires close proximity with other competitive and complementary firms, then the correct strategy for growth is to follow the market forces which reject the Highlands as a site for industrial and economic activity. On this analysis, greater concentration in the Midlands and South-East, at the cost not only of agricultural communities such as the Highlands but of other industrial areas such as the North-East and South Wales, reflects the economic realities of modern industry.

In the mid-1960s the consensus of economists was that this analysis of the optimum distribution of population and employment for the growth objective is broadly speaking wrong: and that there is therefore no significant conflict in designing a regional policy which is optimal by both criteria.

There are a number of reasons for this. First, any large-scale movement of workers to the work would require the provision of social capital – houses, schools, hospitals, roads – in the new area, and the under-utilization of existing social capital in the deserted areas. This would represent an addition to demand on total resources, even taking into account the low quality of such facilities in many areas, and the need to replace a good proportion of them in the near future (so that emigration would only affect where, not whether, the replacement took place).

Secondly, the employment problem of the depressed areas is not only a matter of unemployment, but of activity rates (employees as a percentage of the home population). Male activity rates do not differ much: but the very low number of women in the labour force in such regions as Wales, the North and the South-West represent a substantial pool of unused labour.[1] The most plausible version of a workers to the work strategy involves the migration of the male unemployed – of the kind successfully achieved in the 1930s. The female activity rate will certainly not be favourably affected. It may even be made worse if the emigration of the young and able from the region makes the region less attractive than before for industry, and hence reduces the demand for female labour. Alternatively, it is possible to envisage a long-term policy aimed at large-scale migration not only of the male unemployed but also of their families. But the volume of migration required would have very serious effects on the viability of the regional economy, given the economies of scale – real or supposed – in modern manufacturing, and in the provision of social capital. Many regional markets are already too small to support a local

[1] John Bowers, 'The Anatomy of Regional Activity Rates' (*NIESR*, 1970), pages 17 and 40.

establishment – whether a hospital or a manufacturing plant – of the optimum size: they have therefore to import from other regions. Any further decrease in size would make them even less attractive as a base for economic activity: and the initial emigration would therefore generate a new unemployment problem.

Lastly, whether it is desirable to move the workers to the work depends not only on the difficulty of successfully promoting migration but on the cost of the alternative – that is, of moving capital to where labour is available. The tendency of the market to concentrate economic activity, and the reluctance of industrialists to accept any location other than the one they have voluntarily selected, is prima facie evidence that the mobility of capital is low, and that the economic disadvantages of remoter locations are substantial. But there are good reasons for not basing regional policy on these market indicators. Because of the importance of externalities it is unlikely that the independent commercial decisions of firms will lead to an optimum pattern of location. In considering the costs of expanding production in the South-East an industrialist will ignore the costs of congested or increased social capital which his decision to expand there will put on the local community, because they will not fall on him. More important, a company will reject a distant location if it does not provide the necessary variety of complementary firms and services. Other companies complementary to it will reject the same location for the same reason. Each firm would be willing to choose that location if every other would. The market provides no mechanism for co-ordinating the decisions of these decentralized units so that they achieve the lowest cost location – lowest cost to themselves, let alone to society. There is therefore a strong case for refusing to accept at its face value the market's condemnation of certain regions. The argument is supported by the empirical investigations of Luttrell[1] which show that in general a self-contained branch set up in a new area would not show any persistent cost disadvantage of any substance which could be attributed to an inherent inferiority of the branch location.[2]

The National Plan recognized the possibility of conflicts between growth and other objectives, and showed how they would be dealt with if they arose:[3]

There may at times appear to be some conflict between the national priorities of economic growth and the local claims of certain regions or parts of them. But regional policies will not be concerned with bolstering up small areas which have no economic future; they will be concerned with developing those parts of each region where there is a real growth potential.

[1] W. F. Luttrell, 'Factory location and industrial movement' (*NIESR*, 1962).
[2] Ibid. pages 312 ff. See also *Regional Policy and the Motor Industry* (EDC for Motor Manufacturing, 1969), which concludes (page 1) that '. . . there was little evidence that regional policy had proved disadvantageous to firms expanding into development areas'.
[3] *The National Plan,* op. cit. page 85.

So long as the conflicts relate only to 'small areas', and the local population can move quite readily to neighbouring growth areas, there is not much cause for concern. It is possible to accept the decline of mining villages in Durham provided that adequate alternative employment is available on Tyneside or Teeside. The conflict only becomes serious if the stern pursuit of growth requires the deliberate abandonment of larger areas such as West Cumberland. It is fortunate that at the time the Labour Government came to power in 1964 there was no serious conflict between the requirements of the National Plan, which had growth as its central objective and the wider social and political pressures which required that the authorities maintain a high level of economic activity in such regions as Wales, Scotland and the North.

Policy to 1964

At the time of the change of Government in 1964 the instruments of regional policy were:

(*i*) Control of the location of privately built factories (but not offices) via the issue of Industrial Development Certificates (IDCs). These were required for all factories or extensions over 5000 sq. ft.

(*ii*) The provision of loans and grants by the Board of Trade, under the Local Employment Acts 1960 and 1963, to companies operating in the Development Districts. Loans and grants could be made for general purposes, among others to compensate for unusual initial expenses. Since 1963 there had been available standard grants for buildings, and for plant and machinery – at 25% on cost for buildings, and 10% for plant and machinery (in addition to the investment and initial allowances available throughout the country). The capital cost of plant and machinery in Development Districts could be written off against profits for tax at whatever annual rate the company chose (free depreciation). All loans and grants under the Local Employment Acts (but not free depreciation) depended on the provision of employment by the proposed project.

(*iii*) The building of factories in Development Districts by the Board of Trade for subsequent sale or lease on favourable terms. Some (but few) of these factories were advance factories built speculatively. All leased factories were let at local market rents – which were in most cases below the level which would give a normal commercial return on the cost of the building.

(*iv*) Various small-scale provisions – retraining of labour: transfer of key workers: clearance of derelict sites: improvement of basic services: overseas aid tied to purchase from depressed areas.

All these policies related to the Development Districts, which in 1964 covered about 15% of the insured employees in Great Britain.[1] These districts were defined as '. . . any locality in Great Britain in which . . . a high rate of unemployment exists or is to be expected . . . and is likely to persist. . . .' Broadly, an unemployment rate of 4·5% was the criterion.[2] The districts were small, because based on Local Employment Exchange areas: additions to and deletions from the list were quite frequent.[3]

This package of policies was subject to a number of criticisms which had an important effect on the new Government's thinking.

The substitution in 1960 of Development Districts for the Development Areas not only reduced the proportion of employees covered by the legislation, but also selected for favourable treatment within the problem regions those areas – of high unemployment – which were prima facie least suitable as bases for sustained economic growth. It would be preferable to give incentives over a broader area – even if that involved subsidizing areas which were relatively prosperous even by national standards.[4] Conversely, it was ridiculous to give grants to isolated pockets of unemployment in the S.E. when the area as a whole was chronically short of labour.

The mix of incentives was criticized for its encouragement of capital-intensive projects. Prima facie a regional policy is required to reduce unemployment. Policy should therefore be directed at subsidizing those activities which use labour. This was to an extent done in the administration of Board of Trade loans and grants, which were conditional on the creation of employment. But free depreciation (which was available whether or not employment was created) encouraged the location of capital-intensive processes in the regions, and involved subsidizing activities which might make little contribution to the unemployment problem, whether directly or indirectly.

Others felt that although financial and administrative devices could be used to divert industry to locations which it would not otherwise choose, it would be preferable to lay more emphasis on attacking directly the disadvantages which made companies avoid the depressed regions – in particular, inferior schools, hospitals, roads, communications and general infrastructure – which were at least as important to industry as cost-subsidies.

As well as these detailed points there was a feeling that economic management in general (and hence regional policy) had under the Tories failed to use the quantitative and other expertise available to modern

---

[1] Local Employment Acts, 1960 and 1963: *Fourth Annual Report by the Board of Trade* (HC 314, Session 1963/64), page 4.

[2] *First Annual Report by the Board of Trade* (HC 291, Session 1960/61), pages 3–4.

[3] See the Board of Trade Annual Reports for the changes made each year.

[4] This criticism was only partly met – and then only for N.E. England and Central Scotland – by the assurance given in 1963 that those areas selected as particularly suitable for future expansion (the 'growth areas') would continue to be eligible for such assistance until there was evidence of a sustained improvement in the region as a whole. *Central Scotland: A Programme for Development and Growth* (Cmnd. 2188, 1963), page 10. *The North-East: A Programme for Development and Growth* (Cmnd. 2206, 1963), page 6.

policy-makers, and was therefore to be condemned for ineptitude as much as for wrong-headedness. For regional policy this meant that research into the nature of the regional problem (including the preparation of regional accounts, input-output models, and so on) should be vigorously encouraged. Future decisions should be made on the basis of much improved regional and national statistics, after quantification of the costs and benefits of the alternatives, and with the help of accurate models of the regional economy. Much of this was unattainable in the current state of the art and of knowledge. It was possible, however, to make a start by introducing a greater element of planning – in the sense of taking decisions about the regions in the context of a long-term overall view of how the region should develop, and after considering for each decision how it fits with actions being taken in other areas. In this way it was hoped that piecemeal unco-ordinated measures could be replaced by a coherent regional strategy.

Policy under Labour 1964-70

The sequence of events in the evolution of Labour regional measures is as follows. In the middle of November 1964 George Brown announced the imminent creation of Regional Economic Planning Councils and Planning Boards, and the introduction of a Bill to restrict office building in the South-East.[1] In 1966, the Industrial Development Act substituted Development Areas for Development Districts, and changed regional investment incentives to fit with the new investment grant system. In 1967 the Regional Employment Premium was introduced. Gradations in the definition of Development Areas were made in 1967 by specifying Special Development Areas, and in 1969 by giving subsidies to Intermediate Areas.

The main changes in policy therefore came in 1966/67: and only between September 1967 and June 1970 was the full package in operation. Looking at the period 1964/65 to 1969/70 as a whole, and at the crude changes in budgetary costs of regional assistance, the increase is remarkable – about ten-fold.

For a number of reasons, however, it would be wrong to take this as an accurate indication of the scale of improvement in regional incentives. First, the changes in 1963 – when standard building and plant and machinery grants were introduced and, more important, free depreciation – did not have full effect on the budget figures until 1965/66. This alone makes the increase under Labour more like fourfold – from say £75 million to £300 million.

Secondly, the figures are based on the cost to the budget in the appropriate financial year. They lump together therefore a variety of payments

[1] IDC control was extended to all factory development over 1000 sq.ft. Under the Industrial Development Act 1966 the limit was raised again to 5000 sq.ft., except in the Midlands and S.E., where it was set at 3000 sq.ft.

TABLE 6.1   ESTIMATED COST OF PREFERENTIAL GOVERNMENT ASSISTANCE
TO DEVELOPMENT AREAS (AND FORMER DEVELOPMENT
DISTRICTS)

	£ million	
	1964/65	1969/70
Assistance under Local Employment Acts	27·3	58·4
Investment Grants differential	—	96·0
Regional Employment Premium	—	109·0
SET Premium	—	28·6
Industrial Training[a]	—	4·3
Free Depreciation[b]	3·0	—
Miscellaneous[c]	—	5·2
Total	30·3	301·5

[a] DEP assistance only: excludes Government Training Centres
[b] £45m. in 1965/6 (first full year)
[c] Highland and Islands Development Board: Loans and SET refunds to hotels

Source: *Hansard,* House of Commons, Vol. 801, Col. 643.

of diverse economic and long-term budgetary effects. For example, within
the category of LEA assistance are included grants, repayable loans, and
construction of factories. These figures are not net of repayments, interest
or rents received during the year on previous loans or factories.[1] Plainly
an out and out grant is a very different proposition both for the recipient
company and for the Government than a repayable interest-bearing
loan.[2] More important, free depreciation is computed at its net cost to
the Exchequer (i.e. at the amount of tax foregone): while investment
grants are shown gross (i.e. before taking into account the extra tax paid
because companies cannot write off for Corporation Tax that part of the
capital cost covered by the grant).

Even if they were amended to take these factors into account, there
is a more fundamental difficulty in taking annual figures of the kind in the
table as an index of the intensity of regional policy. To do so would be
analogous to comparing successive annual tax-takes in analysing changes
in discretionary fiscal policy: rather than looking at changes in tax codes,
and their effect on tax-take at some constant level of activity (for example,
full employment). In the case of regional incentives, it is plain that many
factors affect the figures for total assistance other than changes in the terms
on which the authorities will provide it. For example, the major determinant of Board of Trade assistance under the Local Employment Acts

[1] These receipts are substantial. In 1968/69 for example loan repayments were £15 million:
rents £6 million and interest £3 million. See *Local Employment Acts 1960 to 1966: Accounts
1968/9* (HC 100, Session 1969–70), pages 4, 7, 11.
[2] Grants offered (not paid, as in the Table) amounted to about 45% of total assistance
to Development Areas in both 1964/5 and 1969/70 (Fifth and Tenth Annual Reports of
the Board of Trade on the Local Employment Acts) – or absolutely £17 million in
1964/5 and £38 million in 1969/70.

T.L.G—H

in the early 1960s was the overall level of national economic activity, which made companies more anxious to invest in Development Districts, and hence to ask for assistance. In assessing regional policy in those years, the increase in the figures for the cost of regional assistance consequent on such increased demand should not be taken as an indicator of more generous Government regional policy, for which the only criterion is whether or not the terms on which the assistance is provided are made more or less generous.

It is important therefore to recognize that the increase in total expenditure may be attributable to other factors which affect the level of activity in the regions – some of which, such as IDC policy or provision of infrastructure, are within regional policy, while others are beyond government control or unintended by government. And within the total, an increase in a particular category of expenditure (such as investment grants) may represent the automatic result of the favourable effect on regional activity of another category – e.g. the Regional Employment Premium – rather than an improvement in that particular regional incentive.

What then were the changes which the Labour Government made to the terms on which assistance was offered to industry in the regions? The change in 1966 from Development Districts to Development Areas, which covered a larger part of the country even than their pre-1960 ancestors, represents an important change in regional incentives. The coverage of the Development Districts had varied from 9·2% of the total population in 1962 to 16·8% in 1966. The Development Areas in 1966 covered 20%. This reform therefore led to a once and for all rise in the proportion of economic activity automatically eligible for LEA and investment aid (although a good deal of the extra population was agricultural and not therefore likely to get much regional assistance).

Table 6.2 gives details of the financial assistance available to firms in Development Areas (and Special Development Areas and Intermediate Areas) in mid-1970. It is comparable with the list of measures in operation in 1964. The map shows the geographical definition of the relevant areas at mid-1970. (See Fig. 6.1)

Investment incentives were changed radically in 1966. Free depreciation and plant and machinery grants were dropped. Instead, capital investment on qualifying assets in the Development Areas got investment grants at 40% – 20% more than elsewhere.[1] Whether this change represents a change in regional incentives – and in what direction – depends on what difference it made to the differential investment incentive in favour of the regions as it seemed to a company making an investment decision. Such a comparison should be based on the present value of the investment incentives to the typical company before and after the change, keeping everything else (in particular the company tax code and other regional incentives) constant. To get the full benefit of assistance under the old

[1] This differential remained at 20% when the rates were raised to 45% and 25% as a temporary measure in 1967 and 1968.

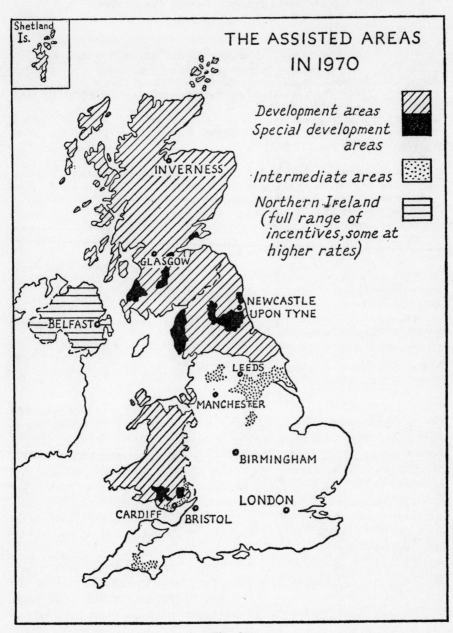

THE ASSISTED AREAS
IN 1970

Development areas

Special development
areas

Intermediate areas

Northern Ireland
(full range of
incentives, some at
higher rates)

Shetland
Is.

INVERNESS

GLASGOW

BELFAST

NEWCASTLE
UPON TYNE

LEEDS

MANCHESTER

BIRMINGHAM

LONDON

CARDIFF
BRISTOL

Fig. 6.1

TABLE 6.2   FINANCIAL ASSISTANCE IN THE DEVELOPMENT AREAS,
SPECIAL DEVELOPMENT AREAS AND INTERMEDIATE
AREAS* OF GREAT BRITAIN AT MID-1970

(1) Investment grants on plant and machinery at 40% (20% elsewhere) for use in manufacturing, extractive and construction industries.

(2) Regional Employment Premium (30/- p.w. for each fulltime male worker in manufacturing industry. Lower rates for women, boys, girls, part-timers).

*(3) DEP and ITB grants for on the job training, training courses, and transfer of key workers.

(4) Local Employment Act incentives (only available where employment will increase).

*(a) Factories for rent or sale at local market value. In the case of some projects new to the area, two years rent-free (five years in Special Development Areas),

*(b) Building grants at 25% (for some new projects 35%),

(c) Low interest loans for plant and machinery or working capital,

(d) Removal grants,

(e) In Special Development Areas, for new projects only

(i) Operational grants at 10% p.a. for first three years on capital costs incurred in first three years.

(ii) Loans towards balance of building costs.

(iii) Building grants at 35%.

From August 1968 assistance under the Local Employment Acts was not available for service industries (unless the project increased employment by at least 50).

(5) Loans, Grants and refunds of SET to hotels in certain rural areas.

Source: Ministry of Technology, *Incentives for Industry*.

regime, a manufacturing project had to create additional employment (to get building and plant and machinery grants): and be profitable, or at least be part of a company with taxable profits elsewhere (to get immediate benefit from free depreciation). For such a project, the relative advantage of the new as compared with the old system will vary with the company's discount rate, the capital intensity of the project, and other factors. Calculations based on the position of a typical company[1] show that the 1966 change made a negligible difference to the incentive in favour of the regions, both in the case of plant and machinery and of buildings.

This central case is, however, only one example of an investment project. For other manufacturing projects, the new system was better whenever one or both of the conditions of employment creation or profitability was not fulfilled. Hence replacement investment in existing plants, and investment by companies without profits for UK tax (for example, some international oil companies), were favoured. On the other hand, little investment in services got anything under the new regime after 1968: under the old, it was subsidized provided it created employment.

It is likely therefore that the investment grant system did not represent any substantial change in the level of incentives to companies to switch

[1] See Annex A to Appendix I to *Evidence to Select Committee on Scottish Affairs* (HC 267-I, Session 1969/70).

investment into the Development Areas – plainly not in the case of the typical manufacturing investment: and probably not overall if the off-setting effects on other types of investment project are balanced against each other.

The increase in budget costs – if there is any after adjustment for the abandonment of standard grants and free depreciation – does not there-fore represent any major change or improvement in policy in relation to specifically investment incentives. It is the result of other factors – includ-ing no doubt genuine changes in other regional incentives – which in-creased the willingness of companies to invest in the Development Areas given the level of investment incentive: and perhaps of increased replace-ment investment by companies already operating there.

Regional Employment Premium, however, is a plain case of improved assistance. It was introduced from September 1967 at a rate of 30/- per week per man (with corresponding payments for other classes of labour) in manufacturing industry, and was accompanied from the time of devaluation by a differential 7/6 SET premium: this was withdrawn in 1970 with the introduction of assistance to the Intermediate Areas. Several characteristics of the REP deserve attention. First, it was intro-duced on a large scale *ab initio*: it was at once one of the most important forms of financial assistance. Secondly, REP/SET is available quite un-conditionally for all employees in manufacturing industry. Until 1964 regional incentives (except free depreciation) had only been available where the Board of Trade was convinced that an increase in employment would be forthcoming: and even free depreciation required the act of in-vestment and the earning of profits somewhere by the claimant company. Thirdly, REP is a subsidy on labour: it went a good way therefore in meeting the criticism that subsidies should encourage the use of the free factor labour rather than scarce capital.[1] Fourthly, payment was guaran-teed for seven years. A firm moving to or setting up a branch in a Develop-ment Area could therefore predict that element of its costs with certainty for a number of years – as it could not predict its capital costs, which would depend on whether investment grants were still available when it replaced or extended capacity in later years.

The REP has been compared with a regional devaluation: and praised as a neat device for reviving that weapon in a country where a common currency dictates the maintenance of fixed exchange rates between regions. It is not clear, however, how the REP differs from other subsidies (for example, the investment grant) in this respect. Any regional subsidy can have any combination of a number of effects.[2] If it raises profits, it will

---

[1] This criticism is supported by the analysis of Professor Brown which shows that an important part of the explanation of the high share of development areas in new capital-intensive industry was attributable to differential investment grants (See Appendix J to *Report of Hunt Committee on Intermediate Areas* (Cmnd. 3998, 1969)).

[2] See A. J. Brown, 'The Green Paper on the Development Areas', *National Institute Economic Review*, May 1967, page 26.

induce companies to switch investment and activity to the region. Or it can have a devaluation effect, by allowing a reduction in prices and a consequent increase in regional exports. Or it can be treated as a direct injection of income from outside, which goes into profits or wages or both, and increases the demand for regional goods.

All these effects stimulate regional activity: but they can be created by any outside subsidy, including investment grants. But the investment grant applies only to additions to capital, and to that extent operates only at the margin: the REP on the other hand is paid on all labour, including the intra-marginal, and is thus more like a devaluation.

The REP amounted to a reduction in labour costs of about 7% as compared with non-Development Areas. This may be about 2·5% of annual operating costs. The present value of the differential element in grants was about 12% of gross capital cost for plant and machinery. These again may be worth about 2·5% p.a. of annual operating costs. So a company in a Development Area typically received an overall subsidy of about 5%.[1] Because the subsidy was greater for capital as a percentage of cost than for labour, capital-intensive industries still got an appreciably better deal.

Amounts spent on training grants and help for transferred workers, although small, represent an important improvement in the attractiveness of the regional labour force.[2] In addition to financial inducements for training, the increase in Government Training Centres – nationally from 26 with 4078 places in 1964 to 40 with 8863 places in 1968, and a planned further expansion to 54 with 13,000 by the end of 1971 – was disproportionately directed towards the Development Areas, which had 1340 places in 1964, 3574 in 1968, and 5700 (planned) by 1971.[3]

Total assistance under the Local Employment Acts can be split between loans, grants and factory building. The Board of Trade is bound by statute to observe certain criteria in approving projects. But it has a good deal of discretion: and there are indications that the general attitude of the authorities to providing assistance under the Local Employment Acts became more generous after 1964 – at least towards manufacturing industry. A major decision between 1964 and 1970 was to exclude completely from assistance service projects which serve mainly a local market, and any which provide less than 50 jobs. This took effect from July 1968,[4] and will make comparison of 1969/70 figures with previous years underestimate changes in assistance to manufacturing industry. Similarly, the substitution of investment grants in 1966 for (inter alia) standard

[1] G. McCrone, quoted in *Evidence to Select Committee on Scottish Affairs* (HC 267–I, Session 1969/70), page 534. See also Ministry of Technology comments on his figures, ibid. Appendix 17.

[2] For an account of Government help with training in Development Areas, see *Employment and Productivity Gazette*, April 1970, page 281.

[3] *Hansard*, House of Commons, Vol. 792, Col. 1685 and Vol. 774, Col. 6.

[4] Ninth Annual Report by the Board of Trade (HC 392, Session 1968/9), page 2.

plant and machinery grants will artificially deflate the increase in total grants between 1964 and 1970.[1]

Taking figures for assistance offered – not paid – Table 6.3 shows the breakdown between 1964/65 and 1969/70:

TABLE 6.3 TOTAL ASSISTANCE OFFERED IN THE DEVELOPMENT AREAS £000

	1964/65		1969/70
Loans		10,429	28,088
Special Grants	632		11,412[a]
Building Grants	10,027		26,247
Plant and Machinery Grants	6,790		103
		17,449	37,762
Factory Building		12,730	17,038
Total assistance offered		40,608	82,888

[a] Includes £10,150,000 Operational Grants for new projects in Special Development Areas.

Source: *Annual Reports on Local Employment Acts.*

The record of factories completed in Development Areas is not quite as good as the figures for offers in this table might suggest. In 1969/70 factories totalling 1,998,000 sq. ft. were completed. This is an improvement on the 1,460,000 sq. ft. of 1964/65: but rather below the peak under the Conservatives in 1961–2 of 2,959,000 sq. ft. But taking annual averages, the Labour rate of approvals over the five years April 1965/March 1970 was 122 projects of 3,031,000 sq. ft. The equivalent figure for the four years 1960/64 under the Conservatives was 58 projects of 1,994,000 sq. ft. The increase on this basis is therefore striking. Part of it is the result of a deliberate emphasis on building speculative factories in advance of demand. The Conservatives approved 46 such factories in the period April 1960/October 1964. Between November 1964 and April 1970, 221 factories were approved – an annual rate of 40 projects. Of these, 59 were still under construction in April 1970: and 55 were completed and unlet. On average, the latter had been empty for about a year.[2] It is likely that this disappointing result represents a relatively low demand for Board of Trade factories in the Development Areas – a demand which is itself determined by other regional policies and above all by the level of national economic activity. Given that Board of Trade factory building must be a relatively passive factor in the overall regional situation, it would have

[1] Plant and Machinery Grants offered were £103,000 in 1969/70, and £6,790,000 in 1964/65. See *Tenth Annual Report* (HC 127, Session 1969/70), page 24: and *Fifth Annual Report* (HC 298, Session 1964/65), page 7.
[2] *Annual Reports on Local Employment Acts. Hansard,* House of Commons, Vol. 800, Col. 366 and Vol. 801, Col. 25.

been futile to adopt a higher rate of building when there was already a good stock of unoccupied advance factories.

Providing better infrastructure is an important element in regional policy. How much of the improvement in roads, schools, hospitals and so on in the Development Areas in the last few years is attributable to regional policy is in principle very difficult to assess. A proper analysis needs first some estimate of the expenditure on infra-structure which would have taken place in the absence of, or neglect of, the regional problem. This cannot be done. Whether or not they were a conscious part of regional policy, some important improvements have clearly been made. Communications with the regions certainly improved substantially in the 1960s. The opening of the Severn Bridge, the development of the motorway system, in particular of the North-West, the introduction of Inter-City passenger services faster than the competitive air links, the development of Freightliners – all these have gone far to meet the demands of the regions for better inter-regional transport. About one-third of the £62 million subsidy to British Rail under the 1968 Transport Act goes to the support of unprofitable lines in Development Areas.[1] Some overall indication of the Government's attitude to regional infra-structure is given by data on public investment in new construction. Between 1965/66 and 1969/70 annual expenditure on new construction – which includes houses, hospitals, schools, roads, power stations – went up by 41% in the UK as a whole. In the regions North, South-West, Wales, North-West, Scotland and Northern Ireland it rose by 57%. In 1969/70 the share of these regions of the total was 47% (compared with 42% of the population).

The Government has a number of more direct methods of influencing employment and the location of industry. One is to support private industry in trouble. The paradigm of this is the case of Upper Clyde Shipbuilders. There were plainly reasons for keeping these yards in business even if employment had been readily available elsewhere for the labour released by a liquidation. But the possibility of losing 10,000 jobs in a Development Area strongly reinforced the argument for support. By the end of 1969 the total aid to UCS in grants and loans, given or promised by the Shipbuilding Industry Board, with the approval of the Ministry of Technology, was £18·7 million.[2] The Labour Government in general showed itself more willing to interfere with – whether by money or not – the activities of private industry. Where this had the effect of keeping alive a plant or factory in a Development Area which would otherwise have closed, it was a useful supplement to more orthodox regional policies, whether or not it was justifiable in terms of general industrial policy.

The Government can further influence the location of employment by using its power to affect the location of Civil Service departments.

[1] *Hansard,* House of Commons, Vol. 778, Col. 135.
[2] *Evidence to Select Committee on Scottish Affairs* (HC 397, Session 1968/9), Appendix 21, para. 13.

A policy of dispersal from London was accepted by the Government in 1963 after the publication of the Flemming Report. It was planned to move 13,500 jobs right out of London, and another 4500 to the periphery. It is claimed that between 1964 and 1970 45,000 government jobs were established outside London, of which 21,000 were in Development Areas.[1]

These included moving the Giro and Inland Revenue to Bootle: the Motor Tax Office to Swansea: and the Royal Mint to Llantrisant.

The most powerful direct weapon is the Board of Trade's control of industrial buildings via the issue of IDCs. An IDC was required to support all applications for planning consent for industrial buildings over 3000 sq. ft. in the Midlands and South-East, and over 5000 sq. ft. elsewhere.[2] The Board of Trade has a statutory obligation to pay special regard to the employment needs of the Development Areas and in general to see that proposals are consistent with a proper distribution of industry. It is not easy to see from any published data with what vigour the policy is pursued, or what its effects may be. Figures for IDCs refused are not much good: most companies will not bother to apply if they know they are going to be turned down – and no such statistics can reveal the modifications to expansion plans made in the light of likely official resistance to the first-choice site. A study carried out by the Board of Trade[3] into the behaviour of 239 firms whose applications for IDCs were turned down in the South-East between July 1958 and June 1963, and whose immediate plans were not clear (i.e. excluding those for whom alternative plans were made or were otherwise apparent at the time of refusal), sheds some light on the problem. Of these projects, 17·7% by floor space went to Government-assisted areas – then Development Districts. Another 25·9% went to some other location preferable on distribution of industry grounds to the congested South-East. 12·2% were abandoned. 34·4% went ahead by one means or another in the South-East.[4]

This evidence suggests that the IDC method can make a considerable contribution to reducing congestion in the South-East – more than the figures suggest, as most of the 34·4% which remained in the South-East did so on a reduced scale: but that Government-assisted areas do not get much of the industry so displaced.[5]

It is plain that the IDC system has a very important effect on the expansionary plans of firms, via abandonment, deferral, and modification: but that diversion to Development Areas and similar desirable effects on location are only a minor part of such modifications. In most

---

[1] Crosland, *Hansard,* House of Commons, Vol. 801, Col. 436.
[2] From 1964 to 1966, over 1000 sq. ft. anywhere. Before 1966, research buildings and certain kinds of non-production space were not within the control.
[3] *Evidence to Select Committee on Scottish Affairs* (HC 267-I, Session 1969/70), Appendix 7: and *Minutes of Evidence of Board of Trade* (HC 397, Session 1968/9), Q 1221 ff.
[4] Appendix 7, Tables 2 and 5.
[5] See also the Birmingham Chamber of Commerce and CBI enquiries for the Hunt Committee (Cmnd. 3998, 1969), page 104.

cases firms manage to achieve their original objectives in one way or another, but by second-best means. One of these means, and by no means the most common, is to build in a Development Area.

Table 6.4 shows that the share of IDCs (by area) going to the Development Areas was somewhat higher in 1965–9 than in the early 1960s: but that this share fell appreciably towards the end of the period. The figures for additional employment in completed buildings show a similar pattern.

To see whether there has been any change in IDC policy during the period, figures for Development Area shares in IDCs granted, or employment created, are only of limited help. An increase in the share of industrial building going to Development Areas can arise either because the Board of Trade has been more stern in its rejection of projects in the South-East: or because other regional policies – REP, investment grants, the extension of preferential treatment to more areas – have made the Development Areas more attractive to industry, and hence increased the demand for IDCs in Development Areas. As applications for IDCs in Development Areas are rarely refused[1] such a change would produce an improved Development Area share.

TABLE 6.4　INDUSTRIAL BUILDING IN DEVELOPMENT AREAS[a]

Year	IDCs approved in DAs (Area in m.sq.ft.)	Col. 1 as % of IDCs approved, in Great Britain	Estimated additional employment[b] (000) in D.A.s
1961	15·0	27	30·0
1962	9·1	24	30·3
1963	12·2	31	32·2
1964	20·2	34	26·5
1965	24·6	40	42·5
1966	28·6	41	} 45·1
1966[c]	29·1	38	
1967	28·9	33	39·0
1968	37·9	34	39·2
1969	33·0	29	20·4[d]

[a] DAs as defined in 1966 and after. Thus an area which was not a Development District, but was after 1966 in a DA (e.g. much of Wales) is included in the 1961–5 figures although it then had no preferential status.

[b] In buildings *completed* for manufacturing industry.

[c] Before August 1966, ancillary space for storage, canteens etc. was included only for some areas: after that date for all. Two figures therefore appear for 1966 – one on the old basis, one on the new.

[d] 6 months only: not an annual rate.

Source: *Board of Trade Memorandum to Select Committee on Scottish Affairs* (HC 397, Session 1968/9), page 122; Annex I to Appendix 14 to same (HC 267-I, Session 1969/70) page 528: *Hansard*, House of Commons, Vol. 795, Col. 317.

[1] See Appendix 16 to *Select Committee on Scottish Affairs* (HC 397, Session 1968/9).

The only evidence whether any such changes are the result of a different attitude to granting IDCs, apart from the assertions of politicians that they were, is the Board of Trade Evidence to the Select Committee on Scottish Affairs.[1]

... The policy [on IDCs] has become tougher during this period overall, tougher in relation to the South-East and Midlands, although relaxed perhaps to some extent in the areas which are now grey areas. As far as its operation in the South-East and Midlands is concerned, it has become tougher over this period. *Q.* When did it become tougher? *A.* . . . I would say that the main emphasis on this was when the present [Labour] administration came into power.

IDC control is one of the few regional policy weapons aimed directly at reducing congestion in the prosperous areas as well as promoting activity in the Development Areas. Although the problems of the South-East and of the depressed areas are recognized to be two sides of the same coin in principle, actual policy measures have concentrated almost exclusively on one side, leaving the other to exhortation. But the introduction of Office Development Permits went some way to shift the balance. This was aimed primarily at preventing expansion and congestion in the South-East, particularly in Central London. Offices within the London Metropolitan region were controlled from November 1964. The West Midland conurbation was added in August 1965: in July 1966 the control was extended to the rest of the South-East and West Midlands, and to East Anglia and the East Midlands. In February 1969, East Anglia and certain areas of the East and West Midlands were excluded.[2] The control therefore at mid-1970 still covered a very large area of the South-East and Midlands. The 48·2 million square feet of office development in the pipeline in London in November 1964 had been reduced to 16·8 million by March 1970. And refusals in the South-East in 1966/70 covered a gross area of 19,566,000 sq. ft., 50% of the area for which permits were issued.[3]

Regional planning

Although the National Plan gave considerable prominence to regional planning,[4] it did not attempt to provide a breakdown of industrial production region by region, nor did it suggest that subsequent regional plans should try to do so. It proved hard enough to produce detailed figures for national output: to have split them geographically would have been an impossible task. The declared purpose of the Regional Economic

[1] Ibid., 1232–4.
[2] *Annual Report by the Board of Trade on the Control of Office and Industrial Development Act*, (HC 389, Session 1968/9), page 3.
[3] *Annual Reports of the Board of Trade*, 1966/67 to 1969/70.
[4] *National Plan* (Cmnd. 2764, 1965), Ch. 8, Appendix B.

Planning Councils was to produce 'firm regional plans for the consideration of Ministers'.[1] It is worth examining what the nature and effect of these plans have turned out to be.

Before 1965 there were a number of studies of particular regions.[2] In 1965 four more appeared – three under the aegis of the DEA[3], and one for the Government of Northern Ireland[4] – which had been in preparation when the Planning Councils were being formed. The scope and purpose of these studies varied a good deal: but all contained a mass of factual information – much not available, or not readily available, before – about the existing economy of the region, a forecast of the way it would develop on existing policies, and some indication of how it would be desirable that it should develop. It is plainly of great interest to carry out exercises of this kind. If regional planning is to mean anything, it must be based on a reasonably accurate assessment of the facts. But two further conditions are necessary if the future of a region is to be affected favourably. First, the policy-makers must have a fairly good model of how the regional economy works – of its internal linkages and of its relationships with the rest of the country and the world. Second, the authorities, or someone, must be able to influence the instruments which affect the target variables which they are interested in. Otherwise the exercise, however skilfully performed, remains of curiosity value only.

To a considerable extent, these three conditions were unfulfilled at the time when regional planning was introduced, and remain unfulfilled. The data are not nearly as bad as they were. Regional Social Accounts now exist for all regions of the United Kingdom – if only for 1961 and/or 1964.[5] The Treasury has produced a Central Government budget for Scotland.[6] And the *Abstract of Regional Statistics* (which started in 1965), the statistics produced for the Hunt Committee, the investigations of the Select Committee on Scottish Affairs, and the official regional studies produced since 1965[7] have between them made things a good deal

---

[1] Ibid, page App–15.

[2] *Central Scotland: A Programme for Development and Growth* (Cmnd. 2188, 1963). *The North-East: A Programme for Development and Growth* (Cmnd. 2206, 1963). *Report of the Committee of Enquiry into the Scottish Economy* (Scottish Council, 1961 – The Toothill Report). *Report of the Joint Working Party on the Economy of Northern Ireland* (Cmnd. 1835, 1962 – The Hall Report). *The South East Study, 1961–81* (MHLG, 1964).

[3] *The North West* (DEA 1965); *West Midlands* (DEA 1965); *Cumberland and Westmorland,* (DEA 1965).

[4] *Economic Development in Northern Ireland* (Cmd. 479, 1965 – The Wilson Report).

[5] Woodward: *Regional Social Accounts for the United Kingdom* (NIESR 1970).

[6] *A Scottish Budget 1967–8* (H.M. Treasury 1969).

[7] It is worth listing the more prominent of these, if only to bring out the scale of the effort directed to regional policy and planning during the period:

The Scottish Economy 1965–70 (Cmnd. 2864, 1966); *The East Midlands Study* (DEA 1966); *A Review of Yorkshire and Humberside* (DEA 1966); *Challenge of the Changing North,* (DEA 1966); *The Lothians* (Scottish Development Department 1966); *A Region with a Future: Draft Strategy for the South West* (DEA 1967); *West Midlands: Patterns for Growth* (DEA 1967); *A Strategy for the South East* (DEA 1967); *Cairngorm Area* (Scottish Develop-

easier for anyone interested in the facts about the regions.

Additional data, although of great descriptive interest, will only help policy if we are able to make good guesses about how regional economies work. The heroic assumptions involved in the estimate of the regional multiplier[1] show how tentative we must be in suggesting how the regional economy operates, and what the effects of policy instruments will be. The processes of economic growth in general, and at the regional level in particular, are obscure. The location decisions of business men, and the effects of infrastructure improvements, grants, threats, on those decisions cannot be explained except in the most general terms. To estimate the consequences of a tougher IDC policy in the South-East, for example, requires knowledge of the congestion costs of allowing expansion at the present rate: the reaction of the companies whose plans are frustrated: the addition to production costs if they have to locate elsewhere: the multiplier effect on the region to which the plant is diverted: the attractive effect on other industry of an increase in the region's output of that particular product: and so on. It would be ridiculous to require precisely estimated values for all these variables. But at present we have very little idea indeed of the magnitudes involved. Hence we have very little to work on when, for example, we have to decide whether to force firms to leave the Birmingham conurbation for overspill towns thirty miles away: or whether to build a motorway from Plymouth to Bristol. Any serious attempt at a comprehensive cost-benefit analysis of regional policy, or any particular act of policy, would be ridiculously pretentious in the present state of knowledge.

The problem of ignorance about how the economy works, and of the costs and benefits involved, is closely linked with the third condition for regional planning mentioned above, that is the adequacy of the policy instruments under the authorities' control. There is a striking contrast between the powers of physical planners and those of economic planners. The central element in British planning has been physical – of housing, roads, green belts, new towns – and has been carried out by legal and administrative means of (in principle) inevitable efficiency. Economic weapons are by comparison flimsy – some administrative devices, but mainly subsidies designed to change the environment within which independent economic units take their free decisions. This freedom of decision

ment Department 1967); *Halifax and Calder Valley* (DEA 1968); *The North West of the 1970s* (DEA 1968); *East Anglia* (DEA 1968); *The Central Borders* (Scottish Development Department 1968); *Grangemouth/Falkirk* (Scottish Development Department 1968); *Huddersfield and Colne Valley* (DEA 1969); *Opportunity in the East Midlands* (DEA 1969); *Doncaster* (DEA 1969); *Humberside* (Centre for Environmental Studies/DEA 1969); *N.E. Scotland* (Scottish Development Department 1969); *Outline Strategy for the North* (DEA 1969); *Yorkshire and Humberside: A Regional Strategy* (MHLG 1970); *Tayside: Potential for Development* (Scottish Development Office 1970); *A Strategy for South West Scotland* (Scottish Development Department 1970); *Strategic Plan for the South East* (MHLG 1970).

[1] Brown in *National Institute Economic Review*, May 1967.

by a myriad of decentralized units makes planning in any real sense very difficult.

The difficulties which economic planning faces are exemplified by the problem of moving industry to new towns. The physical planners can provide the houses, the roads, the factories: but to get the companies to move is more difficult. The nature of the difficulty is, however, complex. The Board of Trade (or its successor Department) has in principle under the IDC and Local Employment Act legislation very wide powers to force or bribe industry to move. Its failure to use them, and the reluctance of outsiders to advocate a strong dirigiste policy in such cases, is based not merely on ideological hostility to administrative direction, but on fear of the unknown consequences of using or extending the existing powers. If for example the Board adopts a very tough line on granting IDCs in the West Midland conurbation[1] in the hope of driving industry out to the nearby new and overspill towns, it runs a number of risks – that the pro‑ ject may be abandoned altogether, or be carried out in a modified form which evades the control, which involves a loss of production to no purpose. If in addition it only offers an IDC in the new town, it arrogates to itself the choice of the best alternative site outside the conurbation: if it makes a mistake, there is again a loss.

All this makes a stern IDC policy – or the precise and rigorous use of any locational policy – unattractive. But not to use policy in this sort of way contradicts the assumptions which lie behind the initial planning decision to create new towns. It may well be that the requirements of the engineering trades in the West Midlands are such that to force them to develop elsewhere has a high economic cost. In this case they should be allowed to grow where they are – and the idea of overspill should be abandoned. But a decision to go for new towns implies that this argument has been rejected. In using its powers, the Board should there‑ fore act on the assumption that industry is to be moved to the new towns: and that the apparent risks and disadvantages in individual cases are outweighed by the wider economic and social arguments which lie behind the plan. If they do not, regional planning is likely to remain inherently self-contradictory.

Since 1964 the hard core of regional planning has been the work of the Regional Economic Planning Councils and the Planning Boards.[2] The Councils, which are made up of individuals with wide knowledge and experience of the region are primarily concerned to produce regional studies and plans.[3] These are not detailed industry by industry blueprints: nor are they at all precise about the location of new firms or activities. They set broad aims – the provision of 100,000 new jobs by 1985: the elimination of outward migration within ten years: – suggest growth

[1] See Lomas and Wood, *Employment Location in Regional Economic Planning* (London 1970), Ch. 7.
[2] See *Economic Planning in the Regions* (DEA 1966).
[3] See page 236, footnote 7.

points: and make a multitude of suggestions to Government, industry. and the local authorities designed to improve the region's economy. The Councils have no executive powers: so the effectiveness of these demands varies. Local planning authorities should statutorily[1] have regard, inter alia, to current policies with respect to the economic planning and development of the region as a whole: but it is not clear how much this meant in practice. The Government took a good deal less notice than the Councils would like – partly at least because the sum of the demands of all the Councils in the country far exceeded the capacity of the Government to meet them.

Whatever the reaction of local authorities or central government was in practice, the purpose and aspirations of such plans must be severely limited so long as these are the only bodies which can in principle be expected or required to take notice of them. These two between them take a large number of decisions crucial for the regional economy: but as in the case of the new towns, so long as private industry is independent and unpredictable, planning will obviously only have limited scope. There is no doubt that the Councils' regional plans have typically provided a good first draft for a broad strategy for the region. How much of the strategy can in practice be put into effect, even with the full acceptance of the public authorities, is a different matter. Consequently the plans are a mixture of pious hope, forecast and blue-print for action, according as they deal with the (relatively) uncontrolled private sector or the (relatively) controlled public sector. The dilatoriness of the Government in commenting on them, and the apparent neglect with which they have been treated, make it unlikely that they have served as fully as they might the purpose of co-ordinating the decisions of the public sector within a broad strategy.

Nevertheless such co-ordination has undoubtedly improved because of the Regional Economic Planning Boards, which are made up of representatives of the Government departments operating in the area – the Board of Trade, Housing, Transport, Education and so on. Until 1969, the representative of the DEA was chairman[2] (except in Scotland and Wales), and could attempt to see that decisions were taken in the light of some overall picture of the region's problems which no doubt took account inter alia of the Council's regional plan. It was not possible for Planning Boards to re-allocate the regional budget, and so spend more on roads and less on housing if they wanted. But both the machinery for co-ordination, and the presence of a neutral chairman was undoubtedly of value. The Boards in effect made it possible for that part of the region's economy under the Government's direct control, viz: public expenditure, to be effectively planned in the light of the expected and desired pattern of that part of the economy largely outside its control, viz: the private sector. This made such policies as a growth point strategy, and detailed

---

[1] *Town and Country Planning Act 1968*, Section 2(4) (a).
[2] Since then, the representative of the Ministry of Housing.

decisions such on the future level of public expenditure in Durham mining villages, more effective because all departments would be working
together.

Under the name of regional planning a good deal of useful progress
was made during the period. Whether the method deserves the grandiose
title of planning is largely a matter of taste or semantics. Given the state
of knowledge and of the art it is doubtful whether any more direct interference would in general have been desirable. But it seems that the
Board of Trade was reluctant to use even that degree of interference
which its authority and the present modest level of expertise in these
matters would have made legitimate. In the evidence to the Select
Committee on Scottish Affairs,[1] the Board made clear that after refusing
an IDC it made no attempt to induce the company to go to a particular
Development Area nor *a fortiori* to any particular part of a Development
Area. The company typically did a grand tour of the local authorities,
which often involved competitive bids for its plant, until it found what
suited it best. This must often have been different from what would
have suited the economy or the region: and in many cases the latter or
something nearer it would have been acceptable to the company. Plainly
the Board of Trade is suited by its experience in location problems,
and its power as the controller of the only discretionary element in regional
financial incentives, to play a leading part in fitting economic activity
to the broad regional strategy. It would be a disaster, given the present
state of ignorance, if a Government department attempted to direct all
industry to precisely the location which it thought best. But it is plainly
wrong to forswear in advance any attempt to use existing powers to put
industry where the regional strategy suggests.

Appraisal

The preceding account shows that between 1964 and 1970 important
changes were made in regional policy, almost all in the direction of making
the climate for the development of the depressed areas more favourable.
The extent of these changes is exaggerated by crude figures for financial
cost. Nevertheless, they are appreciable, particularly when the generally
more enthusiastic and determined attitude of the relevant Ministers to the
problem is taken into account. An important general piece of evidence
for the success of the policy is the persistent complaints of industrialists
that the Development Areas are unfairly advantaged: and of the inhabit-
ants of neighbouring areas (in particular the grey areas covered by the
Hunt report) that their growth is frustrated by regional subsidies.

More precise evidence is hard to come by. There is little hope of testing
in any rigorous way the effects of particular policy changes. But looking
at the regional picture as a whole, there are some signs that things

[1] *Evidence to Select Committee on Scottish Affairs* (HC 397, Session 1968/9), particularly
pages 592 ff.

improved in the last half of the 1960s: and it is reasonable to attribute this in part to regional policy – although such attribution must be tentative so long as we are ignorant of how the regional economies would have behaved on unchanged policies.

TABLE 6.5   UNEMPLOYMENT 1956–70

| | Percentage | | |
	Development Areas	Great Britain	DA as multiple of GB
June 1956	1·9	1·0	1·90
1957	2·2	1·2	1·83
1958	3·3	2·0	1·65
1959	3·7	1·9	1·95
1960	3·0	1·4	2·14
1961	2·5	1·2	2·08
1962	3·4	1·8	1·89
1963	4·3	2·1	2·05
1964	3·1	1·4	2·21
1965	2·5	1·2	2·08
1966	2·3	1·1	2·09
1967	3·6	2·1	1·71
1968	3·8	2·2	1·73
1969	3·8	2·2	1·73
1970	4·0	2·4	1·67
			Unweighted average 1·91

Note: Unemployment is defined as total registered unemployed, expressed as a % of employees, not seasonally adjusted.

Source: *Ministry of Labour Gazette* for July each year, and October 1966, page 666.

The most obvious improvement is in the most sensitive area – unemployment rates. The relationship between unemployment rates in the Development Areas and national rates was in June 1970 as good as it has ever been – and thus a good deal better than in the early 1960s.[1] In particular, the historically very high national unemployment rates of 1967–70 have not been accompanied by a corresponding increase in the Development Area rates. These were lower in 1970 than in 1963, although national rates were higher. The improvement has not benefited every area equally: the 1970 rate was only half as much again as compared with 1966 in Wales, but more than twice as high in the North. In no case, however, did the rate in a Development Area increase proportionately more than the national rate. This is against recent precedent, and the *a priori* prediction that regional unemployment is the last to be taken up in a boom and hence the first to rise in a slump.

[1] This improvement was maintained in general for the remainder of 1970 – except in the case of Scotland, where there was a sharp deterioration in the third quarter. See *National Institute Economic Review*, February 1971, page 19.

The change in the unemployment position, if modest, is clear and welcome. In the case of activity rates there is also some sign of improvement since 1960. Female activity rates, unlike male rates, are reasonably well measured by the Ministry of Labour statistics[1] particularly in Wales and the North. The disparity in female activity rates between regions has been somewhat reduced by the high increase – both proportionately and absolutely – in the North, Wales and Scotland. Figures for average family incomes are less reassuring. There is no sign of a faster rate of growth in the poorer regions than in the UK as a whole – but any proper assessment requires adjustment for regional price levels and their changes.

TABLE 6.6   ACTIVITY RATES (FEMALE)

New Standard Regions	1960 percent	1969 percent	1969 1960=100	GB=100 1960	GB=100 1969
North	31·7	35·5	112	83	89
Wales	27·0	30·1	112	71	75
Scotland	37·3	40·9	110	98	102
North-West	41·8	42·3	101	110	106
South-West	30·3	32·5	107	80	81
West Midlands	42·1	42·7	101	111	107
South-East	40·3	42·6	106	106	106
E. Midlands/Yorks, Humberside	37·2	39·4	106	98	98
Great Britain	38·1	40·1	105	—	—

Figures relate to employees at mid-year as a percentage of home population.

Source: *Abstract of Regional Statistics*, 1965 and 1970

TABLE 6.7   AVERAGE WEEKLY HOUSEHOLD INCOME BY REGIONS

New Standard Regions	1968/69 Shillings	1961/63 UK=100	1968/69 UK=100
North	565	89	90
Wales	544	92	87
Scotland	582	94	93
North-West	604	98	97
South-West	601	96	96
West Midlands	646	113	103
South-East	694	107	111
E. Midlands/Yorks, Humberside	583	96	93
United Kingdom	624	—	—

Source: *Abstract of Regional Statistics 1965*; *Family Expenditure Survey 1969*

These tables at least suggest that things are moving in the right direction. Whether they are disappointing or not depends on how high

[1] See Bowers, *The Anatomy of Regional Activity Rates* (NIESR 1970), page 40.

hopes should be in the first place, and how quickly regional policy can be expected to produce results.

The degree of success to be expected from regional policy in raising the levels of employment and prosperity in the Development Areas is severely limited by the loss of jobs in basic industries – which is at the heart of the regional problem – which took place during the period. Between 1964 and 1969 the Northern Region, for example, lost 45% of its mining jobs, 39% of its railway jobs and 15% of its jobs in metal manufacture. Wales and Scotland suffered similarly: and these five years involved a total national loss of jobs in six basic industries which are concentrated in the problem areas – coal mining, agriculture, railways, textiles, metal manufacture, ports and shipbuilding – of 678,000, compared with 466,000 in the previous five years.[1]

Board of Trade data on changes in manufacturing location[2] suggest that establishments resulting from moves made between 1945 and 1965[3] accounted for about 9·7% of all persons employed in manufacturing at the end of 1966 throughout the United Kingdom. This represents about 41,000 jobs for each of the years 1945–65. Each year's moves could, if history repeats itself, be expected ultimately to generate about 44,000 jobs.[4] Compared with the 200,000 extra jobs envisaged by the National Plan this is small scale. Few moves are over any distance: and of those only a proportion will or can go to Development Areas. Even with a substantial contribution from the growth of existing industries in the region, it is plain that targets of the kind in the National Plan, based on a partial equation of Development Area unemployment and activity rates to those of prosperous regions, would take decades to achieve.[5]

To a considerable extent the criticisms of regional policy current in 1964 had been met by June 1970. The main blemish remaining was the Labour Government's exclusion of service industries from any of its regional policies. Service industries were not only subject to SET, but did not get any investment grants (let alone at a differential Development Area rate): and the Board of Trade would not make LEA assistance available unless there was a good chance of creating at least fifty jobs – substantially more stringent requirements than in the case of manufacturing industry. Yet is it plain from Table 6.8 that a good deal of the growth of employment in the South-East has been in services: and that much of these services must be export industries, in that they represent national activities which serve not simply the local South-East market – unless the

---

[1] Crosland, *Hansard*, House of Commons, Vol. 801, Col. 432.
[2] *The Movement of Manufacturing Industry in the United Kingdom 1945–65* (Board of Trade, 1968).
[3] '... movement meaning approximately the opening of a new establishment in one or other of fifty areas of the country by a non-local firm', ibid., page 35.
[4] Ibid., page 35.
[5] *The National Plan*, op. cit. pages 37–8.

local population has an extraordinarily high income elasticity of demand for services.

TABLE 6.8   EMPLOYEES (EMPLOYED AND UNEMPLOYED)

| | June 1970 thousands | | 1970 (1964 = 100) | |
	Production Industries	Services	Production Industries	Services
North	697	629	99·6	102·3
Wales	506	462	97·3	96·9
Scotland	1,026	1,133	98·8	97·3
North-West	1,564	1,350	94·2	98·3
South-West	574	768	102·5	99·4
South-East	3,391	5,069	95·8	103·5
E. Midlands/Yorks, Humber/ W. Midlands	3,372	2,377	95·4	101·4
Great Britain	11,130	11,788	96·3	101·3

Source: *Ministry of Labour Gazette,* March 1966; *Employment and Productivity Gazette,* March 1971.

The only policy instrument which prima facie might have made a contribution to increasing service employment in the Development Areas was Office Development Permits. The crude figures for the operation of this legislation are given in a previous section. The likelihood is that the policy may have had some effect on moving offices away from London and the centre of the congested areas.[1] But it offered no inducement to make moves to the Development Areas – there was no incentive to go further than the periphery of the controlled area. The experience of companies which have moved routine office operations out of London suggests that with modern communications there is no real difficulty – or at least no more difficulty than faces a manufacturing company which is forced to fragment its activities by the IDC legislation – in making such moves. And the conclusion is confirmed by the successful decentralization of Government departments.

Given the modest signs of success in lowering unemployment, and the problem of the time-scale, it is reasonable to argue that regional policy of the scale and vigour adopted by the Labour Government was desirable, and should be continued. Even before the General Election, however, its increasing cost – £300 million – began to make it doubtful whether it could continue on quite the same scale. £300 million is not outrageously high, as has been pointed out, by comparison with for example agricultural subsidies:[2] but it is a formidable figure. Whether financial cost is the

[1] Ironically at a time when the South-East began to lose population by net migration outward – although not at a rate fast enough to offset the natural increase. See *Abstract of Regional Statistics 1970,* Table 7.

[2] Gavin McCrone, *Regional Policy in Britain* (London 1969), page 198.

appropriate index of the economic cost of the policy is another matter. Much of the financial cost corresponds to transfer payments, not to calls on real resources. In very favourable cases, where a regional project uses otherwise unemployed local labour and not much else, no resources which would have been used elsewhere are pre-empted by the project: and hence the amount of the subsidy required to make the project take place does not represent any cost in real resources. The cost of regional policy can only be properly assessed in terms of its effect on our ability to achieve desired values of other target variables. As was suggested at the beginning of this chapter, hitting the desired regional employment target may involve no costs in terms of the GNP growth target because one helps to achieve the other. But the distribution of income target may be made more difficult to reach if higher regional employment requires paying large sums to the shareholders of oil companies. In 1968 or 1969 two variables which had been in the background – the quantity of money and the level of taxation – became more important for government policy: in the one case because of the Domestic Credit Expansion target imposed by the IMF in 1969, and in the other because of the alleged disincentive effects, or at least the undoubted unpopularity, of high tax rates. Achieving these targets would be made easier by a reduction in public expenditure – including expenditure on regional policy: hence simple financial cost became an important consideration, because the objectives of economic management had changed.

If for these reasons, or any other, public expenditure as a whole is to be cut, there are nevertheless strong arguments that regional policy should not be reduced, nor its structure substantially altered. These arguments are not based on any notion that the purposes of regional policy are peculiarly desirable as compared with other components of government expenditure: but rather on the very great importance of continuity and predictability in an area where results take a long time to achieve, and depend on the long-term decisions of private industry. One of the main reasons that regional policy has not been effective in the past has been that its intensity and structure has varied. The rescheduling and descheduling of Development Districts, the change from free depreciation to investment grants, are examples of relatively minor changes which emphasize the uncertainty and variability of the inducements offered to industry, without achieving very much improvement in the inducements themselves. This uncertainty makes a company very unwilling to relocate. If it invests now in a Development Area it will get free depreciation, or investment grants, or whatever the current incentive is: but there is no way of telling whether this differential will exist in ten years' time when plant has to be replaced or expanded. A decision to locate in a new area involves a commitment to operate there in the long-term. Such a decision cannot be taken without a forecast of the subsidies which will be available in the long-term, for investment and employment undertaken later in the life of the project. It is not reasonable to base these forecasts on a simple extrapolation of existing subsidies when successive governments give constant reminders of how easily such subsidies can be varied. This consideration was given modest acknowledgement by the seven-year guarantee period for the REP. But the chances of making substantial inroads into the problem of the depressed areas are much reduced if repeated alterations are made in the scale and nature of the assistance offered. A stable policy, even if imperfect, is preferable to constant adjustments designed to achieve what is at the time supposed to be a policy nearer the optimum.

7 Policy towards nationalized industries

Michael Posner

At the 1964 election Labour was committed to steel nationalization, and there was much interest, even in the moderate centre of the Party, in 'public enterprise' as an engine of benign economic change. The Party was less interested in the rules for managing public enterprise; but certainly most enthusiasts would have agreed that nationalized industries should act *differently* from private enterprise firms in comparable circumstances. In the event, steel was nationalized after the 1966 election; a major bill to nationalize the docks was nearly on the statute book, but was lost by the 1970 electoral defeat; existing nationalized industries made some small steps towards diversification (particularly in hydrocarbon exploration); and financial rules for running nationalized industries were much developed and codified, and even to some extent enforced. The major experiments in intervention to change the structure of private industry (through the Industrial Reorganization Corporation, the NBPI and MinTech interventionism generally) are outside the scope of this chapter, though in many cases they involved the injection of public capital – even of public equity capital – into private industry on a significant scale.

If steel nationalization was not quite the 'final solution' that many in the industry must have prayed for, after the political yo-yo of the 1950s, it was evident by mid-1971 that no straightforward denationalization was to be attempted by the Conservatives. Policy for the docks, as illustrated by the bankruptcy of the Mersey Docks and Harbours Board in the autumn of 1970, may well develop (via nationalization and municipalization) in a way not wildly different from that intended by Labour. Despite the doctrinal statements from Conservative Ministers on assuming office, the rolling back of the public sector will lead to lively skirmishes around the Coal Board's brickworks and British Rail's hotels, but will leave the main fortresses of the public sector secure and untrammelled.[1]

1 There has been much talk of 'injecting private capital' into the public sector. It seems likely that while by 1975 there may have been some marginal 'divesting' (sales) of public sector assets, and some continuation of Labour's practice of pushing public bodies to borrow abroad in the Euro-bond market, the total subscription, in sterling, from the London capital market to the public corporations will be negligible. To test this prediction, the reader can ask himself the following conundrum: What would be the rights of a private equity holder in the Gas Council? And if the private capital is to be debentures rather than equity, we would be envisaging merely a return to the pre-1956 practice,

Hence the man from Mars will not find the basic ownership pattern of British industry much changed between 1964 and 1974; the main changes have been in the way the industries are run. Here we will show the doctrinal continuity between the White Papers of 1961 and 1967,[1] and the role played in the development of doctrine by the (bi-partisan) House of Commons Select Committee on Nationalized Industries, in successive reports of increasing sophistication and clarity. In 1970, the doctrine was still developing, and was still incomplete and imperfect: some of the problems are intractable, and, in the present state of economic science, systematically ambiguous. The intellectual work on these White Papers was the work of the Civil Service machine, with the co-operation (often somewhat sceptical) of the officials of the nationalized industries; the continuity was in many cases the continuity of persons and official committees. But Ministers took the responsibility (often in the midst of more pressing matters – Treasury Ministers must have given approval to the 1967 White Paper in the same month as the last steps towards devaluation were taken), and created the environment in which certain intellectual ideas flourished.

This is one of the few areas of economic policy where open government flourishes. Officials from the Treasury, sponsoring Departments, and public corporations submit memoranda and appear as witnesses to the Select Committee, and are extensively cross-examined, not only on their actions and their relations with each other, but on the intellectual arguments underlying their actions. The knowledge that such exposure will occur has proved a healthy spur to thought and argument within the Whitehall machine, and the knowledge that backbenchers from both parties will be investigating doctrine has led Ministers to involve themselves closely in this sort of discussion.[2]

The main lines of policy, at an abstract (almost formalistic) level, were briefly as follows. Public corporations should set their prices relative (or possibly precisely equal) to long-run marginal costs; capital investment should be judged according to some test rate of return; and corporations should be set some kind of financial target against which their success could be judged. Of these three strands, the last was stressed in 1961, and the others were particularly developed in the decade that followed.

But neither the theory of 'socialism', nor the interventionist tastes of the

by which the (Government guaranteed) stock of British Railways was floated on the gilt edged market in place of Treasury stock: this would be a minor change (possibly beneficial) for Government debt management, but of negligible importance for nationalized industry management.

[1] *The Financial and Economic Obligations of the Nationalized Industries* (Cmnd. 1337, 1961); *Nationalized Industries: A Review of Economic and Financial Objectives* (Cmnd. 3437, 1967). (Note the reversal of the words 'economic' and 'financial' in the titles of the two papers, doubtless a paper victory for the Department of Economic Affairs.)

[2] Two excellent specimens are the *Report on the NCB* (HC 471—1 and 471—11 of 1969); and on *Ministerial Control* (HC 371—1, 371—11, and 371—111 of 1968). The Minutes of Evidence are far better reading than the reports themselves.

Wilson administration, nor the realities of the needs of nationalized industries, could be satisfied by formal rules for optimum pricing and investment behaviour. The distinguishing feature of the Labour Administration was the adumbration of policy White Papers for the two main nationalized sectors – transport and fuel – and a sturdy attempt to breathe sense into civil aviation through the Edwards report.[1] It is conceivable that if all costs of inputs represented true 'social costs' (after correcting for distortions elsewhere) of economic resources, if all knowledge were available to all decision-makers, and if technical change were continuous and smooth, industrial 'policies' would be unnecessary – the formal rules would suffice. By common agreement, we are not yet in such a position (and most of us doubt whether we ever shall be); it follows that industries need to be put on the equilibrium path before equilibrium policies can be applied.[2]

Three sorts of tension were created by the dual approach of imposing 'financial obligations' while at the same time developing 'plans' for public corporations. First, a tension between managerial autonomy and ministerial control. The device of a public corporation, where day-to-day dealings could not be the subject of Parliamentary question and answer, was after all a creation of the 1945 Labour Administration – the skilful Morrisonian compromise.[3] The Select Committee have probed continuously at the detail of how Ministerial control is exercised,[4] criticizing in particular 'arm-twisting', concealed pressures, Civil Service interference with commercial judgments, and so on. It was a Conservative Government that dismissed Lord Hall of the Post Office[5] in a blaze of controversy. But long before that Mrs Castle had obtained the premature retirement of the head of British Rail, the tension between successive Ministers of Power and Lord Robens of the Coal Board was an open

[1] The main documents are: *Fuel Policy* (Cmnd. 2798, 1965, and Cmnd. 3438, 1967); *Transport Policy* (Cmnd. 3057, 1966, and Cmnd. 3470, 1968); *Civil Aviation* (Cmnd. 4213, 1969).
[2] The National Board for Prices and Incomes, whose investigators were often turned loose on the public sector by the Labour Government (e.g. Report No. 59 on the CEGB, Report No. 153 on the NCB and Report No. 102 on Gas Prices, would probably have agreed that the enforcement by Whitehall of 'best practice' pricing policy and investment assessment would have gone far towards setting the industries right. But many of the NBPI's criticisms could be reduced to the complaint that in their view nationalized industry management was sometimes dim, unaware of modern analysis and methods. A programme merely of 'spreading the light' on investment assessment would probably involve a larger scale of detailed interference by Whitehall, over a whole run of years, than was attempted even by the Ministry of Transport at the height of its interventionist phase.
[3] Analysed at length in W. A. Robson, *Nationalized Industry and Public Ownership* (London 1962).
[4] HC 371—1 of 1968, op. cit., enshrines their conclusions.
[5] It is just worth noting that one of the acts of the Wilson Government was to 'nationalize' the Post Office, changing its constitutional form from that of a Government Department (the Postmaster General was a Minister of the Crown) to a public corporation. Some wits preferred to regard this (politically uncontroversial move) as 'de-nationalization'.

secret, and Lord Melchett's determination to play the steel corporation's cards close to his chest led to his christening as the 'Mattei of the British public sector'[1] by one informed onlooker. This tension had existed before 1964, and continued in accentuated form after 1970; it is perhaps endemic. Our sympathy should extend to both sides in this controversy; to Whitehall, which has a responsibility, say, to ensure a matching between colliery closures and regional employment policy; and to the Coal Board, which has to maintain managerial morale, the recruitment of miners, and a reasonable degree of financial independence.

Secondly, tension appeared between the 'sponsoring departments' (Ministry of Power for the fuel industries, Ministry of Transport for the railways, Board of Trade for airlines) and the 'central economic departments' (the Treasury and the DEA). Often, but not always, angry Board Chairmen can rally their sponsoring Minister to their cause (e.g. the necessity for a price rise, or a new power station 'start', or the electrification of a rail line), only to see the poor chap converted to another view by an adamant Treasury Minister, whose own officials earnestly believe that their colleagues in other departments were mistaken. Hence the wish of Chairmen like Lord Robens, with the support of the Select Committee, to talk directly to the Treasury: a recommendation rejected by Labour, and unlikely to find greater favour with the Tories.

Thirdly, both the 1961 and 1967 White Papers gave unfortunate currency to the notion of 'ordinary commercial criteria' in their description of how public corporations might behave. We may sympathize with the draughtsmen: anyone who has pined in a railway sleeping car for want of a nightcap will be puzzled why it was not until 1969 that a railway official thought that they might make money by selling drinks to passengers in the night watches. But the vogue for commercialism has tended to obscure the way in which the pricing rules differ from those which a profit maximizing firm would follow, and to encourage undue concentration on 'marketing', even from those enterprises in which the minimization of costs was clearly more important than the maximization of sales. This commercial spirit (characterizing particularly Lord Melchett's determination to press price rises and expansion plans against Whitehall reluctance) is better than dreary quiescence and lack of enterprise, but sometimes begs the question of what the public corporations are there to do.

But overriding all these tensions was a major dilemma, which Labour never solved. The rule 'price at marginal cost' does not emerge unqualified from the 1967 White Paper, because of the continuing emphasis on limiting the industries' borrowing requirement; and in a period in which *all* costs were rising (because of inflation) 'prices and incomes policy' needs clashed increasingly with any pricing rule derived from the White Paper. Should prices be set at marginal costs? Should they be used as an alter-

---

[1] Enrico Mattei was until his death in 1961 the head of ENI, the Italian state oil and natural gas corporation. He was widely regarded as a 'baron' quite independent of the Italian Government, or of any outside control whatsoever.

native to explicit forms of taxation? Should changes in costs be immediately reflected in changes in price? These are the major questions of
policy, of the ground rules by which the industries were to be run. To
analyse them, we must look more deeply at the underlying doctrines of
the 1967 White Paper.

The 1967 White Paper[1]

Suppose a public corporation has a new market opened to it by a
technological development from its own research staff. If the product and
its market can be isolated from the corporation's existing business,
management should proceed with their product assessment as follows. For
a prospective plant of efficient size, calculate the present value of all
expenditure ('capital' or 'current') needed to produce capacity output
over expected life of the equipment or the market, whichever is less.
Choose a product price (or a set of product prices which could vary
through time or between sub-markets) whose present value is equal to
that of the stream of costs. This is the 'long run marginal cost' (LRMC)
of output. In doing this sum, use discounting factors derived from the 'test
rate of discount' (TDR), which is the Treasury's estimate of the true cost
of investment resources (like prices, the TDR could – and indeed should –
vary through time: but to this sophistication we do not yet aspire). If the
sales staff believe the product can be sold at this set of prices, make the
investment; if not, not.

This, in a nutshell, is the implicit doctrine of the Select Committee; it
is also a chief ingredient of the 1967 White Paper. But in that White
Paper the Treasury – and Labour Ministers – added an important *extra*
ingredient identical with that to be found in the (Tory) 1961 White
Paper: financial targets. The practice of setting 'financial targets' for the
industries, expressed most usually in terms of a rate of profit on book
assets, supplies a third rule, neatly over determining a model already fully
solved by a combination of the TDR and the pricing rule. The financial
target seems thus either merely to repeat what is already implied by the
other rules, or instead to impose a requirement in contradiction to the
other rules.[2]

The defence of continued financial targetry, despite this analytical
difficulty, is usually expressed in terms of the desirability of laying down
management objectives. Thus we would calculate the financial surplus
which would be expected *if* the pricing and investment rules were followed,
and *if* the technical efficiency (e.g. productivity of labour) remained at its

[1] This section develops an argument from my paper 'Pricing and investment policies
of nationalized industries', in A. K. Cairncross (ed.), *The Managed Economy* (London
1970.)
[2] A point made brutally by the Select Committee (HC 371—1 of 1967–8, *Report*, Chapter
V).

previous level. The financial 'target' would then be set a little *above* the surplus so calculated, so as to induce managers to 'do a little better'. Although we may doubt whether powerful peers and knights (being the Chairmen of public corporations) actually stay awake at nights worrying about their potential achievement of financial targets which they negotiated earlier with their Minister over dinner, this justification of financial targetry is not of negligible importance: in fact many chairmen take their obligations very seriously. There are, however, other more effective justifications:

(*i*) Pricing rules are difficult to define precisely, and there is often a considerable margin of error within which prices could settle and still be said to correspond to the slogan: 'Price equals LRMC'. Financial targets can be conceived of as fixing the surplus requirements of public corporations in a way which will determine where within the range of permissible price levels we eventually choose to settle.

(*ii*) It is true that to charge prices materially above estimated LRMC involves some distortion in the allocation of resources. But the blessing given by economic theory to marginal cost pricing depends, in its strictest form, on the assumption that the marginal cost rule is applied throughout the economy: we know this condition is not fulfilled in practice. We know, moreover, that Chancellors of the Exchequer often make harsh decisions on taxation which must lead inevitably to a certain amount of resource-misallocation. It might be far better to allow the price of electricity or gas to be a little above its long-run marginal cost rather than to raise some other form of indirect taxation. This argument lets a particularly wicked-looking cat out of the bag. Pricing policy by the public corporations must be seen in part as a form of indirect taxation by the Exchequer.

(*iii*) More technically, it is by no means clear that a given TDR uniquely defines the 'capital charge' which forms a component of the true marginal cost of producing a commodity. That the TDR should be earnable on new investment is clear: the public corporation should not invest unless it believes that it could in principle charge a price embodying a 10% return on capital and still sell its goods. But this is quite different from saying that the price actually charged in a market should embody a 10% return not only on capital invested in the recent past, but also on the book value of existing capital assets. One way to crystallize thought on this problem is to ask – 'What should be the natural consequences for nationalized industry pricing of the decision recently taken to raise forthwith the TDR from 8% to 10%?' Reflection suggests that it does not inevitably follow that prices themselves should forthwith be raised so that new higher TDR is immediately earned on existing assets. It follows that, in the relationship between the TDR and the optimal level of prices, there is a considerable amount of flexibility or 'give'. Once again, a role for financial targets is found as a way of choosing where, within a permissible range, prices should settle.

Given that three rules have been used where two might have been adequate, which has been dominant? The gross trading surplus of the public corporations, as a proportion of their total sales, is shown in Table 7.1.

TABLE 7.1 PUBLIC CORPORATIONS, TRADING SURPLUS AND CAPITAL FORMATION, 1959–70 ($£$ billion)

	1959	1960	1961	1962	1963	1964	1965	1966	1967	1968	1969
1. Sales Revenue	3.2	3·5	4·0	4·4	4·7	5·0	5·2	5·5	6·1	7·1	7·5
2. Gross Trading Surplus	0·4	0·6	0·7	0·8	0·9	1·0	1·0	1·1	1·2	1·4	1·5
3. 2/1 as %	12·5	17·1	17·5	18·2	19·2	20·0	19·2	20·0	19·4	19·5	20·0
4. Capital Formation	0·8	0·8	0·9	0·9	1·0	1·2	1·3	1·5	1·7	1·6	1·5
5. 2/4 as %	50	75	78	89	90	83	77	73	71	87	100

Note: 'Gross Trading Surplus' is struck before providing for depreciation or for interest on capital. It is equivalent to the gross profits of a private sector firm which has only equity capital.

Source: *National Income Blue Book*, 1970, Tables 32–4.

The trend has been upwards (although the sharpest change took place around the time of the 1961 White Paper): indeed, in 1969, for the first time, the gross surplus was greater than gross fixed capital formation. The sums involved are large – the change in the surplus between 1965 and 1968 was of almost the same order of magnitude as the tax increases in the 1968 Budget.

But these figures do not prove that marginal cost pricing has been abandoned. LRMC may be above or below accounting costs. Almost certainly electricity prices were well above the costs of generating from a single new power station.[1] But fast and continuous technical progress in electricity inflates LRMC *above* the cost of generating from one specimen new power station – the cheaper we expect tomorrow's plant to be, the more it 'costs' us to invest in today's design, and the nearer is the 'cost' of today's plant to the cost of existing, old-fashioned plant.[2]

In gas, the *average* of all prices charged is probably well above marginal cost.

The Minister concludes that there are good grounds for charging prices close to long-run marginal costs to those consumer classes that tend to be relatively sensitive to price, while setting other parts of the industry's tariffs above marginal costs in order to make a contribution to the industry's overheads.

[1] See HC 381—XVII of 1967, Appendix 43.
[2] See R. Turvey, *Optimal Pricing and Investment in Electricity Supply* (London 1968), Ch. 4.

[It seems clear from the context that by 'overheads' is meant in fact the accounting charges on newly obsolescent town gas plant.][1]

Again, in coal, prices were almost certainly well *below* marginal cost.[2]

In the transport sector, marginal costs are more difficult to ascertain.[3] Implicit in the interesting but curiously evasive *Railway Policy* White Paper of 1967[4] is the notion that prices must be below accounting cost, since demand elasticities are such that higher prices would lead to lower revenues – hence the 'grants' for unremunerative services that were introduced. Increasingly, but seemingly without explicit policy announcements, fares are being pushed (differentially, line by line) towards the costs of creating new capacity for peak demands;[5] the general implication would seem to be that the general price level in 1969–70 was *below* marginal costs.

Perhaps the following summary may fairly represent an evidently diffuse picture.

A general attitude developed in the 1960s, suggesting that the surplus of the public corporations should be increased. At the same time, there was a wish to achieve some correct allocation of resources through the application of the TDR and LRMC. These two sets of ideas were likely to flourish best when they pointed in the same direction, but this happened only in the cases of coal mining and the railways – both signals suggested sharp upwards movements in prices. But in precisely those two cases other arguments supervened: for coal, fuel policy suggested that the rate of decline (that would be accelerated by rapid price increases) should be braked; and on the railways, the high costs of alternative transport (not fully reflected in the price mechanism) led to the subsidy or 'grant' system.

Elsewhere in the public sector, the notions of LRMC pricing were inconsistent with the wish to raise prices rather than taxes. Up till 1967, the weight of incomes policies leant against high financial surplus pressures, and in favour of LRMC pricing; after 1968, with the exigencies of post-devaluation budgetary policy much in Ministers' minds, the pressure was once again towards higher surpluses. The systematic ambivalence of the 1967 White Paper reflected these inevitably divergent pressures, with the result that a clear line of policy was hard to discern. *Mutatis mutandis*, the new Conservative Government has started on the same merry-go-round.

---

[1] *Observations on North Sea Gas* (Cmnd. 3996, 1969).
[2] HC 381—xvii of 1967, Appendix 23, para. 24. Report of Select Committee on Science and Technology.
[3] See the very useful *Road Track Costs* (Ministry of Transport 1968).
[4] Cmnd. 3439, 1967.
[5] Under the Conservatives this process was accelerated by the decision to reduce the subsidy for London Commuter traffic.

Price discrimination

One aspect of the pricing rules stemming from the 1967 White Paper is worthy of brief further examination. In gas, electricity, railways, and steel, aided and abetted by the National Board for Prices and Incomes, the practice of raising prices equi-proportionately for all customers has been progressively abandoned. The reasons for this change are in part supply factors, in part demand. On the supply side, it has become increasingly recognized that not all railway ton-miles, or electricity kilowatts, have identical costs: where the rail track is congested (as it is for many lines for part of the day and for some lines all of the day),[1] the cost of providing incremental services will be relatively high; where extra kilowatts have to be provided to a temperature sensitive customer at winter peak, the cost is greater than night storage generation. Labour gave greatly increased freedom to the public corporations to reflect different relative costs in different prices – exhibiting in doing so a taste for the price-mechanism that did not characterize uniformly the rest of their economic policy. The timing of these changes in electricity and gas had probably more to do with the diffusion of skilled manpower in the industries than with political pressures – the seeds of development of the electricity bulk supply tariff go back to the late 1950s. But in the case of the railways considerable Whitehall 'nudging' did take place, and here the urge 'to make the economy rational' can plausibly be attributed in part to Ministerial taste.

More controversial has been the price discrimination between customers for which the opportunity has been offered purely by different demand elasticities. The most striking case is that of the aluminium smelting plants, who were offered electricity on long-term contracts at prices below[2] those available to the general run of industrial companies. This was a deliberate attempt to get the best of both worlds – to maintain the *general* level of prices (so as to avoid any necessity to raise the general level of taxation, for any given desired pressure of aggregate demand), while still picking out for favourable treatment those customers whose use of electricity was reasonably sensitive to price. Provided that the 'fence' separating the favoured sheep from the unfavoured goats is sturdily built,

---

[1] *London Transport Fares*, Report No. 159 of 1970.

[2] For reasons akin to those already analysed in the relationship between true long-run marginal cost and continuous technical progress, it is in principle possible that a twenty-year fixed price contract for electricity from a 1971 vintage power station would be less advantageous than the right to buy electricity at the going price, from the system as a whole, in each of the next twenty years. But in my view, the smelter electricity contracts were certainly favourable on *any* plausible assumptions about subsequent movements in the general cost of electricity, at least from the point of view of the customer (whose expectations about the future spot price of electricity are less optimistic than those of suppliers). The importance of general inflation, at even a low rate, in this sort of calculation is another reason for believing that the smelter firms received a discriminatory low price from the CEGB, despite partial Ministerial disclaimer (*Hansard*, 20 November 1968, p. 1140 col. 2).

and other users with lower demand elasticities do not succeed in getting equally favourable terms; and provided also that all those prospective customers (including incremental loads from existing customers) who have high demand elasticities are allowed to become 'sheep', the system represents a neat compromise. Perhaps this is the truest example of 'Labour interventionism' combined with 'determination to make the best of the price mechanism' in our field.

Fuel policy

So far we have been concerned with the financial rules for the public corporations: we now have to sketch in the general framework within which these rules were supposed to operate. The best worked-out example (although not necessarily the most successful in practice) was Mr Marsh's shot at fuel policy.

The essence of fuel policy as presented in Cmnd. 3438 was to use the Government's powers over the public sector to enforce a least-cost solution for the fuel industries. Marginal resource costs were calculated for the basic energy activities – oil, nuclear energy, coal, gas – and the results used to estimate the costs of alternative mixes of ways of meeting the final energy bill.[1] There is no doubt that the 50% increase in crude oil prices successfully forced by the OPEC cartel in the autumn of 1970 was a blow to Labour's policy analysis: but so, previously, had been the failure of coal mining productivity to rise as fast as expected and the rise in nuclear energy costs. In fact, with the sole exception of natural gas (where the price rise in new contracts had not been much higher than the overall rate of price inflation), the prices of all fuels have been pushed up, and the overall choice between fuels has possibly not been unduly shaken; but it does seem true that 1967 Review overestimated the rate of decline in the demand for coal (largely because the overall use of fuel for a given level of GDP had been somewhat underestimated).

In this sort of resource cost calculation there arises a basic problem of enforcement: business men (public or private) react to the prices which actually face them on the market, not to 'shadow' prices or marginal resource costs. Hence there is a clash between what the planners think should happen, and what in fact does happen. There are fiscal weapons –

[1] In practice, the technique of analysis was more piecemeal. Different methods of electricity generation were analysed, and a mix (heavily nuclear at the margin) was chosen; natural gas was separately considered, and a (technically) maximum rate of depletion of gas fields decided upon; and the cost difference, at the margin, between coal and oil was tested by asking 'what increase in the fuel oil duty would be necessary to halt the long-term decline of coal', the size of the required duty then being compared with the possible difference between the financial cost and the resource cost of coal. In essence, the crucial choice between oil and nuclear electricity generation was made straightforwardly; the choice between oil and coal was made by contemplating the impossibility of raising the protective duty in oil above 60%.

indirect taxes – which planners can use to bridge the gap: in the fuel case the hydrocarbon duty ('fuel oil tax') on imported oil products was a good way of supporting coal to the extent needed.

But the fiscal device was not in itself sufficient. Special directions (to some extent accompanied by explicit subsidy) were issued to the electricity industry, to increase their coal burn; the timing of colliery closures was a matter of much Ministerial concern; natural gas depletion rates were influenced by Ministerial pressures; the choice between different types of power station was a Ministerial choice. Hence the public corporations shone with a vague effulgent light, attracting interventionist, planning-minded moths, come to admire the chosen instrument of planning in all its glory. Their fascination was alas severely limited by two severe sets of doubts.

The first doubts were almost certainly mistaken: they arose because of the vigorous and powerful objections of Lord Robens and his Coal Board, who claimed loudly and repeatedly, publicly and privately, that the referee's decision was ignorant, incompetent, prejudiced, and most certainly *wrong*. Close to his retirement, in early 1971, Lord Robens rubbed salt in the wounds by asserting that, not only had the planners made mistakes, but they were already paying for them: coal sales in 1970 had been planned at 152 million tons, had in fact attained 155 million tons, and would have gone far higher if stocks had not been so run down in 1968 and '69; foreign coal had been imported, at high cost; the 1970 oil settlements with the OPEC countries had inflated crude oil prices far above the levels assumed by the planners; and a severe fuel crisis had been averted merely because of the good fortune of a mild winter. The planners had certainly got the *timing* of the decline of coal somewhat crucially wrong; no doubt their error had been to concentrate too single-mindedly on a single 'most probable path', ignoring the risks and uncertainties – an error perhaps characteristic of Wilsonian Whitehall in many fields.[1] But, just as oil prices and nuclear costs were revised upwards, so too were coal productivity prospects revised downwards – even apart from inflation, the main error of the 1967 calculations seems to be that the overall level of fuel costs will be higher in the 1970s than had been assumed. The loss of colliery manpower in 1969 was perhaps too great, but the economic conditions of 1970–1 should enable the NCB to retain the men it needs, and the outlook for coal in the late 1970s is unlikely to diverge notably

---

[1] See, for instance, the Treasury's confidence that the 1967 devaluation would quickly produce an overwhelming balance of payments surplus, and that the tax imposts of 1968 and 1969 could safely be analysed by the traditional tools of economic forecasting, despite their unprecedented size and intensity. Some commentators would argue that these guesses were not central, and could have been known to be 'erroneous' in this sense at the time they were made. But the present writer, who admittedly was somewhat involved in these errors (as also in the fuel policy projections discussed above), would instead persist in regarding the original forecasts as good central guesses that turned out to be wrong through bad luck: the error lay in not taking account sufficiently of the strong possibility of bad luck when policy was built on the forecasts.

from the planners' forecasts. Lord Robens' roars are more defensible for their (undoubtedly benign) effect on NCB morale than for their effective criticism of the planners' wisdom.

The second set of doubts, however, are better founded: the extent of intervention was insufficient for the achievement of what should have been the aims of the planners.[1] Consider in particular the way in which coal was protected. The marginal resource costs of coal differs from colliery to colliery; the NCB sells at prices which differ more between customers than according to the colliery origin of the coal; the NCB will choose that pattern of colliery output that minimizes its accounting costs; Government taxes or subsidies can affect the total of coal output, but not its pattern. The result is systematically non-optimal, because the NCB may continue to produce some coal whose accounting cost is low but whose resource cost is high, and yet close some collieries whose resource-cost-per-ton-of-coal is relatively low. By adhering to the managerial doctrine (not without foundation in common sense) of independence and 'commercial freedom' for the NCB management, the regional pattern of coal output may have been seriously disturbed away from the social optimum.

Perhaps it would be possible to devise instruments of intervention (a finely variable Regional Employment Premium on mining manpower) which would reconcile planning aims with devoluted decision-making by NCB management: this is a major question to which more consideration should be given. But it does provide a good illustration of that basic contradiction to which we have already referred – the contradiction between Ministerial control and management autonomy: the independent Morrisonian public corporation can only usefully flourish in a world equipped with a subtle set of price-mechanism tools of intervention.

Transport policy

Until very recently we have not even attempted to plan as a whole the factors which create our environment . . . or to plan different forms of transport in relation to each other . . . New thinking is required, not only about types of public transport, but also about how they should be financed. Those who manage or work on London Transport, British Railways and provincial bus services are struggling to reconcile two mutually contradictory objectives: to provide an adequate service to the public and to pay their way.[2]

Why were the objectives 'mutually contradictory'? Because the demand curve was such that maximum attainable revenue *minus* costs (*equals* surplus or 'target') might turn out to be less than necessary to 'pay their way'. In elementary text books, it is prescribed that such enterprises

---

[1] See, for a good discussion and excellent evidence, *National Board for Prices and Incomes, Coal Prices, Report No. 153* (together with supplements).
[2] *Transport Policy* (Cmnd. 3057, 1966), paras 6 and 9.

should then go out of business when their capital wears out.[1] In transport it can be argued instead that failure of the price mechanism to work throughout the sector[2] (because of externalities etc.) makes the text book prescription absurdly unacceptable. Hence the decision should be made in three stages: first, what is the optimum mix of transport systems for a town or region; secondly, how should passengers optimally be distributed between alternative means of transport; thirdly, if such an optimum cannot be reached when each individual transport enterprise 'covers its financial costs (with a surplus)', then arrange a pattern of subsidies and taxes to produce the required result.

But this decision algorithm requires detailed analysis of each local situation, in all its aspects. The proper distribution of subsidies, and the decision about where the cash required for these subsidies should come from, needs to be made by those who will pay the subsidy and benefit from it – the local community.[3]

Hence the decision to 'sell' the London Passenger Transport Board to the Greater London Council;[4] the decision to subsidize explicitly the provision by British Rail of 'unremunerative passenger services' (at first using national Exchequer funds, subsequently hopefully in part inducing local Passenger Transport Authorities to pay); and the insistence that investment decisions be taken under cost-benefit, rather than private profit maximizing, rules.[5]

Socialist policies?

All this talk about 'policy' has a certain grandeur of conception and design; but, as in the case of fuel policy, its pretensions can be fairly readily deflated. Fuel policy announced that, without any interference at

[1] Because not all capital wears out simultaneously, this rule is in any case hard to formulate precisely: see A. Lamfalussy, *Investment and Growth in Mature Economies* (London 1961).

[2] Two well-known hypothetical reasons may be recalled. First, owners of motor cars (who buy their cars for non-commuting purposes) consider only the short-run marginal costs of driving, while the railways charge long-run marginal costs (equals, approximately, short-run *average* costs) for travel. Secondly, individual road users systematically ignore congestion costs (imperfectly measured by extra travel time) which are external to the marginal traveller but internal for the community as a whole.

[3] So, at least, was Labour's reasoning. But doubtless the policy owed something to Treasury insistence that the subsidies should not come from the national public purse – a view which found favour with the new Conservative Government who in October 1970 announced the end of the Exchequer subsidy to London commuter fares: if the London Planning Authorities thought that road congestion would result, it was open to them to come to some arrangement with British Rail, and with their own Transport Authority, to continue the subsidy. Although we may think the 1970 decision wrong, the principle of 'local finance for local purposes' flows naturally from Labour's Transport Policy, and from the economic theory of 'public goods'.

[4] See *Transport in London* (Cmnd. 3686, 1968).

[5] See *Railway Policy* (Cmnd. 3439, 1967).

all in present pricing arrangements, and allowing full commercial freedom to the Gas Council (in their marketing policy) and the Electricity Council (in their decision on the 'coal burn'), coal was likely to decline very rapidly in the 1970s; that economic analysis suggested that this was a good thing; and that it should be allowed to happen, apart from some temporary 'tempering of the wind to the shorn lambs' (redundant coal-miners). Transport policy consisted in following Beeching to its appropriate conclusion, getting rid of white elephants to local authorities, where possible, and assuming an explicit burden of subsidy on the national Exchequer when local screams became too loud. The basic problems of urban transport were not *solved* by 'selling' the LPTB to GLC (see the April 1971 Report of the London Transport Authority); they were 'passed to you please' in fine Whitehall style, at the price only of agreeing (uncomfortably close to the 1970 election and wage explosion) to the substantial fare increase that was necessary to make the new Authority 'financially viable'.[1]

This is certainly one possible interpretation of the path of policy, in both the fuel and the transport cases; but it is hard to deny that the answers given were broadly right, and that the apparatus of analysis was the correct one to choose. This judgment, if sound, is praise indeed for the Labour Government; but it has very little to do with *socialism* and all that.[2] The sole socialist step of importance was the nationalization of steel.

The Government's case for steel nationalization, the main preoccupation of the British Steel Corporation in its first three years, and the still unanswered question is – the development programme for the steel industry. Should vast integrated plants (on the Japanese or Italian style) be built, on green field sites, with the latest technologies, at vast cost: or should instead Britain be content with improving and adapting existing plant, becoming increasingly a steel importer? Despite big reorganization[3] (designed no doubt in part, and successfully, so to scramble the various pre-nationalization eggs that subsequent denationalization became impossible), the financial situation of British Steel by the end of 1970 was so serious that its development programme seemed at risk. A decision about steel's future – even if it had fallen to a Labour Government to make – would have been made more as a part of a long-run policy for Britain's trade and payments than as a scheme for enhancing one of the 'commanding heights'.

We have come then to a coincidence between nationalization and rationalization which is perhaps inevitable in a mixed economy, where

[1] Incidentally the fare increase (see *NBPI Report No. 149*) contained substantial elements of 'price discrimination' designed to reconcile marginal cost pricing with more old-fashioned financial probity.

[2] The policy for the National Freight Corporation (*The Transport of Freight* (Cmnd. 3470, 1967)), unifying the relics of British Road Transport with the container—freightliner services of British Rail, was a brave attempt at a socialist solution to a technical problem. Its validity remains to be tested by experience.

[3] See *Third Report on Organization, British Steel Corporation*, HC Paper No. 60, 1969.

arguments about the exact drawing of the frontier between public and private sectors cause much furore in Westminster but have little practical effect on the path of industrial development. Labour's success in 1964–70 was in bringing the public sector up to date, in a way which reasonably respected fairness and justice, but was mainly aimed at a sort of Whitehall rationality.

8 Fiscal policy for stabilization

Michael Artis

Introduction

This chapter is concerned with the Labour Government's use of fiscal policy for purposes of stabilizing the economy. Other important aspects of fiscal policy – such as the manipulation of the structure of taxation to secure a more even distribution of wealth and income, for example – are not discussed in this chapter; nor do the longer-run structural effects of such innovations as the Corporation Tax or Selective Employment Tax receive detailed attention. The concern here is with the way in which fiscal policy was used to 'manage' the economy, or more precisely to manage the pressure of demand in the economy, with a view to attaining desirable positions with respect to the balance of payments, the level of prices, the growth of the economy, and the utilization of resources, particularly labour.

This list of objectives indicates a fundamental difficulty in appraising the success of any phase of stabilization policy. To the extent that management of the pressure of demand has a bearing on all these objectives, it is misleading to evaluate its success by reference only to one of them. This is so because given positions with respect to all objectives are not in general simultaneously attainable; the usual situation is that 'more' of one objective can be had only at the expense of sacrificing some part of another: for example, the record of the Labour Government with respect to unemployment could undoubtedly have been better had fiscal policy been more expansive: but then the balance of payments would have been worse. Nor is there any reason to think that the relative weights given to achievement of the different and conflicting objectives are constant over time even under one administration: so there is no way of 'adding up' the separate objectives to provide a single consistent estimate of the target being aimed for.[1]

That there is likely to be a conflict of objectives when the means of achieving them is confined to a single instrument – in this case, fiscal policy – is quite understandable. A wider range of tools should in theory enable better results to be achieved. In the case of the Labour Government, a range of other tools was indeed used: planning, incomes policy, monetary policy, and measures affecting the balance of payments directly. But it is part of the basic theme of this chapter that it was the failure of

[1] Further, the structure of the economy changes over time so that the technical relations between objectives are not constant. For example, the current relationship between the level of unemployment and the rate of price inflation is apparently much less favourable than it used to be.

these other tools to meet their specifications, or failure to use them at the right time, which conditioned the use of fiscal policy in such a way that its natural objective – the stabilization of the pressure of demand at an appropriate level – could not be continuously sustained.

The chapter proceeds in the following way: first there is a narrative account of fiscal actions and their background, which is prefaced by a statement of the original objectives of the Government, the latter representing to some extent the author's rationalizations of a wide set of statements and attitudes associated more or less closely with the incoming Government in 1964. This is followed by a section which attempts a 'bird's-eye' look at the record, where an analysis is given of trends in the fiscal balance over the whole period, and the effects of discretionary tax measures and variations in the growth of public expenditure. Attention is also drawn to the apparent collapse of the familiar British business cycle. Finally, there is a short passage of conclusions drawing together some of the threads of the previous argument.

Narrative of fiscal actions 1964–70

Although this chapter is particularly concerned with fiscal policy, it would be absurd to neglect the contribution of other types of policy both to the management of demand directly, and to the general policy setting in which fiscal policy was supposed to function. Some references are therefore made throughout to these other policies, and the specific actions taken are tabulated in the summary tables of policy measures which appear below (Tables 8.1–8.3).[1]

The course of events between October 1964 and June 1970 lends itself, on the view taken here, to subdivision into three more or less distinct parts. First there is the period from the mini-budget of November 1964 to the May Budget of 1966 when policy was guided, if with steadily diminishing fervour, by the precept of avoiding the mistakes of 'stop-go'. Then there is the phase from the deflationary package of July 1966 to devaluation in November 1967 which began with the reversal of the previous precept of avoiding 'stop-go' and ended with the equally decisive reversal of the policy of maintaining the exchange rate. Finally there is the post-

---

[1] In addition, figures 8.1—8.3 show in graphical form, the state of various indicators of external and internal balance, and the timing and strength of monetary and fiscal (i.e. tax) measures. The external balance indicators are the current account of the balance of payments (quarterly, seasonally adjusted), and net reserves, defined as official gold and foreign exchange reserves *less* short- and medium-term borrowing. Both these indicators, of course, have negative values for much of the period, as shown in the charts. Internal balance indicators are provided by the level of unemployment (wholly unemployed, excluding school-leavers, in thousands and seasonally adjusted) and by the rate of inflation of the consumer price index (the quarter to quarter increase in the implicit deflator of the seasonally adjusted consumers' expenditure series expressed at an annual rate).

devaluation phase when the demands on fiscal policy took on new dimensions and when some success could at last be fairly claimed for it.

To begin with, however, it is useful to summarize the background of objectives and preconceptions with which the new Labour Government in 1964 was identified.

Some objectives and preconceptions.   Most of the 1950s and the early 1960s had been characterized by a regular cycle of economic activity which many observers had come to regard as at least partly, if not largely, the result of government intervention. An influential account by J. C. R. Dow of post-war economic management,[1] published early in 1964, had indeed concluded that 'as far as internal conditions are concerned . . . budgetary and monetary policy failed to be stabilizing, and must on the contrary be regarded as having been positively destabilizing'.[2] However much academic observers might dispute the finer points of this conclusion,[3] it accorded well with the version of events publicized by Labour in opposition. 'Stop-go' was part of the economic inheritance that the Labour Government was intent upon shedding. A number of means for doing so were canvassed and later explored in practice with, as it appears, discouraging results.

Several morals could be drawn from the 'stop-go' experience, and most of them seemed well taken by the incoming Government in 1964. To begin with, there was the question of inflation; here it seemed that an unwelcome burden could be removed from demand management policy by the institution of an incomes policy. Such a policy could take care of, or at least relieve, the effects of demand pressure on wages and prices and permit the economy to be run at a higher level of utilization of resources than would otherwise seem reasonable. Then there was the suggestion that 'stop-go' contributed to the poor record of growth by deterring investment, particularly if the means of enforcing the 'stop' were monetary means, the presumption being that this implied a more severe effect on investment spending. This idea, apart from feeding a probable prejudice of a political character against reliance on monetary methods of control, led to the

[1] J. C. R. Dow, *The Management of the British Economy 1945–60* (Cambridge 1964).
[2] Ibid., page 384.
[3] I. M. D. Little, for example, in a review of Dow's book which was published in the *Economic Journal* for December 1964, regarded Dow's conclusion – which appeared to be based essentially upon positive identification of two or possibly three instances of government over-reaction – as too sweeping and general in relation to the evidence quoted for it. Dow's characterization might have been held to imply that some 'neutral' policy would have been better; but no wholly satisfactory definition of such a standard of comparison exists. Subsequent empirical analyses, incidentally, have arrived at differing conclusions: the study by Hansen for OECD for example (B. Hansen, *Fiscal Policy in Seven Countries 1955–1965*, OECD 1969) gave general support to Dow; Bristow's more recent analysis of the effect of discretionary tax changes (J. A. Bristow, 'Taxation and income stabilization', *Economic Journal*, June 1968) arrived at an opposite conclusion. The theoretical problems of testing for successful stabilization have been spelt out by G. D. N. Worswick in 'Stabilization policy', *Journal of Money, Credit and Banking*, February 1970.

suggestion that some method should be found whereby growth could be given higher priority and 'supply side' problems resolved by appropriate means. The obvious answer to this appeared, in principle, to be 'planning' and later in practice the institutional innovation of the establishment of the Department of Economic Affairs. Closer to the home ground of fiscal policy another moral to be drawn was that some mistakes could be avoided by weakening the adherence to a fixed annual budget time-table.

In essence none of this was new; it represented an extension, and in principle a more determined continuation, of the policies of the previous Conservative administration.

The missing tool from the kit was any policy to deal directly, and in sufficient time, with the balance of payments, the vicissitudes of which were, after all, one of the prime movers of 'stop-go'.[1] Of course no statement could be expected of an Opposition expecting to govern, to the effect that it would devalue, or even thought it might. Nevertheless, in the public mind it is fair to say that Labour's priorities were thought likely to put growth and employment ahead of prices and 'the pound'.[2] That no early earnest was given of a decision to devalue could also be excused; but as it turned out, the decision to devalue had not been concealed, postponed or reserved – rather, policy was based on a positive decision to defend the existing exchange rate. This decision – or series of decisions, as a changing balance of factors probably sustained it through time – was to be the ultimate undoer of all the rest. It was eventually to guide the management of the economy into a new phase of 'stop-go' – or, rather, of 'stop'.

The problem of the balance of payments and the exchange rate was then to prove the major determinant of stabilization policy. But so far as fiscal policy in particular was concerned, another major influence was to be provided by the incoming Labour administration's taste for public spending. The partial identification of Labour thinking with a Galbraithian view of the affluent society, in which public sector expenditure would suffer unless specific steps were taken to prevent it, meant that the incoming administration was not likely to repudiate the plans for expansion already laid down by the previous Conservative Government. Indeed, in the espousal of growth and the publication of the National Plan the commitment to a rapid growth in public expenditure was to become quite firm; and as the original precondition of such a commitment, in the form of a rapid growth of total output, was not in the event to be met, fiscal policy inevitably bore a harsher burden.

[1] It had perhaps only comparatively recently become apparent that the balance of payments represented a real problem. Dow's treatment of the balance of payments in his assessment of policy, written as it was around 1962, displayed an insouciance which may have seemed fair at the time, but by 1964/65 appeared remarkable (compare Robin Marris' review in the *London and Cambridge Economic Bulletin* for March 1965). The Maudling 'experiment' of 1964 was known at the time for a gamble and its failure was clear by the summer of 1964.

[2] See Chapter 1, page 59.

Narrative: October 1964–May 1966

During the period up to the Budget of 1966, the Government was attempting to apply the lessons learnt from the previous cycle of economic activity – whilst yet endeavouring to pull the balance of payments back into balance. Over time the second task began to loom the larger, and the former was given less emphasis, but it was still a discernible part of policy.

The Government inherited power when the economy was at the top of its cycle, and it seemed clear enough that it was vital to avoid repeating the mistake committed in 1961 when government deflationary action aggravated the cyclical downturn from the peak of 1961, producing the recession of 1962.[1] But just as in 1960, so in 1964, was the cyclical peak of activity marked by an adverse balance of payments; moreover, there was a marked difference of scale between the experience of the two years. The current account deficit of 1960 was £255 million, where 1964's was to prove as large as £376 million: and the adverse 'gearing effect' of capital movements was still more disproportionate, the total currency flow over the exchanges – which was unfavourable to the extent of £695 million in 1964 – had actually been strongly favourable in 1960. It seemed clear to most observers that the current account deficit of 1964 was not merely an evanescent sign of gross overheating, but betokened as well a significant decline in competitiveness.

This inheritance was not an easy one. It did not make the best setting for the introduction of Labour's longer-term economic measures; there was little possibility of forswearing some acts of real or still more, apparent deflation whatever was done; there were no easy gains of growth to be chalked up in the short term; and the current and potential tightness of the labour market promised a stern testing of any tentative measure of incomes policy.

There were, broadly, three alternative strategies available, each with implications for fiscal policy. One was to deflate substantially and rapidly until a point was reached at which the payments position was eased: such a course ran right against the Labour prospectus and in itself promised none but a temporary solution. A second course was to devalue; but this would have implied a very drastic reduction in domestic consumption in order to accommodate the reallocation of resources to exports and and import substitution with the economy already running at a high level of resource utilization. The third course, which was the one which appeared to commend itself, was to ease the economy gradually from its over-stretched condition, whilst adopting interim measures to act directly on the balance of payments and borrowing to cover the remaining deficit: implicit in such a course would be reliance on some longer-term measures to right the economy's competitive position, or on a deferred act of devaluation planned to take place in more propitious circumstances.

As it turned out, it was the third of these strategies – but with the

[1] A chart of the cyclical movement of gross domestic product appears below (Figure 8.4).

reliance placed not on deferred devaluation but upon other measures – which governed policy up to May 1966. The assurance with which the Government in this period was attempting to stick to the precept of avoiding 'stop-go' is apparently belied by its overt actions and the budget speeches; but allowance must be made for the need, as it was probably then felt, to present the measures publicly as acts of stern deflation for the sake of 'confidence' (in the pound), and also for the fact that although the mounting sum of discretionary tax changes and promised cuts in public spending seemed to amount to something more severe than the deflationary acts of 1961, the steam behind the expansion of the economy – including in particular the underlying trend of government spending programmes – was much greater than it had been in 1961.

The first acts of policy, in particular, appeared more deflationary than they really were. The mini-budget of 11 November 1964 introduced increases in taxes amounting to £215 million in a full year. The impact of this was, however, more or less fully offset by other changes; an import surcharge and export rebate scheme were brought in, which to the extent they were effective would boost the economy, whilst the net effect of the increases in rates of national insurance benefits and contributions was also expansionary. Informed observers at the time[1] concluded that the total net effect of all these measures was probably neutral, the burden of net effective deflation being left to the restraint of bank advances. There is no reason to think the Chancellor could really have held a very different view although the balance of his presentation suggested that he was thinking of some net deflation. He reserved his position carefully and explicitly for later review, emphasizing that 'I must never forget the fallibility of forecasting, as a result of which other Chancellors have given the economy a deflationary twist just at the moment when it did not need it'.[2]

That the burden resting on other measures was heavy was also made quite clear: the success of the measures was said to depend upon 'a successful and swift conclusion to the discussions on prices and incomes policy that have already begun'.[3] A significant part of the budget speech was – already – taken up with the need to curtail the expansiveness of the public sector spending programmes inherited from the previous administration.

The first full budget, introduced in April 1965, made it still clearer that the short-term tactics of acting by temporary means on the balance of payments whilst easing the pressure of demand (which now became more clearly an objective of policy) were seen as part of a long-term strategy involving incomes policy and 'planning' to improve the competitiveness of the economy. The budget objective was to 'make room' for an improvement in the balance of payments sufficient to produce a zero basic balance in 1966. Further credits had been sought to cover the interim

[1] See, for example, the *National Institute Economic Review*, No. 30, November 1964, pages 5–11; *London and Cambridge Economic Bulletin*, December 1964.
[2] *Hansard*, House of Commons, Vol. 701, Col. 1043.
[3] Ibid.

TABLE 8.1 FISCAL AND OTHER 'DEMAND MANAGEMENT' MEASURES: NOVEMBER 1964–MAY 1966

	Fiscal policy	Monetary policy	Hire purchase terms	Prices & incomes policy	External policy
1964 Q.IV	*Nov. 11* Mini-budget. Rates of income tax (for 1965/66) and of petrol duty raised. Increases in national insurance benefits and contributions announced for January–March 1965. FY effect: £215 m.	*Nov. 23* Bank Rate raised from 5 to 7%. *Dec. 8* Advances restraint request.		*Dec. 16* Joint statement of Intent issued.	*Oct. 26* Temporary import surcharge (at 15%) and export rebate introduced. *Nov. 8* $400 m. loan made available. *Nov. 25* $3,000 m. loan announced.
1965 Q.I	*Feb. 1* Prescription charges abolished. *Feb. 22* Rate of rise of public expenditure 1964/65–1969/70 to be restricted to 4¼% p.a.			*Feb. 11* White Paper on machinery of prices and incomes policy.	*Feb. 10* Renewal of credits negotiated in November; IMF loan to be sought.
Q.II	*Apr. 6* TSR-2 cancelled. *Apr. 6* Increases in rates of tax on tobacco, and alcoholic drinks, and in motor vehicle duties. Restriction of business expenses. Introduction of long-term Capital Gains Tax and Corporation Tax. FY effect: £233 m. *June 15* Defence spending to be held at £2,000 m. (1964 prices) in 1970.	*Apr. 29* Call for special Deposits. *May 6* 5% limit on expansion of advances during 1965/66. *June 3* Bank rate cut from 7 to 6%.	*June 4* Controls tightened: min. downpayment raised from 20 to 25% on cars, from 10 to 15% most other goods.	*Apr. 8* White paper fixes norm for incomes increase at 3–3½%.	*Apr. 6* Tightening of exchange control regulations. *Apr. 27* Import surcharge reduced to 10%. *May 14* Further IMF drawing of $1,400 m. *May 29* Swap agreement with US for $750 m. renewed.
Q.III	*July 27* Public authority investment cuts announced. Local authority mortgages limited.	*July 27* Reminder of advances restraint.	*July 28* Controls tightened: max. repayment period reduced to 30 mths.		*July 27* Tightening of exchange controls. *Sept. 10* New international support for £.
Q.IV					

	Fiscal policy	Monetary policy	Hire purchase terms	Prices & incomes policy	External policy
1966 Q.1	*Jan. 17* Investment allowances withdrawn in favour of grants.	*Feb. 1* Existing limits on advances to be retained.	*Feb. 8* Controls tightened: min. downpayment raised to 25%; max. repayment period reduced to 24 mths. (27 mths. for cars).	*Feb. 24* Prices and incomes bill published.	
Q.II[a]	*Apr. 6* Local authority mortgage limits raised. *May 3* Budget. Introduction of SET, betting and gaming tax. Corporation tax rate at 40%.				*May 3* Programme for voluntary restriction of overseas investment.

[a] Up to May 3.

Source: *National Institute Economic Review; Economic Trends.*

losses of reserves and further measures acting directly on the balance of payments were brought in (these were estimated to 'save' some £100–£200 million).

Deflation of demand was accomplished by raising rates of indirect taxation: the two new innovations – a long-term Capital Gains Tax and Corporation Tax – were not proposed as in themselves the means of raising more revenue. On the side of government spending, some cuts had already been announced: TSR-2 had been cancelled[1] and limitations were shortly announced on total defence spending in the years ahead.

The Chancellor was clearly conscious of the risk of repeating the 'stop-go' mistake, explicitly recalling the measures of 1961;[2] equally it was clear that righting the balance of payments would require more room to be made for the absorption of resources required. His forecasts for the economy (as in the mini-budget speech of 1964) were regrettably guarded, but suggested that he thought the economy would continue to grow at somewhere near a capacity rate provided the balance of payments target was met.

Approval of government policy at this time still required an observer to evaluate very favourably the probable success and time-scale of the Government's efforts, through planning and incomes policy and in other ways, to secure an improvement in the UK competitive position. It was clear that it required an act of faith and of hope to do this.[3] The situation was brilliantly summed up by Professor W. B. Reddaway in his contribution to the *London and Cambridge Economic Bulletin* in June 1965, which was entitled 'Suspended Judgement'. The flavour of this article is conveyed by the summary, part of which reads

The crisis in the balance of payments . . . demanded actions to produce immediate results, unrelated to the Government's long-term objectives, and the long-term policies are necessarily still in the preparatory stages: one must therefore suspend judgement, but even to a sympathetic observer there seems no logical reason for thinking that the objectives can be achieved and the long-term problem of the balance of payments solved by the methods envisaged.

In the text Reddaway added the warning that 'a prolonged and indiscriminate credit squeeze is certainly not the way to do it'. In May–June a new phase of credit restraint had indeed been brought in, and there was to be a further tightening in July.

[1] The usual 'cost overrun' experience with such projects probably means this saved much more than the £35 million credited to it for 1965–6.
[2] *Hansard*, House of Commons, Vol. 710, Col. 288.
[3] This is not churlishness or benefit of hindsight, as the quotation from Professor Reddaway's review given in the text confirms. The August 1965 issue of the *National Institute Economic Review* made a similar point, but summed up its forecast for the period to the end of 1966 as involving near-stagnation of output growth as the price of achieving a near zero balance on basic balance of payments account.

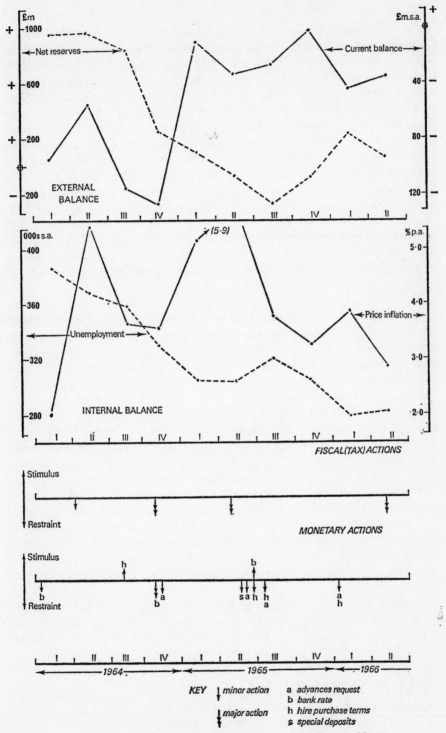

Fig. 8.1   Policy actions and indicators: 1964 I–1966 II
For definitions, see page 263, footnote 1.

The actual out-turn of events in 1965 was afterwards described by the Chancellor in his budget speech of May 1966 as having been 'broadly in accord with intentions'.[1] Taking the year as a whole, data now available show that output grew by about 2½%, with an improvement in the net foreign balance (exports of goods and services minus imports) equivalent to ¾–1% of 1964's output. The current account had improved by over £300 million, the basic balance by £475 million, and the adverse total currency flow had dropped from £659 million to £353 million. The difficulty was that a still considerable *further* improvement in the balance of payments was required, with output growth having already tended to flatten out. Nor was there any sign that the longer-term measures needed to secure a more favourable competitive position were having any effect. It was still too soon for the planning exercise to bear fruit, and the first experiments with incomes policy had not brought wage rises in 1965 anywhere within required limits; a cut in working hours had contributed to prolonged tightness in the labour markets and unemployment had shown no sign of rising.

The budgetary answer to these problems remained essentially the same as it had been in 1965, however. Further measures to deal directly with the balance of payments were taken (the voluntary programme to restrain outward investment), and further action was taken to restrain demand – once more, the necessary (but not sufficient) condition for an improved competitiveness to be realized in a more favourable balance of payments. On this occasion the main burden of deflation fell on a new tax – the Selective Employment Tax – which was estimated to raise revenue in a full year by £240 million. This innovation, whatever the merit of the other advantages claimed for it,[2] had the effect of broadening the tax base; and increases in rates of SET, and the cancellation of premia, were to offer means of substantial further revenue increases in the next few years.

The budget speech indicated once again the hopes being placed upon other arms of policy, but with clear reservations about the results of incomes policy up to that time. Nor was there this time any encouraging reference to avoiding 'stop-go' nor indeed much by way of an assessment of the prospects for output. 'The crucial question' was whether the prospects were 'consistent with the improvement we need in the balance of payments'.[3]

Outside observers found the prospects of achieving the Government's target of a zero basic balance in 1966–7 plausible – but only in the context of a continued low growth rate. The *National Institute Economic Review* for May 1966 argued that 'the main objection to present policies ...

---

[1] *Hansard*, House of Commons, Vol. 727, Col. 1442.

[2] The subsequent investigation of the Selective Employment Tax officially commissioned from Professor Reddaway suggested that the tax had substantial productivity effects in the service sector, but dealt rather coolly with the other advantages claimed for it at different times by different people.

[3] *Hansard*, House of Commons, Vol. 727, Col. 1443.

is that they represent a counsel of despair about the prospects of achieving any acceleration in the British growth rate'. The events shortly to follow, culminating in the measures of July 1966, were only to render this assessment an understatement.

Narrative: June 1966–November 1967

The initial phase of policy, up to the Budget of 1966, was partially successful in its aims; an improvement in the balance of payments was obtained in association with a significant growth of output. This policy added about a year to the normal cyclical period of 'above trend' economic activity. The Labour Government's '1961' came in 1966 rather than 1965 and its '1962' duly followed in 1967.

The deflationary actions of July 1966 mark the threshold when the initial phase of policy was given up. Righting the balance of payments then became the overriding objective of demand management policy. This change in policy reflected the fact that the balance of payments recovery chalked up since 1964 was insufficient and had been obtained in such a way that the needed *further improvement* could not be readily expected. Many of the measures used to act directly on the balance of payments were either once-for-all in nature (like the cuts in government overseas spending) or temporary (like the temporary import surcharge) and had to be removed at some date. Longer-term policies had not evidently set in train any forces making for a lasting improvement in competitiveness. Meanwhile the burden of international indebtedness grew, and with it the needed target surpluses for repayment. The margin for manœuvre and the Government's ability to buy more time diminished.

With other measures ruled out, the sterling crisis which blew up in May 1966 forced further deflation and temporary controls on the balance of payments. The first half of 1966 had seen a pause in the improvement on the balance of payments and a high rate of capital outflow; the seamen's strike, which began on 15 May, was the last straw.

The new measures announced in July to September included a pay and prices freeze, new international credits, imposition of the £50 travel allowance, credit restrictions and, on the fiscal side, cuts in planned public sector investment and an increase of 10% in rates of indirect taxation (the 'regulator'). The deflationary measures were substantial: the regulator alone implied a fall in real disposable incomes of about $\frac{3}{4}$%, and this combined with the credit restraint and the effect of the new Selective Employment Tax precipitated a down-turn in economic activity. In the latter part of 1966 and through 1967 unemployment began to rise very rapidly.[1]

[1] The reasons for this sharp upsurge in unemployment appear rather complex; over and above the deflation of demand, some other factors were at work. But there is no clear agreement on the relative importance of these, and in addition to a threshold 'shake-out' phenomenon, commentators have cited increased unemployment benefits, redundancy payments and the introduction of SET as specific factors.

TABLE 8.2 FISCAL AND OTHER 'DEMAND MANAGEMENT' MEASURES: MAY 1966 TO MID-NOVEMBER 1967

	Fiscal policy	Monetary policy	Hire purchase terms	Prices & incomes policy	External policy
1966 Q.II[a]					June 13 $2,000 m. new credits agreed at BIS.
Q.III	July 20 10% regulator increase. Public investment cuts (by £150 m. in 1967/68).	July 14 Bank rate raised from 6 to 7%, call for special deposits. Aug. 9 Banks reminded of 105% ceiling (in strong terms).	July 21 Deposits increased, and re-payment period for cars reduced.	July 20 Prices and incomes stand still until end of 1966. Sept. 7 TUC supports pay freeze.	July 20 £50 travel allowance to be introduced from Nov. 1. Sept. 13 $1,350m. new swap facilities announced.
Q.IV	Dec. 1 £120 m. increase in invest-ment grants for 1967/68 announced.			Oct. 4 Compulsory provision for Prices and Incomes Act activated. Nov. 22 White Paper on wage and price policy in period of severe restraint; norm for increases nil from Jan. 1967.	
1967 Q.I	Mar. 21 Six months advance in payment of investment grants.	Jan. 20 UK and others agree to lower interest rates. Jan. 26 Bank rate cut from 7 to 6½%. Feb. 3 Credit squeeze on private housing to be eased. Mar. 16 Bank rate cut from 6½ to 6%.		Mar. 2 TUC approves extension of voluntary wage vetting. Mar. 21 Prices and Incomes White Paper proposes year of moderation after June 30.	Mar. 13 $1,000 m. BIS loan renewed for further year.

	Fiscal policy	Monetary policy	Hire purchase terms	Prices & incomes policy	External policy
1967 Q.II	*Apr. 11* Budget. SET refund for part-time employees; 10% regulator consolidated. *June 9* White Paper on Regional Employment Premiums in Development areas, 30s a week for men for at least seven years from Sept. 4. *June 21* National Insurance Benefits to be increased from Oct. 30. £230m. contributions increase.	*Apr. 11* 105% limit on bank advances lifted. *May 4* Bank rate cut from 6 to 5½%.	*Apr. 11* Terms on motor-cycles relaxed.	*Apr. 17* Prices and Incomes Act 1966 to be amended to give power to delay increases for up to 7 mths. *June 30* Period of severe restraint ends, no norm set; TUC vetting.	*June 29* £50 travel limit extended until Nov. 1968.
Q.III	*July 18* Defence White Paper announces £200 m. savings by 1970–1. *July 24* Government expenditure to grow by no more than 3% in real terms over next 3 years.	*Oct. 17* Bank rate raised from 5½ to 6%. *Nov. 9* Bank rate raised from 6 to 6½%.	*Aug. 29* Controls relaxed.	*Sept. 7* All future major price increases in Public Sector to be referred to PIB.	
Q.IV[b]	*Oct. 30* Family allowances to be increased from Apr. 1968. *Nov. 18* £100 m. defence cuts; £100 m. cuts in other public spending; SET premium withdrawn except in development areas, saving £100 m. Export rebates to end April 1968 saving £400 m. Corporation Tax to be raised 2½% in budget.	*Nov. 18* Bank rate raised from 6½ to 8%. Advances limited to all but priority borrowers.	*Nov. 18* Controls tightened		*Oct. 10* Swiss banks lend UK £37½ m. at 5½% for one year. *Nov. 12* UK obtains $250 m. BIS credit to re-finance IMF debts due in December. *Nov. 18* 14·3% devaluation, $3,000 m. credits sought, including $1,400 m. IMF stand by.

[a] From May 4.
[b] Up to Nov. 19.

Source: *National Institute Economic Review; Economic Trends.*

Policy in early 1967, up to and including the budget, resembles with benefit of hindsight that stage of well-being and apparent recovery which a patient reaches just before the final relapse. The errors of sentiment of government policy in regard to the balance of payments were most probably on this occasion compounded by technical forecasting errors. The result, with the Middle-East War and the dock strikes thrown in for good measure, made a shambles of a policy which had, anyway, little real coherence.

At the beginning of the year, the short-term future looked reasonably assuring provided that some reflationary action to halt the trend of unemployment was in prospect. In some ways the situation resembled that of 1962, which provided a reminder of the dangers of delaying reflationary action too long; the big difference was that whereas by July 1962 all debts had been repaid and reflation could begin with 'a clean slate', at the beginning of 1967 the outstanding value of official debt stood at £1481 million. With the past history of three years of substantial deficit, a high premium was inevitably placed on securing a surplus in 1967: failure to do so would be bound to have serious consequences.

Policy remained substantially unchanged in the first five months of the year. The budget provided no significant change and the Chancellor's speech indicated that output growth was expected to pick up from its cyclical trough to reach 3% per annum. At the same time the Chancellor foresaw a reasonable buoyancy in world trade and an increase in imports which was 'unlikely to be large'. The budget speech was a welcome improvement on its predecessors of the previous two years in the amount of detail it gave about the forecasts underlying it. Unfortunately, these proved to be misleading: a retrospective review, adjusting the out-turn for the impact of erratic factors, indicates that the estimates of exports were pitched much too high, and of imports too low; that the growth of output was put too high and that recovery was thought to be coming in earlier than in fact it did.[1] The mistake in the timing of the recovery was easily remedied – by reflationary actions taken in June and August; the balance of payments failure, too, was remedied – at last, by the devaluation of the pound on 18 November. The proximate causes of this included the closure of Suez and the dockers' strikes as well as the unusually slow growth in world trade which affected exports adversely. But even after correction for these factors the fact remains that the underlying behaviour of exports (in relation to world trade) and of imports (in relation to output) was exceptionally unfavourable in 1967. This experience would have made quite clear the need for a fundamental change in policy with respect to the balance of payments even if that change had not been forced.

The devaluation required new fiscal measures. The change in the exchange rate by itself only gave the opportunity for an increase in exports and for import substitution. Demand management had to ensure that room was made for these developments to take place: for apart from

[1] See *National Institute Economic Review*, February 1968, pages 8–10.

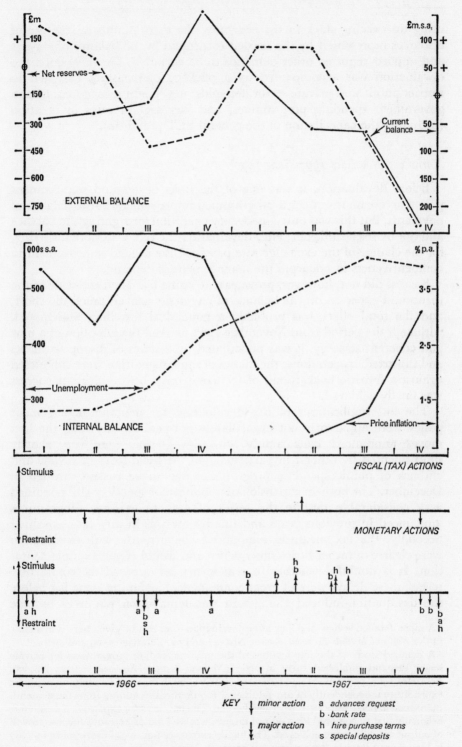

Fig. 8.2   Policy actions and indicators: 1966 I–1967 IV
For definitions, see page 263, footnote 1.

using up existing slack in the economy, the extra claims on the use of resources represented by the needed turnround in the balance of exports and imports required other demands to be curtailed. For this reason the devaluation was accompanied by a package of measures designed to restrict public and private sector demands: new credit restrictions, cuts in government spending programmes, and increases in rates of taxation (including the cancellation of the general SET premium).

Narrative: November 1967–June 1970[1]

Before devaluation, it was one of the tasks of demand management policy to 'create room' for a programmed improvement in the balance of payments. But this was only a necessary condition for righting the balance and not by itself sufficient; after devaluation the role was more satisfying, for the change of the exchange rate provided the needed improvement in competitiveness to underpin the management of demand.

Success did not, however, prove easy to come by. The time-scale of the turnround expected on the balance of payments proved much too short, and the total effect was probably a good deal less than anticipated. Although the period from November 1967 marked the adoption of a new and coherent strategy, it was punctuated by a series of disappointments and thwarted expectations; the tactics of implementation were conducted against a frenetic background of recurrent crisis before ultimate success was finally achieved.

The full implications of the devaluation for demand management policy were apparently not immediately grasped. At any rate, the first moves announced concurrently with devaluation were very shortly supplemented by others: in particular, on the fiscal front, a review and cutback of public spending programmes had to be rushed through in December. The built-in expansion of public sector spending still remained very considerable despite the series of cuts to existing programmes announced in previous years and this review was in any case overdue.[2] Secondly, the tax measures announced concurrently with devaluation were clearly of rather little consequence and would require supplementation. It is doubtful whether in real terms (as opposed to 'confidence' terms) these delays were of great consequence: assuming some lag before the devaluation-induced changes in the demand on resources become

[1] A more detailed review of policy after devaluation than can be given here is available in the *National Institute Economic Review*, Nos. 47 and 51, February 1969 and 1970.

[2] A detailed study of the implications of the public spending programmes for private sector demand published early in 1967 (*National Institute Economic Review*, No. 39, February 1967, pages 23–7) had indicated clearly enough the need for restraint of public expenditure independently of any additional requirement stemming from the demand-management needs associated with devaluation. The public sector expansion programme, originally tied to National Plan output targets, was well out of step with the low growth of output actually being achieved. The highly expansive posture of fiscal policy in 1967 is brought out later in the analysis, pages 292–6 below.

effective, cutbacks in the expansionary effect of fiscal policy were not needed immediately.

The 1968 Budget was the most powerful, and in its presentation, the most coherent and elegant, of any of the budgets delivered in the Labour Government's periods of office. It set out a sophisticated grand design for policy, replete with a quantified set of forecasts for output and its components cast in volume terms. The economy, however, proved churlish enough not to respond in appropriate terms: consumption grew much faster than anticipated and the balance of payments failed to respond at anything like the rate implied by official targets. Import demand grew very fast indeed.

New measures were called for and applied in November 1968: the regulator was used again, and there were further restrictions on credit. Once more a measure bearing temporarily on the balance of payments – the import deposit scheme – was introduced: with the difference, this time, that longer-term measures were in hand to improve competitiveness.

The fiscal actions of 1968 had set in train a radical change in the expansiveness of the public sector. The continued slow improvement in the balance of payments, however, caused further action to be taken. The 1969 Budget again introduced further increases in taxation (Table 8.3); these were superimposed on top of the increases legislated in 1968 and were complemented by heavy restraint of public sector expenditures. Thus it was in 1969, rather than 1968, which witnessed the largest turnround in the fiscal balance towards restriction.[1]

It was not until the third quarter of 1969 that the devaluation gains were plainly seen. Fiscal policy none the less remained highly restrictive – and was complemented by a much tighter monetary policy; no action was taken until the Budget of 1970 to relax these restraints, and even then the amount of reflation involved was very small. Unemployment consequently rose fairly steadily from about the third quarter of 1969 on. One of the reasons for this, as it seems, unduly obstinate stance of policy was the belief that the end of restrictive incomes policy would induce a sharp upsurge not only in money wages but also in real wages and consumption. This belief was not altogether supported: and in the first half of 1970 the cumulative deflationary effect of previous actions had mounted to a scale which involved a new record number of unemployed, and under-utilization of resources.

The narrative of policy actions outlined above, selective and abbreviated as it is, indicates one or two provisional conclusions of some importance. First, fiscal policy was throughout highly active: discretionary tax changes were frequent and large. The predominance of the fixed annual budget time-table was not obviously allowed to influence adversely the timing of policy: substantial policy actions were taken on several occasions between budgets, and the budget actions themselves were typically informed by an

[1] This point is brought out below, in comparing the movement of the weighted budget deficit between 1967 and 1968 and between 1968 and 1969 (Table 8.9, page 295).

TABLE 8.3 FISCAL AND OTHER 'DEMAND MANAGEMENT' MEASURES: NOVEMBER 1967–APRIL 1970

	Fiscal policy	Monetary policy	Hire purchase terms	Prices & incomes policy	External policy
1967 Q.IV[a]	*Dec. 21* £600 m. cuts planned in public spending and £711·5 m. cuts in nationalized industry programme 1968/69.				*Nov. 29* IMF agrees $1,400 m. standby. *Nov. 30* Letter of intent published.
1968 Q.I	*Jan. 16* £700 m. cuts in public spending for 1968/69. *Mar. 19* Budget. Increases in rates involving: purchase tax, customs and excise and petrol duties, SET, betting duties, road fund licences. Special investment levy. Additional family allowances and 'clawback'. FY effect: £923 m.	*Mar. 21* Bank rate cut from 8 to 7½%.		*Jan. 5* 3½% max. for pay rises announced.	*Feb. 12* Basle meetings renew credits.
Q.II		*May 23* Advances restraint request.		*Apr. 3* White Paper lays down nil norms, 3½% maximum for pay rise, with productivity bargain exceptions.	
Q.III		*Sept. 9* Bank rate cut from 7½ to 7%.			*July 8* Basle agreement for insured funding of sterling balances announced.
Q.IV	*Nov. 22* 10% Regulator activated.	*Nov. 22* Advances restraint tightened.	*Nov. 1* Controls tightened. Cars: min. deposit raised from 33⅓ to 40%; max. repayment period reduced from 27 to 24 months. Similar proportional tightening for other goods.		*Oct. 15* £50 travel allowance renewed. *Nov. 22* Import deposit scheme: 50% deposits for 6 months required.

	Fiscal policy	Monetary policy	Hire purchase terms	Prices & incomes policy	External policy
1969 Q.I		Jan. 31 Advances restraint reminder. Feb. 27 Bank rate raised from 7 to 8%.		Jan. 17 White Paper 'In Place of Strife' on strike-curbing legislation published.	
Q.II	Apr. 15 Budget. Change in income tax allowances and rebates; estate duty. Betterment Levy, Capital Gains Tax, purchase tax. SAYE announced. FY effect: £130 m.	Apr. 15 Further reminder of advances restraint request. May 31 Halving of rate paid on Special Deposits as penalty for non-compliance with restraint request.		Apr. 16 Proposals for Industrial relations Bill announced. June 18 Bill dropped.	June 23 Letter of Intent published. DCE maximum (1969/70) £400 m.
Q.III	Aug. 19 TDR for public sector investment raised from 8 to 10%.				
Q.IV	Dec. 4 White Paper puts annual rise in public spending 1968/69–1973/74 at 3%.			Dec. 12 2½–4½% range for wage increases suggested.	Oct. 21 Import deposit percentage cut to 40%; renewed for 12 months.
1970 Q.I	Apr. 14 Budget. Income and surtax allowances increased; abolition of stamp duty; other minor changes. FY effect: –£202 m.	Mar. 14 Bank rate cut from 8 to 7½%. Apr. 14 Bank rate cut from 7½ to 7%.			Jan. 1 Travel allowance increased from £50 to £300.

ᵃ After devaluation.

Source: *National Institute Economic Review; Economic Trends.*

attempt to ensure that the time-scale of effectiveness of tax changes was appropriate to the forecast evolution of the economy. Flexibility is a desirable characteristic of fiscal policy and testifies to a virtue, rather than a defect, in the policy-makers.[1] Secondly, it is fairly clear that for most of the period the objective of policy was not to stabilize the pressure of demand but to right, or assist in righting, the balance of payments. Thirdly, it also seems clear that the policy-makers were apt to learn their lessons, first too slowly, and then too well. The need for a radical change in balance of payments policies was not recognized in practice until the devaluation; nor did it seem that the need to cut back public expenditures – given the 'low growth' context – was fully realized until that point. But then the engines were reversed with a vengeance and the posture of heavy restraint was maintained, in effect, *à outrance*, with predictable consequences for unemployment and output.

A narrative account of policy actions, while it brings out the background of policy decisions can act as a distorting mirror in some respects. The overall view presented in the next section attempts to correct the perspective by pointing to some long-run trends and providing some more formal analysis of the balance of fiscal policy.

An overall view

A good point at which to begin an overall view is with the British business cycle. Figure 8.4 shows the deviations of gross domestic product from its trend value over the period 1958 I–1970 II.[2]

Two important points stand out from this: first, that the duration of the 'above trend' period of the cycle in 1964–6 was longer than in the previous cycle. As argued earlier, it was indeed initial government policy that the cycle downturn from its peak in 1964 should not be aggravated. Secondly, it can be seen that following the downturn in 1966–7, there was no more than a feeble upswing in 1968 followed by renewed decline; that is, the old cycle disappeared.

This is clearly brought out in Table 8.4 which compares the two earlier cycles with the experience following the third quarter of 1967. The growth of GDP in the latest period is above the 'downswing' growth rate of previous cycles, but well below the upswing rate and rather under the trend rate. The behaviour of the components of output is also markedly different. In the former cycle, the behaviour of both private investment

---

[1] This comment may seem obvious. However, its point is often lost sight of when frequent intervention is characterized as following 'loss of control' or 'bad forecasting'.

[2] A 'compromise' measure of gross domestic product was used, and a trend equation fitted to the quarterly observations, of the form $Y = ab^t$, where Y is compromise gross domestic product and t is time, measured in quarters from 1958 I. The figures shown in Figure 8.4 are the deviations of GDP from the calculated (trend) values. These deviations describe the effect of cyclical and other factors on GDP; to eliminate some of the lumpiness of the original series a three-quarter centred average of the deviations has been used. The trend rate of growth implicit in the fitted equation was about 3% per annum.

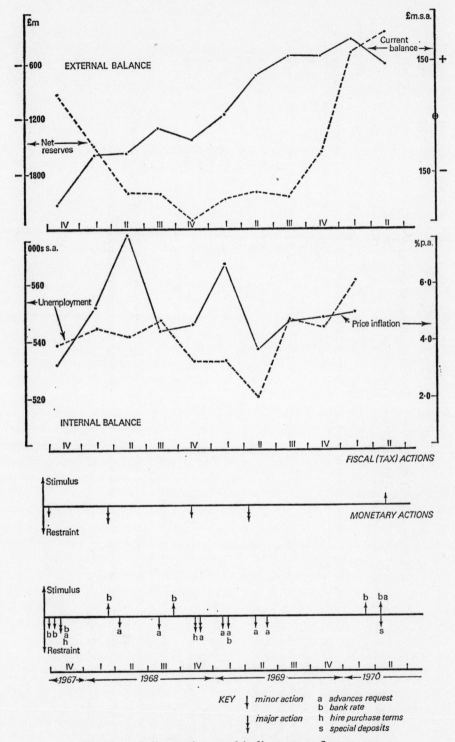

£m   £m.s.a.

Current balance →

EXTERNAL BALANCE

− 600   150 −   +

− 1200

← Net reserves →

− 1800   150 −   −

     IV   I   II   III   IV   I   II   III   IV   I   II

000s s.a.   %p.a.

− 560   6·0

←Unemployment

− 540   4·0

← Price inflation →

− 520   2·0

INTERNAL BALANCE

     IV   I   II   III   IV   I   II   III   IV   I   II

FISCAL (TAX) ACTIONS

↑ Stimulus

                                MONETARY ACTIONS

↓ Restraint

↑ Stimulus

    b   b   b   ba

bb   b   a   a   ha   aa   a   a   s
    a
    h   b

↓ Restraint

     IV   I   II   III   IV   I   II   III   IV   I   II

←1967→ ← 1968 → ← 1969 → ← 1970 →

KEY   ↓ minor action   a advances request
                       b bank rate
       ↓ major action   h hire purchase terms
                       s special deposits

Fig. 8.3   Policy actions and indicators: 1967 IV–1970 II
For definitions, see page 263, footnote 1.

TABLE 8.4 THE UNITED KINGDOM BUSINESS CYCLE

Percentage annual rates of change[a]

| | Average 1958/67 | Two previous cycles | | | | Later period |
| | | Upswings | | Downswings | | |
		1958 III–1960 III	1962 III–1964 III	1960 III–1962 III	1964 IV–1967 III	1967 III–1969 III
GDP[b]	3·2	5·1	4·7	2·0	2·0	2·7
Consumers' expenditure	2·9	4·0	3·7	2·4	2·0	1·1
of which durables	6·1	8·3	13·7	4·3	0·8	−2·2
Private gross fixed investment[c]	5·3	11·9	8·5	3·2	0·0	4·9
Public gross fixed investment	7·7	5·5	10·0	6·1	9·1	−3·2
Public authorities' consumption[d]	2·6	2·2	1·4	3·3	3·2	0·6
Exports[e]	3·5	4·3	3·8	2·7	2·7	10·7
Imports[d]	4·4	9·3	5·0	0·4	3·3	4·6
Stockbuilding (£ m., 1963 prices)	291	284	373	279	267	141
Employment (per cent)	0·5	1·2	0·9	0·8	−0·7	−0·4
Employment (thousands)	13	−44	−51	58	74	25

[a] Between centred three-quarter averages at the dates shown.

[b] A 'compromise' estimate from expenditure, income, and output estimates.

[c] Figures adjusted to smooth out the effect of the modification of investment grants at the end of 1968, on the timing of expenditures.

[d] Excluding US military aircraft.

[e] Figures adjusted to smooth out the estimated effects of the 1967 dock strike on the timing of export deliveries.

Source: *National Institute Economic Review*, No. 51, February 1970, page 33.

and consumer durables expenditure is markedly 'pro-cyclical', stock-building and exports mildly so, public sector spending having no very clear role. In the latest period, however, most of these movements have been reversed or attenuated. Durables expenditure dropped, for example, and private investment sustained a slightly above-average growth. Exports on the other hand grew very strongly and public investment fell sharply.

This apparent disappearance of the cycle, if indeed it was due to government policy, might be regarded as a success for stabilization policy. This would be an unduly complimentary verdict, however, for the reduction of instability implicit in the elimination of the 'stop-go' cycle was evidently achieved largely by eliminating the 'go' phase. The alternating phases of upswing and downswing were substituted by a more or less continuous downswing.

The effect of fiscal actions

It is not really feasible, however, to say what the course of economic activity would have been in the absence of any government intervention. The concept of a 'neutral' policy is not one which commands a universally accepted definition as applied across the whole field of government actions, or even as applied to particular sets of actions such as fiscal policy, monetary policy, etc.[1] This does not mean that nothing useful can be said. But it does imply that the kinds of measurements that can usefully be carried out receive their appropriate justification at a rather more specific, ad hoc and perhaps less grandiose level than as some all-embracing measure of 'fiscal policy'. A number of partial measures are presented below which, when pieced together, provide a reasonably well-rounded indication of the role played by fiscal policy in the period under review.

Discretionary tax changes

A very good case can be made for examining in some detail the effects of discretionary tax changes. First of all, as we have seen in the foregoing narrative sections, frequent and apparently sizeable adjustments were made to rates of taxation by the Labour administrations and so it is at least interesting to know what these amounted to. Secondly, and more important, an argument can be made that in considering the stabilization effects of fiscal policy, it is discretionary tax changes which are far and away the most important item to consider. Variations in the rate of government spending cannot, in general, be undertaken for short-run stabilization purposes but represent the result of long-term plans which are in themselves difficult to alter at short notice; of course this is not wholly true but it is sufficiently the case to justify at least beginning with

[1] See Worswick, op. cit.

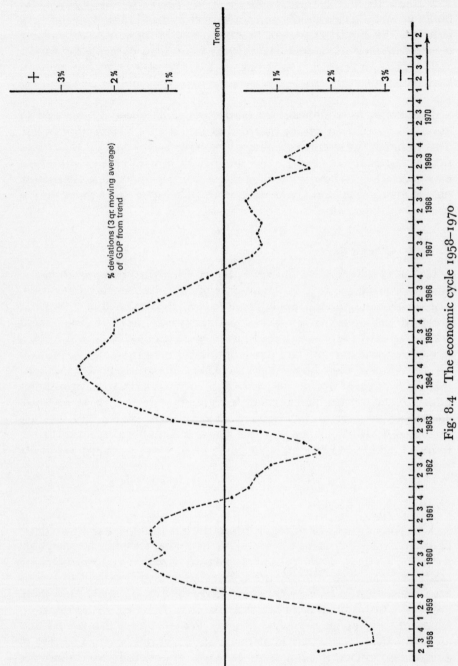

% deviations (3 qr. moving average) of GDP from trend

Trend

+

3%

2%

1%

1%

2%

3%

−

Fig. 8.4 The economic cycle 1958–1970

an examination of tax changes on their own, implicitly treating government spending as given to the system, in much the same way as, for
example, the level of overseas demand.[1] Concentration on the explicit
actions taken in the form of adjusting rates of taxation can be further
justified to the extent that the distinction between discretionary tax
changes and other changes in tax revenues corresponds to a distinction
between 'autonomous' shifts in tax and private expenditure schedules as
opposed to movement along given tax and expenditure schedules. The
distinction sought here is between changes in tax revenues which merely
reflect a restraint of the multiplier process, and are themselves induced by
changes in the level of economic activity, and changes in tax revenues
which initiate a change in the level of economic activity.[2] The correspon-
dence of this distinction to that between discretionary and other sources of
tax revenue change is certainly not water-tight[3] but it does not seem to be
a bad first approximation.

Table 8.5 brings together the main discretionary tax changes brought
into force during the period covered by the analysis, and in Table 8.6 an
attempt has been made to translate them into terms of their total –
cumulative – effect on gross domestic product.

The translation between the figures given in the two tables involves two
main adjustments. First of all, the figures of the 'full year' effect on the
revenue of a given change in tax rates are taken as an indication of the
'autonomous' shift in the tax schedule. Allowance must be made for any
pecularities of timing and adjustments imposed to allow for savings offsets,
import leakages and the adjustment to factor cost in order to derive an
estimate of the 'first-round' impact of the tax changes on gross domestic
product at factor cost.[4] (As we are interested in the effect on the level of
GDP in volume terms, i.e. as now measured at 1963 prices in the official
statistics, an additional adjustment must be made to correct for changes in
the price level.) These estimates have then been cumulated from the
fourth quarter of 1964 onwards. The second stage in the analysis consists
in applying a model of the multiplier-accelerator process to the 'first-
round' effects calculated as above. This is to allow for the fact that the
first-round change in output (GDP) will, in its second and further stages,

[1] At a later stage, we attempt to bring variations in public expenditure back into the
picture.
[2] Of course, a change in rates of taxation will typically have both an impact effect and
result in a modification of the multiplier. But the latter effect is likely to be of very much
smaller significance than the former. A good basic account of these distinctions can be
found in Chapter 9 of G. C. Harcourt, P. H. Karmel and R. H. Wallace, *Economic
Activity* (Cambridge 1967).
[3] One difficulty, for example, arises from the effect of inflation where the tax system is
not proportional. If the system is progressive, then rising nominal incomes and prices
entail increases in real effective rates of taxation comparable in effect to legislated
increases in statutory rates.
[4] This part of the analysis is confined to the effects of tax changes on consumption, since
our knowledge of the effects on other items of expenditure (e.g. investment in the case
of Corporation Taxes) is very sketchy.

TABLE 8.5 DISCRETIONARY TAX CHANGES: NOVEMBER 1964–APRIL 1970

Date	Direct taxes		Indirect taxes		Other		Total FY effect[a]
	Detail	FY effect[a]	Detail	FY effect[a]	Detail	FY effect[a]	
Nov. '64	Increase of 6d. in standard rate of income tax (for 1965/66)	+122	Hydrocarbon oil duty	+93	Temporary charge on imports	+200	+340
					Tax rebates for exports	−75	
Apr. '65	Minor changes in allowances	+42	Tobacco duty	+75			+166[c]
	Capital Gains Tax starting '66–'67[b]		Spirits, beer, wine	+49			
May '66	Temporary extra charges	+26	Betting and gaming	+17	Export rebate	+9	+150
	Minor changes	−6			SET (net)	+240	
July '66			10% Regulator increase	+150			
Apr. '67	Minor changes	−3¼	Minor changes	+1¼	SET (refunds in respect of part-time employees)	−10	−14½
Nov. '67	Corporation tax 42½% for 1967/68				SET (premiums withdrawn except in development areas)		
Mar. '68	Reduction of child allowance and changes	+95	Purchase Tax	+163	SET increase (net)	+152	+923
	Corporation Tax increase to 42½%	+98	Hydrocarbon oils	+76			
	Special surtax charge	+100	Tobacco	+30			
	Other	+38	Wines and spirits	+15			
			Betting and gaming	+30			
			Motor vehicles duties	+126			
Nov. '68			10% regulator	+250			+250
Apr. '69	Corporation Tax increase to 45%	+120	Hydrocarbon duties	+45	SET increase (net)	+130	+346
	Minor changes	−23	Wines	+10			
			Betting and gaming	+12			
			Purchase Tax	+52			
Apr. '70	Increase in Income and Surtax allowances	−183					−214
	Other	−31					

[a] Effect in a 'full year', £m.; + indicates increase in revenue; − indicates decrease.
[b] Yield expected to fluctuate widely from 10 to 125 p.a.
[c] Excluding Capital Gains Tax.

Source: *Financial Statements, Economic Trends.*

lead to consequential changes in incomes, and so to further changes in consumption, imports and output with repercussions on stockbuilding and investment. The resultant estimates of the full effect on GDP of the discretionary tax changes undertaken from the last quarter of 1964 are shown – expressed as a proportion of actual GDP – in Table 8.6. It can readily be seen that the cumulative deflationary effect of these measures was very powerful. The figuring indicates that by the beginning of 1968, output was some 2% less than it would otherwise have been in virtue of these changes, and by mid-1970 something over 4% less.

TABLE 8.6 CUMULATIVE EFFECTS OF DISCRETIONARY TAX CHANGES 1965 II–1970 II[a]

Per cent of GDP[b]

1965		1966		1967		1968		1969		1970	
I	−0·1	I	−0·7	I	−1·6	I	−2·0	I	−3·6	I	−4·2
II	−0·3	II	−0·8	II	−1·8	II	−2·7	II	−4·0	II	−4·2
III	−0·6	III	−1·1	III	−1·9	III	−3·0	III	−4·1		
IV	−0·7	IV	−1·3	IV	−1·9	IV	−3·2	IV	−4·0		

[a] These are the 'full' effects, i.e. after allowing for the working out of multiplier-accelerator processes. The model used for estimating the latter effect is based upon the one described by J. R. Shepherd and M. J. C. Surrey in 'The short-term effects of tax changes', *National Institute Economic Review*, No. 46, November 1968. The initial direct effects of tax changes on gross domestic product were obtained from estimates published in the *National Institute Economic Review*, supplemented by further estimates made by the author and by M. J. C. Surrey of the National Institute. These estimates generally follow the procedures outlined by W. A. B. Hopkin and W. A. H. Godley in 'An analysis of tax changes', *National Institute Economic Review*, No. 32, May 1965.
[b] Figures are rounded.

Thus, the cumulative effect of these measures was more than sufficient to account for the loss of potential output sustained by the economy at the end of the period (reference back to Figure 8.4 shows that by 1970 the economy was operating at some 2% 'below trend').

The computations underlying the figures presented in Table 8.6 can be used to comment upon stabilization, bearing in mind that we are necessarily only concerned with the effects of discretionary tax changes in doing so, and not with other elements of policy.[1] The procedure to be used is similar to that already exploited by Bristow (op. cit.). The computation of the full effects of the tax changes on GDP allows us, by adding these effects back to actual GDP, to construct a series of 'underlying' GDP – 'as it would have been had the tax changes not been undertaken'. A simple way of describing the stabilization effects of the tax policies pursued is then to compare the fit of trend lines passed through each of the two series

[1] Furthermore, the tax changes involved – those detailed in Table 8.5 – are Central Government taxes only (local authority taxes and public enterprise pricing policy is excluded) and 'confidence' effects and other unquantifiable influences are also ignored.

of GDP, actual and 'underlying'. If the fit of the trend line to 'underlying' GDP is better than the fit of the trend to actual GDP, then it would seem that the fluctuations in the level of economic activity have been exaggerated by the tax policies and they could be regarded as destabilizing. Relevant equations are presented in Table 8.7; four equations are given in all, the

TABLE 8.7 STABILIZING EFFECTS OF DISCRETIONARY TAX
MEASURES

Equation no.	Estimation period	Dependent variable	Independent variables		D.W.	R²
			Constant	Trend		
1	58 I–70 II	Y^o	8·643 (0·005)	0·007 (0·00017)	0·412	0·976
2	58 I–70 II	Y^u	8·632 (0·0038)	0·008 (0·00013)	0·646	0·988
3	65 I–70 II	Y^o	8·876 (0·003)	0·005 (0·0002)	2·039	0·961
4	65 I–70 II	Y^u	8·875 (0·004)	0·007 (0·0003)	1·455	0·973

Note: Y refers to 'compromise' GDP at factor cost (1963 prices), an average of estimates from expenditure, income, and output; superscript o refers to observed (actual), and u to underlying values. Data in logarithms. Figures in brackets are standard errors. The estimation period refers to the period over which the trend equations were estimated. The values of underlying GDP differ from those of actual GDP by the amount of the calculated total effect of tax changes only for the period 1965 I–1970 II both in Equation 2 and in Equation 4.

trend equations being measured either over the period 1958 I–1970 II or over the period 1965 I–1970 II, although in both cases it is only the Labour Government's tax changes which are being examined (i.e. actual and underlying GDP are regarded as being equal for sub-period 1958 I–1964 IV), the longer period being brought into the analysis only as a means of extending the observations for measuring the trend. The equations are fitted to quarterly data in logarithmic form[1] and comparison of the fit of the equations for Y^o (actual GDP) and Y^u ('underlying' GDP) indicates that policy could be assessed as marginally destabilizing. This conclusion, incidentally, is the opposite of that reached by Bristow (op. cit.) who found that tax policy over the period 1955–64 had been stabilizing. Both conclusions, however, are subject to the caveat that the detected differences in goodness of fit in the equations appear to be 'small', as well as to other qualifications arising in particular from the fact that the models applied are subject to error. A firmer conclusion in our case would be that no evidence can be found that tax policy succeeded in stabilizing. This conclusion should not be surprising; the narrative section indicated clearly that for much of the time it was not the Government's aim to stabilize the path of output growth. Its concern, rather, was with

[1] An exponential trend was fitted of the form $Y = ab^t$, where Y is GDP at factor cost (1963 prices), t being time measured in quarters.

the balance of payments either under the guise of 'defending the parity' or of 'making devaluation work'.

As the tax increases built up steadily over the period it is not surprising that the coefficients of the trend terms in the equations indicate that policy reduced the rate of growth – by something like $\frac{3}{4}\%$ per annum on average over the period 1965 I–1970 II.

The initial fiscal stimulus

The role of discretionary tax changes justifies special attention for all the reasons given above, but it would obviously be a very partial account of fiscal policy which omitted mention of variations in government spending. After all, the tax increases might be counter-balanced by increases in government spending: indeed, this *is* part of the story, as will be seen. It is also part of the story that towards the end of the period – in 1968 and 1969 – the continued tax increases were accompanied by a sharp change in government expenditure programmes. Taken together, the deflationary impact of the changes on both sides of the Government's accounts was then dramatic.

In the previous section, emphasis was given to the positive action implied in tax rate changes and the point was made that government spending serves various long-term needs which require long-term programmes and inhibit the employment of variations in rates of spending as a short-term weapon of stabilization policy. The measurement of the effect of the tax actions also laid emphasis on their effect on output and called for a weighting procedure to translate the revenue effects into output effects.

In order to bring government expenditure into similar account as the tax changes, then, two points have to be met. First, changes in government spending have to be cast in 'output' terms, with appropriate allowances for import and factor cost leakages and for savings effects in the case of transfer payments.[1] Secondly, there is the question of what benchmark to take, by which to measure a variation in government spending. Although one possibility is to take a position of zero change as the benchmark, the consideration that government expenditure must always be expected to grow along some long-term trend for reasons not connected with demand management suggests that perhaps a more appropriate benchmark would be some positive growth rate. In practice this was taken as just under 3%, a rate corresponding to the trend growth of GDP and also to the trend rate of rise (measured from 1965 to 1970) in the 'output weighted' volume of government expenditure. Whilst the choice of this particular benchmark cannot be defended in detail, it is at least reasonably appealing and, as we shall see, provides some interesting results.

The resultant measure of fiscal policy, combining discretionary tax

[1] As these allowances differ as between components of government spending, account is taken of the change in 'mix' of expenditures.

changes and variations (around a growth benchmark) in government expenditures, can conveniently be called the 'initial fiscal stimulus'.[1] It is presented in Figure 8.5 in the form of a two-dimensional diagram. This shows for each financial year, the first-round effect on output of discretionary tax changes (on the horizontal axis) and the first-round effect on output of variations in government spending on the vertical axis. In both cases the stimulus (or contraction) has been measured as a proportion of actual GDP in the year concerned. The NW and SE quadrants represent 'mixed actions', government spending and tax rate adjustments pulling in opposite directions, whilst the NE and SW quadrants represent cases where both sides of fiscal policy operate in the same direction.[2]

As both the tax changes and the spending changes have been expressed in comparable (output) terms, the dashed 45° line divides off the stimulatory actions (above the line) from the deflationary actions (below it), the total net stimulus or restraint being measured by the distance from the line to the observation.

The chart tells a revealing story, showing as it does that the deflationary tax actions of the early years of the period were offset by expansive spending policies (especially in 1967/68), until in 1968/69 and 1969/70, heavy restraint was applied on both sides. The total restraint exercised in these two years was of a similar order of magnitude although the 'mix' in 1969/70 was more in favour of restraint of spending and less in favour of higher taxes than it had been in 1968/69, and was slightly the larger in total effect.

The total fiscal balance

In this section we leave behind the partial measures of fiscal action, just discussed, in order to examine the total fiscal balance. Perhaps a good place to start is with the trends in sector saving and overall investment. Table 8.8 shows the proportion of total investment (including stockbuilding and the surplus on current account of the balance of payments) as a proportion of GNP, for three sample 'pre-Labour' years, and for the years 1965–9; and it shows the contribution made by the various sectors to the required amount of matching savings. One way of describing the setting for fiscal policy under Labour suggested by the table is that it financed a higher investment ratio in the face of a tendency for the corporate sector contribution to fall, and a cessation of the previous rise in the personal sector's contribution. This was chiefly done through an increase in the

[1] In virtue of its similarity to the measure of fiscal policy described under that name by E. Gerald Corrigan in 'The measurement and importance of fiscal policy changes', *Monthly Review of the Federal Reserve Bank of New York*, Vol. 52, No. 6, June 1970, pages 133–45.
[2] This presentation of fiscal actions follows one used by M. J. Artis and R. H. Wallace in 'Fiscal policy in postwar Australia' in N. Runcie (ed.) *Readings in Australian Monetary and Fiscal Policy* (London 1971).

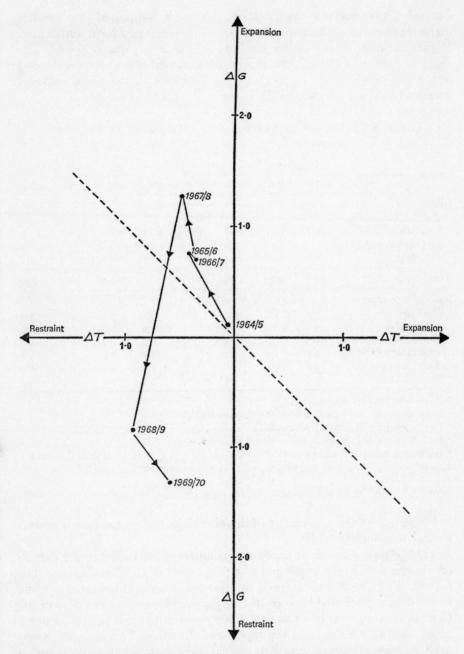

Fig. 8.5   Initial fiscal stimulus, fiscal actions 1964/65–1969/70. Expansion and restraint in taxing ($\triangle$T) and spending ($\triangle$G) decisions;[a] as % GDP, fiscal years.

[a] $\triangle$T, $\triangle$G initially measured as first-round effects on GDP.   See text.

T.L.G.—K*

Central Government's contribution, although supported by smaller increases in the contributions of public corporations and local authorities. Higher taxation was of course one way in which this was achieved. The sharp increases in the Central Government contribution towards the end of the period stand out particularly (and tie in with the sharp restraint exercised in those periods, as discussed in the previous section).

TABLE 8.8 TRENDS IN SAVINGS AND INVESTMENT IN RELATION TO GNP

Per cent of GNP[a]

	1956	1959	1962	1965	1966	1967	1968	1969
Investment								
Total domestic investment[b]	16·1	16·1	16·6	18·7	18·3	18·6	18·8	18·4
Net investment overseas[c]	1·0	0·6	0·4	−0·1	0·2	−0·7	−0·7	1·0
Total investment[d]	17·1	16·7	17·0	18·6	18·5	17·9	18·1	19·4
Saving, by sector[e]								
Persons	3·5	3·4	5·2	5·7	5·6	5·4	4·9	5·0
Companies	9·2	8·8	7·2	8·4	7·0	6·8	6·2	5·5
Public corporations	0·9	0·8	1·4	1·8	1·7	1·7	1·9	1·8
Central government	2·0	2·0	2·3	2·5	3·2	2·6	4·0	6·3
Local authorities	0·6	0·9	0·8	0·8	1·0	1·0	0·9	0·9
Residual error	0·9	0·8	0·1	−0·6	nil	0·4	0·2	−0·1

[a] At current market prices.
[b] Gross domestic fixed capital investment plus stockbuilding.
[c] Equals current balance of payments.
[d] Including residual error in the national accounts.
[e] Including additions to tax and dividend reserves but after provision for stock appreciation. Figures may not add to total because of rounding.

Source: *National Income and Expenditure 1971*.

Inspection of the movement of the overall public sector deficit reveals similar tendencies.

Table 8.9 provides some summary measures of the public sector deficit, on various definitions, expressed as a proportion of GNP in the year concerned. The simplest measure is to take the actual (unweighted) public sector deficit (included here are the receipts and spending not only of the Central Government but also of the local authorities and public corporations), and this is shown in the top line of the table. This measure, however, is open in principle to two crucial objections. In the first place, it implicitly treats every £1 of expenditure (of whatever kind) as equal in impact to every £1 of taxation (of whatever kind): whereas in fact the output-generating (or, in the case of taxes, output-destroying) content differs from item to item. In some 'extreme' cases, for example imports of missiles wholly constructed in the United States, the domestic output content may be zero, and in others, for example, the services of school teachers, the output content may be 100%. Similarly, the output generated by public expenditure as a whole may be judged greater than the reduction in competing demands on output implicit in a matching amount of tax revenues raised by the public sector.

TABLE 8.9 CONCEPTS OF THE BUDGET DEFICIT[a]

As per cent of GNP[b]

	1965	1966	1967	1968	1969
The unweighted deficit	1·9	1·6	3·6	1·7	−1·6
The weighted deficit[c]	8·3	8·1	10·1	8·7	6·3
Crude full employment weighted deficit[d]	8·7	8·3	9·9	8·6	5·9

[a] Whole public sector. Surplus shown with −ve sign.

[b] At current market prices.

[c] See *Note* below.

[d] Weighted receipts raised (or lowered) according as to whether GDP (in volume terms) was below (or above) trend.

Note: The weights used to give the weighted budget surplus or deficit figures were chosen so as to reflect the income-creating or destroying potential of various categories of expenditures and receipts: they reflect 'equilibrium' allowances for import and savings offsets, and were drawn from a variety of sources including input–output estimates, Dow (op. cit.), Hopkin and Godley (op. cit.), and from independent regression and *a priori* estimates. Import offsets of 9, 14, 17 and 20% were assumed, respectively, for public authorities' current spending, fixed investment (public and private), consumers' expenditure and stockbuilding. Savings offsets assumed varied from nil in the case of current grants to 10% in the case of income tax on wages and salaries, 15% in the case of expenditure taxes and gross trading surpluses, 50% in the case of surtax, and over 70% in the case of capital taxes. The weight applied to taxes on corporate income included a small corporate income/investment effect and an allowance for an effect on personal consumption obtained as the product of the marginal dividend pay-out ratio and the marginal propensity to consume out of dividend income. Debt interest and current grants paid abroad were omitted altogether from both the weighted and unweighted versions, as were all expenditures and receipts in the nature of asset swaps and forced loans. Investment grants were treated as negative Corporation Tax receipts.

Source: *National Income and Expenditure 1971.*

The second major objection to the actual deficit as a measure of fiscal impact is that it does not distinguish between changes in tax revenues (and other receipts) and expenditures which are contingent on variations in the level of economic activity and changes which are independent. This is an especially important point inasmuch as the tendency for tax revenues to fall in phases of recession and to rise at times of boom automatically increases the deficit – all other things being equal – when economic activity is low and lowers it when economic activity is running at a high level, giving a spurious impression that fiscal policy has been changed in a 'correct' direction. A measure which overcomes these objections, though it is subject to other qualifications, is the weighted 'full employment' budget deficit. Such a measure not only weights the tax revenues and expenditures of the public sector in an appropriate manner, but also normalizes the level of economic activity at which these are evaluated so as to remove the influence of the economy on the budget. This normalizing procedure, properly carried out, involves a considerable amount of estimation, which is made practically difficult for present purposes by the frequent tax rate changes which are such a feature of fiscal policy in our period. Because of this difficulty the only adjustment attempted here is a crude one, based on the highly simplified assumption that the response of tax revenues (and other receipts) to variations in the level of economic activity is proportional. The resultant estimate of the full employment weighted deficit is given in the third row of the table, with the unadjusted weighted deficit figures appearing in the second row.

Much the most important feature of the table is the variation from year to year (rather than the absolute value in any one year) of the deficit. In this respect, and despite all the considerations detailed above, it will be apparent that all three measures tell much the same story. In particular, 1967 stands out, again, as the year in which the public sector was strongly expansionary; and the story of the subsequent two years is of a drastic reversal with the public sector deficit's role in GDP shrinking by as much as some 4%. The unweighted figures run at a lower level throughout (and for 1969 show a surplus) than the weighted figures, reflecting the greater output weights attributed to the expenditure side of the balance than to the taxation side. Changes in the mix of expenditure and taxation do not, however, seem to have been large enough seriously to modify the movement of the deficit when translated into 'weighted' terms. Nor does the approximate adjustment for changes in the level of economic activity much change the picture given by the unadjusted weighted deficit, though it reduces somewhat the apparent expansionary swing in 1967 and suggests a stronger move in the direction of restraint in 1969.

The swings in the public sector deficit had as their correlate offsetting swings in the surplus and deficit positions of other sectors in the economy. Table 8.10, extracted from the flow of funds figures, illustrates this point. The movements in the last three years of the public sector's net acquisition of financial assets are the most interesting as showing once again the swing into a large deficit position in 1967 followed by a strong movement in the reverse direction both in 1968 and even more in 1969. These movements were reflected most notably in offsetting swings in the position of the corporate and of the overseas sector,[1] the swing being most pronounced in 1969. The connection between the public sector deficit and its borrowing requirement[2] implies a particularly strong connection in British conditions between fiscal and monetary policy. Whilst, during the years up to 1969 the stance of monetary policy was generally restrictive if the continual application of advances controls is any guide (see Tables

[1] The overseas sector's net acquisitions of financial assets is simply the current account surplus with sign reversed.
[2] The difference is the amount of transactions in existing assets.

TABLE 8.10 SECTORAL FINANCIAL ACCOUNTS 1964–9

	Public sector	All companies	Personal sector	Overseas sector	Residual error
	A. Net acquisition of financial assets,[a] by sector (£ million)				
1964	−1,005	− 39	+ 736	+376	− 68
1965	− 848	+ 60	+ 947	+ 52	−211
1966	− 795	−156	+1,045	− 83	− 11
1967	−1,680	+240	+ 970	+298	+172
1968	−1,048	− 12	+ 739	+288	+ 33
1969	+ 365	−701	+ 938	−440	−162
	B. Annual changes[b] in the net acquisition of financial assets (£ million)				
1964	− 173	−421	+154	+500	− 60
1965	+ 157	+ 99	+211	−324	−143
1966	+ 53	−216	+ 98	−135	+200
1967	− 885	+396	− 75	+381	+183
1968	+ 632	−252	−231	− 10	−139
1969	+1,413	−689	+199	−728	−195

[a] Increase in net financial claim on other sectors. Alternatively defined as sector saving plus net capital transfers minus fixed capital formation and increase in stock-building. Sector figures should add across to zero; residual error column shows extent of discrepancy.

[b] A + sign indicates a fall in deficit or increase in surplus, a − sign the opposite.

Source: CSO *Financial Statistics, September 1971.*

8.1–8.3), it was not until 1969 itself that the Bank of England felt both free and disposed,[1] to press its open market operations home to the point where the rate of growth of the money supply was severely restrained. In that year the rate of rise of money supply, at less than $\frac{1}{2}\%$ on average, fell considerably below the rates of increase of 3–5% experienced in the other years.[2]

Summary and appraisal

Appraised by reference to the standard set of policy goals (Table 8.11) stabilization policy had no great measure of success. The growth of domestic output fell well below the National Plan target and failed even to match the modest trend rate of previous years, of around 3%. Because

[1] Both factors are important. In 1969 the official view of monetary policy apparently underwent a major change, with the introduction of the concept of domestic credit expansion (DCE) and a wholly new emphasis on money supply. This conversion was not only related to pressure from the International Monetary Fund but probably also represented a sense of despair at the apparent failure – up to then – of the standard weapons of economic management to produce 'the goods' (a balance of payments surplus).

[2] Using the 'M_1' official definition of money supply. Alternative definitions of money supply (M_2, M_3) yield different figures, but in all cases 1969 stands out as the most restrained year in this respect.

of this, unemployment rose to over 500,000,[1] but price inflation was not abated. On the other hand, the overriding policy aim was to right the balance of payments and in the end, because of the devaluation, this aim was achieved.

TABLE 8.11   POLICY PERFORMANCE, 1964–9

(Annual averages or annual data except where otherwise indicated)

	Average level of unemployment[a] (000s)	Rate of price inflation[b] (%)	Growth of output (%)[c]	Balance of payments on current account (£m.)
1964	362	3·0	5·5	− 376
1965	308	4·8	2·7	− 52
1966	323	4·4	2·1	+ 83
1967	512	3·1	1·8	−298
1968	541	4·0	3·1	−288
1969	535	5·1	1·7	+440
1970	573	7·3	1·7	+579
1970, 2nd qr.	563[d]	8·3[e]	2·4[f]	+452[f]

[a] Wholly unemployed, excluding school-leavers; Great Britain.
[b] GNP (market price) deflator, change on previous year.
[c] GDP at factor cost, 1963 prices, increase on previous year.
[d] Average for second quarter 1970, seasonally adjusted.
[e] Per cent change on same quarter of 1969.
[f] Annual rate, seasonally adjusted.

Source: *National Income and Expenditure, 1970; Department of Employment Gazette; Economic Trends.*

In one way it could be said that there was little technically wrong with fiscal policy. There is no evidence that it was ineffective. Suggestions that it was so, and unfavourable comparisons between the effectiveness of fiscal and of monetary policy based largely on experience in 1968 and 1969, appear in the simplest form in which they are usually expressed, to involve neglect of time lags, an over-identification of fiscal policy with tax rate changes and a misidentification of a poor official forecast with ineffectiveness of the policies based on it. Fiscal policy was very flexible in the sense that large changes could be, and were, introduced at short notice, in several cases between budgets. This flexibility was some safeguard against faulty forecasting, the extent and nature of which it is impossible to comment upon extensively in the absence of a full run of

[1] A good deal has been made of the fact that unemployment since 1967 has been standing much higher in relationship to other labour market indicators (e.g. vacancies) than it previously did. Although the fact is not in dispute there is no agreed explanation of why this should be so and possible causes include the effect of SET, increased social security benefits and redundancy payments. But whilst there may be a partly 'spurious' element in the big rise in unemployment, particularly between 1966 and 1967, the fact remains that policies were deflationary in both intent and effect, so that the direction of movement of the unemployment figure is not in doubt.

published forecasts; although it still seems likely that the most important errors were 'errors of sentiment'.[1]

The technical efficiency of fiscal policy, however, was made to bear the strain of weaknesses in other policies and of inconsistent or unsustainable policy objectives. The two things which stand out most clearly in this regard are the commitment to defend the exchange rate and the concomitant failure of the National Plan. An important ingredient in fiscal policy was, after all, the programme for growth in public spending largely inherited from the previous administration and endorsed in the National Plan. But that programme was conceived of as part of an overall programme for expanding output at a rate far in excess of what was in the event to be allowed. Consequently it had to be accommodated by tax rate increases, until in the end it was drastically cut back when the need to transfer resources to the balance of payments became ever more paramount. The swing in the posture of fiscal policy from expansion to contraction was, when it came, very large indeed, and readily explains the depressed state of the economy – since little was done to modify it – throughout 1970 and the following year.

[1] Forecast errors in 1967, however, were probably particularly unfortunate in flattering an error of sentiment about exchange rate policy, as it appears that the official forecast for imports in that year was unduly sanguine, and better forecasts might have led to speedier imposition of the import deposit scheme in 1968 and to earlier and sharper reflation perhaps in 1969, given the targets of the time. Some comment on the forecast errors in 1968 and 1969, when quantified estimates were published by the Treasury, can be found in the *National Institute Economic Review*, Nos. 47 and 51, February 1969 and 1970.

9 Labour market policies

Derek Robinson

Introduction

The post-war period has been marked by generally high levels of employment and tight labour markets although there have been marked regional differences in the level of unemployment. Productivity growth has been relatively low by international comparisons and the adverse movements in unit labour costs have generally been regarded as leading or contributing to the serious balance of payments problems that have regularly affected the economy. It is commonly held that a series of rigidities on both sides of the labour market have contributed to the slow rate of growth of productivity. However, policies tended to focus upon the *outcome* of labour market behaviour, that is the rate of increase in money wages or unit costs, rather than on the underlying structural problems.

All post-war governments have periodically attempted to implement some form of incomes policy.[1] The previous Conservative administration had introduced a pay pause in 1961 followed by a White Paper, *Incomes Policy: The Next Step*.[2] This urged that wages and salaries should rise by no more than the past trend in productivity growth of 2 to $2\frac{1}{2}\%$ per annum. It contained no proposals for limiting price increases although a paragraph referred to the need for continued restraint in profits and dividends and repeated the statement by the Chancellor in the House of Commons on 18 December 1961 that 'as a part of the incomes policy, appropriate corrective action would have to be taken if aggregate profits showed signs of increasing excessively as compared with wages and salaries'. On 26 July 1962 the Prime Minister announced that a National Incomes Commission would be established to provide impartial and authoritative advice on certain matters relating to incomes.[3] This White Paper did not set out a norm but referred to 'the desirability of keeping the rate of increase of the aggregate monetary incomes within the long-term rate of increase of national production'.[4] The TUC refused to co-operate on the grounds that the NIC 'was supposed to be a body capable of formulating policy and applying policy from the top. It was to take over the function of

---

[1] See for example J. Corina, *The Development of Incomes Policy*, Institute of Personnel Management, London 1966; M. Edelman and R. W. Fleming, *The Politics of Wage-Price Decisions*, Urbana, Ill., 1965.

[2] Cmnd. 1962, 1961.

[3] The terms of reference and membership of the Commission were set out in Cmnd. 1844 in November 1962.

[4] Para. 6.

government, trade unions and employers in determining what that policy was'.[1] The unions believed therefore that the Commission was being empowered to formulate economic policy thereby usurping the right of the Government and social partners. This was a matter of considerable importance that was to influence subsequent developments of incomes policy under the Labour Government. Trade unions are not prepared to surrender their perceived right to participate in economic decision-making to some other body albeit that that body is allegedly impartial. Trade unions believe that they have a right to participate in such decisions and therefore they will only voluntarily surrender that right if they are given similar powers in other areas of decision-taking, or, on a purely temporary basis, if they believe that conditions are so extreme as to demand a temporary abrogation of their rights. So far as the trade unions were concerned therefore incomes policy had become a means for holding down wage and salary increases with no corresponding control over the price level. While the earlier pay pause had some effect on the rate of growth of earnings the work of the NIC does not appear to have had any similar effect.

In 1962 the Conservative Government with the agreement of, and indeed in response to the urging of, employers and unions, established the National Economic Development Council. This tripartite body was originally envisaged as discussing broad economic and social problems and policies and it was hoped that sufficient agreement on causes and cures could be obtained so that policies to increase economic growth and reduce the rate of inflation could be agreed and implemented. The NEDC carried out exercises in 'planning' and in forecasting future growth rates. It also prepared outlines of policies that would be necessary to attain specified rates of economic growth.

In an attempt to reduce some of the structural rigidities in the labour market the Conservative Government introduced the Industrial Training Act in 1964. Many firms did not train new recruits or their existing workers in sufficient numbers or to a sufficiently high degree of skill. Moreover those firms that did provide training complained that other firms which did not lured away the trained men once the original firm had incurred the cost of training. The Act can be seen as an imaginative measure to overcome the reluctance of many firms to provide sufficient training and to ease somewhat the rigid age limits and entry qualifications often enforced by trade unions with employers' agreement on entry to apprenticeships.[2] The actual implementation of the Act through the Industrial Training Boards may well leave things to be desired.

---

[1] From George Woodcock *Report of a Conference of Executives of Affiliated Organisations Held on 30 April 1965, on Productivity, Prices and Incomes* (TUC, London 1965).
[2] For an outside analysis and evaluation of the Act see 'Manpower policy in the United Kingdom', *OECD Reviews of Manpower and Social Policies* (OECD, Paris 1970).

Prices and incomes policy

The incoming Labour Government finding itself faced with severe economic problems sought the co-operation of both sides of industry to secure agreement on certain economic and social policies. The Joint Statement of Intent on Productivity, Prices and Incomes[1] was a tripartite declaration setting out agreement on certain broad issues. The economic objective was to secure a rapid increase in output and real incomes with full employment; and the social objective was to distribute the benefits of faster growth in a way which satisfied social need and justice. The Statement recognized that it was necessary to keep the increases in money incomes in line with increases in real output in order to maintain a stable general price level which was necessary to improve the balance of payments and improve the competitive ability of the country. The Government pledged itself to prepare a National Plan through the NEDC and to establish machinery to keep a continuous watch on general movements in prices and incomes and to examine particular cases. The trade union and management representatives accepted the objectives of the Statement and undertook to support the policies necessary to implement them. From the trade union viewpoint it was important that the National Plan was to be prepared through the NEDC which, being a tripartite body, permitted the unions to participate in the discussion and formulation of economic and social policies.

The Government expanded its views on the criteria and methods of implementation of a prices and incomes policy,[2] stressing the economic objectives. Price stability obtained by slower rates of increase in money wages was regarded as a necessary pre-condition for the attainment of the economic and implied social objectives of the National Plan and of the general range of government policies. Initially it was hoped that moderation in wage and price increases might be secured by the voluntary acceptance of the guidelines on wage and price increases and decreases although the possibility of the Government using tax measures as 'inducements' to observe the policy was provided for.

A special conference of executive committees of affiliated organizations of the TUC met on 30 April 1965 to consider its attitude to prices and incomes policy.[3] The report of the General Council to that conference said that 'the justification for trade union participation in an incomes policy lies in the contribution that it will make to the attainment of economic and social policies which will lead to more substantial and lasting benefits for their members'. They also said that 'the General

---

[1] The text of the Statement of Intent is reproduced in *Productivity, Prices and Incomes: Report of a Conference of Executive Committees of Affiliated Organisations held on 30th April 1965* (TUC, London 1965).

[2] *Machinery of Prices and Incomes Policy,* Cmnd. 2577, 1965 and *Prices and Incomes Policy* Cmnd. 2639, 1965. It is not intended to discuss the detailed provisions of the various policy statements.

[3] *Report of Conference on 30th April 1965,* op. cit.

Council have throughout the discussions made it clear to the Government and to the representatives of the employers' organizations that trade unions would co-operate in a prices and incomes policy only if it appeared to them likely to secure broad trade union objectives more effectively than present policies'. They pointed out that in their view 'the Government was firmly committed to a prices and incomes policy as a major instrument for correcting the unbalance in the economy and for securing economic expansion. Having ruled out the possibility of devaluation and unwilling as it was to resort to deflation, the Government had to find other and more satisfactory means of ensuring stability and, if possible, reductions in industrial costs in order to improve the competitiveness of British goods in overseas markets. If an agreed incomes policy could not be worked out the Government might have to consider alternative and more direct methods of influencing prices and incomes.'

George Brown, Secretary of State for Economic Affairs, spoke at the conference. He made a strong plea for incomes policy on the grounds that it was a necessary part of the general economic strategy of the Government and was linked necessarily to the National Plan. There was a degree of interdependence between these two policies so that each required the other for the full attainment of its objectives. He also advocated an incomes policy as the only effective alternative to devaluation. He summed up the situation by saying: 'I think the question which is basically before us can be put in four words: order or chaos; planning or anarchy.' There was a strong feeling expressed by the supporters of incomes policy at that conference that trade union participation in an incomes policy was an essential condition for the continuation in power of the Labour Government.

George Woodcock emphasized the Government's desire to have an incomes policy voluntarily accepted when he said: 'I saw Mr Brown on 21 October, when he made it absolutely clear that the Labour Government wanted, and in fact desperately needed, a policy for incomes and prices.'

Woodcock emphasized the basic change not only in behaviour but in philosophy that the acceptance of a prices and incomes policy required. He clearly saw that what was being called for was a fundamental change in both attitudes and behaviour. Unlike demand management policies which seek to influence wage and price decisions by changing the level or pressure of economic forces, prices and incomes policy seeks to influence the outcome of decisions without changing the level of pressure of demand. Thus it necessarily and inevitably requires that people take decisions different from those which they would have taken in the absence of the policy and different from those which they could currently take. If it is thought that wage and price decision-takers are unable to take decisions different from those determined by the purely economic conditions then of course prices and incomes policy is doomed to failure from the start. It is a necessary condition for the success of an incomes policy that there is a margin of freedom in decision-taking so that wage and price increases can, by institutional action or by the deliberate decisions of those responsible for taking decisions, be kept lower than they would be, given the prevailing economic conditions.

The attempt to induce decisions different from those that would otherwise have been taken imposes greater problems and strains upon trade unions than upon management in its price decision. Not only the traditions but the ethos of trade union activity strongly encourage negotiators to take such increases in money wages as are available to them. Trade unions are voluntary organizations which must be able to carry their members with them in their policies. Therefore it is not enough to persuade the trade union leadership to accept an incomes policy; it must also persuade the branches and particularly the active members. Otherwise trade union leaders who accept the requirements of the policy and change their behaviour are open to criticism and attacks from below. They can be accused, rightly, of settling for smaller money wage increases than they could have got although the increases in real terms may be greater. The change in attitudes therefore must permeate the whole of the trade union organization or the position of the trade union officials who accept incomes policy becomes impossible in terms of their own place and behaviour in their organization.

The Government's proposals can be seen as having both short-term and long-term effects. The short-term effects were to do with reduction in rate of price increases, while the longer-term effects were to do with the rate of growth of the economy and the implementation of social and economic policies more attractive to trade unions. The emphasis upon the second, the longer-term effects, was necessary in order to secure trade union participation. Indeed, without such benefit there is no advantage to trade unions in participating in an incomes policy. However, the shorter-term aims, concentrating on restraint in money wage increases, were seen as imposing irksome restrictions on trade union behaviour which could be acceptable to trade unions in one of two circumstances. If they were convinced that there was a serious economic crisis and that the Government was not calling for contributions only from trade unionists then they might be prepared to co-operate in a temporary short-term wage freeze. Secondly, they would accept the restrictions only if there were compensating advantages elsewhere. This is a basic dilemma for all trade union movements. They wish to influence social and economic policies of governments in order to further trade union aims and advance the interests of their members. Traditional methods of collective bargaining have not always been particularly successful in achieving this. Participation in a prices and incomes policy which is part of a comprehensive economic policy which satisfies a number of trade union objectives might be the way in which the trade unions can, in a modern integrated economy, best secure their objectives. However, because incomes policy has tended to be introduced for short-term economic purposes it has the connotation of restrictions in money wages and is not seen as part of a general co-ordinated economic programme. In speeches at TUC Congresses Wood-cock emphasized the great difficulties involved in moving from the short-term to the long-term approach to this problem.[1]

Development of the policy

The policy passed through various stages of development in response to the economic situation and the way in which unions and employers reacted to the various policy requirements. The broad provisions were that proposed price and wage increases should be reported to appropriate government departments which could either let them pass, without giving specific approval to them, could seek to obtain some modification, or could refer them to the National Board for Prices and Incomes for investigation. The NBPI could therefore scrutinize only those issues referred to it by government. Moreover it could handle only a relatively few of the many thousands of price and wage changes taking place each year. The overwhelming burden of vetting changes therefore rested with the appropriate government departments although the influence of the NBPI was a significant feature of the policy. The Board's Reports were published and contained the results of detailed examinations of wages or prices and costs in the industries concerned. They shed a spotlight of factual examination into areas of economic activity which had for long remained murky or unknown. The Board's findings had no statutory force in themselves; at various stages of the policy it was possible for the Government to impose a price or wage standstill pending reference to the Board, and, at certain times, for a stated period after the Board had reported, providing that the Board had reported that such a standstill was in the public interest.[2]

Basically, the Government's powers were negative ones in that they could prevent some changes taking place, at certain times according to the type of policy currently applied, but they had very few positive powers, i.e. there was really very little government could do to ensure that certain sort of changes did take place in the absence of proposals from the parties themselves. The positive recommendations of the NBPI were not, in general, capable of being translated into specific directives. There was a somewhat grey intermediate area in respect of some parts of the public sector, but even here any Board proposals affecting pay or working conditions were subject to the agreement of the parties to collective bargaining in the sector concerned.

[1] See for example *TUC Report 1965*, page 468. The reasoning and analysis were carried through at succeeding congresses.

[2] For a discussion of the work of the NBPI, see, Derek Robinson, 'Implementing an incomes policy', *Industrial Relations*, Vol. 8, No. 1, October 1968; Robert B. McKersie 'The British Board for Prices and Incomes', *Industrial Relations*, Vol. 6, No. 3, May 1967; The *General* (later *Annual*) *Reports of the NBPI*, Reports No. 19, 40, 77, 122 and 170; H. A. Clegg, *How to Run an Incomes Policy and Why We Made Such a Mess of the Last One*, (London 1970).

This is a matter of some importance to any future incomes policy of the type introduced by the Labour Government. If the policy consists of certain negative provisions or statutory powers to prevent particular types of changes in prices or incomes occurring and a framework of permissive rules which are intended to allow certain changes to occur, e.g. relatively larger increases to the lower paid, the Government is in danger of appearing to fail to provide some of the 'constructive' side of the total policy provisions and seem to be concentrating exclusively on the restrictive parts of the policy. This is particularly the case in respect of changes in the structure of relative wages. Government spokesmen frequently emphasized the social justice content of incomes policy which would permit a more equitable and desirable distribution of incomes, both between profits and wages and within the wage-earnings groups.[1] However, they had no effective powers to ensure that differentiating increases were given to the lower paid and certainly none to ensure that only the lower paid received any exceptionally large increases. Because of the reluctance to interfere unduly with the *processes* of collective bargaining,[2] although of course they sought to influence the outcome of bargaining, they could in effect only endorse or reject the proposals emanating from bargaining bodies. If these proposals did not further the social objectives of the policy, or if they did so in a way which appeared to government to contain undue inflationary pressures, for example if large increases to lower-paid workers were also to be granted to all or most of the workers covered by the settlement irrespective of whether they were low paid, the Government had little more than persuasive influence at its disposal to seek to obtain a desired settlement. Almost inevitably this meant that government would be criticized for its failure to satisfy the expectations about social justice created by its spokesmen when trying to persuade trade unionists to apply the policy measures.

The powers that a government should adopt to implement a prices and incomes policy are as much a political as an economic issue. But they are also influenced by the type of general policy sought. A voluntary policy presumably seeks reserve powers only to encourage the laggards or as a last resort. Ultimately a voluntary policy stands or falls by the willingness of the parties to change their attitudes and accept new criteria for the determination of incomes and prices. Thus there is a strong desire on the part of government to maintain the existing machinery of collective bargaining, and indeed in some cases to strengthen this by encouraging the development of institutional arrangements that will permit the parties to formal collective bargaining to take decisions which will effectively influence the realities of pay levels and pay structures. The Donovan Report[3] recommended changes in the collective bargaining structure

[1] For example see the speech of George Brown at the TUC Special Conference, 30 April 1965, op. cit., page 30.
[2] Ibid., page 27.
[3] *Royal Commission on Trade Unions and Employers Associations*, Cmnd. 3623, 1968.

which would allow the parties to the bargaining to exercise effective influence or control over the subjects covered by their bargaining, by advocating a move towards formalized plant or company bargaining in some cases. While this was not proposed in order to make incomes policy more effective, or possible, it could have that effect, providing that the policy requirements are accepted by the larger number of plant bargainers. It is easier to persuade a relatively small number of national bargainers to accept the policy requirements but unless they are in turn able to persuade those responsible for bargaining at plant level also to follow the policy relatively little has been gained and a large amount of damage may have been done. Industries where plant bargaining is not possible will undergo a loss of relative earnings unless they are given specifically higher increases under the formal policy provisions. The creation of the wedge between national trade union leaders and the local bargainers will in itself be an undesirable development. Trade unions must be able to carry their members with them and therefore must reflect the views of their members, and, perhaps even more importantly, of their activists.

One of the major problems to be tackled by an incomes policy is the question of differentials or the relative wages of different occupations or people in different industries. We have not found any satisfactory way of reaching general agreement on relative wage levels. Thus decisions taken in one settlement to improve the position of particular groups of workers are in danger of being frustrated by the subsequent actions of other groups which press for consequential increases to restore previous differentials. No incomes policy can succeed until there is some minimum agreement on relative wages; but equally a 'free bargaining' situation without an incomes policy will also have undesirable economic results if groups seek to change their relative earnings position and other groups respond in the usual way. Thus this is not a problem unique to incomes policy. What incomes policy can do is offer a way by which changes in relative wage levels can be secured if there is sufficient agreement between the parties and different interest groups and types of workers. Free collective bargaining cannot do this as there is no way in which the strongly organized groups who have significant economic power can transfer their economic bargaining strength to the less strong and lower-paid sections, even if they should decide to do so. However, while incomes policy provides the possibility for such action it also in some ways makes it more difficult. A policy such as applied in Britain leads inevitably to a greater degree of centralization of decision-taking within the trade union movement. This necessarily involves the unions in formulating common views about a 'fair' or 'acceptable' wage structure so that the problems of relative wages are thrust to the fore. It is not easy to change traditional attitudes to acceptable differentials and there is a great danger that unions will not be able to adapt sufficiently quickly to ensure that the socially desirable changes in wage structures take place.

The TUC responded to the requirements of incomes policy, under the additional impetus of statutory provisions requiring the notification of proposed wage and price increases, by establishing its own vetting machinery to examine wage claims from affiliated organizations. It is not possible to assess what effect, if any, this machinery had on reducing the inflationary aspects of wage claims and settlements,[1] but there is no doubt that the very act of setting up the committee was a considerable step forward in terms of the acceptance of common interests and in the view that wage settlements by a particular group of workers could have direct as well as indirect repercussions on many other workers. This was a somewhat fundamental change in British trade union behaviour, which has always emphasized the autonomy of each affiliated union.

The initial impact of the policy upon wage increases was somewhat less than expected. This led the Government to announce in September '65 that it intended to introduce legislation requiring the notification of proposed increases. Further stages of the policy may be briefly summarized as[2] July–December 1966 a standstill on price and pay increases; January–June 1967 a period of severe restraint; 1 July 1967–March 1968 a zero norm with the exception clauses of Cmnd. 2639; March 1968–December 1969 a ceiling of $3\frac{1}{2}\%$ on wage, salary and dividend increases with possible exceptions where productivity has increased. After 1969 a range of increases of $2\frac{1}{2}$–$4\frac{1}{2}\%$.

Legislative support for the policy came from a series of Prices and Incomes Acts. For example, in the 1966 Act the more important sections were contained in Parts II and IV. Part II permitted the Government to require compulsory notification of proposed increases in prices, charges, dividends and claims and settlements of wages and conditions of employment. The Government could impose a standstill of one month while the department concerned considered the proposed increase. A further statutory standstill of up to three months could be imposed if the proposal was referred to the NBPI. Once the Board had reported or the three months were up there were no legal provisions to prevent the parties from completely ignoring the policy requirements. Part IV of the Act did two things. It protected an employer from civil action for breach of contract for not honouring an agreement entered into but set aside as a result of the Government's period of standstill and severe restraint. Secondly, it allowed the Government to place a compulsory standstill on pay and prices in specific firms or industries, freezing these to the level existing on

---

[1] See Robinson, op. cit.

[2] The appropriate White Papers are *Prices and Incomes Policy: An 'Early Warning System'* Cmnd. 2808, 1965; *Prices and Incomes Standstill* Cmnd, 3073, 1966; *Prices and Incomes Stand-Still: Period of Severe Restraint* Cmnd. 3150, 1966; *Prices and Incomes Policy after 30th June 1967* Cmnd. 3235, 1967; *Productivity, Prices and Incomes Policy in 1968 and 1969* Cmnd. 3590, 1968; *Productivity, Prices and Incomes Policy After 1969* Cmnd. 4237. The last White Paper is the most comprehensive argument put forward by government for a policy that we have seen.

20 July 1966. This part of the Act was intended to compel observance of the policy unlike Part II which had merely sought to induce voluntary co-operation after the requirements of the national interest had been determined by the NBPI.

Part IV was activated in October 1966 and expired in August 1967. Part II of this Act was not activated although similar provisions in the 1967 Act were.

Under the 1967 Act, the temporary standstill of pay and price increases of three or four months under Part II of the 1966 Act was extended to a maximum period of six months from the date of reference to the Board. This was partly because of the difficulties the Board had in producing detailed analytical reports in a short period and partly to compel the parties to spend longer considering the findings of the Board before implementing their original agreement. In addition the Government could, after a report by the NBPI, suspend a price or pay increase which did not accord with the recommendation of the Board for a period of three months. While the Act forbade payment of a wage increase during the period of an Order imposing a standstill there was no legal provision to prevent the employer voluntarily agreeing to pay the increase retrospectively for the full period of the standstill. The 1968 Act continued the provisions of Part II of the 1966 Act until the end of 1969. A standstill Order could be imposed in the context of a reference to the Prices and Incomes Board for a maximum period of eleven months from the date of the reference to the Board. Additional powers were given to Ministers to require a reduction in prices where the Board had so recommended. Powers were also granted to prevent dividend increases and rent increases and particular reference given to local authority rents.

The policy can be seen as having two parts. First, an attempt to induce changes in behaviour on a voluntary basis. Secondly, in cases where the parties were not clear as to the policy requirements, or if they were aware of them chose to ignore them, there was statutory provision, firstly, to spell out the policy requirements by allowing the NBPI to comment, and secondly to prevent people from applying decisions that were regarded as clearly contrary to the public interest.

The results of the policy

It is reasonable to ask whether the policy had any significant effect on the movement of wages and prices. This is a very difficult question to answer. The usual approach is to carry out some econometric analysis which provides some economic relationships, so that, for example, we conclude that if unemployment (or some other measure of the pressure of demand) is at a certain level the expected increase in wages, and/or prices would be of a specified amount. The basic underlying economic relationship is based on an examination of what actually happened over a past period. If it is assumed that the same sort of relationship would hold in the future, it is possible to test what actually happened during the period of incomes policy with what would have happened if there had been no policy and the past relationships had continued.[1]

There has been a series of articles in various academic journals purporting to test the success of incomes policy by using these methods in one way or another.[2] However, most of them use, as the wage variable to be explained, the Wage Rate Index: so that while they may have some technical interest or merit, they have little relevance. There are two main reasons for this. First, the policy was not based on attempts to reduce the rate of increase of the Wage Rate Index as such; it was intended to reduce the rate of increase in money incomes and to reduce the rate of increase in unit labour costs. These are not necessarily the same, but neither is equated to the movements of wage rates and minimum entitlements which is what the Wage Rate Index measures. As long as there is wage drift, and this has occurred either positively or negatively throughout the period concerned, movements in the WRI do not adequately reflect the course of wage earnings. Secondly, even if the WRI is regarded as somehow or other indicating what has happened to wage earnings, it cannot be regarded as having done so in a consistent manner throughout the period of the Labour Government.

The introduction of minimum earnings guarantees changed the basic character of a movement in the WRI. Previously, if the Index rose on account, for example, of an increase in basic wage rates in the engineering industry, it was reasonable to assume that every worker covered by the agreement received that increase. However, with a minimum earnings guarantee only those workers whose earnings in any week would otherwise fall below the guaranteed level receive the increase. The WRI, however, was increased as though all workers in the industry had received that addition to their minimum rates.[3] But if some workers did not receive the make-up pay, it is misleading to regard the movement in the WRI of $x\%$ in the same way as an increase of $x\%$ would have been regarded if

---

[1] The first recent major analysis based on this approach, which has had very considerable, and possibly undue, influence on economic thinking was that carried out by Professor A. W. Phillips, 'The relation between unemployment and the rate of change of money wage rates in the United Kingdom, 1861–1957', *Economica*, n.s. 25, November 1958. This gave us the celebrated Phillips Curve.

[2] The most important of these is probably that by R. G. Lipsey and J. M. Parkin, 'Incomes policy: a reappraisal', *Economica*, n.s. 37, May 1970. A further article taking the analysis further by J. M. Parkin, 'Incomes policy: some further results on the determination of the rate of change of money wages', *Economica*, n.s. 37, November 1970, and it is interesting to note that the November 1970 article by Parkin refers to 'Money Wages' although strictly it should follow Phillips' practice and refer to 'Money Wage Rates'. The distinction is between wage rates, which are the rates negotiated formally in collective bargaining, generally at industry level, whereas money wages might well be taken to mean the total level of wages including plant-level increases, but not adjusted for changes in prices, i.e. not real wages.

[3] This is because strictly speaking the Index measures weekly wage rates and minimum entitlements.

determined by a traditional wage settlement.[1] Thus an analysis based on a time-series of the Wage Rate Index which does not take account of the changes in the types of bargains which are reflected in movements in the WRI is unlikely adequately to explain what has happened. Indeed, such an analysis will find that the Index rose more than it 'should' have done for any given pressure of demand during those periods when this type of wage agreement played any significant part in increasing the WRI.

Two other objections can be raised to this type of study. If it uses registered unemployed as the measure of the pressure of demand and does not take account of the apparent structural shift in the basis of the figures of unemployment,[2] it will conclude that wages are rising faster than they 'should'. If, however, it is accepted that the unemployment figures have somehow altered in a 'structural' sense as indicators of demand, past econometric relationships, unless they are adjusted, cannot be used to form a set of criteria for assessing the performance of incomes policy in the later stages of the Labour Government. Secondly, if it is accepted that one of the aims of policy was to increase the rate of productivity obtained for any given wage increase then it follows that merely to measure what has happened to wages will be an incomplete analysis. The Labour Government's incomes policy did not merely seek to reduce the rate of increase of money incomes for any given level of demand; it also sought to increase the rate of productivity growth for any given level of income increase. It is necessary, therefore, to try to take account of the productivity effects of the policy.

However, it is not really possible to assess the impact, if any, of the policy on productivity. There appears little evidence to suggest that over the policy period as a whole there was any significant increase in productivity growth, after trying to make adjustments for the considerable variations in productivity growth over the cycle. Nevertheless a number of observers would conclude that the policy had a significant effect in changing attitudes to productivity. This could have occurred in two ways: first, by encouraging productivity bargains, even though some of these may have been phoney and produced in order to obtain a wage increase under the productivity exception clause; secondly, there was a change in the climate of collective bargaining. Very great emphasis was placed on the relationship between increases in productivity and real wage increases

[1] We have no reliable information as to whether all workers received a compensating increase when minimum earnings levels were raised in engineering. The NBPI Report No. 104 tried to form some tentative conclusions but admitted that the data on which these were based were unsatisfactory and inadequate.

[2] There is a body of opinion that holds that figures of registered unemployed do not have the same relationship with pressures of demand as they had in the past, and in particular that for any given pressure of demand we have a larger amount of unemployment than we had previously. This may be because of the Redundancy Payments Act, earnings-related social security benefits and the general climate of incomes policy which has encouraged the ending of under-utilization of labour. Certainly the unemployment-vacancies relationship has shifted significantly (See Table 9·1).

and there is a strong impression that this led to changes in bargaining attitudes and behaviour. The NBPI played a significant role in influencing opinion and creating a climate of 'educational work' which altered attitudes. This may not have survived the ending of the incomes policy period, but was believed by many people involved in or connected with bargaining as existing during 1965–8.

A recent study[1] by an inter-departmental working party provides a great deal of econometric evidence about the behaviour of earnings and prices, using figures of earnings or wages and salaries and not the Wage Rate Index. Table 9.1 taken from Annex VIII of the Report presents details of percentage changes in certain economic variables (columns 1–11), and the absolute percentage levels of unemployment and vacancies (columns 12 and 13). This gives a good broad picture of the development of prices and incomes, using various measurements, over the period 1950–69. While the year-to-year variations can be seen easily this sort of statistical presentation cannot say whether the results were better or worse than would have been expected without a policy, and as we have seen it is necessary to formulate some economic model or produce formulae which might allow us to examine this question. Accordingly the Report considered the economic analysis underlying the various econometric models which had been put forward in economic literature and decided which were the most suitable equations for analysing the impact of prices and incomes policy although once basic relationships had been decided there was selection of the best statistical expression and choice of variable. This is a basically different approach from one which tests all conceivable econometric relationships and settles on the one that gives the best statistical fit even though there may be relatively little economic justification for the particular relationships expressed in the equation. The conclusions may be summarized as follows:

(*i*) The use of figures of unfilled vacancies rather than of registered unemployed gives a better fit for the earnings of manual men for periods before 1965 as well as after. This reinforces the belief that there has been some change in the relationship of figures of registered unemployed as indicators of demand on the labour market.

(*ii*) All these models provide results which are consistent in that the earnings of manual men increased less rapidly than might be expected in the years 1965, 1966 and 1967,[2] but more rapidly in 1968 and 1969.

(*iii*) The slowing down of increases in manual earnings was particularly marked in 1966 and 1967, the periods when the policy was applied most rigorously through standstill and severe restraint. Over the three years

[1] *Prices and Earnings in 1951–69: an Econometric Assessment*, Department of Employment, HMSO, May 1971.
[2] The increase was also slower than might have been expected in 1956, 1957, 1961 and 1962, years of other forms of policies to influence wages. The increases were also higher in 1963 and 1964.

Table 9.1 Economic Indicators of Earnings and Price Movements 1950–69

Percentage change on previous year: except cols. 12–13

Year	Wages and salaries employee (1)	Average earnings of all full-time manual workers (2)	Average earnings of full-time manual men in manufacturing industries (3)	GDP/person employed (4)	Income from employment/real total final output (5)	Prices of final output at factor cost (6)	Retail prices (7)	Import prices (8)	Imports of goods and services/real total final output (9)	Gross profits etc/real total final output (10)	Wages and salaries/unit of output (11)	Unemployment in GB (12)	Unfilled vacancies (13)
1950						3·24	3·07	13·08	11·55	-2·19		1·458	1·196
1951	10·21	10·12	9·35	2·20	7·15	12·71	9·14	31·59	35·36	5·39	7·42	1·120	1·392
1952	7·14	7·82	8·01	0·18	8·44	5·68	9·18	-1·87	-8·08	14·46	6·75	1·562	0·959
1953	4·87	6·14	6·68	2·51	1·78	0·44	3·08	-9·62	-6·18	3·42	2·44	1·497	0·919
1954	5·15	6·62	7·46	2·75	2·48	1·58	1·84	-0·38	-0·84	1·71	2·64	1·246	1·071
1955	8·00	9·24	9·14	2·81	4·10	3·85	4·51	2·78	7·71	0·46	5·40	0·970	1·311
1956	7·95	7·97	7·06	0·04	8·42	5·36	4·96	1·35	0·99	2·71	8·15	1·044	1·117
1957	5·55	4·64	4·58	1·40	4·18	3·79	3·69	2·34	3·43	3·24	4·49	1·320	0·845
1958	3·93	3·45	3·27	0·16	4·40	3·08	2·98	-5·14	-3·56	5·51	4·04	1·856	0·625
1959	3·75	4·52	4·97	3·23	0·30	1·39	0·59	0·01	2·01	3·26	0·85	1·966	0·716
1960	5·67	6·55	7·29	4·99	-0·17	1·75	1·01	1·52	5·52	3·04	1·04	1·502	1·020
1961	6·70	6·03	5·59	1·40	6·17	2·64	3·45	0·02	-2·50	-0·66	5·58	1·348	1·023
1962	4·65	3·59	2·76	0·77	4·13	2·73	4·16	-0·30	0·31	1·45	4·08	1·836	0·677
1963	4·51	4·15	4·23	4·09	0·93	2·16	2·02	2·35	1·88	5·05	0·52	2·166	0·625
1964	6·69	8·69	8·77	4·27	1·88	2·74	3·30	3·23	6·16	2·18	2·51	1·552	0·953
1965	6·44	8·05	7·39	2·29	5·05	3·48	4·79	1·20	-0·75	3·21	4·21	1·317	1·132
1966	6·26	5·79	5·39	1·09	5·39	3·10	3·90	1·24	2·13	-1·16	5·14	1·377	1·075
1967	5·41	3·95	3·05	2·38	1·95	3·20	2·48	0·84	4·89	4·86	2·61	2·208	0·749
1968	7·37	8·26	7·96	4·35	2·57	4·13	4·71	11·36	14·35	0·31	2·90	2·343	0·815
1969	7·80	7·82	8·04	2·10	5·15	3·30	5·43	2·64	2·98	-0·65	5·44	2·317	0·864

Source: Department of Employment Report, *Prices and Earnings 1950–69: an Econometric Assessment*.

1965–7 manual earnings rose by about 4% less than expected and by 4% more than expected in 1968–9.

(*iv*) If average wages and salaries per employee are taken as the measure of income rather than manual earnings, the total increase over the period 1965–9 was about 2–4% more than expected based on past relationships with vacancies, although relationships based on unemployment figures would have given a higher result. Average wages and salaries rose faster than manual earnings because of different movements in salaries and wages and because there were changes in the composition of the working population, e.g. changes in the proportions of workers working only part of the year which affects average wages and salaries per employee on a yearly basis.

(*v*) Given the wage increases, factor prices rose rather less than might have been expected. Over the period 1965–9 factor prices rose by something like 2 or 3% less than past relationships would suggest. This meant there was a relative switch of income from profits to income from employment. However, even though factor prices rose less than expected retail prices rose because of indirect taxes. It was not possible to distinguish the effects of prices and incomes policy from other policy measures, e.g. SET or the abolition of resale price maintenance.

This would suggest that as far as actual earnings of manual workers were concerned the policy had little overall effect in the period 1965–9 but slowed down the rate of increase in the first half of the period. It might therefore be argued that the immense stresses and strains imposed on the labour market and on the relations between trade unions and the Labour Government were an excessive price to pay for merely postponing wage increases. A further gain from a trade union view may be the switch of total income from profits to employment incomes. However, the latter point could prove to have some undesirable longer-term consequences if the relative decline in profits leads to a slowing down of growth as a result of a decrease in retained profits to finance investment. This may be a somewhat over-gloomy view of the total effect of incomes policy. We do not know what would have happened to the economy without a policy. The breathing space obtained in 1966 and 1967 may have helped by permitting us to avoid even more drastic economic measures, although it may also have postponed the act of devaluation which could be regarded as undesirable.

During 1969 trade union acceptance of an incomes policy effectively dwindled to the point of no significant contribution. This was in part due to the effects of other policies on real living standards, in part to the controversy over the industrial relations proposals and in part to the increasing institutional difficulties of trying to advocate an incomes policy inside the trade unions. The removal of the immediate pressure on the balance of payments weakened the appeal for restraint of money incomes. Moreover, the Government had been unable to accept the alternative economic policies put forward by the TUC,[1] and in particular had been unable to accept the growth policies at that time.

Those who believe that the incomes policy had some beneficial effects rely on impressions and non-quantifiable factors rather than econometric analysis. The attitudinal change to productivity would be stressed as a gain from the policy,[2] as would the emphasizing of the results of increasing the importance of considerations of public interest in wage and price decisions. Essentially therefore the debate is conducted on two levels using two different approaches, and to some extent the approach adopted is influenced by previously held views as to the desirability of a prices and incomes policy as well as a desire to test the effectiveness of one.

The effects of the policy in redistributing income between different groups, and in particular of helping the lower-paid workers, are even more difficult to assess. The statistical evidence is scanty and inadequate. There are details of the changes negotiated by different groups, but these do not tell us what actually happened to the total earnings or effective standard week pay of the workers covered by them. Figures of average earnings in industries or sectors are not helpful in tackling the question of whether the *distribution* of earnings has changed and the details of distribution which are available from the New Earnings Surveys cover only two dates, September 1968 and April 1970, and therefore are unable to shed light on the effect of the policy.[3] Attempts to link up the distribution of earnings from other surveys are frustrated by the significant differences in coverage so that any conclusions will be misleading. Overall, however, it is unlikely that the policy saw any really significant redistribution of wage incomes,[4] but this may have been due, in part at least, to the policy provisions whereby government had only negative or permissive powers. It was also particularly unfortunate that the two major references to the NBPI on low pay were caught up by the standstill and severe restraint periods.[5] There is also some evidence that movements in minimum weekly rates determined by industry or national bargaining during 1969–70, that is after the effective policy period, actually widened so that the lower-paid groups in traditionally more highly paid industries received larger

[1] See *Economic Review 1969* (TUC, London).

[2] It now looks as though the beneficial effects of this change have been lost as a result of the present Conservative Government's policy of increasing the level of unemployment. Trade unions and workers are increasingly suspicious of any changes which might have the effect of pushing the unemployment figures still higher. It is easier to destroy methods of increasing efficiency through co-operative, albeit antagonistic co-operative, bargaining than it is to create it.

[3] See 'New Earnings Survey, September 1968', *Department of Employment*, 1970, and *Department of Employment Gazette*, November 1970 to February 1971.

[4] See *General Problems of Low Pay*, NBPI Report No. 169 (Cmnd. 4648, 1971). This comes to the same broad conclusion although it seems to suggest some relative gain by the lower paid in the earlier part of the policy. The statistical data are insufficient to permit any reliable detailed analysis.

[5] See NBPI Reports Nos 25 (Cmnd. 3199) and 27 (Cmnd. 3224) on agricultural workers and workers in retail drapery, outfitting and footwear trades.

increases than the lower-paid groups in traditionally low paying industries.[1] In this respect the weaker policy period probably had less effect on overall or general minimum wage rate levels than did the previous three years of the policy.

Manpower and employment aspects

Various policy measures were introduced in order to effect structural changes in the economy or to promote a freer movement of labour and the reallocation of resources. It might be argued that incomes policy itself was working in a contrary direction by creating additional distortions and rigidities in the labour market. Thus some people oppose incomes policy merely because it tries to interfere with the working of economic forces. However, there is much evidence to suggest that the labour market contains so many rigidities, distortions and institutional barriers and forces that the application of naive general economic concepts will be dangerously misleading. The labour market is so imperfect that any distortions that are caused by an incomes policy which contains the types of exception clauses that the British incomes policy contained are unlikely to have any serious consequences.[2]

The Redundancy Payments Act of 1965 established the principle that where employment was terminated because of redundancy employees with more than two years' service would be entitled to a lump-sum compensation. This was the first stage in establishing the principle that employees had certain 'property rights' in their jobs and were entitled to compensation if those rights were removed for reasons other than those within the employee's own control. In addition it was thought that the provision of redundancy payments would reduce trade union and workers' objections to redundancy so permitting a restructuring of industry and a reallocation of resources.

The earnings-related supplements to short-term National Insurance Benefits introduced in October 1966 were also regarded as providing improved safeguards in the event of unemployment (or sickness) thereby removing some of the reluctance of employees to take the risks of changing job or occupation. The scheme provided benefits particularly to the higher-paid workers, who tended to be the higher skilled, to change jobs. There was also the social objective of relating income in times of unemployment or sickness more closely to normal income.[3]

Both these schemes were designed to remove some of the rigidities in

[1] See *Incomes Data Services Report 97*, August 1970. This reinforces the findings of *NBPI Report No. 169*, op. cit.
[2] The question of the distortions in labour markets is discussed in Derek Robinson *Wage Drift, Fringe Benefits and Manpower Distribution*, OECD, Paris 1968; and Derek Robinson (ed.), *Local Labour Markets and Wage Structures* (London 1970).
[3] For a clear and concise summary of these two schemes see OECD, *Manpower Policy in the U.K.*, op. cit.

the labour market by reducing the financial hardships incurred in re-structuring the labour force and in particular in the shedding of under-utilized labour. It was hoped that the increased financial security would reduce the objections to streamlining the labour force and in particular encourage the general policy of increasing labour utilization and productivity by removing the obstacles, institutional or psychological, to the dishoarding of under-employed members of the work force. There are some indications that this occurred,[1] although there is little precise evidence to show that any particular policy measure has caused any structural shift in the unemployment figures.

Other measures to reallocate labour were the Selective Employment Tax, Regional Employment Premiums[2] and the Industrial Training Act. It is difficult to quantify the effects of these measures.[3] The Industrial Training Act appears to have had some effect in increasing the amount and quality of training undertaken by industry although there have been a number of criticisms of particular Boards. The easing of the tight labour market conditions, however, may have prevented the full effects from appearing. Occupational and job mobility reduces as unemployment rises so that the possible reallocative effects of increased and improved training may not have fully manifested themselves. The impact of SET may well have been more significant on the general price level and its repercussions on attitudes towards the incomes policy than its direct effects on the reallocation of labour. Increases in prices, no matter what their cause, will cause workers to reassess their attitudes to money incomes restraint and will raise doubts as to the Government's intention to ensure equality of sacrifice during the incomes policy.

Industrial relations

It is doubtful whether the Labour Government had an industrial relations policy as such when it took office. While in opposition there had been no overriding pressure to decide what Labour policy was towards industrial relations. In some ways it is extremely difficult for the Labour Party to produce an industrial relations policy in the same way that it can produce policies on other subjects. The trade unions dominate Party Conference – they also dominate Party finance. Many MPs are either sponsored by trade unions or feel a degree of attachment to them so that they have an instinctive protective or defensive response when the question of the role of trade unions in a modern society is raised. For while there are people, including some in the Labour Party, who believe that the balance of power between unions and employers, and perhaps

[1] See the earlier comments on the relationship between unemployment and vacancies.
[2] These are considered by Jeremy Hardie in Chapter 6.
[3] See R. D. Sleeper, 'Manpower redeployment and the Selective Employment Tax', *Bulletin of the Oxford University Institute of Economics and Statistics*, Vol. 32, No. 4, November 1970, for some interesting analysis of inter-sector flows of labour.

between unions and society or the state, has now swung so far in the favour of trade unions that there is need of some action to redress the balance, it is clearly the case that many trade unionists reject this utterly and sincerely. They believe that trade unions are still too weak, that employers are waiting to exercise the sort of power they did in the inter-war years and that it is only the constant exercise of militant strength by workers through their organizations that will preserve the existing balance of power or permit an even more desirable one. To some external observers this may seem unreal but in some ways it is one of the crucial distinctions to make within the Labour movement. While some aspects of industrial relations can be relatively easily handled the basic question of trade union reform which seeks to consider the role of trade unions in a modern economy and deal with both the processes and results of collective bargain-ing is one fraught with danger for a Labour Government. It brings into conflict the differing value judgments and priorities of the Labour movement and threatens directly the degree of political unity and organizational solidarity necessary for the effective conduct of govern-ment. However, political parties must respond to public opinion and it was increasingly believed that continued reluctance by a Labour Govern-ment to raise the question of industrial relations would have adverse political effects and open up a debate on whether the unions controlled the Government.[1] Accordingly the Government set up the Royal Com-mission on Trade Unions and Employers' Associations under the chair-manship of Lord Donovan in April 1965.

The Commission can be seen as an investigation of the questions surrounding the processes and methods of collective bargaining. The question of content, whether the settlements were inflationary or not, was not an essential part of the Commission's work. To some extent this reflected the distinction between industrial relations and incomes policy but also indicated the organizational and attitudinal separation inside the Government. 'Industrial relations' was the Ministry of Labour and 'incomes policy' was the DEA. The Ministry preferred the traditional policy of conciliation whereby intervention was confined to peace-keeping rather than the more positive role of intervention in bargaining, not when there had been a breakdown and the aim was to encourage a settlement, but possibly before a breakdown when there was agreement but the agreement contained terms contrary to the incomes policy.

This is a major problem for any Ministry of Labour in an incomes

---

[1] Public opinion is difficult to quantify or even understand on occasions. It may also be 'unduly influenced' by some of the communications media. Notwithstanding it does appear that people were increasingly discontented with the way in which trade unions, officially or unofficially, were exercising power in some industries. The fact that trade unionists are also members of the public does not alter this view. Trade unionists may well respond differently to their own strike than they do to strikes by others. The importance of different value judgments and views on the type of society a Labour Government should be seeking to establish can be inferred from the different attitudes to trade unions held by various contributors to this book.

policy. Should it actively seek to implement those parts of a policy which the parties to bargaining find irksome and risk losing the fund of goodwill it has slowly built up over the years? As long as the prime responsibility for the incomes policy was outside the Ministry of Labour it was possible for the Ministry to continue with its traditional role. The distinction between industrial relations and incomes policy could therefore be maintained. When in 1968 the Ministry became the Department of Employment and Productivity with prime responsibility for the prices and incomes policy there had to be a significant change in attitudes towards intervention. The change of Minister from Ray Gunter to Barbara Castle both permitted and encouraged this change.

The Donovan Report

The Report's analysis concentrated heavily on the 'two systems', i.e. the formal and the informal systems of bargaining, and singled out as the 'central defect . . . the disorder in factory and workshop relations and pay structures promoted by the conflict between the formal and the informal system'.[1] Amongst other things the Commission recommended the establishment of an Industrial Relations Commission[2] charged with the task of advising companies and unions how to improve industrial relations by collective bargaining arrangements. The Report urged that there should be improvements in collective bargaining procedures, which should ensure that many of the causes of unconstitutional strikes would disappear. If unconstitutional strikes persisted after the reforms the question of legal sanctions could be examined more profitably. For the time being it was considered inappropriate to introduce legal sanctions – if the initiative was left in the hands of the employer it would, on the basis of past experience, be impracticable, and if the state were to introduce criminal proceedings experience showed that they would be unsuccessful. An important basic assumption running throughout the Donovan Report is that collective bargaining is in itself a desirable objective as well as being the preferred and most efficient way of settling questions of industrial relations. The state should intervene primarily only to create conditions in which collective bargaining can be widened and strengthened so that the institutions and machinery and procedures of collective bargaining are most efficiently designed to be conducive to the establishment and continuation of free collective bargaining.

The Government's response

As can be seen from Table 9.2 the strike position in this country had not, in aggregate terms, become significantly worse. One of the difficulties

[1] Cmnd. 3623, 1968. For a discussion of the Report see the Symposium in the *British Journal of Industrial Relations*, Vol. VI, No. 3, November 1968.
[2] Later to become the Commission on Industrial Relations (CIR).

when considering whether our industrial relations are good or bad is the determination of criteria. Some people believe that the incidence of strikes[1] is the main sign, and imply that the fewer the strikes the better are industrial relations. Others argue that it is the outcome of the bargaining process that is important so that fewer strikes could mean worse industrial relations if there were much higher wage settlements or if productivity had been impaired. This view would argue that our trouble is that we have too few strikes. It became fashionable to make international comparisons of days lost through strikes. This was, and is, to some extent a futile exercise. Different commentators select different countries for comparison and there are many statistical problems involved in making such comparison in any case.[2] If this approach is pursued, however, the general picture seems to be that as a nation we are not normally at either extreme of the international league table.[3] An alternative approach is to look only at British figures of strikes. Table 9.2 is reproduced from the Department of Employment *Gazette*[4] and shows the trend of strikes during the sixties. The position had not become markedly worse during the decade.

The Government accepted most of the Commission's Report but went further than the Commission in some respects. Public opinion had been hardening on the question of unofficial and unconstitutional[5] strikes and the need 'for something to be done'. Certain disputes had considerable influence on attitudes. The Seamen's strike in 1966 had had considerable adverse effects on the economy. A strike of Liverpool dockers in November 1967 had led to intervention by the Prime Minister in an attempt to obtain a solution. More recently a strike at Girlings in November 1968, over inter-union recognition, had caused widespread lay-offs in the car industry. Political consideration led some members of the Government to the conclusion that measures to provide for government intervention in some forms of industrial disputes were necessary to protect the public

[1] There are different ways of measuring the incidence of strikes as can be seen from Table 9.2. For international comparisons the most useful measure is the number of days lost per thousand men per year.
[2] See for example, H. A. Turner, 'Is Britain really strike prone?: a review of the incidence, character and costs of industrial conflict', *Occasional Paper 20*, (Cambridge 1969) and W. E. J. McCarthy, 'The nature of Britain's strike problem', *British Journal of Industrial Relations*, Vol. VIII, No. 2, July 1970, for a discussion of the results as well as the difficulty of making international comparisons.
[3] See, for example, *In Place of Strife: A Policy for Industrial Relations* (Cmnd. 3888, 1969), page 38.
[4] January 1971.
[5] For our purposes a strike may be regarded as 'unofficial' if it takes place without approval of the official trade union body with appropriate powers to call or support a strike, i.e. it refers to the internal union processes by which the strike decision was made, and 'unconstitutional' refers to strikes which take place in breach of the agreed procedure made between employers and unions for resolving their differences. It is therefore possible to have an official unconstitutional strike; but most unofficial strikes are probably also unconstitutional.

TABLE 9.2 STOPPAGES IN THE YEARS 1960–70

Year	Number of stoppages beginning in year	Number of workers[a] involved in stoppages			Aggregate number of working days lost in stoppages		
		Beginning in year Directly	Indirectly	In progress in year	Beginning in year a	b	In progress in year
		000's	000's	000's	000's	000's	000's
1960	2,832	698[b]	116	819[b]	3,001	3,049	3,024
1961	2,686	673	98	779	2,998	3,038	3,046
1962	2,449	4,297	123	4,423	5,757	5,778	5,798[d]
1963	2,068	455	135	593	1,731	1,997	1,755
1964	2,524	700[b]	172	883[b]	2,011	2,030	2,277
1965	2,354	673	195	876	2,906	2,932	2,925
1966	1,937	414[b]	116	544[b]	2,372	2,395	2,398
1967	2,116	551[b]	180	734[b]	2,765	2,783	2,787
1968	2,378	2,073[b]	182	2,258[b]	4,672	4,719	4,690[d]
1969	3,116	1,426	228[b]	1,665[b]	6,799	6,925	6,846
1970	3,888	1,454	321	1,784	10,844	c	10,970

a The figures in this column only include days lost in the year in which the stoppages began.

b The figures in this column include days lost both in the year in which the stoppages began and also in the following year.

[a] Workers involved in more than one stoppage in any year are counted more than once in the year's total. Workers involved in a stoppage beginning in the year and continuing into another are counted in both years in the column showing the number of workers involved in stoppages in progress.

[b] Figures exclude workers becoming involved after the end of the year in which the stoppage began.

[c] As some stoppages were still in progress at the end of the year this figure is not yet available.

[d] In 1962 about 3,785,000 days were lost through two national one-day stoppages of engineering and shipbuilding workers and a stoppage in the railway industry; and in 1968 about 1½ million days were lost as a result of a one-day national stoppage in the engineering industry.

interest. Accordingly the White Paper issued in January 1969[1] setting out the response to the Donovan Report included proposals for direct government intervention in certain circumstances.

Amongst other things the White Paper said that collective agreements should not be made legally binding unless the two parties decided otherwise and included a written provision to that effect in the agreement. Legal restrictions preventing the conclusion of legally binding agreements between unions and employers' associations were to be removed. Collective bargaining was to be encouraged and it was to become unlawful for an employer to prevent an individual from joining a trade union. The CIR was to be empowered to recommend recognition of trade unions. A

[1] *In Place of Strife*, op. cit.

Trade Union Development Fund was to be established with government finance to assist unions in merging and to improve the quality of their services. The Government rejected the proposal of the majority of the Commission that the protection of Section 3 of the 1906 Trade Union Act should be confined to registered trade unions. Thus, it was not to be possible to sue unofficial strike leaders for inducing others to break their contract of employment. The underlying philosophy was that where an agreed disputes procedure had been followed it would be intolerable to deny the right to withdraw labour, whether the strike then be official or unofficial.[1]

Attempts to prevent constitutional disputes by legislative action may be regarded as undue government interference in a democratic society. Acceptance of the distinction between constitutional and unconstitutional industrial action means that we, as a society, do not seek to limit the freedom to strike, providing the appropriate procedures have been observed. It is very important to emphasize that the Labour Government's proposals were concerned with unconstitutional strikes. In the event of an unconstitutional strike (or lock-out), or one where there was no agreed procedure to follow, the Secretary of State would have been able, if the effects of the strike seemed likely to be serious, to issue an Order requiring a return to work for twenty-eight days on the conditions existing prior to the dispute. The last condition was intended to ensure that where workers had acted unconstitutionally in response to some unilateral action by management affecting, e.g., manning scales, the organization of production or working methods, workers would not be required to accept the management's decision during the twenty-eight days' pause. The purpose of the pause was to enable the DEP to try to secure a settlement. If they were unable to do so the parties were to be free to take such action as they wished.

One of the major complaints of trade unions (and one which is likely to figure prominently in their negotiations in the near future) is the issue of the *status quo*.[2] The question is:

If there is a dispute about changes in working practices, manning scales, etc., should management have the right to implement the change while the disputes procedure is applied so that union members are required to accept the changes they are objecting to, or should management be precluded from actually introducing the changes until the disputes procedure has been exhausted?

This is clearly an important issue of the distribution of power or an aspect of industrial democracy. Unions believe that in some circumstances the existing balance of power in industry is such that current disputes procedures, if made legally binding, would compel their members to accept changes or decisions which they fiercely oppose. The Conciliation Pause

[1] Op. cit., para. 92.
[2] For a discussion of *status quo* agreements see 'Status Quo', *Incomes Data Services Special Study*, April 1971.

provision can be seen as an important departure in that government was offering the *status quo* provision in exchange for a return to work for twenty-eight days in unconstitutional strikes which would have serious effects. It is important to repeat that the Conciliation Pause was to be applicable only to this limited form of strike or lock-out.

The Commission had rejected the introduction of a compulsory ballot before an official strike could be called. The White Paper agreed with this in principle but went on to say that in some situations 'a major official strike (could) be called when the support of those involved could be in doubt'.[1] Accordingly, the Secretary of State was to be empowered in certain circumstances to require the union to hold a ballot, where it was believed that the proposed strike would involve a serious threat to the economy or public interest, and there was doubt as to whether it commanded the support of those concerned. The Secretary of State was also to be empowered to determine the form of the question to be put to the ballot.

Provisions were to be made for inter-union disputes, e.g. over which unions should be recognized and given bargaining rights, to be referred firstly to the TUC and in the event of no satisfactory solution to the CIR. It would be possible for the Secretary of State to make an Order requiring both employers and unions to accept the recommendations of the CIR in these cases. Financial penalties could be applied against both employers and a union which used coercive action to obstruct the implementation of a CIR recommendation in these circumstances.

Two proposals were particularly aimed at providing safeguards for the individual. Legislation was to provide for workers' compensation or reinstatement in the event of unfair dismissal. Dismissal would be unfair unless connected with the capacity or conduct of the employee, or based on the operational requirements of the undertaking (which could come under the Redundancy Payments Act). This carried forward the concept of workers' property rights in their jobs. Secondly, arrangements were to be made for individuals to complain to the Registrar of Trade Unions if they believed they had been unfairly treated by their trade union.

Essentially, the proposals in the White Paper were seen by government as accepting the basic tenets and philosophy of the Donovan Report while introducing additional measures to safeguard the public interest. There was great emphasis placed on the improvement of collective bargaining procedures and machinery, but also an assertion of the interest of the public in the way collective bargaining took place. It was the methods and the repercussions of those methods rather than the outcome of the collective bargains that this White Paper proposed to tackle. It was thought that the proposed safeguards for the public interest were reasonable and that they would be seen as such by both the general public and

[1] *In Place of Strife*, op. cit., para. 97. There had previously been a threatened national strike in engineering where public opinion polls appeared to show that the majority of those involved did not support the calling of the strike.

trade unions. Moreover, the full package of proposals[1] were regarded as providing a number of specific and important benefits to trade unions.

Trade union response to the White Paper was far from favourable. British trade unions have always opposed the encroachment of law in the methods or results of collective bargaining. While the State is, as *In Place of Strife* pointed out,[2] already involved in the processes of industrial relations, unions have a deep, long-standing suspicion of further legal intervention believing that it will, either immediately or ultimately, result in the creation of legislative shackles preventing the exercise of 'free collective bargaining' as they know it. Further, there is absolute abhorrence of the possibility that trade unionists might be sent to prison for the exercise of trade union rights to indulge in collective bargaining and take such action as the unions believe appropriate in the circumstances.[3] Their dissatisfaction with the existing distribution of power in decision-taking in industry strengthens their belief that it would be intolerable for trade unionists to face legal sanctions, even though they took unconstitutional action, if the dispute was regarded as just.

There are two quite distinct sets of values which stem from different premises. On the one hand the 'constitutionalist' or lawyer's approach is to say, 'An agreement is an agreement and if freely entered into should be observed.' On the other hand, the trade unionist response is to say, 'We are primarily concerned about the sheer injustice of the management action which we are opposing.' Because they start from such different premises, discussion between holders of the two viewpoints is seldom fruitful. There tend to be two monologues rather than a constructive dialogue between them. Trade union concern over the justice of their claims and actions lies deep at the roots of their fundamental objection to this sort of legal intervention *per se*.

Trade union opinion also opposed other specific areas of legal intervention previously mentioned. The Conciliation Pause was interpreted as an imported version of the American 'cooling-off period' which would be used purely as a delaying tactic and the fact that it was to be confined only to unconstitutional strikes with serious consequences tended to be ignored in the public debates. Indeed, one of the features of the *public* discussions was that the actual content of the White Paper was discussed much less than the things that people *thought* were in the document. Even

---

[1] We have dealt with only some of the proposals and rather cursorily at that. The White Paper should be read in its entirety for a full understanding. In particular we have dealt unduly briefly with the role of the CIR. This was established in March 1969 and a description of its functions and method of working can be obtained from its *Reports* and the *First General Report* (Cmnd. 4417).

[2] Para. 5.

[3] The Government's proposals tried to meet this by specifying that trade unionists could not be imprisoned for refusing to obey an Order issued during the Conciliation Pause. The appropriate remedy would be a fine. However, trade unions and a number of Labour MPs raised the question of what would happen to those who refused to pay a fine. A solution of attachment of earnings would have been opposed equally fiercely.

so, there were objections genuinely advanced by the unions. Union officials rejected the proposals for compulsory ballots on a number of grounds. If a ballot was necessary to call a strike, was it also necessary to end it? If so, it was likely that some strikes would be prolonged. They argued that in many cases officials tended to reduce the incidence of strikes rather than force them on unwilling members and thus the proposal could lead to more strikes. But perhaps the two most strongly held objections were that by leaving the wording of the question to be put to the ballot to the Secretary of State, there was a danger that some Secretary would be tempted to word it in such a way as to seriously affect the outcome of the vote. Secondly, as the ballot was not compulsory but to be called at the Secretary's discretion, it was believed that ballots would be held only when there was a strong possibility of the strike proposal being defeated. This was regarded as unfairly weakening the union's bargaining position.[1]

The cumulative effect of the opposition to the proposals was that the traditional alliance of trade unions and politically-based socialists in the Labour Party was threatened as perhaps never before.[2] All the instincts of trade unionists were to oppose the creation of the principle of direct legislative intervention in the established processes and machinery of collective bargaining. There were others who believed that trade unions were no longer in the vanguard of social progress but were conservative bodies seeking to defend particular sectional interests irrespective of the damage they did to others. The more doctrinal socialists may also have seen unions as obstacles in the way of fully fledged socialist planning. Yet many of the bitterest trade union opponents of the White Paper regarded themselves as fully fledged socialists and would certainly reject absolutely any suggestion that they were unduly selfish or standing in the way of social progress. They may, in some cases, have recognized the difficulties of fulfilling the double role of furthering their socialist beliefs while protecting the direct interests of their members (which is what trade unions are basically about), but they did not believe that their actions were hindering progress towards a socialist society.

Criticism of the White Paper grew in both unions and the Parliamentary Labour Party. Given the basic trade union objection on grounds of principle, it was not surprising that there were no prominent trade union supporters of the proposals. This was highly significant and important. Even though sections of the trade union movement opposed incomes policy, there were other sections which supported it. Thus debate could take place inside the trade unions and it was possible for the Government to have the constructive aspects of its policy advocated and communicated

---

[1] This was put to me most vividly by one trade union official who said, 'We shall be on a hiding to nowt! They'll never give us a ballot if they think we can win the bloody thing and so *strengthen* our bargaining position.'

[2] Previous differences had been on a 'Left versus Right' basis. This issue altered traditional alignments.

to the rank and file by those unionists who supported it. This was not the case with the industrial relations proposals. They thus appeared, and were presented by most means of mass communications, as a straight conflict between the Government and the unions.

The Government's difficulties went even deeper. The beneficial aspects of the proposals, trade union recognition, protection against unfair dismissal, the granting of compulsory bargaining rights, and the establishment of the Trade Union Development Fund, were not seen as conferring any substantial advantages on the strongly organized and powerful trade unions. These already had recognition, or believed they had in the majority of cases sufficient power of their own to enforce it on reluctant employers. They believed that a strong trade union was the best safeguard against unfair dismissal. Indeed, there were some fears that the provision of too many safeguards by the state might be regarded as proving that trade union membership was no longer necessary as the benefits could be obtained by law and if unions were participating in an incomes policy there might even be disadvantages in membership, as it is probably more difficult to control the incomes of the unorganized work force. Many of the immediate benefits from the industrial relations package would probably have accrued to the weaker sectors of the movement and while they may have welcomed some of them they were not prepared to swallow the other parts.

In his Budget Speech in April 1969 the Chancellor said that a short Industrial Relations Bill would be introduced quickly,[1] before the TUC and Labour Party Conferences. This was seen as necessary to protect the immediate economic situation. The pressures against the proposed Bill mounted and an additional criticism was made that the Bill, whether short or long, could make little if any immediate impact on the economic position. Any contribution a reform of industrial relations might make would be long term, resulting from changed attitudes and behaviour. Not even the 'favourable' items in the short Bill could make it palatable.[2]

After a period of considerable uncertainty as to whether the Bill could actually have been got through the PLP and whether the Government could have survived, a solemn and binding undertaking was agreed between the Prime Minister and the TUC in June 1969. As a result of this, the TUC was to play a more positive and prominent role in the event of unconstitutional stoppages. In some cases they would place an obligation on the unions concerned to take energetic steps to secure an immediate resumption of work. However, it was recognized that there might be some cases 'where they consider it unreasonable to order an unconditional

[1] The fact that the Chancellor made the announcement raised questions as to the reason for the Bill and strengthened trade union fears that it would restrict unions' ability to obtain wage increases. There was a fear of a permanent restrictive wages policy. This may have been unfounded but increased opposition to the Bill.
[2] For a highly stimulating account of this period see Peter Jenkins, *The Battle of Downing Street* (London 1970)

return to work'.[1] This again emphasizes the crucial point that trade unions are not prepared to condemn all unconstitutional action out-of-hand. They wish to consider the circumstances and form a judgment accordingly. As a result of the Statement the short Industrial Relations Bill was dropped.

Whether this was an abdication of previous policy by a government faced with possible collapse or whether it was a constructive development of voluntary collective responsibility by the TUC will no doubt be debated for many years. What appears clearer is that, once again, public opinion misunderstood the nature of the agreement. It was to deal with unconstitutional stoppages. It was not intended to deal with official strikes. Thus, the criticisms made during the Local Authority manual workers' strike, or the Electricity Supply Industry work-to-rule in 1970, that the agreement had not ended strikes, were misfounded. The Labour Party will no doubt be plagued by charges that it 'gave in to the unions' and that it is being hypocritical in opposing the proposed Conservative legislation in 1971. It depends on whether one believes that voluntary action by the unions through the TUC is not only a practical possibility but a preferred way of dealing with unconstitutional strikes whether or not one will support the charges. What is perhaps important is that it should be realized that there is a constructive interpretation that can be placed on the Government's actions.

Collective bargaining and labour market policy

Since 1964 there has been a marked shift in emphasis of collective bargaining away from industry-level to plant or company bargaining. This was recommended by the Donovan Commission and encouraged in statements by the DEP and NBPI. By linking more closely changes in wages with productivity changes at plant or company level there will probably be some positive contributions to increasing productivity either directly or as a result of shedding of under-utilized manpower. The pressures towards more rational and orderly wage structures and wage systems should, in the longer run, have similar effects and lead to a reduction in the rate of increase in unit labour costs. These developments could lead to a more efficient utilization of scarce labour resources and, if bargaining decisions are linked with aspects of industrial training, a general improvement in the quality of manpower resources. The measures to establish formal procedural agreements at company level should make a longer-term contribution to improving industrial relations by removing some of the causes of disputes, but may in the shorter run lead to additional inflationary pressure. If formal procedural agreements at company level also lead to more formal substantive agreements setting out wage

---

[1] Text of Statement, *TUC Annual Report, 1969*, para. 140. The Report gives a clear factual account of the series of meetings, as seen by the TUC.

structures and wage levels, and this will be encouraged by the apparent move away from piecework methods of pay to measured day-work or some other form of generally high basic time rates, there is a strong possibility that the forces of coercive comparison in wage claims at local or inter-plant level in multi-plant companies will increase. This ought, however, in the longer run to improve the situation by permitting more rational economic decisions to be made.

However, if collective bargaining develops in this way there could be new problems to be faced by future incomes policies. Changes in plant-level wages are more difficult to monitor, if only because there are more of them, so the vetting procedures could become greater and more complex as productivity changes would figure more prominently in a number of wage settlements. It is also possible that wages based more closely on plant or company productivity changes would make it more difficult to reallocate wages in a non-inflationary way to sectors which had lower rates of productivity increase or which for some other reason were to be given increases above a norm.

There are changes taking place in the type of agreements. Increasingly minimum earnings level guarantees are being introduced in an attempt to give particularly high wage increases to the lower-paid members of an industry without these increases necessarily being received by all workers.[1] This raises one of the major problems of an incomes policy which has a social content, that of re-allocating incomes to the lower paid. If the agreements work as intended, they can make a significant contribution, but we have insufficient knowledge of how they have actually worked in practice.

Equal pay

Just before the Dissolution in June 1970, the Government enacted its Equal Pay legislation. This provided for the introduction of equal pay between men and women by the end of 1975. The two main methods for preventing discrimination are a requirement that equal treatment be given where men and women are engaged on the same or broadly similar work in the same establishment, or where a woman's job has been rated by a job evaluation exercise as equivalent to a man's job of a different nature from her own; and it will not be possible to specify different pay and conditions so as to discriminate between men and women in collective agreements, or Wage Council Orders.

Various attempts to quantify the effects of equal pay have been made but it is doubtful if these are of much reliability. It is not really possible to decide in advance how such legislation will be applied. Experience in the European Common Market countries suggests that the mere introduction

---

[1] Some unions which have had experience of this type of agreement may refuse to conclude similar ones. This may be because their initial agreement was felt to be unsatisfactory. But others are negotiating them for the first time.

of legislation is in itself insufficient to produce equality of earnings between men and women. It may be that 'job evaluation exercises' will be carried out which will result in the greater majority of men who are in grades which otherwise might be affected by equal pay being regraded into a job with a different title so that a higher rate of pay becomes permissible. To a considerable extent the legislation can only provide a framework within which it will be possible to move to equal pay if workers and management really wish to do so. The Act will end some of the worst abuses of discrimination but will probably not, in the early years at least, be able to ensure that no effective discrimination takes place as a result of collusion between male workers and management.

With the Dissolution of Parliament other proposed industrial legislation had to be dropped. These included the Commission for Industry and Manpower Bill which would have reformed the NBPI and the Monopolies Commission into a single body charged with exercising oversight over both areas of work. This would have enabled a more integrated policy to price and income determination to be developed. The revised Industrial Relations Bill which included the various proposals for strengthening collective bargaining, if necessary by requiring employers to recognize and bargain with trade unions, but which did not include the various 'sanction clauses' of the earlier short Industrial Relations Bill, also lapsed.

Assessment

It cannot be claimed that the Labour Government came into office with a pre-determined socialist labour market policy awaiting introduction. It advocated a voluntary prices and incomes policy, but this was seen primarily as a means towards certain economic and social ends, such as faster growth and the avoidance of balance of payments difficulties, rather than as having positive constructive socialist objectives in its own right. There was no general agreement within the Labour Party that a prices and incomes policy could have such an effect. For the rest, the policy, if it can be described as such, consisted of little more than a general inclination to implement more humane and generous treatment of those affected by redundancy and general regional policies which would stimulate employment in certain areas. There was some success in reducing the regional imbalances in the incidence of unemployment. While the general approach was laudable it cannot be described as a particularly socialist positive drive; it increased the effectiveness of previously considered measures.[1] The labour market policy was seen as being an unemployment-reducing policy and apart from the need to have income restraint there was no fundamental policy position on how a labour market should work

[1] See OECD *Manpower Survey of the UK*, op. cit., and, for a factual account of the earlier years of the Government, Derek Robinson, 'Employment policy: recent developments in the United Kingdom', in *Employment Fluctuations and Manpower Policy, Papers Prepared for an International Conference, London, 24–28 February 1969* (OECD Paris 1971).

or the type of influence that should be encouraged or discouraged. The institutions and mechanisms of the labour market had not been analysed to see how they contributed to or hindered basic socialist objectives; partly because there had been little detailed consideration of what the basic socialist objectives were. In particular there had been little beyond broad generalizations on how a more equitable, and therefore presumably more socialist, distribution of income might be achieved. There had been no hard bargaining or policy preparation with the trade unions to see how far agreement on common objectives was possible.

By the application of quantifiable yardsticks the Labour Government's policies might not appear to have been markedly successful in that the prices and incomes policy does not seem, on statistical tests, to have had any notable effect in reducing the rate of increase of money wage incomes during the period 1965–9, nor did the attempts to introduce legislation for the reform of industrial relations prove successful, although there were some voluntary changes introduced. As we have suggested earlier, prices and incomes policy may have had some more intangible success in changing attitudes and in encouraging the development of the fundamental rethinking necessary if we are ever to come to grips with the vexed problem of inflation with high employment levels. Those of us who believe that incomes policy is necessarily a long-term policy which needs careful encouragement might therefore conclude that some foundations have been laid and some vitally important lessons learned; lessons which might, perhaps, only be capable of being learned by experience. The crucial role of wage differentials and the need to seek some common grounds for their determination as pre-conditions for the general acceptance of revised wage structures necessary if the lower-paid are to be given preferential treatment seems to be much more widely accepted as a key area of policy than was the case in the past.[1]

Overall the labour market policy in the early years of the Labour Government consisted primarily of attempts to implement the prices and incomes policy. This dominated all other considerations, effectively preventing any detailed depth study of other aspects of labour market policy. Trade union concern to proscribe state intervention in labour questions has prevented any penetrating discussion and analysis of the way in which labour markets could work to fulfil socialist as well as what might be called 'trade union' objectives. There has been no public discussion of the possible advantages that could result from applying an active manpower policy, perhaps on the Swedish model.[2] Yet this is both a supplement and a complement to an incomes policy in that it seeks to improve the working of the labour market in order to reduce distortions and frictions. The re-training aspects might permit a greater degree of

[1] See the stress placed on this question by H. A. Clegg, op. cit.

[2] See the Papers for the OECD London conference on employment fluctuations, op.cit., and particularly Rudolf Meidner, *The Role of an Active Manpower Policy in Contributing to a Solution of the Dilemma between Inflation and Unemployment.*

occupational mobility and the general framework would probably lead to a change in attitudes towards unemployment. For example, demand management policies are now introduced on the ground that they are in the public interest, i.e. the public interest requires an increase in unemployment. Why should this lead to hardship on those made unemployed? A socialist policy could ensure that if the public interest required something there should be no private loss in this sort of case.

In the second part of the Government's period of office industrial relations reform played the same role of preventing constructive discussion of wide-ranging and deep labour market policies and indeed so dominated the labour scene that incomes policy itself was perforce reduced in importance and ultimately, in effect, allowed to lapse.

The initial proposals for change aroused such hostility in the trade union movement that incomes policy had to be sacrificed on what proved to be, at least for the Labour Government, the altar of a false god. This arose from the proposal to introduce statutory compulsion or penalties in certain events. There was a great deal of the Industrial Relations Bill which was considered desirable. For example, replying to Mr S. Orme, MP, who said she should forget all her former policies, Barbara Castle was applauded at the 1970 Labour Party Conference when she said:

All of them, Stan? The 90 per cent of that Industrial Relations Bill, which was the biggest charter for trade unionism in this country's history, do you want me to forget that? (Applause) Because I will not. I believe that the Industrial Relations Bill I introduced to parliament just before the election could have transformed the mental climate of this society.[1]

This does not mean that some industrial relations reform by a future government is unnecessary, nor that it will not take place, but rather that the processes of change, as well as the environment in which it will take place, will be very different. One of the vital issues will in fact prove to be whether or not a Labour Government can produce policies which will reconcile the apparent public demand for industrial relations reform with economic and social policies, including a prices and incomes policy, which will permit the traditionally close relations between the Party and the trade unions to continue. There may be grounds for believing that the attitudes of both sides will have changed a little by then so that some area of agreement proves possible. If it does not, then it is probable that a future Labour Government's policies will founder on this rock. It is difficult to see how socialist social and economic policies can be implemented without a prices and incomes policy, even though this might have to be called something else, and it is equally difficult to see how such a policy can be introduced without the co-operation of the trade unions. A statu-

[1] *Labour Party Conference Report 1970*, page 126. Note that the reference was to the second IR Bill, but Mrs Castle's remarks emphasize that the changes were seen as altering attitudes and thus behaviour and not as producing any immediate economic results.

tory policy, while effective for some time, could hardly provide the basis for the Government's general economic and social strategy.

There must be much more discussion of objectives and means within the Labour movement. There is not yet sufficient agreement on practical policy objectives. It is easier to reach agreement, perhaps, on what socialism is and what a socialist society will look like, but much more difficult to reach agreement on what the next Labour Government should do in its labour policy. It is not that the trade unions are wilfully blind and selfishly pursuing their own interests, although of course they have to seek to further their members' interests in order to survive. But they genuinely believe that their approach is best, not only in terms of results but also in terms of desirable methods of working. This difference of view as to how the economic system works was expressed at the 1970 Party Conference:

The most effective redistributor of wealth and incomes in the community is not the incomes policy, but the militant stand of the Trade Union Movement, and until we as a Movement recognise this, and support the trade unions fully, we will get nowhere.[1]

The difference in value judgments between trade unionists and some other sections of the Labour Party is genuine and deep and effective policy requires that both groups try to reach some accommodation. This will not prove possible if either group believes it has a monopoly of enlightenment and truth.[2]

It is inevitable that the need to produce detailed policy proposals which reflect the objectives of various groups within the Labour movement will impose considerable strains on the unity of purpose of the movement. Industrial relations and labour market policies will impose greater strains than any other area of policy as it is here that the danger of a rift between the trade unions and the rest of the Party is greatest. As we have suggested earlier both sides must try and understand the value judgments of the other even though they need not accept them. In particular the 'political' or theoretical socialists must understand why trade unions believe they are the best defenders of the interests of the workers[3] and equally the trade unions must understand that not all their actions, pursued sometimes by small groups for immediate short-term sectional gain, are necessarily part of the advance towards either a socialist or a just society. The traditional hostility to state intervention in large areas of activity surrounding labour

[1] Keith Morrell, prospective Parliamentary Candidate, St Marylebone, *Labour Party Annual Conference Report 1970*, page 116.
[2] 'Unless trade unionists are willing to play their part they have no right to expect the government to pursue the growth policies . . . Equally, trade unions will only be able to persuade their members to abandon the methods which in the past they adopted for the defence of their standards and jobs provided that the government is prepared to reshape its own economic strategy.' *TUC Economic Review*, 1968, para. 79.
[3] The distinction between workers and trade union members is not always drawn.

relations and the determination of incomes is in some respects inconsistent with action to support the election of a socialist government. It is not possible for government to abdicate responsibility for such large and important areas to the two sides of industry themselves.

Trade unions will have to consider which of their traditional attitudes are genuinely needed in modern conditions to defend the legitimate interests of their members and which are out-dated fossils, remnants of some previous type of society and economic order when the balance of power, both economic and political, was different from what it is today. In turn unions may well find that they need new additional powers which their reliance on the traditional independence of collective bargaining cannot give them; such things as the general demand policies with their effect on the level of unemployment, regional policies, industrial training and so on all impinge heavily on the well-being of trade unions and are outside the scope of traditional bargaining. A new arrangement to permit tripartite discussion and decision-taking might emerge to replace the old mixture of bipartite and unilateral decision-taking. It will not be enough to reserve positions until everyone is convinced that a real socialist policy has been produced; it is necessary to produce policies for immediate use by the next Labour Government. Difficult though the problems are in this area the experience of the 1964–70 Government demonstrates that without agreement the Government is effectively prevented from carrying out its basic economic and social objectives and the movement is in danger of tearing itself apart as government believes it must take action and the unions are unwilling to accept the specific proposals made, or even, in some cases, the idea of government intervention at all.

Hopefully the experience of the last Labour Government can be turned to good account. While it was not noticeably successful in this field neither was it as great a failure as is sometimes suggested. The main problems were caused either by omission – there was no clear-cut socialist, or even Labour Party proposal for large areas of labour market policy – or contemporary emergencies so dominated the scene that they used up the fund of goodwill necessary to introduce change in industrial relations and collective bargaining behaviour before any lasting results could be obtained. Next time it might be that the need for change will be accepted, mainly, one hopes, because there will have been lengthy, detailed, constructive and perfectly frank discussions between different sections of the movement as to what a socialist government should do, not in the ultimate ideal society, but when it next comes into office in the conditions that are likely to be then obtaining. Seen in this light the experience of 1964–70 may turn out to have been most valuable in that it prepared the way for sound socialist policies next time. If it does not, then these were indeed the waste years, and even worse, wasted despite the obvious good intentions and socialist objectives of the two politicians most clearly concerned, George Brown and Barbara Castle. Their efforts – whether one agrees with the objectives or not – were clearly motivated by sincere beliefs that the action was necessary to protect the interests of the people of this country and particularly the ordinary working people. Both of them in some way suffered politically for their convictions. Their central role in labour issues proved to be a bed of nails, but proved so because they sought to actively interfere with events. Non-interventionist policies can soften the bed and transform it into a comfortable reclining couch, but a socialist government cannot afford non-interventionist policies.

Index